SALEM'S CENTURIES

In the series *History and the Public*,
edited by Steven Conn

Also in this series:

Robin F. Bachin and Amy L. Howard, eds.,
*Engaging Place, Engaging Practices: Urban History and
Campus-Community Partnerships*

David W. Young,
The Battles of Germantown: Effective Public History in America

EDITED BY **Donna A. Seger and Brad Austin**

SALEM'S CENTURIES

*New Perspectives on the History
of an Old American City*

TEMPLE UNIVERSITY PRESS   *Philadelphia • Rome • Tokyo*

TEMPLE UNIVERSITY PRESS
Philadelphia, Pennsylvania 19122
tupress.temple.edu

Copyright © 2026 by Temple University—Of The Commonwealth System
   of Higher Education
All rights reserved
Published 2026

Library of Congress Cataloging-in-Publication Data

Names: Seger, Donna A. editor | Austin, Brad, 1972– editor
Title: Salem's centuries : new perspectives on the history of an old
   American city / edited by Donna A. Seger and Brad Austin.
Other titles: History and the public (Philadelphia, Pa.)
Description: Philadelphia : Temple University Press, 2026. | Series:
   History and the public | Includes bibliographical references and index.
   | Summary: "A collection of scholarly essays covering the history of
   Salem, Massachusetts, over a period of four hundred years"— Provided by
   publisher.
Identifiers: LCCN 2025045544 (print) | LCCN 2025045545 (ebook) | ISBN
   9781439925591 cloth | ISBN 9781439925607 paperback | ISBN 9781439925614
   pdf
Subjects: LCSH: Salem (Mass.)—History | Salem (Mass.)—Social conditions |
   LCGFT: Essays
Classification: LCC F74.S1 S36 2026 (print) | LCC F74.S1 (ebook) | DDC
   974.4/5—dc23/eng/20251114
LC record available at https://lccn.loc.gov/2025045544
LC ebook record available at https://lccn.loc.gov/2025045545

The manufacturer's authorized representative in the EU for product safety is Temple
University Rome, Via di San Sebastianello, 16, 00187 Rome RM, Italy (https://rome
.temple.edu/).
tempress@temple.edu

♾ The paper used in this publication meets the requirements of the American
National Standard for Information Sciences—Permanence of Paper for Printed
Library Materials, ANSI Z39.48-1992

Printed in the United States of America

9 8 7 6 5 4 3 2 1

*To our students and colleagues
at Salem State University,
the residents of Salem, Massachusetts, and
our families at home.*

—DONNA AND BRAD

Contents

Acknowledgments — xi

INTRODUCTION: *Salem's Centuries* / Donna A. Seger and Brad Austin — 1

THE FIRST CENTURY: 1626–1725

The First Century Introduction — 11

CHAPTER ONE: The Dispossession of Wenepoykin and His Kin / Emerson W. Baker — 15

Interlude 1: Putting Salem on the Maps / Brad Austin — 27

CHAPTER TWO: Gallows Hill's Long Dark Shadow / Emerson W. Baker — 33

Interlude 2: Salem's Regicide: Hugh Peter, 1598–1660 / Donna A. Seger — 43

CHAPTER THREE: **Salem and Slavery** / Bethany Jay   47

Interlude 3: John Higginson: A Seventeenth-Century Salem Merchant and His World / Marilyn Hayward   61

THE SECOND CENTURY: 1726–1825

The Second Century Introduction   67

CHAPTER FOUR: **Salem's Revolution: A World Turned Upside Down** / Hans Schwartz   69

Interlude 4: Jonathan Haraden, Salem's Revolutionary Privateer / Maria Pride and Donna A. Seger   79

CHAPTER FIVE: **The Kinsmans of Salem and China** / Dane A. Morrison and Kimberly S. Alexander   84

Interlude 5: Sabe and Rose / Bethany Jay and Maryann Zujewski   95

CHAPTER SIX: **John Remond, Citizen of Salem: The Personal and the Political in the World of an African American Entrepreneur, 1805–1874** / Donna A. Seger   101

Interlude 6: Mary Spencer: Shipwrecks, Sugar, and Salem / Brad Austin   115

THE THIRD CENTURY: 1826–1925

The Third Century Introduction   123

CHAPTER SEVEN: **Salem and the Civil War** / Robert W. McMicken   127

Interlude 7: The Civil War Service of Luis Fenollosa Emilio / Brian Valimont   139

CHAPTER EIGHT: Immigrant Catholicisms / Elizabeth Duclos-Orsello   144

Interlude 8: Salem's Black Picnic: An American Tradition
/ Donna A. Seger   164

CHAPTER NINE: A Salem Scholar Abroad: The Worldview of Walter G. Whitman / Michele Louro and Elizabeth McKeigue   170

Interlude 9: Salem Willows: Playground of the North Shore
/ Brad Austin   184

CHAPTER TEN: From Shrine to Source: Salem and the Colonial Revival, 1876–1934 / Donna A. Seger   190

Interlude 10: Suffrage Success: The Election of 1879
/ Donna A. Seger   205

THE FOURTH CENTURY: 1926–2026

The Fourth Century Introduction   213

CHAPTER ELEVEN: From Fire to Wind: The Development and Redevelopment of Salem, 1914–2026
/ Donna A. Seger and Brad Austin   215

Interlude 11: Salem's Labor History: The Naumkeag Steam Cotton Company and the 1933 Strike / Aviva Chomsky   226

CHAPTER TWELVE: Salem and World War II
/ Brad Austin and Susan Edwards   231

Interlude 12: The Sixties Come to Salem State
/ Brad Austin and Elizabeth Duclos-Orsello   245

CHAPTER THIRTEEN: Situating the Self in Salem: Identity, Social Justice, and the Descendants of 1692 / Andrew Darien   254

Interlude 13: Salem's Changing Demographics / Aviva Chomsky   269

CHAPTER FOURTEEN: **Salem: Allowing the Past to Haunt Us on Our Terms** / Margo Shea and Theresa Giard 274

EPILOGUE: **It Happened in Town House Square** / Donna A. Seger 285

Salem / J. D. Scrimgeour 295
Contributors 297
Index 301

Acknowledgments

It might seem obvious that historians from Salem's public university would take the lead in the attempt to contextualize this proud city's quadricentennial. As is often the case, however, what is apparent in retrospect is not always clear in the present. This book is the product of a lunch shared by two historians (and friends) who share a passion for understanding Salem's history but who had very different ideas about how they could help commemorate its four hundredth birthday.

When Brad invited Donna to meet him at Concord's historic Colonial Inn for lunch, he thought that he had identified the perfect way for Salem State's History Department to meet this moment: Donna should do it! In Brad's plan, Donna would identify the most engaging essays she had posted to her incredible blog, *Streets of Salem*, and she should publish them as a book. Brad believed that this book would have wide popular appeal, and he very generously (he thought) offered to help her group her essays into book sections. Problem solved, right?

Donna, however, came to the lunch with other grander ideas. After listening patiently and politely to Brad's suggestions, she countered with her own proposal. They should work together, not simply to repackage essays she had already written but to create a work of accessible scholarship that would focus on offering new perspectives on Salem's storied history. As anyone who has met her will confirm, Donna can be very persuasive, and this book is the outcome of the brainstorming that began across a lunch table in Concord, Massachusetts, a relatively young town that won't be able to celebrate its own quadricentennial for another decade, in 2035.

Whatever grand plans were hatched that day over bread rolls and crisp salads, this book is only possible because of the work and contributions of literally dozens of people and several important institutions over the centuries. It is our pleasure to acknowledge their contributions now.

We must begin with the people and institutions who have documented, collected, told, and contextualized the four centuries of Salem's history. While it is impossible to name everyone whose work has inspired and directed us, we want to specifically thank Dane Morrison and Nancy Schultz, whose magnificent collection of essays, *Salem: Place, Myth, and Memory*, was always on our minds (and our desktops) as we conceived and constructed this volume. Their ability to bring together a host of scholars with expertise on a wide variety of Salem topics motivated us to try to do the same, and the fact that their volume authoritatively covered many important topics (colonial encounters with Native Americans, maritime history, architectural history, Hawthorne) freed us to turn our attention to other less examined aspects of the city's past. Moving back a bit, we wish to acknowledge the inspirational breadth and depth of detail achieved by two men generally dismissed as antiquarians: Joseph Barlow Felt, whose *Annals of Salem* (1827) still serves as an assertive rejoinder to the event history of his time (and ours), and Sidney Perley, a tireless miner of property and probate records whose exhaustive (his own term, with which we concur) multivolume *History of Salem* published a century later nevertheless opens with the *natural* history of the North Shore of Massachusetts.

While it is impossible to thank by name *all* the historians who have helped this volume's authors draft their twenty-eight original essays, it is possible to acknowledge the efforts of several key institutions who have collected and preserved records related to Salem's past and who make those materials accessible to historians in the present. One measure of Salem's significance is the number of records relating to its residents that can be found in the nation's foremost archives. The Library of Congress and the National Archives have preserved thousands of documents relating especially to Salem's first two centuries, and their efforts to make many of these records available (and searchable) digitally was incredibly helpful for our authors.

The best Salem collections, however, are local—or regional—ones. Foremost among these is the Phillips Library of the Peabody Essex Museum. This library, removed from Salem to a larger facility in Rowley, Massachusetts, is still, essentially, Salem's "historical society," and there are treasures galore awaiting future Salem historians among its vast collections. We are grateful to Dan Lipcan and the librarians of the Phillips Library for their stewardship and commitment to the ongoing digitization of Salem sources. Readers will note that several of the essays in *Salem's Centuries* are dependent on another local archive, that of our own university headed by the archivist Susan Edwards, which is also committed to increasing access to materials that document Salem history, particularly that of the twentieth century and beyond.

A quick look at our contributors' biographies will reveal that all of them have a Salem State University connection, having either taught at the university or graduated from our master's program on the way to other archives and scholarly pursuits. It's important, therefore, to acknowledge the intellectual atmosphere created at the university, and, especially, in the History Department, where scholarly excellence is valued and supported at a level that is rare in regional public universities. In particular, we thank our colleagues in the History Department, many of whom contributed to this volume, for being great historians, teachers, and role models as engaged scholars. We also want to acknowledge the moral and financial support our provost, David Silva, and our dean, Brian Vanden Heuvel, have given to this project. Their personal encouragement was *almost* as important as the release time they gave Donna to work on *Salem's Centuries*.

It has been a joy to work with the team at Temple University Press, and we are thrilled that this volume will join the impressive *History and the Public* series list there, edited by Steven Conn. Thanks, Steve, for taking on this project and for helping us realize our shared vision of creating a work that speaks to both scholarly and general audiences. From our first conversation with Steve and Aaron Javsicas, the editor in chief at Temple, we have known that our project was in good hands. We appreciate all that they and others at the press, especially Stephen Gluckman, have done to keep us on track and to get the manuscript through production. We also thank the manuscript's external reviewers. Their enthusiasm for this project was a great boost in the middle of a long process, and their thoughtful and constructive suggestions made this a much better volume.

We are, of course, grateful to our families and friends, some of whom have had to live as closely with this project as we have. Donna thanks her husband John, stepson Allen, and parents Tom and Pam, all of whom have served as supportive sounding boards at one time or another, as well as her curious and critical friends in Salem, who contribute to a community where the importance of both place and past and present is always appreciated. Brad thanks LaGina, Stella, and Phoebe for their love and support and for being willing to work around random stacks of documents and books on the kitchen table as he worked on this project. He also thanks Julia, Bill, and Dianne for always being interested in stories that begin, "You wouldn't believe what I just learned about

Salem. . . ." Probably no one is happier that this project is done than Brad's friends who have grown weary of conversations that begin the same way and that, to their minds, never seem to end.

We'd both like to conclude by acknowledging our students who daily bring us a variety of perspectives about Salem's past and who give us optimism for its future. We dedicate this volume to them.

SALEM'S CENTURIES

Introduction

Salem's Centuries

DONNA A. SEGER AND BRAD AUSTIN

Four centuries after its settlement by Englishmen and -women with both economic and ecclesiastical motivations, the impressionistic outline of Salem's history remains largely the same as that established by its most famous native son. Nathaniel Hawthorne's "Custom-House" preface to *The Scarlet Letter* paints Salem with a mid-nineteenth-century brush, its once "bustling" wharves now quiet and decayed but its colonial past still ripe for harvest. Salem had emerged as a flourishing fishing and trading settlement over the seventeenth and eighteenth centuries, but its infamous witch trials, which became the embodiment of the Enlightenment disdain for "superstition," seemed to overshadow its commercial vitality at that time and in the nineteenth century, just as they do today.

Hawthorne was living and writing in the wake of Salem's greatest era of prosperity: the post–Revolutionary era when its fleet of over two hundred vessels bound for the East Indies made Salem the seventh largest city in the United States with the highest per capita income in the new country. His immediate predecessors, including his very own father, knew that they had to go to sea to seek their fortunes and "to go home poor its [*sic*] a curse in Salem."[1] Sadly, Captain Nathaniel Hawthorne Sr. did not come home, poor or otherwise, dying of yellow fever in the Dutch Suriname in 1808. Many members of his son's generation realized that their fortunes could no longer be made at sea: whether because of competition or geography (a deep harbor that nevertheless had a predisposition toward silting and no river valley hinterland), Salem had ceased to be a global port with its orientation fixed squarely on "the farthest port to the rich east" by 1850.[2]

Nathaniel Hawthorne emphasized his native city's decline (or reorientation) more than the legacies of its previous prosperity: its strident architecture, strong social networks based on generational wealth and maritime and mercantile experiences, and knowledge institutions such as the Salem Athenaeum, the Essex Institute, and the "Cabinet" of the East India Marine Society, later the Peabody Museum. He looked away from the Salem of his own time toward a mistier and more distant society of the past and, in doing so, established a firm foundation for the dominance of the colonial in Salem history and culture. Mining his own family for material, Hawthorne noted that his family had "mingled their earthy substance with the soil" of Salem "for nearly two centuries and a quarter." In a preview of how the City of Salem would market the witch trials a century and more later, he could distance himself from "intolerant" Puritanism while also profiting from that characterization. His great-great-great-grandfather William Hathorne, who persecuted Quakers, and his great-great-grandfather John Hathorne, who interrogated "witches," were embarrassing (so much so that he added the "w" to his surname to distinguish himself from them) but also "haunting," memorable, *and* marketable. Despite the fact that his more recent ancestors, his grandfather Daniel and namesake father Nathaniel, were mariners and he himself worked in several custom houses, Hawthorne did not dwell on maritime themes in his works: perhaps the less busy wharves of his own time were too close. His colonial characterizations were enduring, however, shaping depictions of Salem up to the present even though new messengers and mediums now tell the story.

In late nineteenth-century Salem, residents could look back with pride on two famous Nathaniels: the "Great Romancer" Hawthorne and his distant cousin Nathaniel Bowditch, a mathematician and navigator who made his mark with the 1802 publication of *The New American Practical Navigator*, a pioneering work that remains in print (and in use) today. Bowditch's fame, combined with Salem's commercial range and prosperity in the Federal era, established maritime history as another focus of Salem historiography in that era, and beyond. Prior to the emergence of the "new maritime history" in the late twentieth century, the study of Salem and the sea was romantic in its inclinations, focused on ships more than sailors and the open sea more than the coast or the port and offering "fundamentally celebrations and not analyses" in the words of Daniel Vickers.[3]

The dominance of these two topics, the witch trials of 1692 and the maritime ascendancy of the late eighteenth and early nineteenth centuries, has created a limited view of Salem's history over four centuries. While knowledge of the precise details and dimensions of these topics has expanded under this concentrated and continuous focus, their larger context and consequences have received less scrutiny, as has nearly all of Salem's modern history, from its experiences of the Civil War, industrialization, immigration, and civic engagement in the nineteenth century through its urban development and redevelopment in the twentieth century. This is the largely unexplored terrain that we cover in *Salem's Centuries*.

As the editors of this collection of essays, we have perspectives that while intimate are "outside." We are both professors in the History Department at Salem State University, yet neither of us is a specialist in Salem history: Brad is a historian of twentieth-century America with a specialty in sports history and a pedagogical focus on teacher training, while Donna is an early modern Europeanist. Both of us became engaged in Salem's history through more public avenues: Brad through teacher education and the administration of several large local-history-focused grant projects, and Donna through residency, volunteerism, and blogging. In our various roles, we each have had questions, often very basic ones, about Salem's history, yet we could not find the answers for them without doing the research ourselves. Both of us were driven, by and through our various endeavors, to develop a more inclusive and comprehensive framework of Salem's history that expanded on its "signature" eras of witch trials and maritime ascendancy.

We were also inspired by the pioneering editorial efforts of our former Salem State colleagues, Dane A. Morrison and Nancy L. Schultz, who opened a wider window of Salem history with their 2004 volume *Salem: Place, Myth, and Memory*. This collection of essays utilized a multifaceted focus to identify the historical roles and identities that Salem has assumed over its long history and informed our own volume, *Salem's Centuries*. Both books "are centered in the local, examining a single place over time," and both also reflect the times of their publication.[4] The past twenty years have witnessed intensified research into indigenous and African American history as well as the increasing commodification of Salem's history, based on its "Witch City" brand, even beyond that which was apparent at the millennium. With these trends in mind, we felt the call and the need for more and different chapters exploring Salem's history.

Salem's Centuries was also inspired by both a past and upcoming anniversary and an unexpected relocation. Salem's tercentenary in 1926 was so eventful that it left a mark for commemorations to come, but, after the turn of the twenty-first century, it became increasingly unclear as to how a quadricentennial might come about, as the city appeared to be losing access to its own history by way of the Peabody Essex Museum's Phillips Library. One of the foundational institutions of the Peabody Essex Museum, the Essex Institute, had long served as Salem's de facto historical society, as its predecessor, the Essex Historical Society, was bound by its charter to keep both its "library and cabinet . . . in the town of Salem," a requirement that was repeated in the Essex Institute's 1848 charter. The leadership of the Peabody Essex Museum, formed in 1992 by a merger of the Essex Institute and the Peabody Museum, did not recognize this restriction and moved the Phillips Library, constituting the bulk of Salem's archival history, to a Collections Center in Rowley, Massachusetts, in 2018. There was considerable agitation over this move, including a Change.org petition with over five thousand signatures and an appeal from the president of the American Historical Association, Mary Beth Norton (herself a historian of the witch trials), who described the Salem archives as "of national, even international, significance." Yet, it happened, with the Peabody Essex Museum promising increased digitization in compensation for diminished access. Digitization initiatives have, indeed, increased since the relocation, but Salem still found itself without a historical society or "pastkeeper," particularly a keeper of its most recent past, as the four hundredth anniversary of its European settlement approached. Apart from its location, both the comprehensive nature of its collection and the professional stewardship of its librarians have ensured that the Phillips Library remains the essential archive of Salem history. We couldn't have produced this book without the Phillips Library collections and the help of its wonderful archival staff.

All of these factors drove our mission to present as much of Salem history as possible, encompassing both recent historiographical trends and traditional topics that have received minimal attention due to the emphasis on the colonial and the commodifiable. We asked our contributors (all colleagues or former students at Salem State) to connect to at least one of three themes in their chapters: neglected narratives or perspectives, broader historiographical contexts, and examples and examinations of how Salem's history has been lost or distorted in its public presentations over time.

We hope that our sustained focus on these themes delivers on our book's subtitle and offers readers "new perspectives on the history of an old American city." We have adopted a novel and, we believe, accessible approach to telling Salem's stories and to engaging with these themes. The overarching structure of *Salem's Centuries* is chronological, with essays divided into the four centuries of Salem's history. While our volume begins and ends with essays that seek to orient our readers to Salem, and place-based history is evident elsewhere, our focus throughout is on social history, elevating the stories of groups, events, and perspectives that have not been the focus of most traditional histories of the city. Our format features both full-length chapters, which take the form and tone of most traditional academic essays, and shorter pieces, which we have labeled "interludes," that are more focused on individuals or singular events and connect them to the larger themes in Salem and American history.

While one might think that a city of Salem's age and stature would have myriad studies of the American Revolution and the Civil War, that is not the case, and so we included chapters on both wars as well as interludes on some major Salem players from each war, the Revolutionary privateer Jonathan Haraden and the officer and historian of the pioneering Massachusetts Fifty-Fourth Regiment Luis Emilio. While Salem has long been recognized in regional and national histories of the abolitionist movement for its early antislavery societies aligned with William Lloyd Garrison and the inspiring trans-Atlantic orations of two African American sibling agents of the American Anti-Slavery Society, Charles Lenox and Sarah Parker Remond, we sought to expand and align local and individual perspectives with more recent studies in several pieces in *Salem's Centuries*, including a chapter on family patriarch John Remond's quest for citizenship and interludes on Sabe and Rose Derby's passages to freedom, the entrepreneurial abolitionist Mary Spencer (a.k.a. Salem's "Gibraltar Woman"), and the evolution of the venerable "Black Picnic" at Salem Willows. In regard to Salem's most recent history of the twentieth and twenty-first centuries, there was ample opportunity to meet all of our themes as so little historical research has been pursued: studies of immigration, urban development, and tourism trends are largely new contributions to the city's narrative history.

Engagement with recent historiographical trends and topics can be found at both the beginning and the end of the book. For example, in our first century, we have Bethany Jay's survey of "Salem and Slavery" and Emerson W. Baker's two contributions: the first, an examination of Salem's enshrined "Indian Deed" in "The Dispossession of Wenepoykin and His Kin" and, the second, a chapter that bridges the distant storied past and the present through the confirmation of Proctor's Ledge as the execution site of the victims of 1692. Baker sets this discovery, which received national attention in 2016, in context in "Gallows Hill's Long Dark Shadow." In our last century, we have Margo Shea and Theresa Giard's analysis of ghost tourism and Andrew Darien's oral histories of witch trial descendants.

When it functioned as a historical society for Salem, the Essex Institute had little interest in social history (beyond where people *lived*, the subject of a succession of "reminiscences" in its *Historical Collections*) or more contemporary history. This past perspective on institutional and event-driven history has induced us to seek out stories of individuals, families, and communities, with a preference for those representing the relatively unexamined nineteenth and twentieth centuries. Yet, there are many unexplored personalities and territories in the earlier centuries as well, and *Salem's Centuries* seeks to examine their experiences and contexts.

Two lesser-known figures of Salem's first century, the pastor Hugh Peter and merchant John Higginson, are the subject of interludes in the first century, while Salem's "extraterritorial" experience is explored in two settings in the second and third centuries: Macao, the residence of the Kinsman family of Salem in the mid-nineteenth century, and Nanjing, where Salem Normal School science professor Walter George Whitman brought his family in 1925. Dane A. Morrison's and Kimberly S. Alexander's study, "The Kinsmans of Salem and China," reveals the price that was paid to keep up with entrepreneurial expectations when Salem's maritime hegemony was on the decline, while Michele Louro and Elizabeth McKeigue's analysis of the travels and mediation of Whitman illustrates another Western perspective on the East a century later. The latter chapter is based on materials in the Salem State University Archives and Special Collections, now the largest archive of local history in Salem, as are two other studies in Part IV that are focused on the experience of Salem residents during World War II and Salem State students during the 1960s.[5]

The post–Civil War chapters in *Salem's Centuries* are focused on a city shaped more by in-migration than out-migration and groups seldom studied, such as the Catholic parishes of Elizabeth Duclos-Orsello's "Immigrant Catholicisms" and the early twenty-first century Dominican immigrants Avi Chomsky examines in her interlude, "Salem's Changing Demographics." Over this period, there was also an apparent shift in Salem's orientation: away from the sea and toward the land and the development and redevelopment of its own land- and cityscape. The city (from 1836) had to seek new connections to the world around it—via the train in the nineteenth century and the car in the twentieth century—and was consequently reshaped itself.

Both demographic and transportation trends shaped the city, as did a major disaster: the Great Salem Fire of June 1914. The impact of this epic conflagration, which cut a swath through the most densely settled and industrialized section of the city and left nearly twenty thousand people homeless and at least half that number jobless, is examined in two chapters in *Salem's Centuries*, encompassing the perspectives of looking backward and forward. In "From Shrine to Source: Salem and the Colonial Revival," Donna A. Seger explores the material dimensions of Salem's dominant colonial narrative in the early twentieth century, a time when it seemed imperiled by both fire and modernity. Seger and Austin widen the chronological perspective to analyze the dynamic forces that shaped Salem's urban streetscape throughout the twentieth century and into the twenty-first century in "From Fire to Wind: The

Development and Redevelopment of Salem, 1914–2026." This chapter encompasses both the emergence of the historic preservation movement and the experience of urban renewal in Salem, both through the lens of social history.

The final chapters of *Salem's Centuries* consider the city's history and contemporary identity through a public history perspective. From the inception of the annual Haunted Happenings Halloween festival, in the 1980s, through the commemoration of the tercentenary of the Salem witch trials, in 1992, and the installation of the *Bewitched* statue in Salem's most historic square, in 2005, Salem came to embrace its century-old "Witch City" brand more completely than ever before. Somehow, in the words of one contemporary author, the witch trials of 1692, "which constituted a nine-month episode in the city's four hundred years of busy history . . . created a modern identity and an international reputation for Salem."[6] It is impossible for us to explore all the dimensions of that process in a book that is actually dedicated to those "four hundred years of busy history" rather than just 1692, but we offer two different perspectives in our last century, as well as an epilogue that begins and ends with that incongruous yet symbolic statue of *Bewitched*'s Samantha Stephens.

In addition to our stated and more academic themes, we hope readers will discern other trends and connections in this, admittedly, selected and curated view of Salem's history. We discerned several trends and connections as we pieced together our curated view of four hundred years of one city's history. Salem's entrepreneurialism is evident throughout, from the seventeenth-century fisheries to the eighteenth-century privateering to the myriad ephemeral attractions that popped up from the late nineteenth century onward. A broader expression of this entrepreneurialism is an apparent energetic civic engagement on the part of Salem's residents: in local, national, and global initiatives. Whether they were building (or rebuilding) Salem, selling Salem, or serving Salem in efforts extending from charity to defense to preservation, the city's residents seem always intent in their endeavors. A dynamic globalism is also evident throughout Salem's centuries, from its roles in the Atlantic world in the seventeenth and eighteenth centuries through the experiences of its "extraterritorial" residents in the East in the nineteenth century and the participation of its general citizenry in the world wars of the twentieth century. Salem was always, and remains, very much a part of the world, even though it seems as if the world is descending on Salem in these twenty-first-century days of advancing tourism. These trends do not represent either the decline or the lack of diversity evident in Hawthorne's depiction of Salem, so we hope that we have broken that particular spell.

The spell of 1692 remains unbroken by our book, but we hope we have placed the trials of that year in a larger narrative and thematic context. While it may seem odd that a Salem history does not devote a chapter explicitly to the witch trials, we felt that we had nothing to add to the well-established narrative and analysis, and, for those of us who live and work in Salem, this event is less past and more present, a reality that is explored in several chapters in *Salem's Centuries*. While Witch City remains a sturdy construction, we do hope that readers will recall the other interesting stories if they find themselves walking the streets of Salem. There are many absent topics and tales that could have been included, as Salem's centuries were, indeed, full: of merchants and *Monopoly*, inventors and immigrants, books and buildings. Like those who presented Salem's history before us, we were constrained by our format as well as our own perspectives and priorities, and we invite all future Salem historians to join the conversation with theirs.

NOTES

1. Letter from Salem merchant John B. Williams to his brother Henry, June 18, 1849, box 3, folder 4, Henry L. and John P. Williams Papers, MH-238, Phillips Library, Peabody Essex Museum, Rowley, MA. Cited in Nancy Shoemaker, *Pursuing Respect in the Cannibal Isles: Americans in Nineteenth-Century Fiji* (Ithaca, NY: Cornell University Press, 2021), 251.

2. The Salem City Seal was adopted in March 1839, featuring a "A ship under full sail, approaching a coast designated by the costume of the person standing upon it and by the trees near him, as a portion of the East Indies; beneath the shield, this motto: 'Divitis Indiae usque ad ultimum sinum,' signifying 'To the farthest port of the rich east'; and above the shield, a dove, bearing an olive branch in her mouth. In the circumference encircling the shield, the words 'Salem Condita A.D. 1626' 'Civitatis Regimine Donata, A.D. 1836.'"

3. Nathaniel Bowditch, *The New American Practical Navigator* (Printed at Newburyport, Mass., 1802, by Edmund M. Blunt, for Cushing and Appleton, Salem: Sold by every book-seller, ship-chandler, and mathematical-instrument-maker in the United States and West Indies), 1802; Daniel Vickers, "Beyond Jack Tar," *William and Mary Quarterly—Early American History: Its Past and Future* 50, no. 2 (April 1993): 418–424, available at https://doi.org/10.2307/2947085.

4. Dane Anthony Morrison and Nancy Lusignan Schultz, eds. *Salem: Place, Myth, and Memory* (Northeastern University Press, 2004), 9.

5. Salem's experience of World War II is also based on "Salem: The Home Front, 1941–1945," Oral History Project Records, ACC 81023, Phillips Library, Peabody Essex Museum, Rowley, MA. This was an oral history project of the Salem Youth Commission under the direction of Reta Meshon Brill, partially funded by a grant from the National Endowment for the Humanities.

6. J. W. Ocker, *A Season with the Witch: The Magic and Mayhem of Salem, Massachusetts* (Countryman, 2016), iv.

THE FIRST CENTURY

1626–1725

One of the first ministers of the English settlement of Salem, Francis Higginson, described a new world of plenty in his travel journal, part of which was published in London as *New-England's Plantation* in 1630. The shore bordering Massachusetts Bay north of the Charles River featured a variety of soils, among them clay "for the building of our houses" and black earth so fertile that "it is almost incredible what great gain some of our English planters have had by our Indian corn." The local trees provided wood of which there was "no better in the world," and fish were so plentiful that "the least boy in the Plantation may both catch and eat what he will of them." The only entity that wasn't plentiful in New England was people: Higginson noted that "the Indians are not able to make use of a fourth of the land," in large part due to a "great and grievous plague" that had swept many of them away twelve years before. Higginson had landed at a place called Nahum-kek or Naumkeag, also the name of this diminished band of peoples affiliated with the Algonquian-speaking Pawtucket Tribe, but it would soon be called Salem.

The associations with "peace" inherent in the plantation's new English/Hebrew name seem to refer to the projected peaceful coexistence of both the "new" planters of Higginson's company and the native Naumkeag peoples as well as the "old planters" who preceded them, the remnants of the Dorchester Colony's settlement on Cape Ann to the north. With insufficient fishing to sustain them, Roger Conant led a band of planters south in 1626, creating Salem's first English settlement on the North River. The small settlement was relatively isolated and independent until the arrival of John Endecott in 1628 and John Winthrop in 1630, when corporate connections were reestablished, with Endecott and Winthrop representing the New England and the Massachusetts Bay Companies, respectively. Higginson summarized these years succinctly, emphasizing a godly unity:

> When we came first to Naumkeag we found about half a score houses and a fair house newly built for the Governor. . . . And we brought with us about 200 passengers and planters more, which by common consent of the old Planters were all combined together into one Body Politic under the same Governor. There are in all of us both old and new Planters about 300, whereof 200 of them are settled at Naumkeag, now called Salem, and the rest have planted themselves at Massachusetts Bay, beginning to build a Town there which we call Charlestown. We that are settled at Salem make what haste we can to build houses, so that within a short time we shall have a fair town.[1]

The "Body Politic" was also the Body Religious, and Higginson is widely recognized as the author of the Confession of Faith and Covenant of the First Church of Salem, which was agreed on in August 1629. He died just a year later, and, fortunately, his contract with the Massachusetts Bay Colony included provisions for his widow and children. His son John Higginson served as minister to the First Church for an impressive forty-eight years (1660–1708), during which he weathered a succession of challenges to the unity of the congregation, most notably the witch trials of 1692.

The life and work of both one of Higginson's predecessors, Hugh Peter, and his son and namesake, John Higginson Jr., represent more secular and "Atlantic" perspectives on Salem's first century. Peter had arrived in Salem full of plans to advance the plantation's economic position and heal the divisions over Roger Williams's short ministry in 1635, but he could not extricate himself from parliamentary politics during what was supposed to be a brief return to England at the opening of the Civil War and eventually died as a regicide. Later in the century, Higginson maintained a productive commercial and civic life in a Salem that was no longer an isolated outpost.

There are estimates for Salem's population over its first century, but they are just estimates and do not include its most marginalized peoples, both the Pawtucket peoples, who were further diminished after the English settlement by the disease, displacement, and war that accompanied the arrivals, and the enslaved Africans, including those in the household of Hugh Peter. After the negotiations that resulted in Salem's 1686 "Indian Deed," we seldom hear of the former, while the latter were included in a provincial census only in 1754.

Francis Higginson estimated the population of Salem to be "several hundred" after the arrival of his fleet, and the more specific number of 179 members of the First Church in 1637 indicates a larger population of over 700 people. At the end of the seventeenth century, Salem's population had increased to over 2000, and, by 1754, the same year as the Massachusetts Slave Census, it was in the realm of 3500.[2]

NOTES

1. *Nevv-Englands Plantation: Or, A Short and True Description of the Commodities and Discommodities of That Countrey—Written by Mr. Higgeson, a Reuerend Diuine Now There Resident*, Early English Books Online, University of Michigan Library Digital Collections, available at https://name.umdl.umich.edu/A03330.0001.001, accessed July 19, 2024.

2. Eben Putnam, "Note on the Population of Salem in 1637," *Essex Institute Historical Collections* 57 (1921): 149–150; 1754 Massachusetts Slave Census, Primary Research, available at https://primaryresearch.org/slave-census-all/, accessed July 19, 2024; Daniel Vickers, *Young Men and the Sea: Yankee Seafarers in the Age of Sail* (Yale University Press, 2007), 265.

CHAPTER ONE

The Dispossession of Wenepoykin and His Kin

Emerson W. Baker

On October 11, 1686, eight heirs and family members of the late Wenepoykin, the sagamore of Salem and neighboring communities, met in Beverly, possibly gathering for the first time since the sagamore passed away at Natick two years earlier. It was a sad occasion, for they gathered to sell part of their ancestral homelands to the town of Salem, something Wenepoykin had refused to do. However, they did so with the realization that they had long been effectively dispossessed.[1]

Today, there is a growing interest in acknowledging Native Americans as the first inhabitants of America and recognizing their dispossession. People ask who were the Native inhabitants of our town? What tribe lived here? What happened to them? These are important questions as communities begin to address ancient wrongs by acknowledging the Native presence on the land known as Turtle Island (present-day North America) countless generations before the arrival of Europeans. A consideration of the life of Wenepoykin and the land sales his heirs and kin executed provides some complicated if incomplete answers to these seemingly simple questions. This chapter is an excursion into the difficult history of seventeenth-century New England, an era of profound change for both the Native inhabitants and the English settler colonists who would establish Salem.[2]

The Salem deed is one of many of the Essex County documents where the Native owners of the land sold their rights for very little compensation. While these transactions tell a dark story, there is a bit of a silver lining. To prove they were the heirs who had the right to sell, these deeds and the accompanying depositions specify in detail the family relationships of the grantors to their parents and grandparents who ruled the land in the early seventeenth century. Thus, these tools of dispossession also provide a rare opportunity to reconstitute Native kinship networks and gain a better understanding of the bounds of the territories they inhabited.[3]

Wenepoykin was born somewhere on the North Shore of Massachusetts sometime in the 1610s to a woman whose name has been lost to time. The vagueness around his birth exemplifies how little we know today about life for Native Americans in early seventeenth-century New England. Unfortunately, this dearth results from the lethal and unsettled nature of these years, which would lead to great suffering for Wenepoykin, his family, and their people. We do know that Wenepoykin was the youngest son of Nanepashemet, the supreme sagamore of the North Shore, a region that was a borderland and disputed ground between several groups of Native Americans as well as English settler colonists. The land was so contested that, to this day, two Native American groups—the Massachusett Tribe at Ponkapoag and the Cowasuck Band of the Pennacook-Abenaki (descendants of the Pennacook and Pawtucket Wabanaki)—both claim Naumkeag as part of their ancestral homeland.[4]

In his early years, Wenepoykin survived epidemic diseases as well as Native American warfare. From 1616 to 1619, a great plague raged among the indigenous population of coastal Massachusetts, New Hampshire, and southern Maine. Native Americans had been isolated from peoples in Europe and Asia for thousands of years, so they lacked resistance to their diseases, resulting in what are called "virgin soil epidemics," which devastated Native populations with no natural immunity. Experts have not been able to identify the vector, but even relatively harmless childhood diseases brought by European explorers and fishermen proved lethal when exposed to a new population. As much as 70 percent to 90 percent of the indigenous population of the North Shore may have died from 1616 to 1619. In 1632, one colonist estimated that Wenepoykin's family had perhaps thirty to forty warriors under their command, suggesting a total population of perhaps two hundred had survived the epidemic.[5]

Increasing the demographic horror, Wenepoykin's people were on the losing end of a war that began in 1607, against the northern groups of the Wabanaki peoples. At the time, English observers referred to them as the "Tarrentines," but they were the Micmac of Nova Scotia and their allies. These raiders regularly ventured far south by boat to attack Native villages. Wenepoykin's father Nanepashemet was killed during one such attack, which took place about 1619. It is unclear exactly where he died, but it was in his fort, located not far from the northern bank of the Mystic River, likely in present-day Medford.[6]

Fortunately, Wenepoykin had a remarkable mother, who became the leader of her family and their peoples following the death of her husband. English settlers referred to her simply as the "Squa Sachem" or the "Massachusetts Queen," but never by her given name, so we refer to her as the Massachusett Sunksqua. Regardless of her name, as Lisa Brooks put it, "She was an influential female leader who helped to orchestrate a series of marriage alliances in the wake of devastating epidemics which rewove the network of relations on the Massachusett coast, enabling the survival of her kin."[7]

The Massachusett Sunksqua and Nanepashemet were Salem's first power couple. Although there has been long-standing disagreement over the group identity of Nanepashemet and his neighbors, there has been a growing consensus among scholars that he was the supreme leader of the Pawtucket, the southernmost group of the Wabanaki peoples whose lands stretched from present-day Nova Scotia to Vermont. In addition to his own homelands in the Salem-Lynn area, his alliance included the Wabanaki peoples of the Merrimack River Valley and southern New Hampshire, known as the Pennacook. His influence stretched eastward into southern Maine and westward toward the Concord River. His wife was from a leading Massachusett family, whose principal territory mostly lay south of the Mystic River and along the Massachusetts Bay. She was a close relative, perhaps even the sister, of Chickataubut of Neponset, the leader of the Massachusett.[8] She would rule over her and her late husband's lands until her death, as sunksqua—a female sachem or sagamore. It was an uncommon circumstance, one that indicates both the political power of her family and her own wisdom and leadership abilities.[9]

She definitely needed that wisdom. The widow had to safeguard her three sons and three daughters, as she was both confronted with invaders from the north and considered an enemy by the Massachusett to the south. While they were her own people, these Massachusett belonged to the Wampanoag alliance of the south shore led by the powerful Ousamenquin, better known today by his title Massasoit (meaning "great sagamore").[10]

One important strategy for the Massachusett Sunksqua was to continue the local tradition of strengthening ties with other groups by marriage alliances among leadership families. Her oldest son married a daughter of Masconomet, who was the sagamore of Agawam (present-day Ipswich and surrounding towns). Her second son and Wenepoykin both married daughters of Passaconaway, the sagamore of the Pennacook of the Merrimack River. These marriages were important, for Passaconaway had become the supreme leader of a confederacy that included much if not all of Nanepashemet's former domain. Wenepoykin's first wife presumably died young, for he subsequently married Joane, the daughter of Poquanum, the sagamore of Nahant. Finally, Wenepoykin's sister Yawata married Tahattawan, the sagamore of Nashoba (the area around present-day Littleton, thirty miles west of Salem). Through these marriages, the family and their kin were the leaders of a vast domain stretching from central Massachusetts to southern New Hampshire.[11]

Unfortunately, the family and their people were devastated by a smallpox outbreak in 1633. Both of Wenepoykin's brothers and almost all of their families and followers perished. The Massachusett Sunksqua survived and retained leadership over their ever-dwindling people, though her relative Chickataubut also perished. After the smallpox epidemic, only roughly two hundred Massachusett and Pawtucket were left in Greater Boston and the North Shore. Just one or two Native families remained in Salem, and Wenepoykin appears to have usually resided in the Lynn-Saugus area. He was sometimes called George Rumney Marsh, after the name the English settlers gave to the great coastal marshland in Saugus, Romney Marsh, which had been named after a huge wetland on the coast of Kent, England. Meanwhile his mother resided in the southern limits of their domain, closer to the Mystic River. It was a demographic, political, and spiritual crisis, one that must have seemed worse when they looked at their English neighbors. As the Native population dwindled, between 1630 and 1633, three thousand English settlers arrived in Massachusetts Bay.[12]

The colonial government believed that they owned all the territory within the Massachusetts Bay charter, granted by King Charles I in 1629. The Salem minister Roger Williams disagreed and was banished from the colony in 1635, in part, because he argued that the Native inhabitants owned it, and the colonists needed to purchase the title from them. Still, a few towns soon strengthened their ownership claim by purchasing the Native title as well. Between 1637 and 1640, the Massachusett Sunksqua sold her rights to land in Cambridge and neighboring Charlestown as well and in Concord (twenty miles west of Cambridge). Her second husband Webcowet, the shaman or spiritual leader of her group, cosigned these deeds. Presumably, they were her territories to sell on behalf of her people, but English law recognized husbands as holding the right to sell their wives' holdings. So local officials probably added Webcowet as a signatory as a safeguard.[13]

The Massachusett Sunksqua understood the English legal implications of these sales. In the deed to Charlestown, she reserved the right during her life for her people to continue to plant crops, hunt, and fish on part of the land. She also left out of that sale the territory to the west of the Mystic Ponds, where she resided. The implication is that her group was so small that she believed they all would be gone or forced to leave the area by the time of her death. This was a safe assumption, given the intrusions the English were making into their lives. Notably, the English cows often got into Native American cornfields and destroyed them. In the same May 1640 meeting of the General Court (the Massachusetts legislature) where Edward Gibbons reported the successful purchase of Cambridge and Watertown, they also voted that towns were liable for the damages English cattle caused to Native American crops. Presumably, the Massachusett Sunksqua had raised this concern in her deed negotiations with Gibbons. In 1643, Cambridge paid her eight bushels of corn for damage by cows and built a half-mile long fence along the town's boundary with her. But, clearly, this was a problem that would only get worse and that likely led to some Pawtucket and Massachusett moving inland, away from English settlers. The Massachusett Sunksqua died around 1650, making her son Wenepoykin the leader of his dwindling people.[14]

Many remaining Native Americans moved into the interior to join the new "Praying Indian" townships, where Native Americans converted to Puritanism and lived lives as settled farmers, like their English neighbors. The adoption of Christianity by so many survivors of the epidemics and warfare of the early seventeenth century suggests that many Native Americans felt that their traditional gods had forsaken them. The missionary effort was led by the Puritan minister John Eliot. He oversaw the translation of the Bible into the Massachusett language and encouraged the establishment of the first "praying town" at Natick, about twenty miles southwest of Boston. Wamesit became an important praying town for the Pawtucket and Pennacook on the Merrimack River, ten miles west of Andover in present-day Lowell.[15]

While the dwindling Pawtucket had a diminished need for coastal lands, the rapidly growing English population had a hungry appetite for real estate. And, after the near-destruction of the Pequot tribe of Connecticut in the spring and summer of 1637, no Native American doubted the lengths the English settlers would go to take their land. The Massachusett Sunksqua likely decided it was best to cooperate with the English, so she might at least have some control over the process of land transfer. Also, by the mid-1630s, beavers had been overhunted on the North Shore, limiting the pelts available to trade to the English for their manufactured goods. Selling their land allowed them to continue to receive English goods. In the sale of Cambridge, the town agreed to provide a new coat to the Massachusett Sunksqua each winter while she lived. And at the time of signing the deed she received twenty-one coats, three bushels of corn and nineteen fathom of wampum for Charlestown. Presumably, that was a new winter coat for everyone in her dwindling group. Wampum was the beads Native Americans made from shells, which functioned as a currency of the fur trade.[16]

Wenepoykin, the Massachusett Sunksqua's only surviving son, did not cosign or even witness any of her deeds. Rather, he fought to maintain the ownership of land. In 1651, he petitioned the General Court for the return of lands that he said he inherited from his brother Wonohaquahan, sagamore of Saugus and Malden. The English residents petitioned the General Court for relief for what they called Wenepoykin's "unjust molestation" and "pretending title to certain lands."[17] They indicated that this was the latest of the sagamore's many efforts to defend his ownership. The petitioners warned that if Wenepoykin's claim was upheld, he would sue for lands in Lynn and elsewhere. Furthermore, "other Indians will be incouraged to lay clayme, not only to the farmes belonging to other townes, but to the townes themselves." This "may prove of very bad consequence to divers townships, if not to the whole country." The General Court did not want to put into question the ownership of all the land in the colony. It ruled in favor of the English settlers but ordered them to lay out twenty acres of good planting ground to Wenepoykin, a token acknowledgment of his claim. The next year he suffered another setback when he had to mortgage Nahant for an old debt. When the sagamore could not meet the obligation within the twenty-day limit specified, he lost this land.[18]

Despite these setbacks, Wenepoykin did not give up. On May 19, 1669, the General Court responded to another of his petitions, ruling that they could not act on his request, rather it was up to "the proprietors of the land to give him as they and he shall agree." His petition does not survive, so we do not know what property was under dispute. What is clear is that Wenepoykin was still trying to assert his ownership over his homelands.[19]

Meanwhile, the English population throughout southern New England continued to grow, making it even less likely he could ever recover his patrimony. English settlers came increasingly in contact and conflict with the Native population over land and natural resources. Tensions would erupt into open violence in 1675, as many Native Americans of southern New England rose up against the English, following the example of Metacomet, the supreme sagamore of the Wampanoag whom the English called King Philip. While the war initially went well for the Native cause, it would ultimately lead to defeat and disaster.[20]

There is no evidence that Wenepoykin or members of his family fought against the English. However, a 1686 deposition supporting the Native sale of Salem indicated that Wenepoykin had only recently died, after returning from enslavement in Barbados. At the end of King Philip's War, many Native Americans had been enslaved and sent to Barbados and other English colonies in the Caribbean. Most of those sold had not taken up arms against the English. Rather, they had kin who had been combatants or had claims to lands held by the English. As a sagamore who had repeatedly tried to get his land back, Wenepoykin certainly would have been a target for deportation.[21]

Wenepoykin was one of a very few who returned from Barbados as a free man. It is unclear how this happened, but, apparently, his kinsman James Rumney Marsh (a.k.a. James Quananpohit or Muminquash) was able to see to his release and return home. James was a Christian Indian living in Natick. The depositions and deeds of the 1680s make it clear that he was close kin of Wenepoykin, though the exact relationship is never given. Regardless, he had risked his life as a spy for the English during the war, so his voice carried weight, and he was somehow able to ensure that Wenepoykin lived his last days at Natick. Writing in the 1830s, Samuel G. Drake said, "He died soon after his return, in 1684, at the home of Muminquash, aged 68 years." Drake provides no sources for this statement, but we do know that Wenepoykin had passed by the summer of 1684, when James and other heirs sold the family's claim to the town of Marblehead.[22]

Wenepoykin's heirs signed four deeds in all. In addition to ones for Marblehead and greater Salem, in 1686 they also signed one deed for part of Lynn and another that contained the rest of present-day Lynn, Saugus, Lynnfield, Nahant, Swampscott, and Reading. Both the grantors and the grantees were well motivated. In the wake of King Philip's War, no Native peoples remained in these towns. The deeds indicate that all the signatories lived at either Natick or Wamesit. So, they had been essentially dispossessed and presumably decided they might as well see if they could at least receive some compensation for legally signing over their rights. Soon after Wenepoykin died, James led a contingent of heirs, in 1684, who approached Marblehead with their claim of ownership. He had likely incurred considerable expenses in bringing the old sagamore home, so perhaps he needed money to cover these costs. Regardless, times were tough for the Native survivors of King Philip's War, even for those who had been English allies. The meager £16 they received for signing away their claim must have been a welcome if bittersweet windfall. Meanwhile, the king's revocation of the Massachusetts charter, in 1684, led to tremendous uncertainty over the ownership of land, for all towns held the title to their lands through the charter. Purchasing the title from the Native inhabitants was a way to bolster their claim.[23]

In a series of similar transactions, Masconomet's grandsons deeded their rights to the towns north of Salem, from Beverly to Newbury and west to Boxford. Combined with some of the earlier deeds, signed by the Massachuset Sunksqua, to land along the northern shore of the Mystic River, these define Wenepoykin's domain—the domain he inherited from his brothers and their father Nanepashemet. Indeed, one Native deponent testified in 1686 that he had heard Wenepoykin say that his lands ranged from the "Nahumkeke River" (present-day Bass River between Salem and Beverly) "up to Malden Mill Brook running from a pond called Spot Pond" (present-day Malden River). Notably, he did not claim the lands his mother had occupied and sold, west of the Malden River.[24]

While the Massachusett Sunksqua sold land in Charlestown, Cutshamake—the sagamore of the Massachusett around Boston and the south shore—received 10 shillings in 1639 "for his planting ground within the bounds of Charlestowne." The fact that a Massachusett sagamore had a planting ground on the north side of the Mystic River, in the same community where the Massachusett Sunksqua sold land, helps confirm her identity as a Massachusett. The fact that she only sold land in the southernmost part of her domain may well indicate that the lands she sold were those that she held the hereditary right to, as a Massachusett, rather than from her marriage to the Pawtucket leader Nanepashemet. Only later would the heirs of Nanepashemet's son Wenepoykin sell Nanepashemet's domain.[25]

The use of the term "Nahumkeke" rather than the abbreviated version of "Naumkeag" also helps identify Nanepashemet as a Pawtucket of Wabanaki heritage rather than as a Massachusett.[26] Fannie Hardy Eckstorm noted the term was a Wabanaki word derived from "nahurmo," meaning eel, and the locative suffix, "eag" meaning "runs out." That is, the place to catch eels, at the outlet of a stream or river. As eels are a preferred food for bass, this makes perfect sense that the English would call it the Bass River. However, we know of two other locations the Wabanaki called Nahumkeke or Nehumkeag. One was near the Pawtucket village Wamesit on the Merrimack River, and the other was on the Kennebec River in present-day Pittston, Maine.[27]

While Nehumkeag was a Wabanaki word, the people of this borderland had both Massachusett and Pawtucket heritage, as exemplified by Wenepoykin's parents and his many relations throughout the region. The deed to Salem indicates some of his heirs resided at Wamesit in the Pawtucket territory, while others lived in the Massachusett territory at Natick. So it is understandable that both the Cowasuck Band and the Massachusett claim Salem as part of their homeland.[28]

We probably will never know what Wenepoykin and his family considered their cultural identity, Indeed, determining it may be more important to us than it was to them for they pledged their principal allegiance to their local bands, which were part of a group of interrelated people who had similar traditions, religion, and lifeways. Even if we could determine an answer

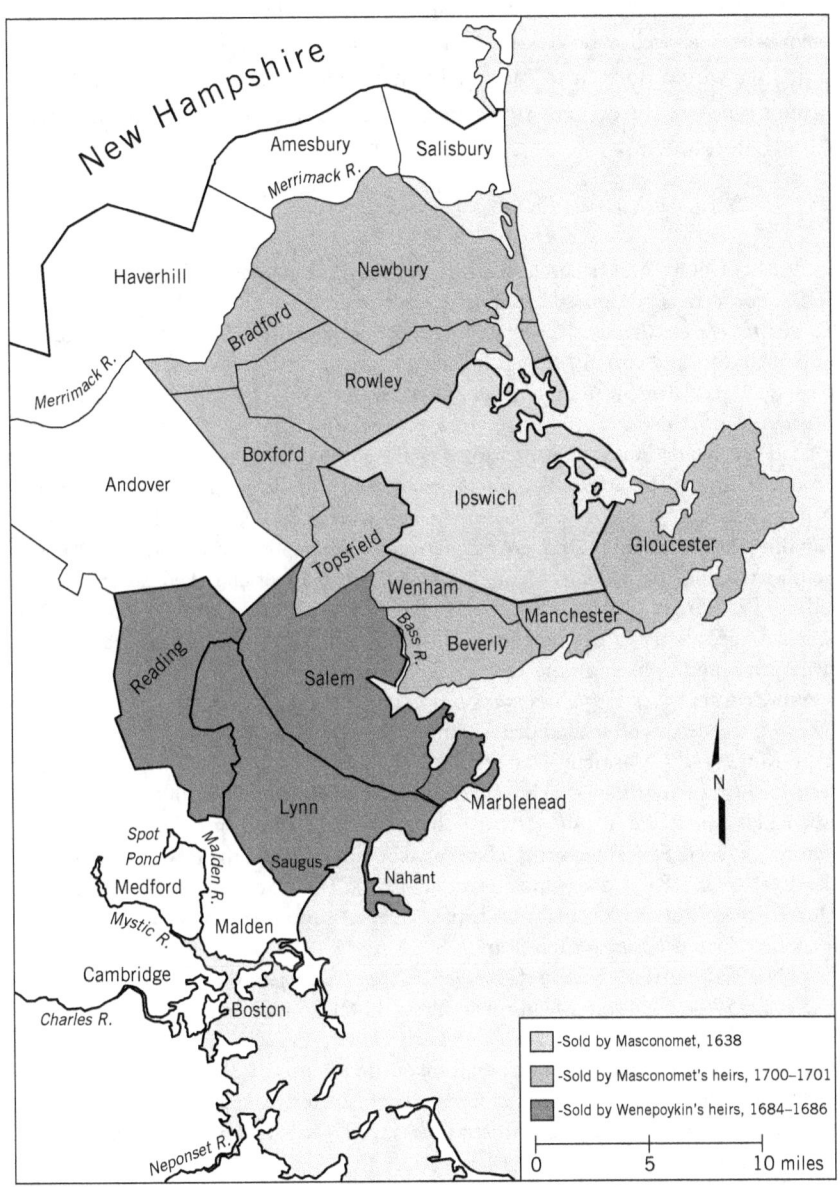

Major Native American land sales in Essex County; map based on township boundaries in 1700. *(Drawn by Emerson Baker.)*

for 1626 or 1686, we have no idea of the political landscape of the region one thousand or ten thousand years earlier. The ancestors of the present-day Massachusett and Cowasuck were among those inhabitants, but there may have been others, as well, whose names have been lost to time. In the spirit of inclusivity, we would do well to cast a wide net and honor not only those Native groups who are the current stewards of Salem but also the ancient ones who came before them.

NOTES

1. Essex County Massachusetts Registry of Deeds, Salem, Massachusetts, Essex Deeds, 7:125. For a transcription and supporting documents, see Sidney Perley, *The Indian Land Titles of Essex County, Massachusetts* (Essex Book and Print Club, 1912), 77–88. The original of the deed currently hangs in Salem City Hall. For an overview of Native dispossession, see Allan Greer, *Property and Dispossession: Natives, Empires and Land in Early Modern North America* (Cambridge University Press, 2018).

2. This chapter builds on earlier work by the author. See Emerson Baker, "Salem as Frontier Outpost," in *Salem: Place, Myth, and Memory*, ed. Dane Anthony Morrison and Nancy Lusignan Schultz (Northeastern University Press, 2004), 21–42; Emerson Baker, "Finding the Almouchiquois: Native American Families, Territories and Land Sales in Southern Maine," *Ethnohistory* 51, no. 1 (2004): 73–100; Emerson Baker, "A Scratch with a Bear's Paw: Anglo-Indian Land Deeds in Early Maine," *Ethnohistory* 36, no. 3 (1989): 235–256. See also Peter Leavenworth, "'The Best Title That Indians Can Claime': Native Agency and Consent in the Transferal of Penacook-Pawtucket Land in the Seventeenth Century," *New England Quarterly* 72, no. 2 (1999): 275–300.

3. All the deeds and related depositions are in Perley, *Indian Land Titles*.

4. More on the Massachusetts Tribe at Ponkapoag is available at https://massachusetttribe.org/we-are-the-massachusett. More on the Cowasuck Band of the Pennacook-Abenaki is available at https://www.cowasuck.org/homelands.html. For Wenepoykin's family, see David Stewart-Smith, "The Pennacook Indians and the New England Frontier, 1604–1733" (Ph.D. diss., Union Institute, 1998), 79–87. See also Ron Wiser Research Home Page, Rootsweb, available at https://freepages.rootsweb.com/~raymondfamily/genealogy/wiser/WiserResearch.html.

5. Neal Salisbury, *Manitou and Providence: Indians, Europeans, and the Making of New England, 1500–1643* (Oxford University Press, 1982), 25–28; Bert Salwen, "Indians of Southern New England and Long Island: Early Period," in *Handbook of North American Indians*, ed. Bruce Trigger (Smithsonian Institution Press, 1978), 15:160–166; "Letter of Thomas Dudley to Lady Bridget, Countess of Lincoln, March 28, 1631," in *Letters from New England: The Massachusetts Bay Colony, 1629–1638*, ed. Everett Emerson (University of Massachusetts Press, 1976), 68–69.

6. For the maritime capabilities and raids of the Micmac, see Matthew R. Behar, *Storm of the Sea: Indians and Empires in the Atlantic's Age of Sail* (Oxford University Press, 2019). Nanepashemet's fort, and his nearby burial site, were visited by a contingent from Plimoth Plantation, led in September 1621. See Dwight B. Heath, ed., *A Journal of the Pilgrims at Plimoth* (Corinth, 1921), 77–80; Salisbury, *Manitou and Providence*, 68–72, 105; Kris-

tine Malpica, "Uncommon Ground: Pawtucket-Pennacook Strategic Land Exchange in Native Spaces and Colonized Places of Essex County and Massachusetts Bay in the Seventeenth Century" (M.A. thesis, University of Massachusetts, Boston, 2021), 49–50.

7. Lisa Brooks, "The Saunkskwa of Missitekw," at Our Beloved Kin: Remapping A New History of King Philip's War, available at https://ourbelovedkin.com/awikhigan/missitekw. The terms "sagamore" and "sachem" are interchangeable and refer to a Native American leader.

8. The work of the late David Stewart-Smith is critical to the understanding of the Native groups of southern New Hampshire as well as northeastern Massachusetts. See Stewart-Smith, "Pennacook Indians." The charts on pp. 86–87 summarize his findings on the families of Nanepashemet as well as Passaconaway. See also Lisa Brooks, *Our Beloved Kin: A New History of King Philip's War* (Yale University Press, 2018), 73–75, 366; Brooks, "Saunkskwa of Missitekw." Mary Ellen Lepionka is currently writing a history of the Native peoples of the North Shore. Much of her work in progress can be found at her website, Indigenous History of Essex County, Massachusetts: From the Last Ice Age to 1700, Cape Ann History, available at https://capeannhistory.org/.

9. Mary Ellen Lepionka, "How Were the Pawtucket Organized and Led?" Cape Ann History, available at https://capeannhistory.org/index.php/how-were-the-pawtucket-organized-and-led/#Squaw_Sachem_and_Passaconaway.

10. Heath, *Journal of the Pilgrims at Plimoth*, 78; Ron Wiser Research Home Page.

11. Stewart-Smith, "Pennacook Indians," 86. The name of Wenepoykin's first wife is unknown. Stewart-Smith suggests that Wenepoykin may have been in a polygamous marriage. However, the fact that Joane survived him, and that Passaconaway's daughter is virtually unknown, it seems likely Passaconaway's daughter was Wenepoykin's first wife, who died young.

12. Salisbury, *Manitou and Providence*, 183; Baker, "Salem as Frontier Outpost," 24–27. Wenepoykin would later be known as George No-Nose, or George who lost his nose, after some unrecorded injury.

13. *Suffolk Deeds* (Rockwell and Churchill, 1880), 1:43; Middlesex County Massachusetts Registry of Deeds, Cambridge, Massachusetts, Middlesex Deeds, 1:175, 2:384; Nathaniel B. Shurtleff, ed., *Records of the Governor and Company of the Massachusetts Bay in New England* (Press of William White, 1853), 1:196, 201, 254, 292, 317; Salisbury, *Manitou and Providence*, 199–200, 287; Hamilton Hurd., comp., *History of Middlesex County, Massachusetts* (J. W. Lewis, 1890), 1:8.

14. Middlesex Deeds, 1:175–177, 2:384; Shurtleff, *Records of Massachusetts Bay*, 1:292–294; Brooks, *Our Beloved Kin*, 80; Salisbury, *Manitou and Providence*, 199–201; Virginia DeJohn Anderson, *Creatures of Empire: How Domestic Animals Transformed Early America* (Oxford University Press, 2004), 158–163, 188–199; *The Records of the Town of Cambridge (Formerly Newtowne) Massachusetts, 1630–1703* (City of Cambridge, 1901), 48. In a separate transaction she deeded the land she inhabited to the son of her friend Edward Gibbons but only after her death. Richard Church deposed in 1656 that the Massachusett Sunksqua died in 1650, "to the best of his remembrance." See *Middlesex County, MA: Abstracts of Court Files, 1649–1675* (online database available at AmericanAncestors.org, New England Historic Genealogical Society, 2003), 1:110.

15. For Praying Indians, see Dane A. Morrison, *A Praying People: Massachusett Acculturation and the Failure of the Puritan Mission, 1600–1690* (Peter Lang, 1995).

16. Middlesex Deeds, 1:175; *Suffolk Deeds*, 1:43; Salisbury, *Manitou and Providence*, 149–152, 201–202, 218–222; William Cronon, *Changes in the Land: Indians, Colonists, and the Ecology of New England* (Hill and Wang, 1983), 91–99, 101–104.

17. Shurtleff, *Records of Massachusetts Bay*, 3:233, 252 (quotes), 4, pt. 1: 52; Massachusetts Archives, 30:19, 19a, 26; Malpica, "Uncommon Ground," 110–112.

18. Massachusetts Archives, 30:26 (quotes); Malpica, "Uncommon Ground," 111–112; *Suffolk Deeds*, 1:205.

19. Shurtleff, *Records of Massachusetts Bay*, 4, pt. 2: 428.

20. Recent treatments of King Philip's War include Brooks, *Our Beloved Kin*; Christine M. DeLucia, *Memory Lands: King Philip's War and the Place of Violence in the Northeast* (Yale University Press, 2018).

21. Perley, *Indian Land Titles*, 10; Brooks, *Our Beloved Kin*, 336–338; Margaret Newell, *Brethren by Nature: New England Indians, Colonists, and the Origins of American Slavery* (Cornell University Press, 2015), 185–186; DeLucia, *Memory Lands*, 297–300.

22. Brooks, *Our Beloved Kin*, 338; Newell, *Brethren by Nature*, 187; DeLucia, *Memory Lands*, 300–304, 317–320; Samuel G. Drake, *Book of the Indians* (Antiquarian Institute, 1836), bk. 2: 47–48.

23. Perley, *Indian Land Titles*, 51–77; Baker, "Salem as Frontier Outpost," 34–35.

24. All of the deeds are in Perley, *Indian Land Titles*. For the deposition, see p. 10.

25. Shurtleff, *Records of Massachusetts Bay*, 1:254.

26. For early use of the terms "Nahumkeke," "Nehumkeag," and "Nehum-kek," see Shurtleff, *Records of Massachusetts Bay*, 1:391; Francis Higginson, *New-England's Plantation, or a Short and True Description of the Commodities and Discommodities of That Country*, in *Letters from New England: The Massachusetts Bay Colony, 1629–1638*, ed. Everett Emerson (University of Massachusetts Press, 1976), 38; Richard Dunn, James Savage, and Laetitia Yeandle, eds., *The Journal of John Winthrop, 1630–1649* (Harvard University Press, 1996), 35.

27. Fannie Hardy Eckstorm, *Indian Place Names of the Penobscot Valley and the Maine Coast* (University of Maine, 1941), 143–144; Middlesex Deeds, 10:8; Wilson Waters, *History of Chelmsford, Massachusetts* (Town of Chelmsford, 1917), 638.

28. Perley, *Indian Land Titles*, 77–88.

INTERLUDE 1

Putting Salem on the Maps

Brad Austin

One of the books I love to use in my historical methods classes is John Lewis Gaddis's 2002 *The Landscape of History: How Historians Map the Past.*[1] The book appeals to my students because of its brevity (clocking in at a mere 150 pages of text), but its attractiveness to me is the way it helps all of us think about what it is that historians actually do. In Gaddis's analysis, historians operate much more like scientists than most believe; we just don't operate as *lab* scientists. Instead, our work is more like that of astronomers and paleontologists, in that historians both try to construct persuasive theories explaining what sometimes scant evidence reveals about our subjects and always have to be willing to revisit our explanations when new evidence (or new questions) demand it.

While that aspect of Gaddis's argument is certainly relevant to this volume's larger project (after all, we've subtitled the book *New Perspectives on the History of an Old American City*), another part is more pertinent to this particular essay. In *The Landscape of History*, Gaddis also compares historians' work to that of cartographers, suggesting that they must be both selective in what they include and intentional when deciding the scale of their project. While he argues that the accuracy of both maps' and histories' representations of their subjects is what determines their utility, he also notes that "there is no such thing as a single correct map. The form of the map reflects its purpose . . . [and] no map tells you everything it's possible to know."[2]

Our work on this book has reminded each of the authors that there is also no *single correct history*, certainly not one that tells all readers everything they want to know. We have had to, in Gaddis's words, be selective about our topics and the volume's scale. Just as one could question what our editorial choices reveal about our perspectives, academic interests, and knowledge gaps, in an effort to learn more about history writing in the twenty-first century, we can use maps to ask similar questions about the early years of Salem. The rest of this essay does precisely that, introducing readers to three (selected) maps of Salem and suggesting ways we can read these maps as evidence of their creators' mindsets and perspectives as they considered the area that would become Salem and its harbor.

Salem Map Number One: Samuel de Champlain (1607)

Samuel de Champlain was "perhaps the most accomplished and meticulous cartographer of northeastern North America" in the early seventeenth century, and his maps reveal a great deal about European perspectives, interests, and knowledge gaps in this era.[3] During a series of voyages between 1604 and 1607, Champlain conducted the "most comprehensive examination of the New England coast and some of its rivers that had so far been attempted," experiences that allowed him to make the "fullest written and cartographic record of eastern North America" created to that point.[4] The map he produced covered North

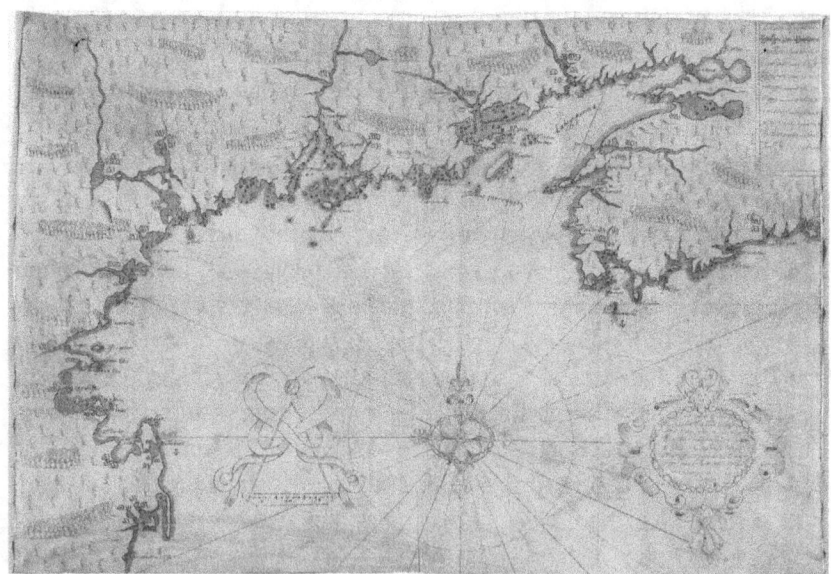

Samuel de Champlain, *Descripsion des costs, pts., rades, illes de la Nouuele France faict selon son vray méridien: avec la déclinaison de la ment de plussieurs endrois selon que le sieur de Castes le franc le démontre en son liure de la mécométrie de l'emnt*, 1607. *(Library of Congress, available at https://www.loc.gov/item/2006629903/.)*

America from just below what is now called Cape Cod up through Cape Breton, and it does so, according to David Quinn, "in significant and largely correct detail, allowing for compass variation."[5]

No one would ever describe this map as a "map of Salem," but it certainly includes what we now call Salem Harbor, and its creation tells us a lot about Europeans' ideas about the area. A few details are worth highlighting. First, all writing on the map is in French, reminding us both that the land that became Salem was part of a multicultural and multicontinental struggle for control and that the outcome of this was not predetermined. Second, the map reflects Champlain's personal experiences and skill as a cartographer. As Quinn explains, he got most of the coastline right, and that accuracy testifies not only to his abilities but also to his interests. His audience back in France was incredibly interested in what he could tell them about his observations of the coastline and its harbors, including the one that the English would later name Salem.

What is most interesting, however, is the way that Champlain's map of the region's interior lands displays simultaneously both specific knowledge and almost complete ignorance. We know that Champlain sometimes worked closely with the local indigenous populations to get assistance navigating up rivers and to learn about the lands he could not observe that were far from the coast. This practice explains how he was able to map harbors and their islands quite well and to indicate with some general accuracy some of the geography of the interior (vast woodlands, prominent mountains, etc.) without seeing these features himself. It's noteworthy that Champlain's maps document a variety of native settlements along the waterfront, acknowledging that the land the European monarchs claimed was already occupied.

In short, Champlain's map highlights how Europeans were coming to understand the lands and waters of North America, using both direct observation and intelligence gathered from the native populations, and that their focus was on the harbors, the existing settlements, and some of the natural resources of the area. Later maps would highlight different interests and perspectives.

Salem Map Number Two: "Map of New-England" Attributed to John Foster, 1677

John Foster's map of New England is generally considered to be the first map of New England published in North America, and the title of the work in which it appeared gives a sense of why Foster rushed it into print. It accompanied the text of William Hubbard's *Narrative of the Trouble with the Indians*, an account of the early battles of what the colonists called King Philip's War. In this conflict, the native peoples (led by Metacomet of the Wamponoag) banded together and attempted to expel the British colonists who were increasingly encroaching on their land. They almost succeeded, attacking and burning more than a dozen colonial settlements, before eventually succumbing after Metacomet was killed. Scholars agree that this war had a tremendous effect on the British colonies, noting that it was the deadliest conflict per capita in colonial/U.S. history and tracing its ripple effects to the Salem witch trials about fifteen years later.[6]

Foster's fascinating map allows us to put Salem's development by the 1670s in a variety of perspectives. The most striking aspect of this map is the fact that it is oriented so that someone sailing the waters of Massachusetts Bay could recognize what is in front of them. While the map's compass rose clearly indicates which way is North, Foster's image is rotated ninety degrees, so that it might make more sense to sailors and to its eventual British audience. Much like Champlain's drawing, this map's accuracy increases when it depicts coastlines and rivers, although viewers now see English place names, including Salem,

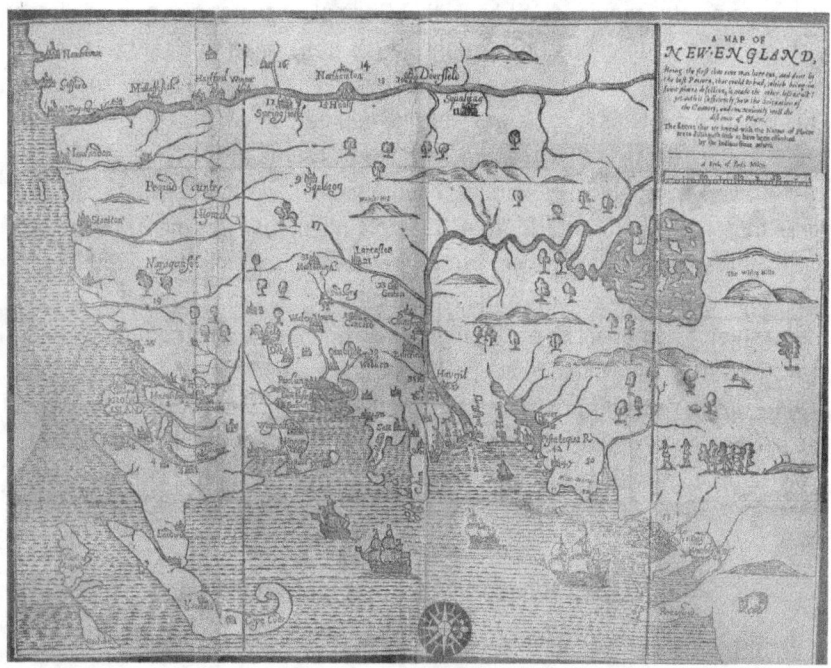

John Foster, *A map of New-England, being the first that ever was here cut, and done by the best pattern that could be had, which being in some places defective, it made the other less exact; yet doth it sufficiently shew the scituation of the countrey, and conveniently well the distance of places*, 1677. *(Norman B. Leventhal Map and Education Center at the Boston Public Library, available at https://collections.leventhalmap.org/search/common wealth:3f462s808.)*

across the landscape. Most important, the map depicts Salem by its place in an extended network of colonial outposts that is encroaching on native land, marked as "Pequid Country," "Nipmuck," and "Naraganset," and New England by both images of indigenous fighters and a legend that indicates exactly which of the towns had been attacked. Despite the fact that Salem was already fifty years old when he created it, Foster's map reminds us that the British colonial experiment wasn't guaranteed to succeed and that many in the 1670s understood this precarity.

Salem Map Number Three: Nathaniel Bowditch, 1806

Jean Lee Latham's novel *Carry On, Mr. Bowditch* won the 1956 Newbery Award for its dramatization of the life of Salem's Nathaniel Bowditch, a young man who progressed from a trading clerk to a sailor and navigator to the author of one of the most important nautical books ever published, *The New American Practical Navigator* (1802). Thomas Jefferson referred to Bowditch as "a meteor of the hemisphere," and the subtitle to Tamara Thorton's 2016 biography of Bowditch

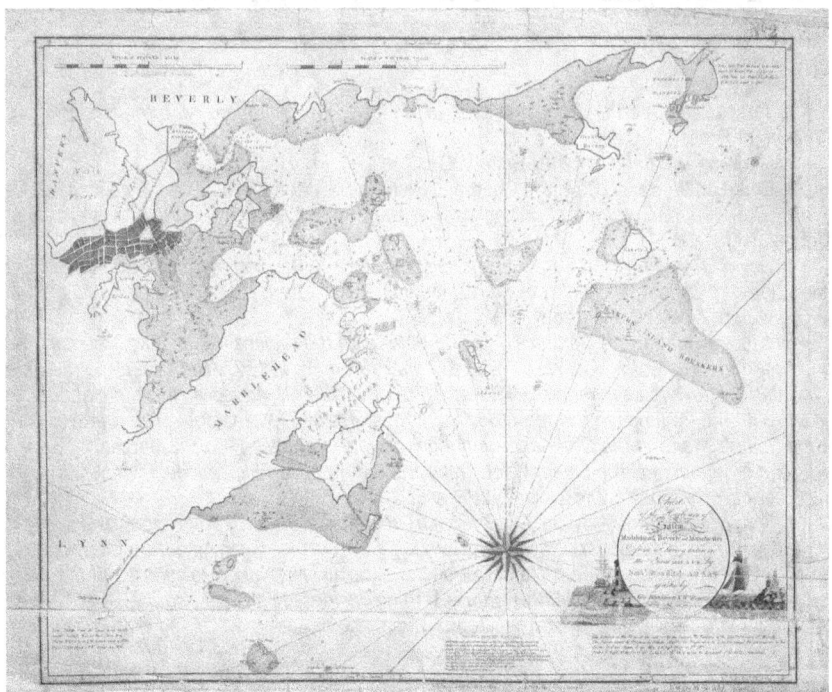

Nathaniel Bowditch, *Chart of the harbours of Salem, Marblehead, Beverly and Manchester*, 1834. *(Norman B. Leventhal Map and Education Center at the Boston Public Library, available at https://collections.leventhalmap.org/search/commonwealth:9s1619634.)*

speaks to his larger significance, as she considers "How a Nineteenth-Century Man of Business, Science, and the Sea Changed American Life." For this essay's narrow purposes, a close look at one of his maps is illustrative.[7]

In this "Chart of the Harbours of Salem, Marblehead, Beverly and Manchester," we can see a more focused representation of Salem in its second century of existence as a port city. Again, while the map includes literal landmarks, showing roads, place names, and political boundaries, the focus is on the sea. It provides detailed depictions of wharf locations and, characteristic of Bowditch's work, incredibly precise renderings of islands and measurements of harbor channel depths. Drawn when Salem was at its absolute peak of its economic and cultural influence in the Americas and in Asia, the details in this chart (and the hundreds of others Bowditch created) were instrumental to those participating in the global commerce that provided Salem its immense wealth.

Taken together, these three maps offer an accessible and useful introduction to Salem's early years. They provide viewers with a sense of how Salem transformed from a nameless (at least to Europeans) harbor on a vast continent, to a town spared by a deadly regional war, to a well-known and populated harbor that was vital to American economic development and global trade.

NOTES

1. John Lewis Gaddis, *The Landscape of History. How Historians Map the Past* (Oxford University Press, 2002).
2. Gaddis, *The Landscape of History*, 33.
3. Emerson W. Baker, Edwin A. Churchill, Richard S. D'Abate et al., eds., *American Beginnings: Exploration, Culture and Cartography in the Land of Northunbega* (University of Nebraska Press, 1994), xxx.
4. David B. Quinn, "The Early Cartography of Maine in the Setting of Early European Exploration of New England and the Maritimes," in Baker et al., *American Beginnings*, 51.
5. Quinn, "Early Cartography of Maine," 53.
6. William Hubbard, *A Narrative of the Troubles with the Indians in New-England, from the First Planting Thereof in the Year 1607, to This Present Year 1677. But Chiefly of the Late Troubles in the Two Last Years, 1675 and 1676. To Which Is Added a Discourse about the Warre with the Pequods in the Year 1637* (John Foster, 1677); Jill Lepore, *The Name of War: King Philip's War and the Origins of American Identity* (Vintage, 1999); Emerson W. Baker, *A Storm of Witchcraft: The Salem Witch Trials and the American Experience*, Pivotal Moments in American History (Oxford University Press, 2014).
7. Jean Lee Latham, *Carry On, Mr. Bowditch* (Houghton Mifflin, 1955); Nathaniel Bowditch, *The New American Practical Navigator* (Edmund M. Blunt for Cushing & Appleton, Salem, 1802); See the introduction to Tamara Plakins Thorton, *Nathaniel Bowditch and the Power of Numbers: How a Nineteenth-Century Man of Business, Science, and the Sea Changed American Life* (University of North Carolina Press, 2016).

CHAPTER TWO

Gallows Hill's Long Dark Shadow

Emerson W. Baker

In 2016, I was part of a team of scholars who announced that, "after centuries of conflicting beliefs and more recent internet speculation," they had "verified the site where nineteen innocent people were hanged during the 1692 witch trials at Proctor's Ledge, an area bounded by Proctor and Pope Streets in Salem, Massachusetts." The announcement quickly went viral and garnered publicity around the world. At the end of the year, *Archaeology Magazine* would name it one of its top ten discoveries of 2016. However, the site had really never been lost. Several generations of scholars regularly reminded the public of that fact, trying to break through the collective amnesia of a community that hoped to heal by forgetting this troubling landmark. For Gallows Hill has truly cast a long dark shadow over Salem.[1]

Four sets of executions took place at the site, one for each of the four sittings of the Court of Oyer and Terminer, which heard the witchcraft cases from June through September. On June 10, Bridget Bishop was the first to die. Five would be executed on July 19, five more on August 19, and, on September 22, the final eight would perish. A large audience viewed these hangings with people coming from as far away as Boston. Indeed, society felt it was important for them to be public, both to assure the community that it was protected and to serve as a deterrent for those who might be tempted to become a minion of Satan.[2]

Despite the many witnesses, little information exists concerning the executions. Close to one thousand documents survive in the court papers yet only a couple refer to the hangings. Bridget Bishop's death warrant only mentions she was taken to "the place provid[ed] for her execution."³ Robert Calef is the one contemporary who gives at least some details of the executions in his *More Wonders of the Invisible World*. Calef completed the book in 1697, but it was not published until 1700. He noted that, on August 19 and September 22, a cart carried the victims from the Salem jail along Prison Lane (present-day St. Peter Street), "through the streets of Salem to execution." On September 22, he said that the cart—loaded with eight victims—got stuck "going up the Hill" to the execution site.⁴

Calef describes the drama on August 19, when Rev. George Burroughs "was upon the Ladder, [as] he made a Speech for the clearing of his Innocency," which he ended with the Lord's Prayer. Burroughs's speech "was very affecting, and drew Tears from many (so that it seemed to some, that the Spectators would hinder the Execution)." After Burroughs was "turned off" the ladder and hanged, Rev. Cotton Mather addressed the crowd from horseback to calm them and remind them of Burrough's guilt, saying "that the Devil has often been transformed into an Angel of light." According to Calef, "this did somewhat appease the People, and the Executions went on." When Burroughs "was cut down, he was dragged by the Halter to a Hole, or Grave, between the Rocks, about two foot deep, his Shirt and Breeches being pulled off, and an old pair of Trousers of one Executed, put on his lower parts, he was so put in, together with Willard and Carryer, one of his Hands and his Chin, and a Foot of one [of] them being left uncovered."⁵ Calef also recorded the Salem minister Nicholas Noyes's reaction to the September 22 executions: "What a sad thing it is to see Eight Firebrands of Hell hanging there."⁶

While Calef's account demonstrates the high drama of this tragedy, it is not much help in pinning down locations. He suggests that the executions took place on a hill that was accessible by cart, and, most likely, somewhere on that hill stood a tree large enough to have all eight victims hanging together. Alternatively, Sheriff Corwin ordered carpenters to build a large gallows. However, such a structure would have been expensive, and there is no mention of a gallows in the court's expenses, though even small items such as shackles for the accused are listed. Somewhere near the execution site, there was a small shallow hole in the rock where some of the bodies at least temporarily resided. Unfortunately, we do not know how much to trust Calef. He did not publish his account until five years later, and it is unclear if he was an actual eyewitness. What is certain is that this Boston resident was an Anglican who opposed the witch trials and was a fierce critic of the Puritans, particularly Cotton Mather.⁷

Calef is known to have stretched the truth elsewhere to make his opponents look bad, and this may be the case in his description of the bodies being hastily thrown into the hole. Even if it did happen, it appears to have been a necessary temporary expedient. Samuel Sewall was in Boston on August 19, but he did confirm in his diary that Cotton Mather and other ministers were "among a very great number of spectators" and that Burroughs's speech and prayer moved people and raised concerns about the executions. However, Sewall also noted that a friend in Boston died the night of August 15 and was quickly buried the next day, without the usual waiting period or arrangements, as the "body could not be kept," due to extreme heat. Under such conditions, it would be important to get the five victims in Salem underground as quickly as possible.[8]

At the time of the executions, all of what is now called Gallows Hill was part of a great common pasture, a barren tract owned by the town. Near the foot of the hill, Proctor's Ledge was close to the palisaded wall that the town had built for protection from Native attacks during King Philip's War (1675–1678). The ledge was only about three hundred feet from the gate in the palisade built for the only road into or out of Salem Town, as it was located on a neck of land between two rivers. As such, it was a perfect place for an execution, an elevated spot safely outside the gates of town on common land but close enough to be easily accessible for observers. Similar locations had been used for executions throughout history. Most notably, Christ was crucified at Golgotha, a rocky hill just outside the gates of Jerusalem.[9]

In 1718, the Proprietors of the Town Commons sold the parcel that contained Proctor's Ledge to Samuel Pope, a blacksmith who lived nearby. In 1737, Pope sold it to Moses Steward, and, sometime before 1774, the lot was purchased by Thorndike Proctor Jr., the grandson of John Proctor who lost his life at the site in 1692. The property would pass, in turn, to two of his sons and, ultimately, to his granddaughter Martha Ann Proctor Nichols who would own it until her death in 1892. Although Thorndike Jr. was born eight years after the executions, oral tradition indicates that members of the family passed along the knowledge that the place that came to be known as Proctor's Ledge was the execution site. It is possible that Thorndike Jr. may have purchased it specifically because of this connection. This difficult truth was never forgotten by at least some residents of Salem.[10]

Others knew the site as well. In August 1766, John and Abigail Adams visited Abigail's sister Mary and brother-in-law Richard Cranch in Salem. John recorded in his diary that one night after dinner they "walked to Witchcraft Hill—An Hill about 1/2 Mile from Cranches" and visited the execution site, where someone had recently planted "a Number of Locust Trees over the Graves, as a Memorial of that memorable Victory over the Prince of the Power of the Air."[11] While the research of the Gallows Hill team suggests that no one remained buried at Proctor's Ledge in 1766, Adams was correct that locust trees had recently been planted there. However, the trees were not a memorial. Rather, in 1748, the Proprietors of the Great Pasture had encouraged their planting to help establish a windbreak on the hill. They offered a bounty of two shillings and six pence when each locust was planted, and the same amount again if the sapling survived fifteen months.[12]

While Adams's use of the term "Witchcraft Hill" was not common, locals used "Witch Hill," throughout the eighteenth and nineteenth centuries, as well as "Gallows Hill." The earliest surviving use of the term Gallows Hill was in the July 13, 1773, edition of the *Essex Gazette* which noted that a tree on "Gallows Hill" was struck by lightning and "was shivered and tore into a thousand Pieces, so that the Upper part of the Trunk resembled a Broom."[13]

Nathaniel Hawthorne used the term Gallows Hill in his popular short story, "Alice Doane's Appeal," which he penned around 1825. The narrator of the story climbs to the top of the hill in the company of two young ladies to tell them a sad tale he has written. On the way home, he bemoans the fact that on the "barren summit, no relic of old, nor lettered stone of later days" or "memorial column" marks the site. While John Adams was still alive and the Proctor descendants continued to own Proctor's Ledge, the Salem native and witch-judge descendant Nathaniel Hawthorne wrongly believed the execution site was at the summit. Collective amnesia was clearly setting in, as the community did its best to forget those painful sights associated with the witch trials.[14]

In 1885, the first memorial to the Salem witch trials was erected when the descendants of Rebecca Nurse, erected a monument to her in the cemetery on the Nurse farm in modern-day Danvers. The descendants were not done. In 1892, the bicentennial of the witch trials, they erected a companion monument that included the names of the forty friends and neighbors of Rebecca who dared to risk accusation by signing the petition stating she was innocent.[15]

Not to be left out of the bicentennial, in Salem, members of the Essex Institute (one of the forerunners of the Peabody Essex Museum) initiated an effort to build a memorial to all the victims of the Salem witch trials. However, as John Proctor's descendants could have told them, they planned to build it at the wrong site, the top of Gallows Hill. The memorial was to take the form of a forty-five-foot-high stone lookout tower, with the names of the victims inscribed on bronze tablets. A lookout tower may seem to be an odd memorial today but not to Union Civil War veterans. At the time, they were building memorials to their fallen comrades, including lookout towers on battlefields. In fact, an elaborate stone tower was dedicated on Gettysburg's Little Round Top in 1893, in memory of two New York regiments.[16]

An artist drew a rendition of the proposed Gallows Hill tower to help with fundraising, but it was never built due to the strident opposition by many Salemites. They felt that "the whole affair ought to be cast into oblivion as too horrible to contemplate; a shame on Salem and our community" and feared that descendants of the accusers might be offended. Incredibly, two hundred years after the trials, memorializing the victims was still too controversial for the community to support. So strong was this sentiment that Salem held no official commemoration of the bicentennial of the witch hunt, though local merchants did use it as an opportunity to encourage tourism and sell souvenirs such as the famous witch spoons sold by Daniel Lowe. Indeed, tourism related to the witch trials really took off in Salem in the 1890s. Meanwhile, people increasingly forgot the actual site of the executions.[17]

Fortunately, Salem did not have long to wait for a reminder. In 1901, the local lawyer and antiquarian Sidney Perley wrote an article where he argued that Proctor's Ledge was the execution site. Twenty years later, he published a much more detailed piece of research to make a strong case for Proctor's Ledge. He drew on the scanty surviving court records and did extensive property research to establish the chain of the title to the land, showing how it passed through members of the Proctor family. Perley also pursued local traditions and oral history, including John Adams's diary and the tradition in Joshua Buffum's family, where his descendants understood that he had observed the executions from his home on Boston Street and at night helped the victims' families remove the bodies. This agreed with the traditions in the Nurse, Proctor, and Jacobs families that they took their loved ones home for burial. Buffum was related to Rebecca Nurse by marriage, so it makes particular sense that he would have helped her sons in this effort. The nights in Salem in 1692 would have been dark and quiet. Anyone up on Proctor's Ledge with lanterns and shovels would have been quickly seen and heard by Buffum and other neighbors.[18]

Perhaps, most important, was Perley's interpretation of the November 25, 1791, letter written by Dr. Edward Augustus Holyoke of Salem, who observed that John Symonds, who was born in 1692, had recently died. During his long life, Symonds had often said that the nurse who attended Symonds's mother during his birth said "she saw, from the chamber windows, those unhappy people hanging on Gallows Hill." Perley knew the location of the North Street home the Symonds lived in when John was born. He studied the topography and determined that it would be impossible to see the peak of Gallows Hill from the Symonds's house, as Ledge Hill—present day Mack Park—obscured the view. However, Proctor's Ledge would have been readily visible from the home site.[19]

In preparation for his 1901 article, Perley also interviewed residents in the neighborhood who remembered the tradition that Proctor's Ledge was the execution site. The Stevens family, who lived on Pope Street just below the rock face, reported that, many years before they took down some old trees (Perley assumed locust trees) and cleaned all the soil out of a crevice in the rock, one of the trees grew out of the crevice (Perley assumed this was the hole in the rocks described by Calef). In sum, drawing from a wide variety of evidence, Perley made a convincing case for Proctor's Ledge being the execution site.[20]

Local officials clearly believed Perley, for, in 1936, the City of Salem purchased two small parcels on Proctor's Ledge, between Proctor and Pope Streets. Both deeds specifically state that the land was "to be held forever as a public park." Subsequent annual reports for the City of Salem refer to the property as "Witch Memorial Land." Yet, the city never did anything to the parcel, and, in 1980, it was almost sold as surplus property.[21]

People seemed to overlook Perley's work and ignore "Witch Memorial Land," so the debate continued on the location of the execution site. In 1963, Historic Salem Inc. formed a committee that tried to determine the site but only complicated matters by using Perley's research to add Ledge Hill as a possibility. Two years later, the *Boston Globe* noted that Rebecca Nurse was executed on Gallows Hill in Danvers. In 1976, Robert A. Booth Jr. brought Perley's work back to people' attention when he carried out a small archaeological excavation at the crevice at Proctor's Ledge. On the tercentenary of the trials in 1992, the *Boston Globe* got a bit closer to the truth by writing, "The hanging site of legend is Gallows Hill, a grassy bluff high up in the Witchcraft Heights area. But theories conflict on just where on the hill the hangings took place—or whether they happened lower in the area, or perhaps even in neighboring Peabody."[22] Perhaps the debate helps explain why, when Salem finally dedicated a memorial to the victims of the Salem witch trials on the tercentenary, they chose a downtown location with no association with the trials. By 1992, witchcraft tourism had become a major industry in Salem, peaking every October when hundreds of thousands of visitors are drawn to the city for "Haunted Happenings," which culminates on Halloween.

In 1997, while researching her book, *The Salem Witch Trials: A Day-by-Day Chronicle of a Community under Siege* (2002), Marilynne Roach found a key court record that supported Proctor's Ledge as the execution site. Boxford resident Rebecca Eames was brought into Salem on charges of witchcraft on August 19, the date of the execution of five people. The summary of her questioning later that day included the following: "She was askt if she was at the execution: she was at the house below the hill: she saw a few folk." Apparently, as Eames and her guards came into town on Boston Street the guards left her off at a nearby house while they watched the hangings. Thanks to Perley's research, we know there were several houses on Boston Street, in 1692, from which you could view Proctor's Ledge, but you could not see the top of Gallows Hill. Here, finally, was a solitary eyewitness account that confirmed Proctor's Ledge as the site. Roach published a pamphlet with this information and an interview with her was published in the *Salem Evening News* on October 31. Still, this news spread slowly.[23]

In 2010, Elizabeth Peterson, the director of the City of Salem's Witch House museum, read the works by Roach and Perley. Convinced that Proctor's Ledge was the site, she was disappointed that nothing had been done to mark the parcel that the city still owned. Instead, it had become a forgotten urban jungle where people threw their trash. Peterson had recently helped in the filming of a documentary on the witch trials, so she asked others involved in that project—the filmmaker Tom Phillips as well as Marilynne Roach, Professor Benjamin Ray (University of Virginia), and this author—if they could work together to confirm the site. If it was the actual site, it needed to be cleaned up, treated with respect, and given a proper memorial.

This newly formed Gallows Hill Project Team began its work. Initially, Roach, Ray, and this author worked independently, drawing upon all the data, to see if they agreed on the Proctor's Ledge site. To further clinch the argument, Ray and Christopher Gist of the University of Virginia's Scholars Lab used GIS to create a viewshed analysis that showed what Rebecca Eames or anyone in one of the homes on Boston Street in 1692 would be able to see. The viewshed analysis confirmed that while Proctor's Ledge was viewable, the area upslope from it, including the top of Gallows Hill was beyond the line of sight from Boston Street. The historians now turned things over to another team member, Salem State Geology Professor Peter Sablock, an expert in geoarchaeological remote sensing. The team knew that when they announced their findings, they would be asked where the victims were buried. Calef indicated that some bodies had been at least temporarily buried at the execution site. Although there were family traditions of removing their loved ones, they needed to know if graves might remain on the hillside.[24]

Sablock and his Geology students carried out extensive fieldwork at Proctor's Ledge. They used ground-penetrating radar and soil resistivity. These techniques indicate the depth of soil before bedrock, the soil nature and stratigraphy, and any subsurface features or anomalies. The results indicated that not only is much of the site exposed ledge; even in those areas with soil, the deepest pockets found were at most eighteen inches deep, not even deep enough for a shallow grave. Indeed, the soil in those pockets was completely disturbed, through the actions of worms and rodents. In the unlikely event that human remains had been left on the parcel, there was no trace of them. Furthermore, the trash on the site included dog's meat bones, which meant it was useless to run chemical tests for high levels of calcium in the soil, which might otherwise suggest human remains. Nor did Sablock find evidence of any structures, which supports the idea that no gallows was constructed, though admittedly the soil was so shallow that a gallows might not have left a footprint under the ground, so the possibility cannot be ruled out.[25]

The team completed its work in 2015. They agreed both that Proctor's Ledge was the location and that no human remains were there. They met with Salem Mayor Kimberly Driscoll to inform her of the findings and to discuss the next steps. The mayor concurred with the team that the site needed to be marked with a memorial. Indeed, Mayor Driscoll insisted that it be the responsibility and duty of the city to undertake this work. The confirmation of Proctor's Ledge as the execution site was announced via a press release on Monday, January 11, 2016. By Wednesday, Gallows Hill was trending on Facebook, as the story went viral with media coverage around the world. Numerous descendants of the victims contacted the Gallows Hill Project Team and the city, to express their thanks and support for the work. They considered it unfinished business that was helping correct an ancient wrong.

Fortunately, Martha Lyon, a talented landscape architect was working on a project for the city, so she was also tasked with developing the memorial. She had discussions with the city and the team and held public forums to gather feedback from neighbors, descendants, and all stakeholders. The task was made difficult by the small irregular piece of land, with rocky and uneven ground, unsuitable for a walking trail. The resulting memorial lies just below the rocky face of the ledge, next to Pope Street. The name of each of the victims is listed on an individual piece of granite, with their execution date. Also cut into stone are the words, "We Remember." While everyone wanted a memorial where people could come and pay their respects, given the nature of the memorial and its location in a residential neighborhood, it would not have been appropriate to turn it into a large tourist destination.[26]

The Proctor's Ledge Memorial was dedicated on July 19, 2017, the 325th anniversary of the first mass execution on the site. I made brief remarks as a representative of the Gallows Hill Project Team and concluded by saying:

> Finally, it is my sincere hope that today marks a new chapter in how Salem treats the witch trials. We became the "witch city" in 1892 on the bicentennial of the trials. While done largely for commercial reasons, I see it as Salem's self-imposed scarlet letter. The term "witch hunt" is synonymous with Salem, and stands as a symbol of persecution, fanaticism, and rushing to judgement. But with that title also comes responsibilities.
>
> From this time forward, I hope that the residents and visitors to Salem will treat the tragic events of 1692 with more of the respect they

are due. We need less celebration in October, and more commemoration and sober reflection throughout the year, for there are tragic lessons to be learned from this story. So, our job is to make sure that this site and what happened here is never, ever, ever forgotten. Only through actions like today, where we acknowledge and confront a troubled past[,] can Salem truly become the city of peace.

NOTES

1. The author thanks his fellow members of the Gallows Hill Project Team—Elizabeth Peterson, Tom Phillips, Benjamin Ray, Marilynne Roach, and Peter Sablock—who made this project and this paper possible. For the full press release, see "The Gallows Hill Project," Salem State, available at https://web.archive.org/web/20220525204509/http://w3.salemstate.edu/~ebaker/Gallows_Hill. "With UVA's Help, Salem Finally Discovers Where its 'Witches' Were Buried," available at https://news.virginia.edu/content/uvas-help-salem-finally-discovers-where-its-witches-were-executed.

2. Marilynne K. Roach, "Gallows Hill Project: [Re-]Discovering Proctor's Ledge," *American Ancestors* 18, no. 1 (2017): 40. For the quote, see Robert Calef, "More Wonders of the Invisible World," in *Narratives of the Witchcraft Cases, 1648–1706*, ed. George L. Burr (Charles Scribner's Sons, 1914), 369. For an overview of the trials and the executions, see Emerson W. Baker, *A Storm of Witchcraft: The Salem Trials and the American Experience* (Oxford University Press, 2015).

3. Bernard Rosenthal et al., eds., *Records of the Salem Witch-Hunt* (Cambridge University Press, 2009), 394–395.

4. Calef, *More Wonders of the Invisible World*, 361–362, 366–367, 369.

5. Ibid., 360–361.

6. Ibid., 369.

7. Baker, *Storm of Witchcraft*, 225–226.

8. Samuel Sewall, *The Diary of Samuel Sewall, 1674–1729*, ed. M. Halsey Thomas (Farrar, Straus and Giroux, 1973), 1:294; Baker, *Storm of Witchcraft*, 35–36, 225–228.

9. Sidney Perley, "Where the Salem 'Witches' Were Hanged," *Essex Institute Historical Collections* 57 (1921): 6–7; Baker, *Storm of Witchcraft*, 50–51. The approximate location of the fortification wall can be seen in Sidney Perley and William Freeman's map of "Part of Salem in 1700," published in James Duncan Phillips, *Salem in the Seventeenth Century* (Houghton Mifflin, 1933).

10. Perley, "Where the Salem 'Witches' Were Hanged," 10; Roach, "Gallows Hill Project," 40. The deed to Proctor is lost, but the land is included in his probate records from when he died in 1774.

11. John Adams diary 13, August 7 or 14, 1766 [electronic edition], Adams Family Papers: An Electronic Archive, Massachusetts Historical Society, available at http://www.masshist.org/digitaladams/.

12. Perley, "Where the Salem 'Witches' Were Hanged," 10; Roach, "Gallows Hill Project," 40–42.

13. *Essex Gazette*, July 13, 1773, 3.

14. The short story was not published until 1835. Robert Fossum, "The Summons of the Past: Hawthorne's 'Alice Doane's Appeal,'" *Nineteenth-Century Fiction* 23, no. 3

(1968): 294; Nathaniel Hawthorne, "Alice Doane's Appeal," in *The Token and Atlantic Souvenir*, ed. Charles Bowen (Charles Bowen, 1835), 84–101. The quote is on p. 101.

15. William P. Upham, "An Account of the Rebecca Nurse Monument," *Essex Institute Historical Collections* 21:151–160; Baker, *Storm of Witchcraft*, 272–273.

16. Baker, *Storm of Witchcraft*, 273–274; John M. Rudy, "Dan Sickles, William H. Tipton, and the Birth of Battlefield Preservation," *Adams County History* 20 (2014): 33–34.

17. Baker, *Storm of Witchcraft*, 273–274.

18. Sidney Perley, "Part of Salem in 1700, Number 7," *Essex Antiquarian* 5, nos. 10–12 (1901): 147–149; Perley, "Where the Salem 'Witches' Were Hanged," 1–18; Roach, "Gallows Hill Project," 39–41.

19. Perley, "Where the Salem 'Witches' Were Hanged," 8–9.

20. Ibid., 11–14.

21. Roach, "Gallows Hill Project," 41.

22. *Boston Globe*, September 5, 1965, 152; David W. Johnson, "Witch Execution Site Believed Found," *Salem Evening News*, A1; Richard Carpenter, "Salem Plays Up Witch History," *Boston Globe*, May 10, 1992, B30 (quote).

23. Marilynne Roach, *The Salem Witch Trials: A Day-by-Day Chronology of a Community under Siege* (Cooper Square Press, 2002); Tom Dalton, "Site Unknown: Author Says Salem Witchcraft Victims Not Hanged atop Gallows Hill," *Salem Evening News*, October 31, 1997, A1; Marilynne Roach, *Gallows and Graves: The Search to Locate the Death and Burial Sites of the People Executed for Witchcraft in 1692* (Sassafras Grove, 1997).

24. For a map showing the viewshed analysis, see Caroline Newman, "X Marks the Spot," UVA Today, January 26, 2016, available at https://news.virginia.edu/content/x-marks-spot.

25. Peter Sablock, "An ElectroMagnetic Geophysical Survey of the Execution Site of the Victims of the 1692 Salem Witch Trials, Salem, Massachusetts, USA," Geology Department, Salem State University, 2015.

26. "Proctor's Ledge Memorial: Site of the 1692 Salem Witch Trial Executions," Martha Lyon.com, available at https://www.marthalyon.com/portfolio/remember/Proctor's+Ledge+Memorial:+Site+of+the+1692+Salem+Witch+Trial+executions.

INTERLUDE 2

Salem's Regicide

Hugh Peter, 1598–1660

Donna A. Seger

The first four pastors of Salem's First Church were Cambridge educated, well connected, and true believers in its foundational covenant and congregational structure. Francis Higginson and Samuel Skelton were the founders of this spiritual community, which had "bound itself together in the presence of God," according to Higginson's wording of the Salem Covenant. Over his tenure (1634–1636), Roger Williams pushed the church from mere congregationalism toward more radical separatism, both from other churches in Massachusetts and from the civil authorities, resulting in his banishment to Rhode Island. Hugh Peter reaffirmed and expanded the original covenant but did not dwell long in Salem: he had work to do on both sides of the Atlantic.

Peter's Salem appointment, in 1636, came a year after he had arrived in America, a year spent preaching in various settlements as well as advocating for a more productive fishing industry: he was enthusiastic about both pursuits, so the Salem congregation knew what (or who) they were getting. Once there, he was active in both spiritual and material matters, preaching enthusiastically and at length, both in and outside of his meetinghouse, working toward making his many land grants more profitable, advocating for intensified fishing and shipbuilding industries in Salem, and serving both on the committee that would draw up the Massachusetts Body of Liberties and as an overseer of the newly founded Harvard University. Peter was the absolute opposite of his predecessor Roger Williams in two important respects: he had no reluctance about claiming land long owned by Native Americans (and, for that matter, no reluctance about utilizing the coerced labor of Native Americans on these same lands), and he drew no line between the interests of church and state, or the ministry and the magistracy. He expanded the Salem Covenant in 1636 with an admonition that members of the congregation should "carry ourselves in all lawful obedience, those that are over us, in Church or Commonweal." He was popular, likely more for his charismatic preaching than his disciplinary focus. Against the wishes of his own congregation, he departed for England, in 1641, as part of a colonial delegation to represent the economic, political, and religious interests of the Bay Colony before private and public entities in London, never to return to America.[1]

The first American historians of seventeenth-century Salem did not cast Peter in a very flattering light, for some of the earlier reasons and more. He excommunicated Roger Williams and was one of the more forceful interrogators of the Antinomian exile Anne Hutchinson, so any modern focus on toleration will not favor him. As part of the proceedings to commemorate, in 1929, the three hundredth anniversary of the founding of the First Church, the present pastor Thomas Henry Billings calls Peter a "violent and bigoted Puritan" who nonetheless "took in hand and established on a more secure foundation" all of Salem's industry and was also "unwearied in extending the influence of the church."[2] A more recent study calls Peter "a tireless pioneer for New England," but, ultimately, it was his role and fate in Old England that shaped his historical identity: he became a regicide, one who encouraged and consented to the judicial murder of King Charles I, in 1649, for which he was executed by death and dismemberment in the opening months of the Restoration.[3]

Peter became involved in the simmering Parliamentary opposition to the Crown almost as soon as he returned to England, largely through his preaching and successive appointments as a military chaplain. Eventually, he became the chaplain of the New Model Army, which placed him in close proximity to Oliver Cromwell. Their relationship remained close until the latter's death, leading to much access and activity for Peter during both the Second Civil War and the Protectorate, but it also made it impossible for him to acquire amnesty afterward. Peter did not sign the death warrant of King Charles I in 1649, but, nonetheless, he was seen as complicit by Charles II and the Restoration Parliament. He had supported the Army's occupation of London following the Second Civil War, Pride's Purge, and the trial of the king; he fell ill and did not attend the execution in late January 1649, and this absence was the source of much speculation that Peter was actually the masked executioner. Peter served as the chaplain to Cromwell's Council of State during the Commonwealth and preached both the victory sermon following the Battle of Worcester in 1651 and Cromwell's funeral sermon in 1658. It was impossible for him to dissociate himself

Portrait of Hugh Peter with windmill, part of a broadside titled *Don Pedro de Quixot, or in English the Right Reverend Hugh Peters*, 1660. *(@National Portrait Gallery, London.)*

from Cromwell, and he did not attempt to do so. Consequently, Peter became the target for some very creative Royalist propaganda, which attributed his inspirational preaching to his training for the stage rather than the pulpit and characterized him as both quixotic and demonic in *Don Pedro de Quixot, or in English the Right Reverend Hugh Peters*, a particularly dramatic Restoration broadside.[4]

Facing a brutal execution, Peter reached out to his New England daughter Elizabeth, his only child and the product of his arranged union with Deliverance Sheffield, whom he married after the death of his first wife in Salem. From prison, Peter wrote her a letter, published as *A dying fathers last legacy to an onely child* in 1660. Peter had essentially abandoned his wife and child in Massachusetts, so there is a bit of explaining after many pages of life advice. He insists that he had never intended to stay in England but was forced to stay in the "nation embroiled in those civil discontents" to accomplish his mission and please a succession of patrons even though he would have been better off in New England: "It hath much lain to my heart above any thing almost, That I left that People I was engaged to in New-England, it cuts deeply, I look upon it as a Root-evil: and though I was never Parson nor Vicar, never took Ecclesiastical promotion, never preach'd upon any agreement for money in my life, though not without offers, and great ones; yet I had a Flock, I say I had a Flock, to whom I was ordained, who were worthy of my life and labours." He makes no reference to Cromwell but says, "[I] had access to the King about my New England business: he used me civilly; I, in requital, offered my poor thoughts three times for his safety: I never had [a] hand in contriving or acting his Death, as I am scandalized, but the contrary (to my power): I was never in any Councils or Cabal at any time." He closes with blessings for the present king, who may look to promote goodness in religion, good learning, and relief for the poor, "and if I go shortly where time shall be no more, where cock nor clock distinguish hours, sink not; but lay thy head in his Bosom who can keep thee: for he sits upon the waves. Farewell."[5] Hugh Peter was hanged, drawn, and quartered before a jeering crowd on October 16, 1660.

NOTES

1. Hugh Peter supported the enslavement of both indigenous and African American peoples and was an enslaver himself. He wrote to his friend John Winthrop and also is listed as the enslaver of a woman named Hope in Harvard University's report, *Harvard and the Legacy of Slavery* (2022), 63.

2. *Exercises in Commemoration of the Three Hundredth Anniversary of the Gathering of the First Church in Salem, Massachusetts, May 26–June 3, 1929* (Riverside, 1930), 38–39.

3. Malcolm Gaskill, *Between Two Worlds: How the English Became Americans* (Basic Books, 2014), 156.

4. For Peter's Commonwealth career, see Raymond Stearns, *The Strenuous Puritan: Hugh Peters, 1598–1660* (University of Illinois, 1954).

5. Hugh Peter, *A Dying Fathers Last Legacy to an Onely Child, or, Mr. Hugh Peter's Advice to His Daughter Written by His Own Hand, during His Late Imprisonment in the Tower of London, and Given Her a Little before His Death* (London, 1660).

CHAPTER THREE

Salem and Slavery

BETHANY JAY

Though the history of permanent English settlement in North America began in Virginia more than a decade before either the Pilgrims or the Puritans settled in Massachusetts, Americans favor a national story that begins with the founding of Massachusetts.[1] This is not accidental. Since World War II, Massachusetts' dual pillars of religious freedom and the First Thanksgiving have provided a foundation on which to build the nation's identity as a bastion of liberty and an exemplar for the world. Historians have argued for decades that this celebratory narrative of the American nation obscures history, ignoring its contradictions and nuances as well as the diversity of its population. Within Massachusetts itself, this incomplete version of its colonial history has also masked the complexity of its past. Nowhere is this more the case than with the history of slavery in Massachusetts. In Salem, where well-preserved historic neighborhoods offer the allure of authenticity to millions of visitors each year, the historical failure to consider the city's history of slavery has had a huge impact, crafting an image only of religious trailblazers, wealthy merchants, and later fervent abolitionists. A close look at the history of slavery in Salem reveals a city that from its earliest moments thrived not only on the presence of slavery within the city itself but also by participating in an economy built by enslaved labor elsewhere.[2]

Movements to uncover the history of slavery often begin with questions about its origins. Nationally, the 1619 Project has focused the country's attention on the arrival of Africans to Jamestown in its eponymous year. In Massachusetts, the story of slavery begins with John Winthrop's simple journal notation about the arrival of a "Salem ship" from the Caribbean on February 26, 1638:

> Mr. Peirce, in the Salem ship, the Desire, returned from the West Indies after seven months. He had been at Providence, and brought some cotton, and tobacco, and negroes, etc. from thence, and salt from Tertugos.[3]

Winthrop's matter-of-fact listing of "negroes" among the cargo of cotton, tobacco, and salt is the first evidence of the presence of enslaved Africans in Massachusetts. And while it often has been used to mark the beginning of African slavery in the colony, the vessel is part of a larger story of the enslavement of both indigenous and African people.

That story begins with the need for labor. While Salem's landscape eventually would bring prosperity to the colonists, early settlers struggled to capitalize on its resources. Even lumber and fishing—the most immediately profitable industries—necessitated intense labor, as did the farms that sustained early settlers. Colonists devised several solutions to deal with this labor problem, including encouraging immigration, contracting for English indentured servants, and hiring indigenous people as a source of short-term labor.[4] These sources proved inadequate to the demand. The 1636 Pequot War began a transition away from the dwindling sources of English labor and ad hoc agreements with individual native people and toward the legal involuntary servitude of both indigenous people and Africans. The historian Margaret Ellen Newell writes, "The Pequot War coincided with a period of particularly acute labor shortages in New England when political leaders and entrepreneurs sought to tighten their grip on existing sources of labor and find new ones." Certain precedents in war, including "the Christian tradition of the just, defensive war," that permitted Christians to enslave non-Christians motivated colonists to make taking captives a priority of war.[5] Hugh Peter, who was serving as the pastor of the First Church of Salem when the Pequot War broke out, expressed his desire to enslave the Pequots who had been taken captive. In a July 15, 1637, letter to John Winthrop, Peter wrote, "Mr. Endecot and my selfe ... have heard of a dividence of women and children in the bay and would bee glad of a share viz. a young woman or girle and a boy."[6] Peter also suggests trading Pequot captives for enslaved Africans: "I wrote to you for some boyes for Bermudas, which I think is considerable."[7]

Other prominent leaders must have shared Peter's inclination to enslave the Pequots within Salem (and Massachusetts in general) and leverage the enslaved Pequots in an international market. On July 31, 1637, soon after the *Desire* departed Salem, John Winthrop wrote to William Bradford, updating him on the course of the war. Having detailed a gruesome battle that resulted in several captives, Winthrop comments on the *Desire*'s voyage, "The [Pequot] prisoners were devided, some to those of the riuer, and the rest to vs; of these we send the male children to Bermuda, by mr. William Peirce, and the women and maid children are disposed aboute in the townes."[8] Taking Winthrop's journal together with his letter to Bradford, it becomes clear that under direction from Winthrop and other leaders, Peirce sold fifteen boys, captured during the Pequot War, into slavery in the Caribbean. Those boys likely were not combatants themselves but instead were sold because their fathers had been identified as "murderers of English."[9]

However they ended up on the *Desire*, the Pequot boys were part of a larger trade that resulted in the arrival of enslaved Africans in Massachusetts. And, while the young Pequots were destined for enslavement on sugar plantations in the Caribbean, "the [Pequot] women and maid children" were kept in servitude "in the townes." Newell argues that Salem's elite were among those who received the most Indian captives from the Pequot War.[10] Those enslaved indigenous people would have provided essential labor through their work in "ironworks, fisheries, livestock raising, extensive agriculture, [and] provincial armies." The enslaved indigenous women would have worked and lived within the household, preparing meals, watching young children, and making "crucial contributions to small-scale household economies" by sewing and spinning, dairying, and other tasks.[11] In doing so, indigenous people introduced colonists to new foods, like cornmeal, venison, squash, and pumpkin, and integrated indigenous language and customs into daily life.[12]

The appearance of enslaved indigenous and African people in Massachusetts necessitated laws regulating the practice. The Massachusetts Body of Liberties, enacted in 1641 was the first legal code in the English colonies to define who could be enslaved:

> There shall never be any bond slaverie, villinage or Captivitie amongst us unless it be lawfull Captives taken in just warres, and such strangers as willingly sell themselves or are sold to us. And these shall have all the liberties and Christian usages which the law of God established in Israell concerning such persons doth morally require. This exempts none from servitude who shall be Judged thereto by Authoritie.[13]

The wording of the law is indicative of the context in which it was created. The Christian custom of enslaving those taken in a "just war" became codified in Massachusetts in 1641, justifying the enslavement of Native American captives from the Pequot War and other such conflicts. Similarly, the description of "strangers... sold to us" allowed for the enslavement of Africans, who were "strangers" by nature of their foreign birth. The inclusion of the word "strangers" in the 1641 statute may have precluded the children of enslaved parents born in the colonies to be enslaved. After all, they were not foreign born. Revisions to the law in 1670 accounted for this problem, removing that term from the statute so that it read, "lawful captives taken in just warres and such as willingly selle themselves or are sold to us."[14] In this way, slavery as a heritable status was rendered legal in Massachusetts. And, though it has been ignored in many of Salem's histories, before 1700, Native Americans accounted for most of the nonwhite labor in New England.[15]

Indigenous slavery was vital to the growth of New England's economy and culture, but it has largely been absent from the historical narrative. The changing conversation around the racial identity of Tituba is a good example of the way the historical record of indigenous slavery and popular memory of the institution have been in competition. Tituba, of course, is remembered today for her role in the Salem witch trials. In many modern narratives of this event, she is portrayed as a Black woman—a Barbadian provocateur who practiced voodoo within the Parris household and began the rash of early accusations that would escalate the crisis.[16] Documents from the 1692 trials, however, call this depiction of Tituba into question. Contemporary sources consistently described Tituba as an "Indian." The word appears fifteen times in relation to Tituba and differentiates her racial identity from two other women who were identified as "Negro" in the same documents.[17] In modern attempts to rescue Tituba's native identity, many historians have argued that she was an Arawak native from the Caribbean, who had been enslaved in Barbados. Even Tituba's Barbadian origins have been questioned by historians who find that "no direct proof" of that fact exists.[18] The historical conflation of Tituba's enslaved status with an African racial and cultural identity, despite evidence to the contrary, is representative of the larger cultural forgetting of indigenous enslavement in Salem and beyond.[19]

This forgetting may be due to the fact that it was an African-descended population that dominated eighteenth-century Salem's unfree workforce. Enslaved Africans were a significant and visible part of Salem's community. An analysis of the 1754 census found that 123 people, or 3.5 percent of Salem's population, were African American.[20] This community had public cultural practices like "Negro Election Day," perhaps the best-known celebration of African traditions in Salem, ably discussed by Donna Seger elsewhere in this volume. Many of the homes that serve as reminders of the city's illustrious past were sites of slavery. Two enslaved people at the Derby House, now a part of the Salem Maritime National Historic Site, appear on a 1771 tax document.

Enslaved people lived and worked in the mansion that is known as the House of the Seven Gables. While many tourists recognize the Ropes Mansion from the movie *Hocus Pocus*, they probably do not know that several people were enslaved there. Enslaved people in Salem had a diverse set of skills, families that they loved, and a desire for freedom.

Unlike Southern plantation economies, slavery in Massachusetts was concentrated in coastal cities like Salem, where enslaved people participated in a wide range of professions. Even those enslaved on the region's farms often were hired out as cobblers, coopers, tailors, or household servants in the winter. In an analysis of "Slave for Sale" advertisements in the *Boston Gazette* between 1704 and 1781, the historian Robert DesRochers enumerated the advertised skills of enslaved people. Even accounting for exaggerations on the part of eager sellers, the individual enslaved people participated in a number of industries: 36.3 percent of enslaved people were advertised as "versatile labor," while 19.1 percent were listed with specific skills ranging from carpenters and shipbuilders to cart drivers, bakers, and blacksmiths.[21] Advertisements in Salem's *Essex Gazette* demonstrate that Salem's slave economy reflected this larger trend. In 1769, the paper advertised a "Likely Negro Lad, about eighteen or nineteen Years of Age" who could work as a cooper or "in the Field or Garden." Captain David Britton of Salem advertised a "Likely, strong, healthy Negro Woman . . . who understands all sorts of housework." Another Salem woman was advertised as being able to "cook, wash, and do in-door Business as well as most of the Colour." In 1773, Jonathan Phelps leased his Salem blacksmith's shop. He included the hire of "Alfo a Negro Man, who is an excellent Workman," along with the shop. In 1774, "A healthy Negro Man, who is a good Hair-Dresser for Men and Women," was advertised for sale in the *Essex Gazette*.[22]

Just as slavery was visible in Salem, it also was cruel. The value of enslaved labor fluctuated with the seasons, and enslavers sometimes chose sale when faced with the cost of maintaining an enslaved person. Several enslaved people in Salem, including "A Negro Man about 22 Years old," described as "a strong healthy fellow and can be recommended," were advertised as "To Be SOLD, for Want of Employ." Children who couldn't perform valuable labor were particularly vulnerable. "A Very likely healthy Negro Boy, about 7 Years of Age," was sold alongside a "handsome new Chaise," when the estate of John Punchard was being settled. Whether that boy already had been separated from his family or whether separation would result from this sale is unknown. Parties interested in purchasing a "strong, healthy, likely Negro Boy, about 9 Years of Age," or "A very likely, healthy Negro Girl, about 6 Years old," were asked to inquire of the printer. Given the small-scale nature of slavery in Massachusetts, it is likely that these children were siblings. Benjamin Daland advertised that his "Likely, strong, healthy, young Negro Woman" would be sold "together with her Child, a hearty strong Boy, about three Years and a half old." The same was not the case for a woman "about 21 or 22 Years old, and a female Negro Child about 3 years old," who were offered "at a very reasonable rate." This pair, presumably mother and child, may have been separated. Such was certainly the case with "A NEGRO CHILD, of a good Breed, to be given away."²³

Slave-for-sale advertisements provide evidence of enslaved people's daily labor as well as the existential uncertainty of slavery in Salem. But they also serve as evidence of enslaved resistance. Unlike runaway slave advertisements, slave-for-sale postings after 1740 rarely name the enslaved person or the enslaver. In general, interested parties were told to "inquire of the printer." In his discussion of advertisements in Boston, Robert DesRochers has attributed this general trend toward anonymity to the fact that "both word and slaves got around." Literacy was more common among enslaved people in colonial Massachusetts than it would be in the South during the heyday of antebellum slavery. News of impending sales could, and likely did, travel among the enslaved community, and "armed with such information, slaves might force masters to broadcast not sales but flights."²⁴ In short, remaining anonymous was the enslavers' response to the fact that enslaved people fled when faced with the prospect of being sold.

Salem's enslaved people ran away for many reasons. After the death of Samuel Aborn, Joseph Aborn put an advertisement in the *Essex Gazette* to bring outstanding accounts to him for settlement. He also noted, "A Negro Boy, named Douglas, about 18 Years of Age, is run away from his Master, Joseph Aborn, under a Pretence of being free, but is not."²⁵ Prior to running away, Douglas must have told Joseph Aborn that he believed himself to be free. Perhaps Samuel Aborn had promised Douglas his freedom upon Aborn's death but had not codified that in his will? Perhaps Douglas believed that he was working toward a promised freedom in another way? Whatever the reason for Douglas's claim, Joseph Aborn was confident that his word would be sufficient evidence to ensure Douglas's return to slavery. John Hodges did not leave such dramatic evidence when he advertised for the return of "A Negro Boy named Scip," who at twenty years old ran away from enslavement in Salem. Hodges's ad does, however, give a detailed description of the clothes Scip "had on when he went away, a ragged Jacket, a speckled shirt, velvit [*sic*] Breeches, white Stockings, and a small Hat, the Brim about 2 inches wide." By including this detailed description, Hodges was helping ensure Scip's return. The inclusion of physical details was common in Salem's newspapers. And while they described a single person, they placed Salem's entire Black population at risk and under surveillance by suggesting "close inspection of Black bodies as readers compared published descriptions to the flesh-and-blood people who stood before them."[26] Richard Derby, whose house still stands on Derby Street in Salem, certainly expected that people in Salem and beyond would look out for Obed. Derby describes Obed's physical appearance as "about 25 years old, Somewhat tall, his Skin very black, his Nose more in the Shape of a white person's than a Negro's." Derby likely included this description because he was "uncertain what Cloaths he had on, as he carried a considerable Quantity with him, among which were a red Coat with brass Buttons, green Jacket and Breeches with white Buttons." The most important detail of Derby's advertisement may have been that Obed "was born at Cohasset in this Province." That detail enlisted the white citizens of Cohasset in the search for Obed, who may have fled to reunite with his parents.[27]

Runaway slave ads around Salem show that, even as white men were carefully considering the value of their own freedom before the American Revolution, they did not extend that consideration to their enslaved people. Already at war in Massachusetts, the colonists were willing to risk the full wrath of the British military in pursuit of their freedom. On July 16, 1776, Salem's *American Gazette and Constitutional Journal* printed the full text of the Declaration of Independence. While the declaration occupied the front page, the rest of the newspaper contained business as usual. On its final page, Salem's John White Jr. advertised that he "has a Negro Woman to part with." Having carefully considered the value of his own freedom, White did not recognize that his enslaved woman also would value hers. Similarly, Beverly's Benjamin Raymond advertised for the return of Caeser, "A thick well set Fellow, about Twenty-Five Years of Age," and offered two dollars as reward for his return. While we cannot know the specifics of Caeser's flight, we can presume that he was aware of the ubiquitous chatter about liberty and independence. He may have served in the rooms where Raymond entertained. He may have been literate. Whatever the case, Caeser's decision was his own declaration of independence, though it was not recognized as such by Raymond.

The 1780 Massachusetts Constitution, which stated, "Men are born free and equal," offered enslaved people a legal claim to freedom. The Massachusetts Supreme Judicial Court acknowledged this fact in 1783 when deciding the case of Quock Walker, who believed he was illegally enslaved. When giving instructions to the jury, Chief Justice William Cushing declared that "slavery is in my judgment as effectively abolished as it can be by the granting of rights and privileges wholly incompatible and repugnant to its existence." Cushing's instructions did not constitute a legal end to slavery, and Massachusetts did not subsequently pass a law ending slavery. Though this case has been the story of the "end of slavery" in Massachusetts, Salem complicates that narrative. The lives of Sabe and Rose Derby, discussed elsewhere in this volume, provide insight into the tentative and undefined nature of freedom in Salem after 1783. Elizabeth Dunkin's fate similarly muddles this simple story of abolition. On July 29, 1800, seventeen years after the Walker case and ten years after a 1790 census reported no enslaved people in Massachusetts, Salem's James Barr advertised for the return of Dunkin: "Run away from the Subscriber, Elizabeth Dunkin, a negro girl, of a pale black, about 15 years of age." Determined to retrieve her, Barr ran his ad through mid-August.

The 1808 obituary of Rose Derby, likely written by William Bentley, acknowledges the lasting impact of slavery in Salem. Describing Rose as "formerly belonging to Elias Haskett Derby," it also notes that her funeral included a "procession [that] did honor to the people of Colour," providing evidence of an enduring West African tradition. As members of Salem's Black community claimed the streets as their own to celebrate Rose, they made visible the legacy of slavery in Salem.

As a merchant city, Salem profited as much from slavery outside of the city as it did by the presence of slavery within it. We can return to the voyage of the *Desire* for some of the first evidence of this fact. In addition to carrying captive Pequots to trade for enslaved Africans, the *Desire* also carried "dry fish and strong liquors" to the Caribbean.[28] This cargo predicted the exchange of New England fish for goods from the Caribbean that would become a staple of Salem's economy. The historian Ronald Bailey has used the term "slave(ry) trade" to denote "participation in the slave trade and slavery-related commerce." Putting the slave trade itself aside for a moment, Salem's eighteenth-century wealth, visible in many of the city's most historic neighborhoods, was built on trade in goods made by or for enslaved people. The Caribbean played a central role in this trade network, and travel between Salem and the West Indies was continuous. Bailey notes that "more than half of the shipping of Salem—entrances and clearances—was destined for this West India trade." This pattern would persist until the American Revolution. The Caribbean was a valuable market for Salem's merchants because the islands' monoculture—the production of sugar for an international market—consumed the entire labor force and landscape. Salem's merchants played a role in connecting West Indian planters with food and other supplies from mainland North America.[29]

An examination of the voyage of the Schooner *Pembrock*, which sailed from Salem to Dominaco (Havana) in 1764 is illustrative of this trade.[30] The *Pembrock* was owned by Elias Hasket Derby and sailed with Henry Elkins at the helm. When the schooner arrived in Havana in February 1764, it brought, among other items, fish (unspecified), lumber, alewives (herring), cod, rice, hoops, and staves. The vast majority of the foodstuffs listed on board the *Pembrock* would be used to feed the island's enslaved population. Cod and other food that merchants deemed unfit for a European market because of their quality or freshness often were destined for centers of slavery. Importantly, the rice on board would have been grown by enslaved people in the southern colonies, likely South Carolina or Georgia. The cooperage supplies (hoops and staves) would be used to make barrels to transport the sugar, rum, and molasses produced by enslaved people in the Caribbean. In fact, sugar, molasses, and coffee were exactly the products on board the *Pembrock* when it left Havana in April 1764. The *Pembrock*'s trade within Havana is important because it was ordinary. On the whole, 90 percent of Massachusetts imports, namely, rum, molasses, and sugar, were derived from the Caribbean trade in the years 1761–1765.[31] As one of the colony's largest ports, Salem accounted for a significant portion of this trade. The historian Eric Kimball's analysis of trade records notes, "Between 1768 and 1772 over 44% of all the voyages made from Salem and Marblehead were to the West Indies, the single largest destination. The coastal trade was the next largest export zone: nearly 39% of all voyages clearing from Salem and Marblehead were to other ports in British North America, with a heavy concentration toward the southern slave colonies."[32] Salem's merchants, then, were deeply involved in the trade of goods by or for enslaved people, with 83 percent of their voyages over Kimball's period of analysis headed for centers of slavery. Much of the city's celebrated history and architecture was built from the profits of the slave(ry) trade.

Salem's participation in the slave(ry) trade was more extensive than its participation in the slave trade itself, though there is ample evidence of slave trading among Salem's merchants. While limited by available records, the Trans-Atlantic Slave Trade Database lists eighteen slave trade voyages that departed from Salem between 1763 and 1802, destined for African ports like Gambia and Sierra Leone. Captain George Crowninshield was listed as the owner of the *Polly and Sally*, which departed from Salem in 1787 for unspecified ports on the African coast. The *Polly and Sally* likely met an unfortunate end, as it was never heard from once it left Salem. Joseph and Joshua Grafton appear in the database as owners of three vessels that made four separate trips to the African coast. The Grafton's *Favorite* left Salem in 1785 and 1787 for West Africa.[33] Records for the 1787 voyage tell us much about the workings of Salem's slave trade. William Robinson, the captain of the *Favourite*, which is spelled differently in the documents than it is in the database, received clear instructions from the Graftons before departing Salem. The Graftons directed Robinson to find favorable trade for his cargo of tobacco and lumber in various ports on the West African coast. They advised, "If on your arrival you find you can procure slaves and lay in the necessary stores for them and make dispatch, we would have you do it—if you can not procure as many, we would then have . . . you go down the Coast." Once he had completed his trade on the African coast, the Graftons wanted Robinson to go to Demarara, a Dutch colony on the north coast of South America, now Guyana, and "trade their [sic], as we would not have you run any great risqué. We would have you lay the net Proceeds of your Cargo out in Cotton and Coffee." Knowing about the unpredictability of trade, the Graftons noted, "We trust to you Prudent Management."

In many ways, the *Favourite*'s voyage resembled any number of Salem ventures that were part of the slave(ry) trade. Only the addition of "35 pair Leg Irons" and "44 Pair Hand Cuffs," presumably procured from a Salem blacksmith, among the *Favourite*'s supplies demonstrate the very different nature of its voyage. Robinson wrote to the Graftons from Sierra Leone four months after the *Favourite* left Salem. He noted that he had some trouble finding markets for his lumber, tobacco, and rum, and he "cannot tell the exact number of slaves [the cargo] will purchase but suppose from fifty to sixty prime." Apparently abandoning the Graftons' plans to trade in Demarara, Robinson sold sixty-nine enslaved people—twenty-six men, fifteen women, twenty boys and eight girls—in Martinique.[34]

Shortly after the *Favourite* returned to Salem, the Massachusetts General Court passed a law "to prevent the Slave Trade, and for granting Relief to the Families of Such unhappy persons as may be Kidnapped or decoyed away from this Commonwealth." The law, which was prompted by the kidnapping and subsequent enslavement of three Black men in Boston, did not stop the trade out of Salem.[35] Half of all recorded slave trade voyages from the city left after 1788. While these voyages appear not to have had legal repercussions, they did breed contempt among members of the Salem community. The Reverend William Bentley noted his scorn for those who engaged in the illicit trade, who he variously referred to as morally depraved, sinners, and "of contemptible character." Invoking the recent ban, Bentley complained, "Notwithstanding the laws of the Commonwealth, there is not one man of spirit to stand forth and make enquiry into these detestable practices."[36]

The Salem schooner *Felicity*, owned by Joseph White, was part of this illicit trade out of Salem. Bentley was no fan of White. He wrote of the *Felicity*'s voyage, "It is supposed from the Cargo . . . and the character of the owner, that this Vessel is intended for the slave trade." Noting that, despite his great wealth, White "has no reluctance in selling any part of the human race," Bentley determined that White "betray[s] signs of the greatest moral depravity."[37]

The *Felicity* is not only notable because of its illicit nature; it is a remarkable example of violent insurrection aboard a Salem slave trade vessel. Historians estimate that rebellions occurred on as many as 10 percent of slave trade voyages, though available evidence is scant.[38] Captives on board the *Felicity*, which left Salem for Sierra Leone in 1789, briefly took control of the ship. Captained by William Fairfield, the *Felicity* was en route from Cape Mount to a slave market in the French Guiana with thirty-five enslaved people on board. In a letter to his mother, Captain Fairfield's son, also named William, recounted the insurrection, which he referred to as "a very bad accident." Thirteen days into their voyage, "the Slaves Rised against us. . . . Three of the Slaves took Possession of the Caben, and two upon the quarterdeck." The younger Fairfield gives a fairly detailed description of the rebellion: "Them in the Caben, handed up Pistels to them on the quarter Deck. One of them fired and killed my honoured Sir." Presumably, this is how Rebecca Fairfield learned that her husband had died. After a struggle on the quarterdeck and the death of three captives, the rebellion was squashed and the crew "put them In Irons and Chained them and then the Doctor Dressed the Peoples Wounds." A short time later, Captain Robinson was "buried as decent as he could be at Sea." Having detailed the violent death and "decent" burial of his father, William immediately tells his mother of his own troubles: "The 16 of this month I scalt myself with hot Chocolate but now I am abel to walk about again." He ends his letter noting that they have sold some of the enslaved and he, at least, will be home soon.[39]

Historians often talk about revealing "hidden" histories, as though diverse or difficult narratives have been concealed in hard-to-find places. It's true that the public memory of Salem's past has ignored the presence and impact of slavery in favor of "witches," adventures at sea, and the impressive wealth brought by those voyages. But, the history of slavery always has been a part of these stories. We just have not acknowledged it. This chapter has endeavored to make that history visible, not only to tell us about slavery but to tell a more accurate story of Salem itself. Slavery and its associated trade networks were visible in Salem. Voyages to the Caribbean were common experiences for Salem's young men, and the city's economy depended on a steady supply of Caribbean sugar and molasses. Enslaved people were a visible part of the community, working in a variety of jobs, raising families that they loved, and resisting their enslavement. In short, members of Salem's seventeenth- and eighteenth-century community lived in a city where slavery was a daily part of life.

Even as Salem changed, slavery remained integral to the city. In 1826, after a trade decline brought about by the limitations of Salem's shallow harbor, the disruptions of Jefferson's embargo, and the War of 1812, Salem's power brokers met to discuss their future. Led by Benjamin W. Crowninshield, they appointed a committee to "ascertain if it will be practicable and expedient to establish Cotton or other Manufactures in this town."[40] The move signaled the end of trade as the motor of Salem's economy, but it did not end the city's association with slavery. Many of those who met—members of the Derby, Ropes, Pickman, Dodge, and White families, to name a few—would invest money made in the slave(ry) trade into new industry. When factories like the Pequot Mills, run by the Naumkeag Steam Cotton Company, opened in 1847, its machines were fed by cotton grown by enslaved people in the American South. Indeed, Salem's connection to slavery lasted as long as the institution itself.

NOTES

1. *The 1619 Project* has ably made the case for the importance of Virginia's early history in our national narrative. See Nikole Hannah-Jones et al., "The 1619 Project: New York Times Magazine," *New York Times*, August 18, 2019; Massachusetts was originally two separate colonies, Plymouth Colony and Massachusetts Bay Colony, which merged in 1691.

2. Ronald Bailey calls this the slave(ry) trade in his essay "'Those Valuable People, the Africans': The Economic Impact of the Slave(ry) Trade on Textile Industrialization in New England," in *The Meaning of Slavery in the North*, ed. David Roediger and Martin H. Blatt (Garland, 1998) 3–27.

3. John Winthrop, *Journal "History of New England" 1630–1649, Vol. 1: Normal School*, ed. James Kendall Hosmer (Charles Scribner and Sons, 1908; repr. 2017), 259.

4. For examples of indigenous labor in Massachusetts prior to the Pequot War, see Margaret Ellen Newell, *Brethren by Nature: New England Indians, Colonists, and the Origins of American Slavery* (Cornell University Press, 2016), 65.

5. Newell, *Brethren by Nature*, 29.

6. Ibid., 44.

7. Hugh Peter to John Winthrop, July 15, 1637, Winthrop Papers Digital Edition, Massachusetts Historical Society, available at https://www.masshist.org/publications/winthrop/index.php/view/PWF03d354.

8. John Winthrop to William Bradford, July 31, 1637, Winthrop Papers Digital Edition, Massachusetts Historical Society, available at https://www.masshist.org/publications/winthrop/index.php/view/PWF03d358.

9. Newell, *Brethren by Nature*, 69.

10. Ibid., 64.

11. Ibid., 5.

12. See Margaret Ellen Newell, "Slave Codes, Liberty Suits, and the Charter Generation," Southern Poverty Law Center, Learning for Justice, *Teaching Hard History* (podcast), available at https://www.learningforjustice.org/podcasts/teaching-hard-history/american-slavery/slave-codes-liberty-suits-and-the-charter-generation.

13. *The Colonial Laws of Massachusetts*, repr. from the 1660 ed., sec. 91, p. 124, in Lorenzo Johnston Greene, *The Negro in Colonial New England* (Columbia University Press, 1942; repr. Atheneum, 1968), 63.

14. For a more detailed discussion, see Greene, *Negro in Colonial New England*, 65.

15. Newell, *Brethren by Nature*, 5.

16. Several sources counter this narrative, including Bernard Rosenthal, "Tituba's Story," *New England Quarterly*, Vol. 71, No. 2 (June 1998), 190–203.

17. Rosenthal, "Tituba's Story," 195.

18. Though the specifics of Tituba's identity may never be known, the documentary record is clear that the Puritans saw her as "Indian." If this is the case, why has Tituba been redefined as a black woman? The historian Bernard Rosenthal has offered several reasons for this depiction. As a black woman, Tituba was a useful scapegoat, "the dark outsider, the intruder who could be blamed for the community's troubles." But, she also could become the hero, "convert[ed] from a trouble-making victim into a noble woman powerfully resisting oppression." See Rosenthal, "Tituba's Story," 202.

19. Ibid., 202.

20. Salem, MA, Census, MSS 0.432. Courtesy of Phillips Library, Peabody Essex Museum, Rowley, MA.

21. Robert DesRochers, "Slave-for-Sale Advertisements and Slavery in Massachusetts, 1704–1781," *William and Mary Quarterly*, 3rd Ser., Vol. 59, No. 3 (July 2002), 631.

22. *Essex Gazette*, "To Be Sold," October 3, 1769, Vol. 2, No. 62, 39; See also DesRochers, "Slave-for-Sale Advertisements," 657; *Essex Gazette*, "To Be Sold," October 22, 1771, Vol. 4, No. 169, 51; *Essex Gazette*, "To Be Sold," May 26, 1772, Vol. 4, No. 200, 176; *Essex Gazette*, "To Be Let," October 19, 1773, Vol. 6, No. 273, 48; *Essex Gazette*, "To Be Sold for Want of Employ," June 7, 1774, Vol. 6, No. 306, 176. All in *America's Historical Newspapers* database.

23. *Essex Gazette*, "To Be Sold," September 27, 2774, Vol. 7, No. 322, 4; *Essex Gazette*, "To Be Sold," October 22, 1771; *Essex Gazette*, "To Be Sold," February 21, 1769, Vol. 1, No. 30, 122; *Essex Gazette*, "To Be Sold," December 12, 1769, Vol. 2, No. 72, 79; *Essex Gazette*, "To Be Sold," November 27, 1770, Vol. 3, No. 122, 71; *Essex Gazette*, "To Be Sold," January 4, 1774, Vol. 6, No. 284, 92; *Essex Gazette*, "To Be Sold," January 3, 1775, Vol. 7, No. 336, 4.

24. DesRochers, "Slave-for-Sale Advertisements," 634.

25. *Essex Gazette*, "To Be Sold," September 29, 1772, Vol. 5, No. 218, 35.

26. Carl Robert Keyes, "Additional Commentary—Clothing in Runaway Advertisements," *The Adverts 250 Project: An Exploration of Advertising during the Era of the American Revolution, 250 Years Ago*, available at https://adverts250project.org/tag/clothing-in-runaway-advertisements/.

27. *Essex Gazette*, "Run Away from the Subscriber," March 1, 1774, Vol. 6, No. 123, 123.

28. The *Desire* was intended for Bermuda but got off course and ended up in "Providence Island," now the Barbados. See Newell, *Brethren by Nature*, 51.

29. Bailey, "Those Valuable People," 11.

30. Account of the Sale of the Schooner Pembrock Cargo at Dominaco, February 29, 1764, Derby Family Papers 1716–1925, MSS 37, Box 6, Folder 6, Phillips Library, Rowley, MA.

31. Bailey, "Those Valuable People," 12.

32. Eric Kimball, "An Essential Link in a Vast Chain: New England and the West Indies, 1700–1775" (Ph.D. diss., University of Pittsburg, 2009), 272, available at https://d-scholarship.pitt.edu/7256/1/EricKimballDissertationMay12.pdf.

33. The Trans-Atlantic Slave Trade Database also lists the *Favorite* as leaving in 1794, though the vessel owner is not specified in that record. Available at slavevoyages.org.

34. All documents related to this voyage can be found in Ward Family Papers 1718–1946, MSS 46, Box 4, Folder 2—Favorite (Brig) 1787 to September 1788, Phillips Library, Rowley, MA.

35. Chernoh M. Sesay Jr., "The Revolutionary Black Roots of Slavery's Abolition in Massachusetts," *New England Quarterly*, Vol. 87, No. 1 (March 2014), n. 130.

36. Elizabeth Donnan, "The New England Slave Trade after the Revolution," *New England Quarterly*, Vol. 3, No. 2 (April 1930), 262–263.

37. Donnan, "New England Slave Trade," 262.

38. David Richardson, "Shipboard Revolts, African Authority, and the Atlantic Slave Trade," *William and Mary Quarterly*, Vol. 58, No. 1 (January 2001), 72.

39. "A Strange Epistle of a Century Ago," *Essex Institute Historical Collections*, Vol. 25, Nos. 10–12 (October–December 1885), 311–312. See also Donna Seger, "A Salem Slaver," *Streets of Salem*, available at https://streetsofsalem.com/2022/06/06/a-salem-slaver/; Donnan, "New England Slave Trade," 251–278.

40. Report signed by John Pickering and others, pp. 21–25 contain "An Act to Incorporate the Salem Mill Dam Corporation," passed by the legislature in March 1826, Goldsmiths'-Kress no. 24906.17, reproduction of original from Kress Library of Business and Economics, Harvard University.

INTERLUDE 3

John Higginson

A Seventeenth-Century Salem Merchant and His World

Marilyn Hayward

The seventeenth-century Salem merchant John Higginson Jr. (1646–1719) created the well-worn and -handled account book with faded sepia-toned pages and brown ink lettering that sits on the desk in the reading room of the Phillips Library, the principal archive of Salem's history.[1] The pages feel soft, old, and delicate as they are slowly turned. The covers are missing, and many of the pages appear to have been ripped out of the book, but the writing is legible and much of the text is still intact. This venerable work relates the story of Higginson's trade. He owned a shop in Salem to which local customers would come to buy produce and goods made in the area as well as items that Higginson sourced from other merchants and from his ships that were sent to the Wine Islands of Madeira and the Azores, to Bilbao in Spain, and to Barbados and other ports in the West Indies. His account book lists his customers' names, the items they bought and sold, and their payments in cash but more frequently barter. His customers came from Salem, Marblehead, Lynn, Gloucester, Ipswich, and other local communities.

John Higginson Jr. had a reputation as an honest, hardworking, and religious man, which must have helped his trade. His illustrious Puritan family included John Jr.'s grandfather Francis Higginson, who immigrated to America from England in 1629 and became, along with the Rev. Samuel Skelton, one of the two first spiritual leaders in Salem. John Jr.'s father was the well-known Puritan orator and longtime Salem minister John Higginson Sr. His siblings included sister Sarah, the wife of a wealthy Boston Anglican merchant and land speculator Richard Wharton, and brother Nathaniel, who left America and became a merchant and president of Madras for the East India Company. Three other brothers, Thomas, Francis, and Henry, all died young: Thomas was lost at sea while engaging in privateering, and Francis, a pastor, died in England at the age of twenty-five. Henry, a factor working for John Jr. in the West Indies, died in Barbados from smallpox at the age of twenty-four.[2] Last, there was sister Ann Dolliver, deserted by her husband, a "melancholy" mother who confessed to witchcraft during the Essex County witch trials.[3]

John Jr. did not follow in his father's footsteps as minister; instead, he became a colonel in the local militia, a civic leader, and a merchant. He was a lifelong resident of Salem and, in 1672, married Sarah Savage, the daughter of the wealthy Boston merchant Major Thomas Savage. John Jr. and Sarah had seven children, but just four survived into adulthood. An upstanding member of the First Church in Salem, John's children were all baptized in the Puritan church. As a sign of his own faith, he renewed his own original covenant with God and the church and received full communion in the First Church when he was sixty-six years old.

We get a first reference to his public life at the outbreak of King Philip's War in 1675, when twenty-nine-year-old John Jr. became an ensign in the militia.[4] He rose in rank until he was promoted to colonel in 1701. In this capacity, one of his major responsibilities was to train the militia on Salem Common. The colony engaged in Indian wars for much of his adulthood, and, when not actually at war, the threat of Indian attacks and the Anglo-Dutch Wars often raised the anxiety level of the colonists. John Jr. clearly held the esteem of his fellow citizens as he was appointed or elected to a number of civil offices. His various occupations included keeping Salem's town books, being elected a selectman, and being named a deputy from Salem to the General Court, a member of the colony's Council, a Justice of the Peace, and a notary. He was appointed a registrar of probate and a commissioner of the General Court and also served as the county treasurer and as a justice of the Court of Common Pleas. During the witch trials of 1692, he had an eyewitness view as a court officer.

In addition to his mercantile business, which encompassed his shop, sailing ships, a wharf and warehouse on the shore of the South River, and a fishing shack on Winter Island, John Jr. also had financial interests in a brewhouse and a gristmill. He had considerable investments in land, both in Massachusetts and in northern New England. The trading and investment activities recounted in the account book reveal something of the atmosphere of seventeenth-century Salem, hinting at the sights, sounds, and even the smells of a complex community at the edge of the Atlantic and an interconnected Atlantic world. One can imagine the sounds of the wharf ringing out as waves slapped and boats creaked against the docks, workers sawed boards as they repaired and built ships, orders were shouted, and boots stomped along the wharves as shoremen loaded the vessels with fish, provisions, supplies, and Higginson's wares for an imminent voyage.

Indulging our imaginations a bit more, John Higginson Jr.'s recorded business and life can suggest busy Salem streets, shops bustling with people hurrying to complete their tasks and head home, and the sounds of church bells, celebrations, and civic and sacred rituals. Perhaps the air was also rent with disagreements, such as anger at the Quaker Friends who refused to stop their gatherings and often lashed out at icons of the church (e.g., Reverend Higginson) or fights in the streets that resulted in presentments and confessions at the quarterly courts. Fornication, theft, slander, and violence were committed by some of the people mentioned in his account book. The sounds of order ring out, too, as military training was held on the Common near Higginson's home, bell ringers noted the time, constables served warrants to unruly citizens, jurymen deliberated the fates of the accused, and Salem's selectmen considered the possible paths of new roads and surveyed the town's fences.

John Higginson Jr. had a busy civic life, but his business life was social as well. He provisioned his vessels with salt for fish preservation, mackerel for bait, fishing lines and hooks, brandy, foodstuffs, and so on, and, in return, received fish from the master mariners who captained his boats. Higginson then sold fish to other major merchants and received goods that he could not source himself but desired for his shop or trade. Local trades- and craftsmen made his Atlantic ventures possible. They produced the foodstuffs, built and maintained his vessels, labored on board during the voyages, and provided the outlet for his purchases.

His account book indicates that John Jr. was always on the lookout for new opportunities and suggests the possibility of an earlier foundation for Salem's famed trade with the East. In their correspondence during the 1690s, John Jr. and his brother Nathaniel discussed at length their interest in creating an operation sourcing goods from Europe and East Asia to sell back home in America, a century before the China trade that brought Salem so much fame and prosperity. John Jr. suggested there was a market in New England for exotic goods, such as aligers [malt vinegars], pepper, nuts, cloves, toys, calicos, silks, plain, striped, and flowered muslins, and worsted damask in lively colors.[5] Unfortunately, Nathaniel Higginson died of smallpox in 1708, and their plans came to naught.

Closing the cover of the account book, we conclude our story of a fascinating Higginson clan embroiled in most of the major events and trends of the time period: the Great Puritan Migration and the settling of a strictly Puritan colony, the frontier wars that continued from the late 1630s through the lives of all the men named here, the English Civil War, the impact on the colony of Edmund Andros and then the Revolution of 1688, Atlantic trade, the East India Company's trade and exploitation of India and the Far East, the Salem witch trials, the building of political and economic connections through the use of marriages and personal relationships, and even the exploits of pirates and privateers.

NOTES

1. John Higginson Family Papers, MSS 442, Phillips Library, Peabody Essex Museum, Rowley, MA.

2. As a factor, Henry acted as agent for John Jr., receiving and selling goods abroad.

3. In a letter to Nathaniel, Reverend Higginson wrote, "She [Ann] is alas by overbaring malloncolly crazed in her undrstanding." See Letter from Reverend John Higginson to His Son Nathaniel Higginson in Madras, August 31, 1698, Salem, Massachusetts; for the transcription, see *Salem Witch Trials Documentary Archive and Transcription Project*, available at http://salem.lib.virginia.edu/letters/higginson_letter.html, accessed on July 5, 2021.

4. "List of souldiers liable to train under the command of Captain John Higginson," 1694, Phillips Library broadside.

5. John Higginson Jr. to Nathaniel Higginson in Madras, October 3, 1669, Salem, Massachusetts, Higginson Family Papers, *Collections from the Massachusetts Historical Society*, ser. 3, vol. 7, 209. There is a transcription error in this letter. The date is not 1669 but 1696.

THE SECOND CENTURY

1726–1825

Salem was incorporated as a city only in 1836, but it seemed like it had attained that status years, even decades, before. The growth of both its population and its maritime economy in the eighteenth century paved the way for its postrevolutionary hegemony, and it remained in the top ten of the most populous American urban centers until 1820. The fortunes of Salem's most celebrated families were built over this second century, including those of the Derbys, the Phillipses, the Crowninshields, the Cabots, and the Pickmans. Some of these families advanced their financial and political interests with the Revolution, while others fell behind, but all were impacted one way or another.

The pre-Revolutionary period exposed divisions in Salem, as the town became the official provincial port and capital by the passage of both the Boston Port Act and the Massachusetts Government Act in the Parliament in 1774, an "intolerable" combination of measures designed to punish Boston for the Boston Tea Party but in effect unifying British America. When General Gage, the new provincial governor, entered Salem in early June of that year, he was greeted by dueling welcomes from 48 Loyalists and 127 Whigs, after which he was compelled to travel to his temporary home in nearby Danvers as certain inhabitants of Salem had declared that "they will not sell, or let a house or lodgings to any persons that may remove thither in consequence of the passing of the Boston Port Act."[1] Representatives from across Massachusetts met at the General Court for only ten days in May before Gage dismissed them, and, after a large and illegal town meeting in mid-August, he was done with rowdy Salem and left for Boston. New voices emerged over that revolutionary summer, including that of Timothy Pickering, who would go on to become the quartermaster general of the Continental Army and secretary of war and state under Presidents Washington and Adams. Despite Gage's retreat, Salem was still the colonial capital, and, in October 1774, representatives of a discharged General Court resolved themselves into a Provincial Congress, among the first autonomous assemblies of the thirteen colonies.

Once the Revolution began, Salem's chief military role was in the realm of privateering, sending out more than a quarter of all Massachusetts vessels and capturing over 450 prizes, the largest tonnage of any American port. Elias Hasket Derby was Salem's preeminent privateering entrepreneur, outfitting an estimated eighty-five vessels alone, and Jonathan Haraden emerged as the "perfect hero" of privateers, in the words of one of his crew. Derby paved the way for a post-Revolutionary transition to maritime hegemony for Salem, played out on an expanded global stage. Cut off from the British Caribbean ports after 1783, the Salem shipowners and captains compensated by establishing new trading connections in Asia, Africa, and Europe and increasing their port's registered tonnage fourfold by 1810. While there were only two Salem wharfs in 1784, there were thirty at the beginning of the War of 1812. Salem's commercial cosmopolitanism in this "great" or "golden" age was conspicuous and cultural: in his 1812 book, *Travels in the United States*, the Scottish-born cartographer John Melish noted, of the town's "very extensive shipping trade, more business being done here in that line than any town in the New England states, Boston excepted"; he also described Salem's architecture as "uncommonly elegant." The built landscape created and inspired by the architect and woodcarver Samuel McIntire would continue to characterize Salem, but Melish also visited the shipyard of "Billy" Gray, "reputed the greatest shipowner in America" and took note of his large fleet of square-rigged East Indiamen. He observed the return of one of these vessels and the "considerable difficulty" with which it was navigating the "shallow" entrance to Salem Harbor and noted that "in consequence of this circumstance, Mr. Gray was about to remove to Boston."[2]

NOTES

1. *Maryland Journal*, May 28, 1774.
2. John Melish, *Travels in the United States of America in the Years 1806 and 1807, and 1809, 1810 and 1811*, vol. 1 (Philadelphia, 1812), 94–95.

CHAPTER FOUR

Salem's Revolution

A World Turned Upside Down

Hans Schwartz

The seaports of New England were powder kegs that the spark of the Revolution ignited in 1775. As the second-largest city in Massachusetts, Salem added a disproportionate share of fuel to the revolutionary flame. As avid participants in resistance to the Stamp and Townshend Acts, Salem residents took center stage in the politics of 1774 when their city became both the official colonial port and capital following the passage of the Boston Port and Massachusetts Government acts, designed to punish Boston for its Tea Party. A long Revolutionary Salem summer was followed by even more dramatic resistance in the winter of 1775, when the British Colonel Alexander Leslie attempted in vain to seize cannons rumored to be stored just beyond Salem's North Bridge, and "Leslie's Retreat" became a storied preview of Lexington and Concord. Once the Revolution began, Salem proved the most effective port for privateering, dramatically affecting the war at sea. Within Salem, a revolution no less dramatic or important in the life of the town and its inhabitants occurred, as the leading clans of Salem's first generations threw their lots in with the king and found themselves exiled or, at best, supplanted in the political and economic leadership of the town, the colony, and the new nation. Revolution was in the best interest of the rising magnates of the town and all of those whose fortunes stood to grow alongside them. Salem's most successful privateer, the *Grand Turk*, captured sixteen enemy vessels single-handedly and later became the first ship to master the China trade, making its owner, Elias Hasket Derby, America's first millionaire without ever going to sea himself.[1]

The story of Salem in the Revolution is also the story of the revolution in Salem. Families whose fortunes were founded on trade overthrew the older landed and grounded families that had dominated Salem's local government for decades. This revolution is reflected in the names of the streets of Salem today. Washington, Lafayette, and Derby Streets are its major thoroughfares, though shorter connecting streets such as Lynde and Pickman still bear witness to the pre-Revolutionary authority of those Loyalist families.[2] At the local level, the politics of the Revolution were very personal in Massachusetts. In Boston, James Otis, John Adams, and their rising circle felt unfairly excluded from power and its opportunities by Thomas Hutchinson and Andrew Oliver's clique of the more established families. A similar power dynamic existed in Salem, where Derby Wharf extended eight hundred feet into the sea and adventurous merchant mariners controlled 10 percent of the colony's lucrative fishing trade and held large stakes in the triangle trade and every other angle of colonial commerce, yet the town's elder clans and their kin held sway in local politics. The Seven Years' War had hastened the ascendance of the new commercial elite of merchants and artisans, whose goods and services allowed them to rise on the tide of trade. The older elites, including the Browne, Turner, Lynde, and Lindall families, had left commerce to these new families, yet, like their counterparts the Hutchinsons and Olivers in Boston, still dominated local politics as the "new" men came to dominate Salem's maritime economy.

Molasses returned from the West Indian trade meant rum distilleries prospered, as did all manner of tradesmen providing goods and services to the thriving Salem community. Just as the Bostonian artisans, like the silversmith Paul Revere, saw a glass ceiling in the deferential culture of Thomas Hutchinson's Boston, so did the Salemites, such as the blacksmith Colonel Robert Foster, Ship Captain John Felt, or a self-educated and self-made man like Colonel David Mason, who taught himself both enough about electricity to have a lucrative side business lecturing on the subject and enough about artillery to have served as a captain in a British artillery unit only to turn down a permanent commission and return home to Salem. Just as the far wealthier new money merchants found their ambitions stymied by nepotism and their fortunes threatened by customs collectors and imperial placemen, these ship captains and "mechanics" felt the glass ceiling of the hierarchical British world weighing heavily on them.

The Stamp Act and Parliament's promise to enforce customs laws more vigorously threatened the profits and even the livelihoods of Salem's merchants and all those who depended on them, from the ships' captains like Felt and their crews to the artisans who made sails, barrels, and rope to the rum distillers who depended on cheap, albeit illegal, French molasses. Richard Derby Sr. and, indeed, most of Salem's rising commercial class, including the Crowninshields, Dodges, Williamses, and Gardners, quietly took the Whig side. Their views are represented by the instruction, dated October 21, 1765, to Salem's representatives in the General Court, Andrew Oliver and William Browne (both Esq.), requesting: "Do everything you legally and prudently may, towards obtaining a repeal of the STAMP ACT, trusting you will use your whole influence on this important occasion, that the evils we so just dread may be avoided, which this town must largely partake of beyond most others in this government." Thus began a sustained effort to oppose royal power over the colony, utilizing the influence of the city's more conservative older elites, at this point, while undermining them later.[3]

Expressions of popular resistance in pre-Revolutionary Salem can seem muted only when compared to Boston. An early adoption of tarring and feathering occurred in September 1768, when a petty customs officer named Robert Wood, who had informed on a ship in the harbor holding a particularly large cargo of molasses, was seized, rolled in tar, feathered, and carted through town with a halter around his neck.[4] The following January, John Hathorne's brig *Bradford*, newly returned from the Caribbean, was searched for stamped paper or "marks of tyranny"; once found, they went up in flames in a bonfire prepared by "a large Company of respectable people."[5]

The Townshend Acts encouraged both more protests and more division. The Massachusetts General Court drafted a petition to Parliament against the duties, but Lieutenant Governor Thomas Hutchinson refused to cooperate and insisted that the court rescind it. The court voted 92–17 against such an action, but among the seventeen conspicuous "rescinders" were William Browne and Peter Frye of Salem. When a town meeting was called for the sole purpose of censuring the two, Browne's old guard allies presented a remonstrance against censure. Even as the moderator and Browne ally Benjamin Pickman Sr. "fell into the greatest heat and passion, treating the town with great indecency" and addressing the crowd "with language fit only for Bull Dogs," the censure succeeded: Browne and Frye found themselves replaced by Richard Derby Jr. and Timothy Pickering, whose wealth and influence was of a more recent vintage. A revolution in its own right, this clash marked a turning point in Salem's march toward independence. Richard Derby Jr. would go on to offer his fastest ship, the *Quero*, to carry the news of Lexington and Concord to London in the late spring of 1775, and Timothy Pickering would serve as the quartermaster of the Continental Army under General George Washington and as both secretary of war and secretary of state to Presidents Washington and Adams.[6]

A policy of the nonimportation of British goods was adopted in Salem in the spring of 1770, after the Boston Massacre (of which the ensuing trial was presided over by Judge Benjamin Lynde of Salem) and on a volunteer basis. An inspection committee of Richard Derby Jr., Jonathan Ropes, and Colonel David Mason inspected shops and warehouses, confiscated goods, imposed fines, and published the names of noncompliant merchants. Lawsuits ensued and the boycott was not effective, but its implementation forced anyone who hoped to remain neutral to pick a side. Those who still hesitated to support the increasingly radical Patriot leadership, men including no less than Judge Nathaniel Ropes, faced verbal and even physical abuse from their formerly deferential neighbors.

The Boston Tea Party and consequent Intolerable Acts soon cast Salem as center stage in the political drama playing out between the newly appointed Governor General Thomas Gage and the ever-bolder Massachusetts General Court in 1774. With the passage of the Boston Port Act moving the official port of the province from Boston to Marblehead, Parliament underestimated the resolve of Salem Whigs, who saw in the closure of Massachusetts's largest port not the opportunity to seize Boston's business but the threat that, if Boston succumbed, they must surely be next. Likewise, Salem residents chafed at the Massachusetts Government Act, which replaced the colony's revered charter with a British military governor. When Governor Gage announced his intention to move the provincial capital to Salem, as it was now the entrepôt of Massachusetts, "certain inhabitants" of Salem declared "that they will not sell, or let an house or lodgings, to any person that will remove [t]hither, in consequence of the passing of the Boston Port Act, they being determined to show their distressed brethren in the capital city, every possible mark of their sincere sympathy."[7] Gage was forced to reside in nearby Danvers.

Despite this dislocation, Salem greeted Gage with two quite different addresses, one signed by 48 Loyalists (Tories) and the other by 127 Patriots (Whigs), when he arrived on June 2. The first was laudatory and sycophantic, pleasing *his excellency* greatly. The tone of the second offered superficial formalities over the understated but clear opposition. Gage penned a complimentary reply to the first but found the Patriot address infuriating. Of the 48 Loyalists who signed the first address, 29 were bonded by marriage or blood to Salem's four old elite families, led by William Browne, Benjamin Lynde, John Turner, and Peter Frye, and, thus, to Boston's Hutchinson-Oliver clique. Others included several port officials and British merchant factors. The signers of the first address owned more property and were ten times more likely to have graduated from Harvard than those of the second. They were also far more likely to own stock in trade, to have lent money at interest, and to have been born outside of Salem. Among the leading new money merchants, only Francis Cabot welcomed Gage to town. Artisans comprised over half the signers of the Patriots' address, while 30 percent were ship captains. The signatures on Gage's less welcoming letter represented Salem-born members of the Dodge, Ward, Gardner, Derby, Crowninshield, and Proctor families, among other common names, and a pair of Pickerings.

It was soon apparent to Gage, and others, that his informant William Browne had painted a too-rosy picture of Salem's loyalty to the Crown, and it was difficult for him to find his bearings thereafter. The first (and only) assembly of the General Court met in Salem on June 7, 1774, and lasted ten days. Unbeknownst to Gage, a special subcommittee of the assembly was focused more on planning for participating in the Continental Congress than on doing his bidding. So the General Court was dissolved on June 17, but not before it had approved both sending five delegates to the Continental Congress in Philadelphia and boycotting the purchase and consumption of tea and other imports from Great Britain and the East Indies. Tea selling and tea drinking became even more precarious in Salem, with reports of occasional break-ins causing a certain commodity to be strewn on the streets of Salem or set ablaze in bonfires.

Governor Gage's June 29 declaration, "For Discouraging Illegal Combinations," provoked strong reactions up and down the East Coast, as patriotic papers protested "the most alarming Process that ever appeared in a British government." In late July, a detachment of the Sixty-Fourth Regiment of Foot under Colonel Alexander Leslie joined Gage in Salem, an indication that "illegal combinations" were still occurring, and the Fifty-Ninth Regiment would soon follow. Once he assumed more authority with the enforcement of the Massachusetts Government Act in August, Governor Gage banned town meetings in Massachusetts to one per year; consequently, Patriots began organizing *county* conventions. To elect representatives to the upcoming Essex County Convention in Ipswich, the freeholders and merchants of Salem called an "illegal" town meeting for August 24, which concluded its business before soldiers from the Fifty-Ninth Regiment could dissolve it forcibly. Nevertheless, Governor Gage ordered members of the Salem Committee of Correspondence to be arrested. Judge Peter Frye, a committed Loyalist but also a Salem man, caved to the pressure of his friends and neighbors (as well as hundreds, and perhaps thousands, of Essex County militiamen who poured into Salem) and urged the governor to let them go. After a day of deliberation, Gage did so, demonstrating "prudence," in the perspective of one observer: "Seeing them [the five incarcerated Patriots] resolute and the people so determinate, he was willing to give up a point rather than push matters to extremities."[8]

Governor Gage removed himself to Boston at the end of August 1774, but Salem remained the provincial capital. On September 1, Gage summoned

John Dixon, engraver. *A Political Lesson.* / J. Dixon invenit et fecit. United States Massachusetts, 1774. [London: Printed for John Bowles, at No. 13 in Cornhill, Sept. 7]. Photograph. *(Library of Congress, available at https://www.loc.gov/item/2004672699/.)*

representatives from throughout Massachusetts to convene for the election of a new General Court in Salem, on October 5, but reconsidered by the end of the month, "given the present disordered and unhappy state of the province."[9] He excused and discharged all representatives from the scheduled meeting in Salem and indicated that he would not be in the capital himself. Some ninety representatives showed up in Salem on October 5 regardless and gave Governor Gage an additional day to arrive before they declared themselves not a royal General Court but rather an autonomous Provincial Congress, among the first in the thirteen colonies. Business concluded, the new congress resolved to meet next in Concord, ending Salem's role at the center of the storm.

Salem was the site of one more notable pre-Revolutionary moment a few months later—its most storied moment—the incident known as Leslie's Retreat. Had British Colonel Alexander Leslie not retreated, the Revolution might well have begun in Salem rather than Lexington. On February 26, 1775, Leslie brought a contingent of the Sixty-Fourth Regiment back to Salem in search of between twelve and seventeen cannons that Loyalists, most likely William Browne and/or his brother-in-law John Sergeant, as well as Boston's archtraitor and British spy Benjamin Church, had informed Governor Gage were hidden at the home of the blacksmith Robert Foster on the North River, where they were being fitted with new carriages. The regulars landed in Marblehead on a Sunday morning and marched toward Salem on the Marblehead "highway," arriving when Salem's residents were still in church. The Marbleheaders raced to Salem well ahead of the column, and there was ample time to remove the cannons. By the time Leslie arrived at the North Bridge, it had been drawn and secured on the other side, and a scuffle between his troops and the taunting Salem residents ensued. Blood was drawn by a British bayonet to the chest of a distillery worker named Joseph Whicher, a small cut that he boasted about proudly forever after as the first blood spilled in the War of Independence.

Colonel Leslie's orders were to pass over the North Bridge to commandeer the cannons, which were, of course, long gone. He informed the crowd that he would fulfill these orders before returning to Boston, "if I remain here until next autumn," threatening a temporary occupation of Salem. In an exchange with Captain John Felt of the Salem Militia, Leslie declared his intentions, to which Felt replied, "You must acknowledge that you have already been baffled."[10] As darkness approached, the deliberations between Leslie, the militia officers Felt, David Mason, and Timothy Pickering, and the Reverend Thomas Barnard Jr. of the nearby North Church resulted in a compromise: the townsmen would lower the bridge, allow the Sixty-Fourth Regiment to cross it and march fifty rods up the road, thus honorably fulfilling their orders. They would then return to their ships in Marblehead and set sail for Boston. This they did, and just in time, as contingents of militiamen from Beverly, Danvers, and Marblehead were nearby and many more on the march. As the British departed Salem, their band played *The World Turned Upside Down*, a tune Leslie heard again six years later when General Cornwallis surrendered at Yorktown.

The colonial press made much of the incident, preaching the point that British soldiers would back down if faced with determined Yankees. The British officers learned a different lesson—that they too might be humiliated or "baffled" if they showed as much restraint as Colonel Leslie. Had the regulars fired on the crowd in Salem, the war might well have begun then and there rather than in Lexington. Instead, Leslie's restraint and retreat averted a bloody confrontation at the price of personal humiliation, a price other British officers were loath to pay. Just two months later, a bloody confrontation would occur between emboldened Patriots and British regulars determined not to back down at Lexington Green. When the alarm came on April 19 to march to intercept the regulars who were retreating from Lexington and Concord, Salem's militia under Timothy Pickering's command was tasked with taking up a position atop Menotomy Hill in Arlington. As a high steep slope, it would have allowed them to finish the rout of the beleaguered English, had they arrived in time. Instead, Pickering wasted time deliberating, set out late, stopped at several taverns along the way, then failed to engage when he finally arrived. Whether Pickering suffered from nerves, inexperience, or cowardice on that day is not clear, but he rose from this ignominious beginning to become Washington's quartermaster general and adjutant general of the Continental Army.

Salem contributed few men to the Battle of Bunker Hill and never met its quota for the Continental Army, probably because the men were off fighting at sea. Its naval record was far more impressive, with as many as 158 privateering vessels sent out from Salem, in the realm of 10 percent of the entire American fleet. The port's most famous privateer, Jonathan Haraden, won spectacular battles against the Royal Navy. The loss of trade during the war hurt the town, but privateering kept the economy afloat. Elias Hasket Derby, who owned seven ships at the beginning of the war, invested in privateering to counteract his commercial losses, reaping a fortune by financing 85 privateering vessels for 110 voyages and ending the war with 40 ships in his fleet. His ship *Grand Turk*, originally fitted out as a privateer, became a pioneer of American trade with Asia. On a strategic scale, the privateer war at sea helped bring victory at Yorktown. The exponential increase in insurance rates led the British merchants to demand the Royal Navy disperse its ships to protect commerce. Parliament's acquiescence not only made privateering far more dangerous but also deprived Britain of a fleet ready and able to evacuate Cornwallis's trapped army until well after the French arrived to cut off any hope of retreat and impel his surrender.[11]

Salem's merchant-Patriot leaders, the Derbys, the Crowninshields, and their associates, stood poised to amass greater fortunes and take on the political leadership of the town during and after the Revolution. The artisans who had stood at Leslie's Retreat, men like John Felt, Robert Foster, and John Mason, likewise watched their stations rise. Some who had remained loyal or sat on the fence joined the cause, apologized for their Loyalist leanings, and got in on the privateering market. A number of Salem Tories, led by Francis Cabot, Ebenezer Putnam, and William Pickman, appealed to the Salem Committee of Safety on May 30, 1775, that they wished "to live in Harmony with our neighbors" and "to promote to the utmost of our Power, the Liberty, the Welfare, and the Happiness of our country, which is inseparably connected with our own." This recantation was published in the *Essex Gazette*, along with Committee Chair Richard Derby Jr.'s statement that "said Gentlemen ought to be received and treated as real friends of the Country."[12]

Other Loyalists were not welcomed back into the fold so easily. A local ballad illuminates the state of Tory life after Leslie's Retreat: "The Tories in the town / were all put to flight / some left their houses / And others watched all night. / Prince, he kept close, / John Sargent, he fled, / And Grant was afraid / for to sleep in his bed."[13] Many left voluntarily for London, or Halifax, or elsewhere in the empire. The Banishment Act of 1778 targeted the Salem Tories John Sargeant, William Browne, Samuel Porter, and Benjamin Pickman, and the Confiscation Act of the following year stripped them of their estates. The crown rewarded Browne's loyalty, appointing him governor of Bermuda, while Sargeant died in Nova Scotia and Samuel Porter in London. Not all remained in exile, however: Benjamin Pickman returned to Salem after the Revolution, as did Samuel Curwen, with Timothy Pickering arguing in favor of both as valuable members of the community. Curwen's return was facilitated in part by William Vans, the former Loyalist "addresser" (signer of the 1774 Tory welcome letter to Governor Gage) who recanted and profited off privateering. Vans informed Curwen that he had been judged not so hostile to liberty as simply too cowardly to take a stand. The cause of one's loyalism, as well as their personal connections and reputations, were key factors in the redemption or eternal damnation of Loyalists in Salem as elsewhere.[14]

In the end, Salem played large pre-Revolutionary and Revolutionary roles. Leslie's Retreat nearly started the war and significantly influenced how commanders on both sides acted on the day that it did start. Salem privateers wreaked havoc on both the Royal Navy and the British trade. No less profound was the revolution *in* Salem. The old leadership that had taken the town from its seventeenth-century foundations through the imperial conflicts of the following century had been dethroned. New names, new men, and new families stood poised to lead Salem and the young United States into an era of global commerce and high sea adventures.

NOTES

1. Robert E. Peabody, *The Log of the Grand Turks* (Houghton Mifflin, 1926), 1–112, 231–233.

2. Charles M. Endicott, *Account of Leslie's Retreat at the North Bridge in Salem, on Sunday, February 26, 1775* (William Ives and George W. Pease, 1856); Peter Charles Hoffer, *Prelude to Revolution: The Salem Gunpowder Raid of 1775* (Johns Hopkins University Press, 2013); Richard J. Morris, "General Gage Comes to Salem: Interests, Ideologies, Identities, and Family Alliances Collide on the Eve of the American Revolution," *Early American Studies: An Interdisciplinary Journal* 20, no. 2 (2022), 263–304; Richard J. Morris, "Social Change, Republican Rhetoric, and the American Revolution: The Case of Salem, Massachusetts," *Journal of Social History* 31, no. 2 (Winter 1997), 419–433.

3. *Boston Evening Post*, October 28, 1765; Hoffer, *Prelude to Revolution*, 14.

4. *The Boston Chronicle,* September 12, 1768; also reported in *The Pennsylvania Gazette* on September 22, 1768.

5. James Duncan Phillips, *Salem in the Eighteenth Century* (Essex Institute, 1937), 288–289.

6. *Boston Evening Post*, August 15, 1768.

7. *Maryland Journal*, May 28, 1774.

8. John Andrews to William Barrell, August 25–27, 1774, in *Proceedings of the Massachusetts Historical Society* (1866), 8:346–348.

9. *The Massachusetts Gazette; and the Boston Post-Boy and Advertiser*, September 26, 1774.

10. James Barr, "Reminiscences of Capt. James Barr of Salem, Mass," *Essex Institute Historical Collections* 27 (1890), 123–148; Endicott, *Account of Leslie's Retreat*, 20–42; James Duncan Phillips, "Why Colonel Leslie Came to Salem," *Essex Institute Historical Collections* 90 (October 1954), 314; Susan Smith, "Biographical Sketch of Colonel David Mason of Salem, by His Daughter . . . June 1824," *Essex Institute Historical Collections* 48 (1912), 197–203.

11. Eric Jay Dolan, *Rebels at Sea, Privateering in the American Revolution* (Liveright, 2022); Richard McKey, "Elias Hasket Derby and the American Revolution," *Essex Institute Historical Collections* 97, no. 3 (July 1961), 166–196; Peabody, *Log of the Grand Turks*, 1–112, 231–233; James Duncan Phillips, *The Life and Times of Richard Derby, Merchant of Salem* (Harvard University Press, 1929).

12. James H. Stark, *The Loyalists of Massachusetts and the Other Side of the American Revolution* (James H. Stark, 1910), 126–127.

13. Endicott, *Account of Leslie's Retreat*, 32.

14. Thomas B. Allen, *Tories: Fighting for the King in America's First Civil War* (Harper Collins, 2011), 75–91; Endicott, *Account of Leslie's Retreat*, 31–33; Morris, "Social Change, Republican Rhetoric, and Revolution."

INTERLUDE 4

Jonathan Haraden, Salem's Revolutionary Privateer

Maria Pride and Donna A. Seger

Visitors to a downtown Korean barbecue restaurant in Salem might be surprised to see a bronze plaque to their left as soon as they open the door, its antique finish conspicuous in the modern interior. If they took the time to read it before or after their meal, they would struggle to discern what this plaque outlining the life and exploits of Jonathan Haraden (1744–1803), one of Salem's most renowned ship captains and privateers, was doing in this precise location on Essex Street. Salem is a dynamic city, and its main street has never been preserved in amber: this plaque was simply removed from its original location, the large Georgian house in which Haraden lived and died, after its demolition in 1928, and placed on its replacement structure and then *that* building's replacement structure. As the plaque reads, Captain Haraden "was a hero among heroes and his name should live in honored and affectionate remembrance" by whatever means possible (and in whatever *location* possible).[1]

Jonathan Haraden was, indeed, "a hero among heroes," the most celebrated ship captain and privateer in a city of ship captains and privateers. Well before the Continental Congress passed the Privateer Act of 1776, authorizing designated private American vessels to "attack, subdue, and take all Ships and other Vessels belonging to the Inhabitants of Great-Britain, on the High Seas" as well as "all Ships and other Vessels whatsoever carrying Soldiers, Arms, Gun-powder, Ammunition, Provisions, or any other contraband Goods, to any of the British Armies or Ships of War employed against these Colonies," Bay State privateers were in operation, licensed by the Massachusetts Committee of Safety, as British forces were laying siege to Boston in 1775.[2] The Revolutionary nation had a negligible navy, as constructing a navy takes time, and privateering was an Anglo-American tradition. Revolutionary privateering was extraordinarily important to the war effort, with as many as three thousand American authorized ships fitted for privateering, resulting in the capture of some eighteen hundred British ships and their valuable cargoes. It was also lucrative: their official "letters of marque and reprisal" enabled privateers to raid *and* trade. Massachusetts sent out around seventeen hundred ships during the Revolution, and Salem's captains made 276 privateering voyages alone, capturing 458 prizes, the largest prize tonnage of any American port. While the man often acknowledged as "America's first millionaire," Elias Hasket Derby, is recognized as Salem's preeminent privateer *owner*, outfitting an estimated eighty-five vessels for 110 voyages during the Revolution, Jonathan Haraden emerged as the preeminent Salem *privateer* and the "perfect hero," in the words of one of his crew.[3]

Haraden began his military career on an official Massachusetts Navy sloop (one of only two), the *Tyrannicide*, on which he served successively as lieutenant and then captain. By all accounts, he distinguished himself in service (e.g., news reports and letters seem particularly impressed by his capture of the British transport ship *Sally*, with its four thousand blankets on board), but, apparently, he "preferred greater freedom of action" and left government service.[4] He then served as the captain of the privateers *General Pickering* and its sister ship, *Julius Caesar*, capturing many lucrative enemy ships and cargoes, including gunpowder and firearms, sugar, chocolate, cognac, molasses, ginger, and rum, among other valuable consumer goods. He never turned away in the face of much larger and well-armed ships, capturing three British ships during a skirmish off Sandy Hook, New Jersey, in the fall of 1779, and then engaging in a spectacular two-day battle on the other side of the Atlantic, off the privateer haven Bilbao, the next spring. After first capturing a British vessel "without firing a shot," he encountered the thirty-six-gun British ship *Achilles* and dug in, taking that ship too with "superhuman" determination. When Benjamin Franklin, then the minister plenipotentiary in France, heard the news from Bilbao, he wrote that "Captain Haraden—whose bravery in taking and retaking the Privateer gave me great pleasure—is very good in offering the Spare Room in his Ship for the Service of the States."[5]

On the way back home, Haraden captured three more British ships, bringing them into Salem Harbor to great acclaim. The *General Pickering* was captured in the Dutch Caribbean in the following year, and Haraden was briefly imprisoned, but he lived to fight another day on the *Julius Caesar*. Upon his return to Salem after the Revolution, Haraden opened a ropewalk, which supplied the rigging for the sole warship made in Salem, the *Essex*. He died of consumption (present-day tuberculosis) at age fifty-nine, after which Salem newspapers noted the passing of "a distinguished naval commander during the Revolution."[6] The always-reliable Reverend William Bentley noted Haraden's death in his diary on November 23, 1803: "He was one of our most intrepid Commanders of the Revolution. He was an accomplished gentleman, of cool temper, of generous courage, & a most successful Officer in all his engagements at Sea. No man had a higher reputation or could have greater favor among all who were under him."[7]

The location of the bronze plaque dedicated to the memory of this maritime hero seems to indicate that Captain Haraden is forgotten in Salem, a city with an attraction dedicated to the "real" pirates of Cape Cod but not to the genuine privateers of Salem. His house is gone, but, if you look around, you can see his traces. The triumphant captain, returned from Bilboa, received a splendid silver tankard and two canns engraved with the *General Pickering* and his cipher by its grateful owners, now in the collection of the Peabody Essex Museum in Salem with numerous other maritime trophies. Also in Salem is his grave at the city's second-oldest burying ground, the Broad Street Cemetery, which bears the inscription of his obituary. On many occasions of Revolutionary commemoration in the nineteenth century, the achievements and attributes of Captain Haraden were recalled and exalted. In his July 4, 1842, address before the Salem City Council, Charles W. Upham, the pastor, politician, and author of the first substantive history of the Salem witch trials, asserted that "never should the people of this place assemble to commemorate the War of Independence without bearing in honored and affectionate remembrance the name of this dauntless hero and virtuous citizen." In his lengthy oration, later printed, Upham goes all the way back to Salem's seventeenth-century founding to provide a context for Haraden's heroism, and he dwells on all the dramatic details of the Bilboa battle, even increasing the size of the crowd that watched from the shore to one hundred thousand. Haraden emerges as "invincible," and, beyond brave, possessing the ability to make everyone in his company brave as well: "So evident and certain was it that he knew no fear, that fear vanished from the breasts of all under his command."[8]

Despite this depiction, there is a sense that Haraden slipped away from collective memory after the Civil War, only to be resurrected at the beginning of the next century with the 1909 publication of journalist turned maritime historian Ralph Delahaye Paine's *Ships and Sailors of Salem: The Record of a Brilliant Era of American Achievement*, the same year as the placement of the restaurant plaque. Paine was not a professional historian, but his journalistic training led to a preference for firsthand accounts, and his narratives of Haraden's exploits are "compiled from the stories of those who knew and sailed with this fine figure of a privateersman."[9] Paine devoted an entire chapter to Haraden, and it is very much a heroic depiction but also full of a lot of little details that surface in later works: his pioneering use of painted-canvas "camouflage," his battle bluffing, the elaborately embroidered waistcoat he would wear into battle (also in the collection of the Peabody Essex Museum), his calm demeanor in the most challenging situations, and all about Bilbao. Paine's apparent aim was to raise Haraden to the level of John Paul Jones in naval heritage, and those references follow his publication, as does the christening of two USS *Jonathan Haraden*, one of which was launched just after World War I and the other during World War II.

The most remarkable memorials to Jonathan Haraden are those of his own making: well-preserved logbooks in the collection of the Phillips Library of the Peabody Essex Museum, now located in Rowley, Massachusetts. There are two Haraden logbooks, for the brigs *Tyrannicide* (1778–1779) and *General Pickering* (1778–1779), both digitized by the Phillips Library with the support of the Salem Marine Society (of which Haraden once served as master), and additional ships papers in other collections.[10] The *General Pickering*'s logbook is written in his clear hand with the first entry of November 22, 1778, in Salem Harbor. The "intended voyage" was to Martinique but the ship appears to have run off course, as privateers were prone to do. Nevertheless, the logbook reveals the general pattern of sail for trading and raiding: south to the Caribbean, then eastward toward Spain, and, finally, home to Salem. On Christmas Eve, in 1778, Haraden and his crew were in the waters near Barbados, where they captured several prizes; in February, the *General Pickering* was near the Virgin Islands; and, by March 14, it was battling "Nasty weather—11 pm the gale increases very much hove over 6 cannons and got the fore yard down—middle part a heavy gale attended with squalls, rain & hail" off the coast of the Carolinas. By the end of that month, Captain Haraden and his crew were safely in port in Portsmouth, New Hampshire.[11] From there, it was a relatively quick voyage back to Salem, in calmer waters cleared of enemy ships.

NOTES

1. Haraden's plaque was placed on his Essex Street house by the Massachusetts Society of the Sons of the American Revolution on September 25, 1909. A field day and reception in Salem also marked the occasion.

2. *Instructions to the Commanders of Private Ships of Vessels of War, Which Shall Have Commissions or Letters of Marque and Reprisals, Authorizing Them to Make Captures of British Vessels and Cargoes* (Philadelphia, 1776). Massachusetts privateers were authorized to "equip any vessel to sail on the seas, attack, take and bring into any port in this colony all vessels offending or employed by the enemy" by *An Act for Encouraging the Fixing Out of Armed Vessels to Defend the Sea-Coast of America, and for Erecting a Court to Try and Condemn All Vessels That Shall Be Found Infesting the Same*, Massachusetts General Court, November 1775, State Library of Massachusetts, Acts and Resolves of the

Massachusetts General Court (1692–1780), available at https://archives.lib.state.ma.us/items/5efdcc3b-60f3-47f4-8c36-75f57d932562.

3. Eric Jay Dolan's *Rebels at Sea: Pioneering in the American Revolution* (New York: Liveright, 2022) opens with Jonathan Haraden's exploits and includes the "perfect hero" assessment of Israel Thorndike, his first lieutenant on the *Tyrannicide*. Richard McKey summarized Elias Hasket Derby's privateering in "Elias Hasket Derby and the American Revolution," *Essex Institute Historical Collections* 97 no. 3 (July 1961): 166–196: "Derby, in outfitting his eighty-five vessels for their one hundred and ten cruises, supplied personally over fifty percent of Salem's entire privateering activity (and thus twelve percent of Massachusetts' effort and five percent of all the colonies together). Over eight thousand men shipped on his vessels; capturing twenty-nine ships, fifty-eight brigs, ten snows, twenty-five sloops, and twenty-two schooners" (195). Privateering numbers are difficult to pin down with certainty due to incomplete records, the distinction between privateering ships and privateering *voyages*, between those ships that were bonded and those that were not, and between ships that received commissions from the Continental Congress and those that received state letters of marque. In *The Untold War at Sea: America's Revolutionary Privateers*, Kylie A. Hulbert observes that the "vessels engaged" in privateering from 1776 to 1783 range from "1151 to 1697 to over 2000" (Athens: University of Georgia Press, 2022), 9–10. Maria Pride's recent dissertation asserts higher numbers for both Massachusetts and Salem: 975 Massachusetts ships undertaking 1569 voyages, and 1095 privateering voyages departing from Salem over the course of the war: "Privateering in the Eastern Ports of Massachusetts during the Revolutionary War, c. 1775–1783" (Ph.D. diss., University of Stirling, 2024).

4. National Archives, Founders Online; Ralph M. Eastman, *Some Famous Privateers of New England* (Boston: State Street Trust, 1928), 15. Eastman asserts that "no less than a thousand enemy cannons were captured by this splendid seaman."

5. "From Benjamin Franklin to Joseph Gardoqui & *fils*, 4 July 1780," Founders Online, National Archives, available at https://founders.archives.gov/documents/Franklin/01-33-02-0014. [Original source: *The Papers of Benjamin Franklin*, vol. 33, July 1 through November 15, 1780, ed. Barbara B. Oberg (New Haven, CT: Yale University Press, 1997), 22–23.]

6. *Salem Register*, November 24, 1803.

7. *The Diary of William Bentley, D.D.*, vol. 3 (Salem: Essex Institute, 1911), 62.

8. Charles W. Upham, *Oration Delivered at the Request of the City Authorities of Salem, July 4, 1842* (Salem: Chapman and Palfray, 1842), 29–31.

9. Ralph D. Paine, *The Ships and Sailors of Salem: The Record of a Brilliant Era of American Achievement*, 2nd ed. (Chicago: A. C. McClurg, 1912), 84.

10. Phillips Library, Peabody Essex Museum, Rowley, MA: *Tyrannicide* (brigantine) privateering logbook, 1778–1779, Log 3000+; *General Pickering* (brigantine) logbook, 1778–1779, Log 3000+. Papers related to Haraden's last ship, the *Julius Caesar*, can be found in the Ward Family Papers, MSS 46, Phillips Library, Peabody Essex Museum, Rowley, MA.

11. Phillips Library, Peabody Essex Museum, Rowley, MA: *General Pickering* privateering logbook, 1778–1779, Log 3000+.

CHAPTER FIVE

The Kinsmans of Salem and China

DANE A. MORRISON AND KIMBERLY S. ALEXANDER

"How plainly I can see those dear County Street parlors as thee describes them, and oh! How inexpressible are my longings to look in upon them and their dear inmates.... The ties that bind us to home, are very strong and not easily severed."[1] Writing in 1844 from Macao, the Portuguese colony nestled on the outskirts of the Chinese empire, Rebecca Chase Kinsman was feeling homesick and longed to see her beloved Salem. The port was her birthplace and held fond memories of all that was dear to her. Six months earlier, in July 1843, the Kinsmans—Rebecca (1810–1882), Nathaniel (1798–1847), and their children, Natty and Ecca—had boarded the ship (*Probius*) that would carry them across three oceans to China. Their story reveals much about Salem during the era of the Old China Trade (1784–1844), when Americans first traveled to China, India, the East Indies, Oceana, and beyond.

Living in two worlds—a distant world of memories and a real world of "strange" people and places—the Kinsmans used the material culture of the familiar but distant Salem to navigate the exotic but immediate world of Macao. Home became the touchstone against which they made sense of their expatriate experiences. Everything they saw in China they described in reference to Salem, as when Rebecca wrote, "They have no idea of comfort in their houses, according to our notions of it," or observed (much to her daughters' disappointment) that "there are no such things as dolls to be had here (is it not strange?)."[2] In this chapter, we examine four forms of material culture that served as the connective tissue of Salem's expatriate experience: letters, landscapes, likenesses, and foodways.

From Salem . . .

What was this place called Salem? By 1843, the glories of the once-bustling port, enriched by the China and Indies trades, were fading. Those who called Salem home included Nathaniel Hawthorne, whose *Scarlet Letter* (1850) appropriately began with "The Custom House," an essay that notoriously documented the city's decline.[3] Salem had become a place that people were *from*, as the port sent out more and more residents to the eastern frontier of the Indian and Pacific Oceans or the western frontier of Ohio and Indiana. For residents like Rebecca, however, the town still held its particular charms, and her letters recalled the coordinates of her identity—the family's County Street home, East India Marine Hall, Derby Street, and India Wharf. For Nathaniel, although he was born in Salem in 1798, the associations with the town might have been less deeply etched; at age twenty, he made his first East Indies voyage and, thereafter, spent most of his life pacing the confined spaces of a ship's deck.[4] Even so, significant moments bound both to this place. On one of his infrequent visits home to Salem, in 1834, Rebecca and Nathaniel met at a party at the residence of mutual friends on Church Street, and they were married in June 1835. They lived in a new Greek Revival townhouse on Summer Street, a modest home by the standards of the seaport's wealthy merchants, but it was located near their families and friends, Nathaniel's business interests on the wharves, and Rebecca's beloved Pine Street Quaker Meeting House. Here, she gave birth to their first child, Willie, some ten months after the wedding. In addition to their growing family, Nathaniel, as an aspiring sea captain and merchant, continued his lengthy travels to Amsterdam, London, Jakarta, Calcutta, Hong Kong, and Macao, requiring Rebecca to manage the household for extended periods of time, and she found solace in the comfort of the accustomed sights and sounds.

. . . to China

It appears that Nathaniel's 1839 trip to China, an unprofitable venture, had much to do with the couple's decision to bring their family to Macao and Canton.[5] Money remained a constant challenge.[6] On his last cruise, Nathaniel had bet on the prospect of high prices for Chinese teas in New York; when these failed to materialize in 1840, he made the decision he had long hoped to avoid, agreeing to join Wetmore and Company in Canton. Rebecca Kinsman Munroe, the great-granddaughter of Nathaniel and Rebecca, assessed their situation over a century later: "So after all, Kinsman had been obliged to take his wife, she was only thirty-four, and two of their very young children from the

Salem of polite society and Quaker meetings to the extraordinary land of China, where there were many varying conventions, and no Quaker meetings."[7]

What was this place, Macao, where Rebecca and her children found themselves in late 1843? Established as a Portuguese enclave in 1556–1557, the hilly peninsula on the outskirts of the Celestial Empire featured a pastiche of architectural tropes graced by Buddhist temples, Chinese pagodas, and Catholic churches as well as traditional Chinese villages and European-style villas. In addition to the resplendent strangeness of the scenery, the Western visitor often felt overwhelmed by the babel of Macao's inhabitants:

> [There were] representatives, as it would seem, of almost every nation on earth. Jews, Parsees, (who are descendants of the ancient Persians and are fire worshippers) Malays, Bengalees, Lascars, (these all dressed in their several native costumes) then there are Coffers, slaves to the Portuguese, to say nothing of Europeans, English, Scotch, French, Germans, Swedes, etc., distinguishable only by some slight differences of feature and complexion. [And] Portuguese [who] vary very much in complexion, some of them as dark as any colored people in Salem.[8]

It is unclear from the Kinsmans' correspondence whether Macao ever felt like home. Rebecca reflected on her sense of this strange world: "Everything here is so unlike what we have been accustomed to. . . . I wish I could give you an idea of [the inhabitants'] appearance but as this would be impossible by any description of mine, I intend sending home a clay figure, dressed in the costume worn by them."[9]

Letters

Letters transcend the bounds of literary and material culture. As correspondence, they recalled the voices of loved ones and connected one to the emotions of distant people; as artifacts of remembrance, they were held—even fondled—and kept, catalogued, and treasured. As long as letters kept coming, the relationships they represented could be preserved. For expatriates such as the Kinsmans, the difficult decision to leave Salem to "mend [Nathaniel's] fortunes" came at a great personal cost.[10] Dismay at the prospect of interrupted or broken relationships appears throughout the journals and letters they sent back to Salem. The sense of loss was reciprocal, and Rebecca lamented that "our dearest mother took our separation so much to heart."[11] She begged for news from home, writing her family, "And now I have a special charge to give you—write often even when you do not hear of an opportunity to send." Typical was Rebecca's missive of November 4, 1843, urging, "Among 4 brothers and sisters surely there can be no reason why we may not hear every month—I beg of you not to fail."[12] The displaced family rejoiced when they received accounts of the yearly Quaker meeting or John Greenleaf Whittier's poetry, and Rebecca noted, "We are very glad to get the newspapers, the sight of a Salem paper was really refreshing."[13] To prevent delays, the China branch of the family provided careful instructions for transmitting correspondence: "Letters sent in that way, should be directed beside to the care of Fletcher, Alexander & Co., London, who will forward the letter to China. If directed to Canton, they will be liable to be sent there, and then we must wait until they can be sent back here."[14] Indeed, every scrap of gossip or rumor that connected them to Salem was treasured, as Rebecca observed when she wrote, "Horace Story our fellow passenger, received a letter from his father by the Overland mail the other day mentioning a piece of news, an elopement at Salem, but giving no names. We feel quite curious to hear who it can be."[15] Their letters were significant tokens of family, connecting loved ones across thousands of miles and saved as artifacts of remembrance.

Finding Their Place

Initially, the Kinsmans recorded the novel sights and sounds of Macao even as the family settled into routines. Yet, every experience was seen through a Salem lens; the interesting strangers, curious foods, novel clothing, and household goods with which they surrounded themselves were all compared to their beloved Salem. Their daily strolls around Macao, in particular, unfolded a landscape that Rebecca described as exotic and "strange," but the bells that rang out on Catholic holy days "remind us so pleasantly of home."[16]

The timing of their arrival was fortuitous in one regard. The Philadelphia merchant William Lejee had earned his "lac," or fortune, and planned to return to the United States within six months. He welcomed the Kinsman family into his elegant villa, one of the more prominent domiciles in Macao—an imposing pillared house along the Praya Grande. Of her new quarters, Rebecca confided to her family, "I have now what I have always wished for, a spacious sleeping apartment—it measures 23 feet by 26—and we have a bedstead to correspond, seven feet wide and eight long."[17] The efforts to bridge the seas of separation were confined neither *to* Salem's expatriates nor *by* gender. The footprint of the spacious six-columned house far exceeded the area of their Salem townhouse: "Nathaniel was pacing the parlor last evening, and he re-

Lam Qua, *Veranda of Nathan Kinsman's residence in Macau*, circa 1843. *(Photo Courtesy of Martyn Gregory, London.)*

marked that the whole floor of our Summer Street house might easily be put into that room, parlors, entries, closet and all."[18] The happiest times that Rebecca spent during her Macao sojourn were those that recalled Sundays in Salem—the entire family was gathered on the veranda, Nathaniel playing with the children, talking among family or visitors, engaging in board games, reading or scanning the horizon for familiar vessels (especially those from Salem) with the telescope (simply called "the glass") over the Praya Grande and to the harbor.[19]

The Kinsmans' improved lifestyle appeared to cause the Chase family back home in Salem some consternation, and Rebecca frequently tried to reassure her Quaker mother and sisters that exotic comforts had not damaged her soul. As to their villa, she reflected, "For rather would I sit down in silence in our own dear little Pine Street meeting house, and there endeavor to wait upon the Lord, than to worship in any other place." On August 3, 1844, she wrote to her father, "We have, it is true, many luxuries and enjoyments here, which it is part of wisdom to enjoy and appreciate, but I shall be quite willing to relinquish them all and return to our more humble home and good old Yankee customs by and by." As a Quaker in China, Rebecca lived between two worlds. She continued to dress modestly, favoring subdued hues, and the strict simplicity of her dress elicited pointed comments from the cosmopolitan Macao expatriates, even as her Salem family feared that she had become used to far too many comforts. For his part, Nathaniel concurred, writing to "My best beloved" from Canton in January 1847, "I am not very worldly minded now, and my expectations are very moderate, and my desires equally so."[20]

The Art of Connection

One of the most important means of connecting expatriates with folks at home was sending and receiving "likenesses" of distant kin, sent as framed portraits or embedded in mantel pieces and lockets. Before their departure, the Kinsmans commissioned Salem's renowned portraitist, Charles Osgood, to produce images of Rebecca and Nathaniel as mementos. Once they had settled into Macao, they wrote to Osgood for a likeness of the absent "darling boy," Willie, initiating what would be an extended period of anticipation.[21] The portrait would have been costly for them. Osgood had increased his fees after the successes of his portraits of Nathaniel Bowditch and Nathaniel Hawthorne launched him into the upper tier of local artists.

The parents' anticipation was documented in ongoing correspondence. In November 1843, soon after arriving in Macao, Rebecca sent explicit instructions: "We wish Osgood to paint his picture, have it placed in a plain gilt frame and send it to us as soon as you can."[22] By mid-December, Rebecca followed up with, "We are longing for dear Willy's picture, but I suppose it will be long before we shall receive it—Give the darling boy a great deal of love from his mother and his father too, and tell him we think and talk of him many times a day."[23] She wrote to "My dearest sister," on December 22, with further directions: "Most important of all—[send] Willy's picture. . . . And ask Osgood to pack Willy's picture himself, or see to it, so that it may be sure to come safely—Oh, what an inexpressible comfort that will be to us. I hope he will be able to get a *good likeness*."[24]

The long-awaited arrival of the portrait in October 1844 was celebrated as if the boy himself had landed on Macao's shore, as Nathaniel's letters confirmed with a dramatic flourish:

> The "Coquette" from Boston, 26th June, arrived here yesterday and we received a P.S. in the handwriting of Edward, which announced the gratifying intelligence that Willie's picture would be put on board the "Coquette." Immediately after breakfast this morning I dispatched a boat and with an order for the box containing *the precious and much longed for treasure*, with my glass [telescope] I watched the progress of the boat to the ship, saw the case handed into the boat and did not lose sight of her until she reached the beach in front of our house, the coolies seized it and in a moment of time it was put down in my room, where Johnny, agreeable to my directions, had a hammer and chisel all ready. The box was soon opened, and without removing the cloth with which

the picture was covered, I took it into Rebecca's room that she might enjoy the first sight of the features of our dear absent boy.[25]

Letters like this enabled distant kin to participate in a powerful and emotional moment for the entire family, vicariously reuniting the geographically extended family.

Upon arrival in Macao, they also sought to commission a likeness of five-year-old Ecca, another means of maintaining their links to their family and hometown. Rebecca's December 16 letter to her sister included a surprise: "We have had [daughter] Rebecca's portrait painted, which we intend sending to her dear auntie, and I do not doubt it will be the most acceptable present we could offer thee. Father and mother too will not be less pleased."[26] Rebecca appears to have been the coordinating force behind getting the portraits painted and dispatched, although clearly in consultation with "dear hubby." She was gaining experience in the Asian import-export business. With the "absent hubby" spending more time upriver in Canton, the site of Wetmore and Company's offices, she had taken on so many of the firm's operations in strategically located Macao, "as I am now virtually Wetmore & Co. in Macao."[27]

Foodways

Foodways provided particularly potent experiences that could be shared among the travelers in China and the homebound family in Salem, engaging the senses of smell, taste, texture, and even sound. Rebecca's letters described their morning meals, which had a way of feeding memories as well as stomachs. In an 1844 letter, she spent several pages describing an expatriate breakfast of both familiar and exotic fare. Beginning just before 9:00 A.M. with tea ("such tea!") and bread, her letter detailed:

> Bread, tea and coffee—then some kind of preparation of Indian meal, sometimes fritters or Johnny cake, but usually waffles baked in an iron precisely like the one we used at home. . . . We usually conclude with very nice waffles of Indian meal, and dry toast made of a sort of rusk, baked by Portuguese women here, which is extremely light and nice, and reminds me of the cake cousin Rogers of Tewksbury used to make, but not quite as sweet.[28]

Dinners at 3:00 P.M. were even more sumptuous. In time, their Malaysian servant, John Alley, mastered a patois of New England and Chinese cuisines, and Rebecca complimented him:

We are getting more and more in the way of having home dishes—Astor House cornbread takes its place on the breakfast table every morning and hasty pudding is a favorite dish—Bread puddings and custards John makes just as we used to have them at home, and far better than any concoction of the Chinese cooks.[29]

It was a great comfort to the Kinsman family that Alley could adapt his cooking to reflect a taste of Salem, and she wrote in July 1844, "sitting in loose deshabille," with Nathaniel unwell on the veranda, and "John is nearby, attending to some duty, I believe making some 'cold sauce' for dinner, which I wished, to give the pudding a home taste, and which our [Chinese] cook does not understand making."[30]

Apparently, Rebecca's efforts to feel connected to Salem through her own cooking were less successful, and she wrote in December 1843, "What do you think I have been doing this morning? Why nothing less than making a *bread pudding* for the children's dinner, but unfortunately it was not very nice."[31] She persisted, however, writing to her parents and sisters soon after, "What do you think I did yesterday? Nothing less than *assist* in making some *Minced Pies*. Our cook made some the other day, by way of experiment, with reference to the approach of Christmas." When the Chinese cook's efforts at this New England specialty proved wanting—these did not taste just right—Rebecca stepped in and "superintended the mixing," as the family observed the proceedings, "and we had quite a merry time, seasoning and tasting, and fortunately the pies proved very nice" by Salem standards.[32] Other treats sealed the Salem connection. In the spring of 1844, Rebecca noted, "In place of butter, we have guava jelly, which we get from Manila, and this reminds me of mother, who I recollect used to be fond of it."[33] Confections from Salem were especially treasured, and prompted notes of appreciation, such as, "Many thanks to my dear Mother for the nice gingerbread, Nath'l will be delighted I am sure."[34] Learning that a gift of Salem's trademark candies awaited her on the wharves of Macao, Rebecca Kinsman pined, "We have a box of Gibraltars sent out by Mrs. Brown in the 'Natchez'—, which has been in Canton for several weeks, and has not been sent down—I long to taste them."[35]

Conclusion

The Kinsmans' time in China ended tragically. By March 1846, Rebecca was reporting home with disturbing news: Ecca's health was failing. She was succumbing to "China fever," an ailment that killed many Western visitors. "It seems evident that the child ought to go home," she wrote, but the "state of my husband's health is such that it is very desirable that I should be near him."³⁶ And, so, reluctantly, the Kinsmans sent their despondent seven-year-old back to Salem, accompanied by trusted servant John Alley. Letters and gifts followed as the distant parents waited anxiously to hear that Ecca had arrived in Salem in improved health. In November 1846, they received news that the child had died on the voyage. Eventually, John Alley returned to Macao bearing mourning goods—"the clothes which my darling had worn and still more the bright locks of her sunny golden hair."³⁷ Within months, Nathaniel's own continuing malaise worsened. On January 2, 1847, from his quarters in Canton, he penned a hopeful note to Rebecca to reassure her, noting their good fortune in losing "only one child." He reflected on the time he had spent with "My best beloved," recalling memories of Salem: "I flatter myself that I am just as much a lover now as I was eleven years ago, twelve indeed—only think, it is nearly 13 years since we first met at Martha Webb's, does it seem possible it can be so long?"³⁸ Nathaniel died in April and was buried in the Protestant Cemetery in Macao, leaving Rebecca to return to Salem with two surviving children.

For many Americans of the antebellum era, China was imagined through blue-and-white decorative montages pictured on bits of porcelain or on lacquered screens or silk banyans. Yet, the accounts of Salem's China traders and travelers such as the Kinsmans add texture to the imagined China of museums and antiques auctions. Their letters, more than the goods they dispatched home, represent a more complicated legacy of what this place meant to generations of its residents. Expatriates left behind stories of both commercial success and burdening loss. The great wealth accrued by Salem's China and Indies traders was matched by the sacrifices of reluctant travelers like Rebecca and Nathaniel Kinsman, and many more.³⁹ They lived and died far from Salem's shores, but they were Salemites and part of the Salem experience. The challenges and losses experienced by their generation are emblematic of Hawthorne's expressions of decline but as fact rather than fiction.

NOTES

1. Rebecca Kinsman to "My Best Beloved Friend," March 7, 1844, *Essex Institute Historical Collections* (hereafter *EIHC*) 86, no. 1 (January 1950), 118.

2. Rebecca Kinsman to "My Dear Parents and Sister," December 1, 1843, *EIHC* 86, no. 1 (January 1950), 32; Rebecca Kinsman to "Daughter and Sister," December 7, 1843, *EIHC* 86, no. 1 (January 1950), 36.

3. Nathaniel Hawthorne, *The Scarlet Letter. A Romance* (Ticknor, Reed and Fields, 1850).

4. Nathaniel's seafaring family hailed from neighboring Ipswich, and his father moved to Salem in 1797, the year before his birth. Mary Kinsman Munroe, "Nathaniel Kinsman, Merchant of Salem, in the China Trade," *EIHC* 85, no. 1 (January 1949), 10–13.

5. M. Kinsman Munroe, "Nathaniel Kinsman, Merchant of Salem," *EIHC* 85, no. 2 (April 1949), 121–124.

6. Nathaniel Kinsman to Eliza Kinsman, May 19, 1819, in M. Kinsman Munroe, "Nathaniel Kinsman, Merchant of Salem," 85, no. 1 (January 1949), 18.

7. M. Kinsman Munroe, "Nathaniel Kinsman, Merchant of Salem," 85, no. 2 (April 1949), 124.

8. Rebecca Kinsman to "My Beloved Parents, Sisters and Brothers," Nov. 4, 1843, *EHIC*, 86, no. 1 (January 1950), 22.

9. R. Kinsman to "My Beloved Parents, Sisters and Brothers," 18.

10. M. Kinsman Munroe, "Nathaniel Kinsman, Merchant of Salem," 85, no. 2 (April 1949), 124.

11. R. Kinsman to "My Beloved Parents, Sisters and Brothers," 21.

12. R. Kinsman to "My Best Beloved Friend," *EIHC* 86, no. 1 (January 1950), 21.

13. Rebecca Kinsman to "My Dearest Parents and Sisters," December 16, 1843, *EIHC* 86, no. 1 (January 1950), 39.

14. R. Kinsman to "My Beloved Parents, Sisters and Brothers," 21.

15. Rebecca Kinsman to "My Dearly Beloved Mother," November 13, 1843, *EIHC* 86, no. 1 (January 1950), 24.

16. R. Kinsman to "My Beloved Parents, Sisters and Brothers," 16.

17. R. Kinsman to "My Dearly Beloved Mother," April 21, 1844, *EIHC* 86, no. 3 (July 1950), 273.

18. R. Kinsman to "My Dearly Beloved Mother," February 14, 1844, *EIHC* 86, no. 3 (July 1950), 264.

19. Featured in a famous painting, *Verandah of Nathan Kinsman's Residence in Macau, circa 1843*, by Lam Qua, or Kwan Kiu Cheong, (1801–1860). Patrick Conner, *The China Trade 1600–1860* (Royal Pavilion, Art Gallery and Museum, 1986), 42–44.

20. Nathaniel Kinsman to "My Best Beloved," January 2, 1847, *EIHC* 88, no. 1 (January 1952), 66.

21. In 1851, Rebecca's family (the Chases) enlisted Osgood for a family portrait. Rebecca Kinsman to "My Dearest Sister," December 22, 1843, *EIHC* 86, no. 1 (January 1950), 29–30; Nathaniel Kinsman to "My Dear Father and Mother," October 7, 1844, *EIHC* 86, no. 4 (October 1950), 314.

22. R. Kinsman to "My Beloved Parents, Sisters and Brothers," 20.

23. R. Kinsman to "My Dearest Parents and Sisters," 38.

24. R. Kinsman to "My Dearest Sister," 29–30.

25. Rebecca Kinsman to "My Dear Father and Mother," October 7, 1844, in Mrs. Frederick C. Munroe, "The Daily Life of Mrs. Nathaniel Kinsman in Macao, China," *EIHC* 86, no. 4 (October 1950), 314.

26. R. Kinsman to "My Dearest Parents and Sisters," 38.

27. Rebecca Kinsman to "My Beloved Mother," December 13, 1844, *EIHC* 86, no. 4 (October 1950), 324.

28. R. Kinsman to "My Beloved Parents, Sisters and Brothers," 17.

29. Nathaniel had purchased Alley out of slavery in Sumatra. Rebecca Kinsman to "Beloved Sister," April 1, 1845, in Mrs. Frederick C. Munroe, "The Daily Life of Mrs. Nathaniel Kinsman in Macao, China," *EIHC* 87, no. 2 (April 1951), 123.

30. R. Kinsman to "My Beloved Sister," July 26, 1844, in Rebecca Kinsman Munroe, "The American Mission to China: Letters and Diary of Rebecca Kinsman," *EIHC* 86, no. 2 (April 1950), 136.

31. R. Kinsman to "Daughter and Sister," 35.

32. R. Kinsman to "My Dearest Parents and Sisters," 37–38.

33. R. Kinsman, letter to "My Dearly Beloved Mother," 86, no. 3, 270.

34. Rebecca Kinsman to "My Dear Darling Sister," January 24, 1847, *EIHC* 88, no. 1 (January 1952), 66.

35. Rebecca Kinsman to "My Dear and Darling Sister," August 29, 1845, *EIHC* 87, no. 2 (April 1951), 145.

36. R. Kinsman to "My Dear Darling Sister," March 13, 1846, in Rebecca Kinsman Munroe, "The Daily Life of Mrs. Nathaniel Kinsman in China, 1846," *EIHC* 86, no. 1 (January 1950), 391.

37. R. Kinsman to "My Dear Darling Sister," January 24, 1847, *EIHC* 88, no. 1 (January 1952), 65.

38. N. Kinsman to "My Best Beloved," 68.

39. Lucy Stickney, *The Kinsman Family: Genealogical Record of the Descendants of Robert Kinsman, of Ipswich, Mass. from 1634 to 1875—Comp. for Robert Kinsman by Lucy W. Stickney* (A. Mudge and Son, 1876).

INTERLUDE 5

Sabe and Rose

Bethany Jay and Maryann Zujewski

The Salem Maritime National Historic Park (Salem Maritime) was established in 1938 as the first national historic site in the National Park System. Like many institutions of the time, it focused on sharing the stories of the wealthy and well known—in this case, the Derby family and their elite peers. By focusing on a prominent white family and their material culture as examples of American success, Salem Maritime resembled many museums of this era. But this story represented only a fraction of the history—it was a complete picture of neither the Derbys' lives nor the city's maritime trade. This incomplete narrative persisted until recently, when, as part of a larger National Park Service initiative, the staff began to research the history to enable the park's interpretation to reflect the diversity and contributions of all its inhabitants. Examining the role of slavery as both an economic motor and a way of life for Northern families like the Derbys was key to this work. This story of the National Park Service's changing interpretations of the Derby family is a story not only about the past but about how some Salem institutions have begun sharing an increasingly complex and less celebratory narrative of the city's past.

One of the most prominent buildings at Salem Maritime is the 1762 Derby House, built as a wedding present for Elias Hasket Derby and Elizabeth Crowninshield. For nearly a century, the interpretations of the home as well as the substantial wharf that bears the Derby name revolved around the industry and lifestyles of Salem's elite. Elias Hasket Derby, whose "Yankee ingenuity" and entrepreneurship established Salem as a leader in global trade, personified that history. A Salem Maritime brochure in use from 1984 through 1993 discussed

Derby's role as a successful privateer in the American Revolution and then noted, "After he took the lead in opening up new markets for Salem, 'King' Derby's preeminence was undisputed. He was an imaginative and demanding shipowner who evoked great loyalty from his captains."[1] Derby was celebrated as a singular figure whose intellect and skill brought great wealth to his family and his city and also helped bring independence to his country.

By the time brochures like this were in circulation, several generations of scholars had written about the North as a place where economic success depended on the work of those enslaved within the region and elsewhere. In 1942, just four years after Salem Maritime's founding, the historian Lorenzo Johnston Green demonstrated that the success of individuals such as Elias Hasket Derby was much more complicated than the park's narrative indicated. Rather than being the result of individual business acumen, the accumulation of wealth, property, and status by Salem's merchant class depended on the local to global economy of enslavement. Green's discussion of the slave trade itself hints at the importance of the institution to the larger merchant industry, "On the eve of the American Revolution [the slave trade] formed the very basis of economic life of New England; about it revolved, and depended, most of her industries. The vast sugar, molasses and rum trade, shipbuilding, the distilleries, a great many of the fisheries, the employment of artisans and seamen, even agriculture[,] are all dependent on the slave traffic."[2] Despite this clear discussion of the economic impact of slavery, Salem Maritime's brochure elided its importance saying only, "Before the Revolution, the Derbys were active in the European and West Indies trade," and noting that Salem "ships carried native products . . . along with rum and molasses from the West Indies, to ports all over the world."[3] While discussing both centers of slavery and the products of enslaved labor, the brochure failed to name the institution.

These interpretations began to change in 2011, when, at the invitation of the National Park Service, the Organization of American Historians published a study titled *Imperiled Promise: The State of History in the National Park Service*. The study found that many National Park Service narratives represented "a misperception of history as a tightly bounded, single and unchanging 'accurate' story, with one true significance."[4] The singular focus on the Derby family was evidence of this fact in Salem. To uncover other stories at Salem Maritime, the park staff began to research into the two "Servants for Life," listed in a 1771 Massachusetts Tax Inventory as enslaved within the Derby House.[5] While some Park Rangers referred to these two enslaved people as Sabe and Rose, the "negro man" and "negro woman" mentioned in Elias Hasket Derby's 1799 will, they seemed to know little more.[6]

Partnering with Salem State University to research the subject opened unexpected new avenues of interpretation. For example, research showed that the two enslaved people listed in 1771 were not Sabe and Rose. The time frame did not fit, and it seemed that they may never have lived in the Derby home. Instead, an even more fascinating story about Sabe and Rose emerged—not only a story of slavery but a story of the first generation of freedom in Massachusetts. Historians mark the beginning of this era in 1783, when the state's Supreme Judicial Court acknowledged that the 1780 Massachusetts Constitution, which included the declaration that "men are born free and equal," offered enslaved people a legal claim to freedom (see Chapter 3 in this volume for a more thorough discussion). Despite the perception that slavery ended in Massachusetts in 1783, Joanne Pope Melish and other historians have remarked on the liminal nature of freedom in this era: "The judicial interpretations of the Massachusetts and New Hampshire state constitutions, ambiguous as they were, may have been intended by their authors to end slavery definitively, but they did not. The ambiguity was never resolved in Massachusetts."[7] In Salem, Sabe's and Rose's lives remained intertwined with the Derby family for many years—the line between enslaved and free was blurred indeed.

An examination of several key documents finds demonstrations of this tentative freedom. The earliest document, dated 1783, is a receipt for "to schooling Sabe," followed by two 1788 receipts for "to one quarters schooling your Black girl" and "to one quarters schooling Rose," who are likely the same person.[8] During the colonial era, providing for enslaved people's educations was relatively common in New England. As New Englanders later contemplated the end of slavery, at least some considered educating the potentially free people, "as a sort of property improvement that would incur obligation; it must be paid for by the service of the recipient."[9] Efforts to educate Sabe and Rose as free people, then, reveal the contested nature of freedom. Certainly, providing for their education benefited Sabe and Rose, but it also made them more valuable to Derby as laborers. Importantly, Elias Hasket Derby likely expected that even in freedom, his investment in Sabe and Rose would be paid for by their future labor and obligation to him.

The next mention of Sabe and Rose comes in Elias Hasket Derby's 1799 will. Referring to them with the possessive "my" sixteen years after the "end" of slavery, Derby states, "I do hereby give and bequeath unto my negro man Sabe the sum of 250 dollars" and "I do hereby give and bequeath unto my young Negro woman Rose the sum of 250 dollars." Derby, however, did not provide for immediate payment to Sabe and Rose, as he had with his white gardener's legacy. Instead, the next paragraph states, "I order and direct my executor to pay the two last mentioned legacies given to the said Sabe and Rose unto my said daughter Martha; and my will is that my said daughter Martha pay out the same . . . in such proportions and at such times as she may think proper."[10] Although Martha received the money as evidenced by a $500 receipt "for a legacy left to his Negro Servants Sabe & Rose," evidence of Sabe and Rose receiving that money from Martha has not surfaced.[11] Like their schooling, Derby's legacy for Sabe and Rose may have come with the expectation of continued service or obligation to the Derby family. Melish has noted that this kind of financial support would have been fairly common, as would the proverbial strings attached to it: "In the 1780s and early 1790s the families of former slaves quite commonly provided financial assistance for them. . . . Although such assistance was humanitarian and at the very least a form of reparation to which all former slaves were surely entitled, nonetheless the continuing support and responsibility of former owners for free persons of color tended to blur the boundaries between free and slave."[12]

While self-interest or obligation may have kept them tied to the family, after the deaths of Elias Hasket and Elizabeth Crowninshield Derby, Sabe and Rose seem to have taken greater control of their lives. On December 9, 1799, they married in Salem's St. Peter's Episcopal Church, and, like many formerly enslaved people, took their enslaver's surname as their own.[13] This choice may have formalized an existing practice of referring to the two in association with Derby— that is, "Derby's man" or "Derby's Sabe." Or, it may have been a way to capitalize on the Derbys' prestige. A month before their marriage, Sabe received sixteen months' worth of back wages as well as $200 plus interest from a 1797 account with Derby.[14] In 1800, armed with the Derby name, education, and money, Sabe purchased land and opened a shop with a partner. One year later, the business partnership was dissolved.[15]

We do not know why the business failed, but Sabe and Rose obviously struggled during the transition from slavery to freedom. In the years after this failed business venture—more than twenty years after the legal end of slavery—Sabe and Rose appear financially dependent on and bound to the Derby family. In 1807, the Derby children contributed portions of their father's estate to pay for a house for Sabe and Rose.[16] Did the Derby children go to them? Or did Sabe and Rose seek their help? If so, was this a desperate move after the failure of the business and the erosion of potential independence? We probably will never know, but the historian Jared Hardesty indicates that their predicament was not unique. While Sabe and Rose had the advantages of some education, money, and, perhaps, connections, freedom came with "the systemic racism and discrimination of the early American republic. Once again pushing many African Americans into a dependent state. The chains of dependence may have been broken, but its vestiges lived on . . . in a new nation dedicated to liberty."[17]

Even though discrimination affected their lives, Sabe and Rose made their mark as leaders in Salem. In 1806, as the secretary of the Sons of the African Society, Sabe Derby announced the organization's first anniversary in a Salem newspaper. This prominent early Black benevolent society brought members of the free Black community together "for the mutual benefit of each other . . . behaving ourselves all times as true and faithful Citizens of the Commonwealth in which we live."[18] Through his involvement in the society, Sabe made a claim to equal citizenship and fought against the inequities that newly free Black people faced. When Rose died in 1809, her death notice made it clear that she also was a prominent figure in the community, noting "the good qualities of this woman had gained her just esteem." The notice also highlights the ambiguity of her position as a free Black woman, referring to "Rose, wife of Saib [sic] Derby, free blacks, both formerly belonging to Elias Haskett [sic] Derby, an eminent merchant of Salem." More than twenty-five years after the "end" of slavery and a decade after Elias Hasket Derby's death, Sabe's and Rose's identities were still defined by their race and former enslaved status. Rose was defined by her relationship to both her husband and her enslaver. Viewing Rose and the other mourners as exemplars to free people, the obituary applauded their "decent manners" and the funeral itself as "proofs of the good habits and rising hopes of a once oppressed part of civil society."[19]

After the death of Rose, Sabe boarded a ship as a crew member bound for Canton, China.[20] Though mourning Rose's death, he may have seen the voyage as an opportunity to leave Salem and the hold of the Derbys. After a year away, Sabe returned—but not to Salem. Evidence indicates he lived on the north slope of Boston's Beacon Hill, a prominent nineteenth-century African American community, where he worked as a boot black and remarried. Sabe died in 1821. The death record indicates his age (47) but not the cause of his death.[21]

Sabe and Rose's story is never going to be complete. Why they made certain decisions or exactly how they felt about the Derby family will never be fully known. Still, Salem Maritime's work demonstrates the possibilities that come with examining and sharing their story, which is represented by the park's enhanced interpretive tours, educational and digital resources, and school programs. While the accomplishments of Derby and his peers are still part of the interpretation of Salem Maritime, the addition of Sabe and Rose's story affirms the presence and impact of persons of African descent and their unique experiences as the first generation of free Black men and women. By sharing these stories and continuing to question assumptions and gaps in knowledge, a more complete history of Salem has emerged.

NOTES

1. *Salem Maritime National Historic Site Brochure* (National Park Service, 1984), available at https://npshistory.com/brochures/.
2. Lorenzo Johnston Greene, *The Negro in Colonial New England: 1620–1776* (1949; repr., Athenaeum, 1968), 68–69.
3. *Salem Maritime National Historic Site Brochure.*
4. Organization of American Historians, *Imperiled Promise: The State of History in the National Park Service* (National Park Service, 2011), 6.
5. "Massachusetts State Archives Collection, Colonial Period, 1622–1788—v. 132–134—Valuation of Towns, 1771," Database, *FamilySearch* https://FamilySearch.org.
6. Derby Family Papers, MSS 37, box 19, folder 1, Phillips Library, Peabody Essex Museum.
7. Joanne Pope Melish, *Disowning Slavery: Gradual Emancipation and 'Race' in New England, 1780–1860* (Cornell University Press, 1998), 76.
8. Derby Family Papers, MSS 37, box 17, folder 1, Phillips Library, Peabody Essex Museum. Derby Family Papers, MSS 37, box 17, folder 4, Phillips Library, Peabody Essex Museum.
9. Melish, *Disowning Slavery*, 61.
10. Derby Family Papers, MSS 37, box 19, folder 1, Phillips Library, Peabody Essex Museum.
11. Ibid.
12. Melish, *Disowning Slavery*, 99.
13. "Massachusetts, Town Clerk, Vital and Town Records, 1626–2000," Database, *FamilySearch* https://FamilySearch.org.
14. Derby Family Papers, MSS 37, box 19, folder 1, Phillips Library, Peabody Essex Museum. Derby was likely acting as a "bank" for Sabe, holding his money and paying interest. Of course, Sabe's access to his money was then controlled by Derby.
15. *Salem Gazette*, April 21, 1801.
16. Derby Family Papers, MSS 37, box 22, Phillips Library, Peabody Essex Museum.
17. Jared Hardesty, *Unfreedom: Slavery and Dependence in Eighteenth-Century Boston* (New York University Press, 2018), 182.
18. "Laws of the African Society, Instituted in Boston, Anno Domini 1796," *Massachusetts Historical Society Collections,* available at https://www.masshist.org/database/viewer.php?item_id=573&pid=42; *Salem Gazette*, March 18, 1806.
19. *Essex Register*, June 3, 1809.
20. "Massachusetts, Salem and Beverly Crew Lists and Shipping Articles, 1797–1934," Database, *FamilySearch* https://FamilySearch.org.
21. The Boston Directory (1816, 1818, 1820, 1821); Massachusetts, U.S., Town and Vital Records, 1620–1988 available at: https://www.ancestry.com/search/collections/2495/.

CHAPTER SIX

John Remond, Citizen of Salem

The Personal and the Political in the World of an African American Entrepreneur, 1805–1874

DONNA A. SEGER

In a letter to the editor of *The Liberator*, dated February 16, 1833, explaining his perspective on a recent clash between two opposing abolitionist orators whom he had invited to Salem, John Remond relayed that "while I cannot boast of its being my native town; I can say that it is my beloved home" and also a place where the people are "high-minded, well-disposed and friendly to the colored people." His praise is understandable: having arrived in Massachusetts from his native Curaçao as a lone ten-year-old in 1798, he managed to establish himself in a number of professions and positions, from hairdresser to property manager to caterer to purveyor and one of Salem's first restaurateurs over the first few decades of his residence. His roles multiplied and expanded largely due to his appointment as the resident caretaker of Salem's newest assembly hall and social center, Hamilton Hall, built between 1805 and 1807 on equally new (and fashionable) Chestnut Street. In partnership with his wife, the former Nancy Lenox of Newton, daughter of an esteemed African American veteran of the Revolutionary War and baker of "fancy cakes," John transitioned from mere caretaker to celebrated caterer by the 1820s, when he was notably and invariably addressed as "Mr. Remond" in all the newspaper accounts of Hamilton Hall events. The hall was home to John and Nancy and their expanding family, and it was also the foundation of their family businesses: Salem residents lined up for turtle soup sold out the back door every morning at 11:00 A.M., and they purchased Newark cider, baked goods, smoked beef, pickled oysters, and lobsters from their ground floor shop/kitchen/home.[1]

Remond was always looking around for opportunities, and he expanded his sights and sites beyond Hamilton Hall both before and after he took up residence there. He continued in his original profession of hairdressing and opened an "oyster house" on Front Street on the South River leading to Salem Harbor in 1817. He began dealing in porter, ales, and wines and referring to the Hamilton Hall store as his "cider and porter vault." He provisioned both ships and households, citing the premier cooking apparatus (a Rumford Roaster) installed at the hall. By 1833, he was well situated in more ways than one: he lived and worked in overlapping circles of service workers and suppliers, merchant princes and mariners, and men and women of both races and had purchased properties in both Salem's major commercial district and its emerging African American neighborhood. Salem's African American population was small but concentrated, primarily in two areas: an older neighborhood, occasionally and pejoratively referred to as "Roast Meat Hill," located just to the south of Hamilton Hall along adjoining streets that ran down to Mill Pond at the head of the South River, and an emerging one across the pond, along a rise called Mill Hill. Remond had a foot in both.[2]

John Remond's career was a Salem variant of a narrative that played out in several cities along the East Coast in the nineteenth century, as African Americans took advantage of the myriad roles and opportunities associated with the occupation of "caterer" to advance both their own and their families' positions in society as well as their causes—chiefly, the cause of abolition. W.E.B. Du Bois, in his book *The Philadelphia Negro: A Social Study* (1899), saw the emergence of the successful African American caterer as a more corporate process achieved through "as remarkable a trade guild as ever ruled in a medieval city," the Guild of the Caterers, which "raised a crowd of underpaid menials to become a set of self-reliant, original business men, who amassed fortunes for themselves and won general respect for their people."[3] Remond's rise in Salem was more individualistic, though there were parallels and even some connections to his counterparts in Philadelphia, New York, and Boston. In Philadelphia, Robert Bogle is credited widely with establishing the first African American catering business, expanding upon the role of "public waiter" or "public butler" to the realm of a commercial establishment in 1813. West Indian émigré Peter Augustin purchased Bogle's successful business five years later, and, by all accounts, took it to the next level with expanded provisioning services for both food and embellishments. African American competitors and colleagues dominated Philadelphia's catering industry for the next century, including Thomas Dorsey, Henry Jones, Henry Minton, James Prosser, and John S. Trower. In New York, Thomas Downing reigned as the oyster king in the mid-nineteenth century, succeeded by his son George, who expanded the family business into Rhode Island, where Isaac Rice was the pioneering caterer of Newport. Boston's "prince" of caterers was Joshua Bowen Smith, who also served in the Massachusetts legislature.[4] Remond certainly knew Smith, Rice, and both Downings, and he had trading ties to another notable African American culinary entrepreneur in New York City, Henry Scott, a major pickle producer to whom he supplied onions and cranberries.[5] All of these men were working toward abolition in the 1830s, but they were also striving for more specific local and personal goals: the desegregation of public education and access to all of the amenities of their respective locales. These issues had the potential to drive a wedge between John Remond and his "beloved" home, as Salem's characteristic worldliness was countered by equal forces of tradition and hierarchy.

The early 1830s were a turning point for Remond and his family: a time when local successes could no longer compensate for larger universal goals. Aside from all of his provisioning and retail pursuits, there had been a succession of public dinners that had established his reputation above and beyond Salem: beginning with his first event for the Salem Light Infantry, in 1809, and their guest, the Massachusetts Governor Christopher Gore (an event that set a precedent for annual infantry events up to 1863) and proceeding through the grand dinner planned for President Andrew Jackson in 1833. Remond's first presidential function was the anniversary of the East India Marine Society in October 1825, an event that also marked the opening of East India Hall, a magnificent "cabinet" where the society's collections would be displayed from that time until the present. President John Quincy Adams was perhaps the most notable guest, and the event began with a procession through the streets of Salem from Hamilton Hall to the new hall on Essex Street, "where a splendid dinner was served up by Mr. John Remond, which for variety, elegance, and *taste* was allowed by the competent judges to surpass everything of the kind witnessed in our country."[6]

In terms of reporting, an even more magnificent event had occurred the year before, when the Remonds prepared an elaborate feast for the Marquis de Lafayette on his grand American "farewell tour" in 1824. Lafayette arrived in Salem on August 31 and was honored at a Hamilton Hall dinner featuring a menu and interior embellishments so elaborate that the *Salem Gazette* opined that "the whole effect was beyond our powers of description."[7] Salem celebrated the two hundredth anniversary of John Endicott's arrival at what was then Naumkeag in 1828 with a succession of events capped off by a crowded dinner at Hamilton Hall "provided by Mr. Remond," which was not only "sumptuous and worthy of our forefathers" but also "truly a feast of reason and a flow of soul." The *Gazette*'s account featured all the usual toasts and

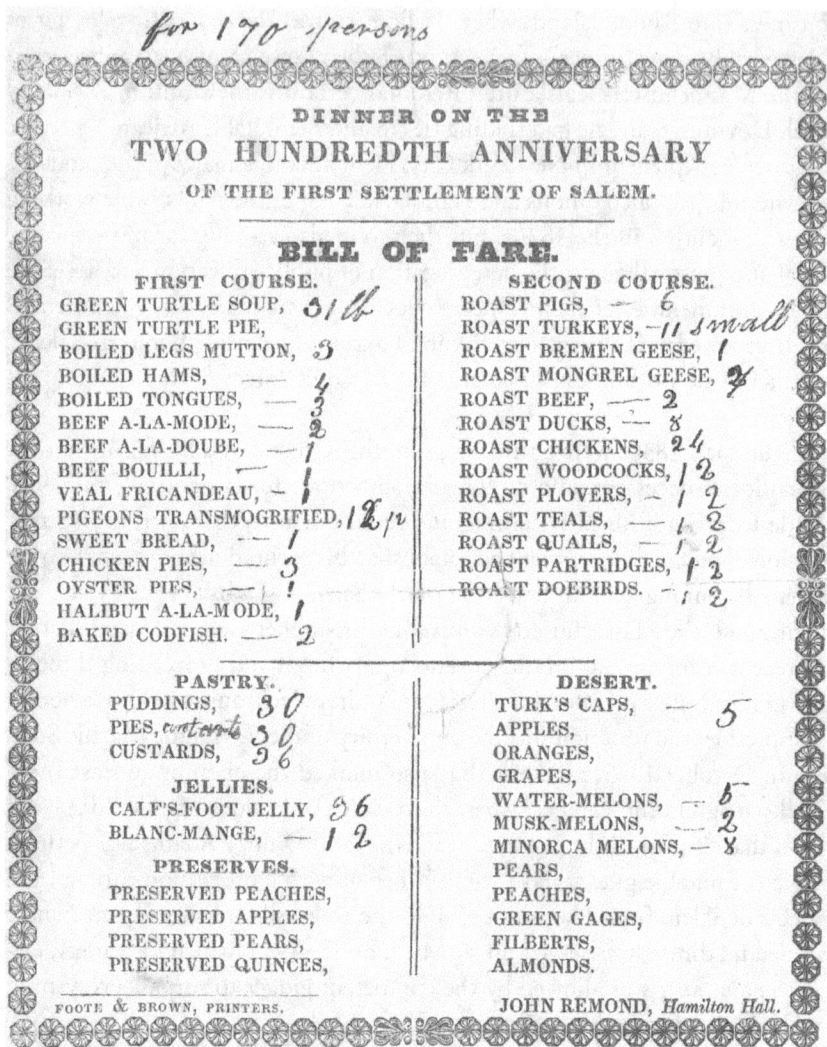

John Remond's menu for dinner on the two hundredth anniversary of the first settlement of Salem, September 1828, Remond Family Papers, MSS 271, box 1, folder 3. *(Phillips Library, Peabody Essex Museum.)*

speeches by the dignitaries present, while the *Salem Observer* published "Journal of a Day in Salem," a more metaphorical account of the day and the dinner by an anonymous Bostonian who found himself "amazing hungry" and "resolved to eat all before me and get boozy by way of pennyworth" at day's end. John Remond did not disappoint: our Bostonian found all sorts of "savoury viands" and "dainties of all climes" at Hamilton Hall, and after he "went through a whole bill of faire from oyster patties to transmogrified pigeon," he *"thought Remond best cook in the universe."*[8]

The preparations for the dinner for President Jackson's visit to Salem in June 1833 do not seem as detailed or extensive (or joyous) as those for previous affairs: Remond made a contract for the dinner only on June 20, promising to furnish a "handsome and good dinner including mock turtle soup" for 150 attendees on June 26. The host subcommittee also requested cherries and strawberries, sherry and champagne, and cigars. but everything else was left to his discretion.[9] The dinner would go on, but the principal guest was absent, having arrived in Salem too ill for entertainment. His great opponent, the former president John Quincy Adams, later expressed his doubts about Jackson's debility, which he called "politic," at best.

We have no knowledge of Mr. Remond's opinion: we can only discern his views by his actions and affiliations, and 1833 marks the beginning of a more political focus in his activities, beginning with his life membership in the New England Anti-Slavery Society and the intensification of fundraising efforts to support the work of William Lloyd Garrison.[10] The commitment to abolition was familial: Remond's wife and elder daughters became members of the integrated Salem Female Anti-Slavery Society in the following year, and, as the remaining Remond children aged, they too became associated with the cause, with Charles Lenox Remond and Sarah Parker Remond evolving into pioneering trans-Atlantic orators and agents for the Massachusetts and American Anti-Slavery Societies. Their fame would eclipse that of their father, who remained tethered to his commercial pursuits, the material foundation of the family's commitment to equal-rights advocacy.

Prior to his formal and financial commitment to the abolitionist cause, John Remond's first community engagement effort was as a member of the building committee for the Union Bethel Church, which was seeking subscriptions to build a chapel on Mill Street in 1827–1828. One can understand his interest in contributing to the creation of a worshipping and gathering place for Salem's small African American community, to be located near the Mill Pond neighborhood, where both many of its representatives lived and he himself owned property. Right across from Hamilton Hall was the magnificent South Church built by Salem's famed architect and woodcarver Samuel McIntire in 1804: its congregation "welcomed" African Americans, but one congregant later observed that "the Blacks of that period were quite church-going people and after the new South Church was built in 1804, a semi-circular gallery was built directly over the Singing Seat, and not far under the ceiling capable of containing 40 or 50 people which on Sabbath morning was always pretty well-filled, looking somewhat like a dark cloud from the floor pews."[11] We have no insights into his faith, but Remond was clearly interested in community, to which he had obligations, but from which he could also draw strength: the stories in the pioneering *Freedom's Journal*, written by free Blacks for free Blacks and for which Remond was an agent, note every "African" church foundation and highlight the myriad roles played by these institutions in unifying and celebrating their communities.

With eight children, the other cause that drew Remond in was public education, both its provision and its setting. In the late eighteenth and early nineteenth centuries, Salem had developed a loose system of private and public grammar schools, characterized by an informal segregation. Charles Lenox Remond and his elder sisters had attended public schools for brief periods, but the general public preference was for segregation. Salem's first "African School" was established in 1807 on High Street by a formerly enslaved woman named Clarissa Lawrence at the request of public authorities: it existed until Lawrence's retirement in 1823, enrolling classes of between thirty and forty students, mostly from the neighborhood.[12] The 1827 Massachusetts Act to Provide for Instruction of Youth, requiring all towns with five hundred or more families to set up free public high schools, forced the segregation issue and the resolution of just what "public" meant. Salem responded robustly with the creation of new public high schools for both young men and young women, and three of the Remond daughters, Sarah, Maritchia, and Caroline, all passed the entrance examination and were admitted to the East Female School in the spring of 1834. This must have been an exciting development for the entire family as well as a promising one: the principal of the school, Rufus Putnam, was then secretary of the four-hundred-member Anti-Slavery Society of Salem, so the presumption must have been one of a supportive environment.

And it was, until the girls were expelled, quite dramatically, after only a few weeks of classes, following a town meeting held on July 24 to discuss a remonstrance by Daniel Beckett and 175 other residents of Salem asking that the Salem School Committee "remove the colored girls from the High Schools for girls and provide them instruction in a separate school."[13] The meeting voted to support the remonstrance, the Remond girls were expelled, and a "separate but unequal" formalized system of segregation became Salem law for the next decade. In a recent study, Kabria Baumgartner interprets this proceeding as a personal affront to the Remond family, and it's difficult not to come to this conclusion given the discourse at the time as well as their preeminence, Sarah Remond Parker's later reminiscences, and John Remond's action: he packed up his family and the portable tools of his trades and left Salem, the city and community he had described as being "well-disposed and friendly to the colored people" just the year before.[14]

The Remonds relocated to Newport, Rhode Island, where John purchased a house as well as a commercial property for his business, but their time in exile was temporary: the family returned to Salem even before its era of educational resegregation was over. Certainly, the mistreatment of his daughters was a key factor in his decision to depart, but John Remond had other concerns. In the fall of 1833 the East India Marine Society, for whom he catered one of his most splendid affairs in 1825, resolved that "people of Colour shall be excluded from visiting the museum of this Society, during the usual hours of admission, excepting as attendants upon visitors."[15] For a man who worked for members of this same society, supplying both their houses and their ships, and with whom he had lived in such close proximity, this reduction to the status of mere and occasional attendant must have been unsettling at the very least, particularly so together with the other events of the year. But how far the public address of "Mr. Remond" revealed a genuine and unencumbered respect is unknown or unknowable: the memoirs of the doyens and doyennes of Chestnut Street in later years characteristically refer to Remond with lines that contain *ifs*, *buts*, and *hads*: "He was very shrewd and active and had he been educated would no doubt have been a rich man."[16]

Newport remained the Remonds' home from 1835 until 1841. John's business was confined primarily to his hairdressing salon and perfumery at 137 Thames Street, where he offered both ornamental hairdressing for men and women and a selection of European waters. He maintained private rooms for the ladies and a selection of the daily papers for the gentlemen. The advertisements he placed in the *Rhode Island Republican* over these years also indicate that he was always seeking rose and peach waters, and, more mysteriously, mushrooms. There was also a short-lived confectionary and a brief offering of oysters at the perfumery. Remond certainly saw his fellow restaurateur and abolitionist Isaac Rice, who would become involved in his own struggle against school segregation a bit later; in fact, their families were merged in 1843 with the marriage of John L. Remond, the Remond's youngest son, and Ruth B. Rice.[17] The Newport years saw the rise of the eldest Remond son, Charles Lenox, as he became an agent for the Massachusetts Anti-Slavery Society in 1838 and the only African American delegate to the World Anti-Slavery Convention in London in 1840. Charles Lenox Remond would dedicate his lifetime to the causes not only of abolition but also of equal rights in every avenue of life, including education, transportation, and suffrage, and the family businesses supported him in all his missions.

Back in Salem in 1841, John Remond was welcomed with a notice in the *Salem Register: Returned. Remond, the celebrated Remond, has returned to Salem, his first love. After an absence of several years in Newport, he comes back to us and intends to shine out in more than his former glory*.[18] Several of his advertisements read: *Remond at home!* This enthusiastic return masks serious challenges facing Remond in Salem. The segregated school system that prompted him to leave was still in place, although a boycott of the "African School" had undercut its financial foundation. Though they were not referred to by name, the Remond Family's experience with the Salem schools in 1834 was referenced in a detailed letter to the *Salem Register* during a renewed discussion about the segregation policy a decade later. Now a grandfather, Remond ("a colored man who had been absent for a few years") demanded that his two grandchildren be allowed to attend the primary school closest to their residence as "I have lived in this city many years, demeaned myself well, and paid my taxes." A school official visited the Remond residence to explain the city's position and was met by not only an "affected" John as well as his wife but also the Misses Remond, who asked "why should we be subject to this baneful distinction? When we were young our father would have us educated; the public schools, and, indeed the private schools were shut against us; and we had to be educated at home at ruinous expense. And now we do not allow, and so help us we will never allow, for a moment, that our children, or any colored children, can, with justice, be shut out from participating freely and in fair open competition in all the advantages of the public schools. A distinct school is more debasing than none."[19] The policy of "distinction" or segregation was at last abandoned that very spring in both Salem and Nantucket, and John Remond's grandchildren attended desegregated public schools.

This had been a long struggle and, as one of the Misses Remond had asserted, a *ruinous* one. The Remonds' return to Salem well before the issue that drove them away was resolved is explained by John's declaration of bankruptcy in December 1842. After being cast away from the businesses and the community that had sustained the Remonds for decades, Newport became ruinous for John and his family. They returned to Salem to try to repair the ruin, but apparently it was too late. In the bankruptcy notice, John is referred to as a "trader" and ordered to appear in a Boston courtroom in the new year.[20] This legal setback does not seem to have affected his entrepreneurial initiatives: he reestablished himself at his former "headquarters" in Hamilton Hall, and, when that facility underwent necessary repairs and embellishments, he established his own hall in Higginson Square, adjacent to Salem's central market. This venue was distinguished from Remond's other establishments because of its adoption of the "strictest temperance principles," and the grand opening, featuring a typically sumptuous Remond dinner and an appearance by the "eloquent anti-slavery advocate" Charles Lenox Remond, apparently went on for hours, proving that "intoxicating liquors are by no means necessary to enliven a meeting at the festive board."[21] A temperance attraction was an odd choice for someone who had maintained a lucrative trade in wines, beer, and cider, but the new hall was flexible in its offering of "refreshments" and seems to have been a busy place for civic events like the annual Election and Training Day at the end of May, for which "Remond did the honors . . . at his Refectory and Oyster and Ice Cream Saloon in Higginson Square."[22] Remond maintained a more spirited venue nearby, at Fourteen Derby Square and "the sign of the Big Lantern," and Nancy Remond began offering her various fancy cakes, from the popular "Election Cake" to the unique "Clay Cake," at both of these locations as well as on her own, as customers could order and pick them up at Five Higginson Square on a daily basis. The entire family catered for the community to which they had returned for a succession of July Fourth festivities.

The late 1840s and 1850s were a time of diversification and stratification for the Remond family. The elder daughters Nancy and Susan continued their culinary activities, both with their parents and on their own, while the younger daughters Maritchia, Cecelia, and Caroline ventured into the other family business—hair work—both together and separately. Their brother John Lenox Remond pursued hairdressing in both Salem and Gloucester, Massachusetts, before his untimely death.[23] Sarah seems to have wavered between helping her mother and helping her sisters before she followed in her brother Charles's footsteps and emerged as an inspirational trans-Atlantic abolitionist orator after 1856. Once again, Sarah's movement out into the world enables us to glean her father's (the diligent businessman) perspectives on the forces that are outside of his control but still in his "world." We can only guess at John's reaction to his children's protests against segregated seating, including Charles's 1842 appearance before the Massachusetts legislature protesting segregated railway cars and Sarah and Caroline's May 1853 expulsion from Boston's Howard Street Athenaeum, when they attempted to sit in their ticketed seats for the evening's opera performance. The pioneering testimony of Charles and the winning civil suit of Sarah are indicators of his approval and advocacy, of course, but Remond went about his business.[24]

Sarah's brilliant career forced Remond to confront his and his family's status as "colored citizens" again: Was this a contradiction in terms? Her two-year tour of New York, Ohio, and New England as a lecturer for the American Anti-Slavery Society, in the company of her brother and other well-known abolitionists of both races and genders, was by all accounts successful, and she received an invitation to continue her lectures in Britain in 1858. Both her lectures and her departure should be seen in the context of the urgency of the 1850s felt in the African American abolitionist community following the passage of the Fugitive Slave Act and the Dred Scott decision, which denied the status and rights of citizenship to all African Americans. Nonetheless, Sarah had acquired a passport, the ultimate confirmation of citizenship, before her departure in December 1858, as had her father several years before. John Remond's passport was part of a pattern of a proactive documentary quest that began in his early adulthood: despite the restriction of the 1790 Naturalization Act to "free white persons," he obtained a certificate of naturalization in 1811, he urged his son John Lenox to acquire a Seaman's Protection Certificate in 1839 (even though he was not, to my knowledge, a seaman), and then he acquired a passport for himself in 1854. Most studies agree that the citizenship status of all free Blacks before the Civil War was "murky" at best, but John's was especially so given that he was an émigré: he sought "affirmations of citizenship" at every opportunity.[25]

The Remond passports became powerful symbols of the paradoxical situation African Americans found themselves in after Dred Scott, when Sarah applied for a visa to travel to France from Britain, along with her younger sister Caroline Putnam and her son, and was denied on the basis that she had no citizenship as a "person of color," when, in fact, the U.S. State Department simply failed to recognize the passport that it had issued her just the year before. As Sirpa Salenius demonstrates, Sarah transformed this individual conundrum into a "collective" one very effectively, especially as the British press was intent on embarrassing the American officials.[26] The local angle is also very revealing: while the *New York Times* identified Sarah as "a colored young lady of Massachusetts, who devotes a good deal of her time to the pleasing task of teaching the English idea of freedom to shoot unvenomed arrows of scorn at the American fact of Slavery" and concluded that the American diplomats in London were simply doing their jobs, the *Salem Register* focused on the family dilemma and the perspective of an anguished father, grandfather, and *citizen*, John Remond. He had shown his precious passport and naturalization papers to the editors of the *Register* and asserted that his two daughters and grandson "should have the protection that they are entitled to as citizens of the United States." There was no question of his status in Salem—the *Register* simply gave him a forum: "He himself has been a citizen, duly acknowledged for half a century, and he very pertinently asks, 'if we cannot be citizens either home or abroad, what is to become of us?'"[27]

John Remond became an unassailable citizen, as did his daughter Sarah (albeit a British one) and all of his children; Nancy Remond died a year before the ratification of the Fourteenth Amendment. But Mr. Remond's claim of citizenship predated this constitutional landmark. He had *made* himself one by acquiring the necessary documents, paying his taxes, meeting his civic

Photograph of John Remond, n.d. *(Courtesy of Hamilton Hall, Inc.)*

obligations, building businesses, raising a family, defending his rights, and catering to the community. The praise and toasts showered upon Mr. Remond at each and every anniversary dinner of the Salem Light Infantry as he navigated the "venerable" stage of his life and career are a preferable testimony of the esteem in which he was held than what was said in his obituary in the *Boston Traveler*, which concludes by identifying him as a "West Indian negro" rather than an American citizen, the citizen of *Salem*, that he was. Better still are the local reports of a party he threw for himself on the occasion of his eighty-first birthday in 1868, at which Salem's "best citizens were present, and passed the hour to their own pleasure and to the gratification of their host."[28]

NOTES

1. "Letter to the Editor," *The Liberator*, February 16, 1833. For an overview of the Remond Family, see Dorothy Burnett Porter (Wesley), "The Remonds of Salem, Massachusetts: A Nineteenth-Century Family Revisited," *Proceedings of the American Antiquarian Society* 95, no. 2 (October 1985): 250–295. The Remonds had eleven children

between 1809 and 1826, with three dying in infancy and early childhood: Nancy Remond Shearman (1809–1878), Charles Lenox Remond (1810–1873), Susan H. Remond (1811–1879), John Lenox Remond (1812–1856), Maritchia J. Remond (1813–1895), Cecelia Remond Babcock (1816–1912), Cornelius Remond (1817–1821), Mary Remond (1819–1820), Sarah Parker Remond (1824–1894), and Caroline Remond Putnam (1826–1908), and an unnamed infant; *Salem Gazette*, June 2, 1825.

2. An anonymous letter published in the first African American newspaper *Freedom's Journal* narrating a "short visit to Salem" in 1827 estimates the number of "persons of color" to be in the realm of four hundred, a number that is repeated in successive articles. Remond was an agent for the newspaper throughout its run (1827–1829); *Freedom's Journal*, November 9, 1827.

3. W.E.B. Du Bois, *The Philadelphia Negro: A Social Study* (Oxford University Press, 2014), 19.

4. For surveys and studies of African Americans in the catering business in the nineteenth century, see Diane M. Spivey, *At the Table of Power: Food and Cuisine in the African-American Struggle for Freedom* (University of Pittsburgh Press, 2022); David S. Shields, *The Culinarians: Lives and Careers from the First Age of American Fine Dining* (University of Chicago Press, 2017); Jessica B. Harris, *High on the Hog: A Culinary Journey from Africa to America* (Bloomsbury), 2.

5. Phillips Library, Peabody Essex Museum, MSS 271, Remond Family Papers: includes four pieces of correspondence between John Remond and Henry Scott from the fall of 1831.

6. *Salem Literary and Commercial Observer*, October 15, 1825.

7. *Salem Gazette*, September 1, 1824.

8. *Salem Gazette*, September 19, 1828; *Salem Observer*, September 27, 1828. John Remond was always the acknowledged cook in contemporary accounts, but, in her 1887 memoir, *A Half Century in Salem*, Marianne Silsbee noted that "Mrs. Remond, the wife of the caterer, will be remembered for her charming manners and good cooking. Her mock-turtle soup, venison or alamode beef, and roast chickens, with perhaps ducks, and light, not flaky pastry, made an ample feast for a dozen gentlemen at the fashionable hour of two o'clock," 94. Two of the Remond daughters, Nancy and Susan, followed their mother into culinary careers, and Mrs. Remond also operated her own fancy cake bakery out of their property on Higginson Square in central Salem.

9. Phillips Library, Peabody Essex Museum, MSS 271, Remond Family Papers.

10. Boston Public Library, Anti-Slavery Collection: Letter from John Remond to William Lloyd Garrison, dated April 17, 1833: a rather convoluted letter explaining a donation of $50, "for your unwearied services in endeavoring to promote our cause."

11. Letter of John D. Clarke of Malden, Massachusetts, to Francis H. Lee of Salem, dated January 6, 1886. Francis Henry Lee Papers 1848-1912, MSS 128, Phillips Library of the Peabody Essex Museum.

12. Clarissa Lawrence School Records, Fam. MSS 883, Phillips Library of the Peabody Essex Museum.

13. *Salem Gazette*, July 25, 1834.

14. Salem's path to school segregation and desegregation is explored thoroughly by Kabria Baumgartner in *In Pursuit of Knowledge: Black Women and Educational Activism in Antebellum America* (New York University Press, 2019) and by Rebecca R. Noel in

"Salem as the Nation's Schoolhouse," in *Salem: Place, Myth, and Memory*, edited by Dane Anthony Morrison and Nancy Lusignan Schultz (Northeastern University Press, 2004), 129–162.

15. James M. Lindgren, "'That Every Mariner May Possess the History of the World': A Cabinet for the East India Marine Society of Salem," *New England Quarterly* 68, no. 2 (June 1995), 197.

16. Letter of John D. Clarke of Malden, Massachusetts, to Francis H. Lee of Salem, dated January 6, 1886. Phillips Library, MSS 128, Lee Family Papers.

17. *Newport Herald of the Times*, February 9, 1843.

18. *Salem Register*, August 16, 1841.

19. "The Colored School," *Salem Register*, March 14, 1844; The eldest Remond daughter, Nancy, had married James L. Shearman in 1834, and they had five children of school age by this time. Shearman had partnered with Charles L. Remond before his marriage, and he partnered with his father-in-law in the 1840s and 1850 in various victualing businesses, eventually succeeding him in his catering business.

20. *Salem Register*, January 9, 1843.

21. *Salem Register*, February 5, 1844.

22. *Salem Register*, May 30, 1844.

23. Nancy Remond Shearman was working primarily with her husband, who was the occasional partner of her father, while Susan Remond, listed as having "no occupation" in a succession of federal censuses, was actually quite renowned for her culinary, baking, and confectionary talents, according to the unpublished memoir of New York City educator Maritcha Remond Lyons (obviously a friend of the Remonds!). Lyons wrote that Susan's "bread, cakes, pastry, jellies and confections and more substantial desserts were in constant demand and brought excellent prices. She also served, in a small dining room, where none were eligible to entrance save the most exclusive of townsmen and their specially invited guests." Maritcha's mother, Mary Joseph Marshall, had worked at the Remond's confectionary in Newport and taught the Remond girls the special hairdressing techniques she had learned in New York from a French master. Maritcha Remond Lyons, "Memories of Yesterdays: All of Which I Saw and Part of Which I Was"; Harry A. Williamson Papers, New York: the Schomburg Center for Research in Black Culture, New York Public Library. Cecelia, Maritchia, and Caroline Remond opened their own hairdressing shop as early as 1846 and, from 1849 to 1851, were all working together in what became known as the "Hair Manufactory" on Washington Street, as they specialized in hair pieces and wigs. In the latter year, Caroline went out on her own, with the help of Sarah Remond, and the Hair Manufactory became "Remond & Babcock," after Maritchia Remond and Cecelia Remond Babcock, who had married James R. Babcock in 1843, and later the Ladies Hair Work Salon. Caroline married Joseph Hall Putnam, in 1846, and, therefore, the namesake of her popular "Mrs. Putnam's Medicated Hair Tonic."

24. "Remarks of Charles Lenox Remond. Before the Legislative Committee in the House of the Representatives, respecting the rights of colored citizens in travelling etc.," *The Liberator*, February 25, 1842; "Rights of Colored Persons," *The Liberator*, May 13, 1853; "The Opera Ejection Case," *The Liberator*, June 10, 1853. See also Elizabeth Stordeur Pryor, *Colored Travelers: Mobility and the Fight for Citizenship before the Civil War* (University of North Carolina Press, 2016) for longer discussions on both Charles Lenox Remond's and Sarah Parker Remond's transportation struggles.

25. Martha Jones, *Birthright Citizenship: A History of Race and Rights in Antebellum America*. (Cambridge University Press, 2018), 12.

26. Sirpa Salenius, *An Abolitionist Abroad: Sarah Parker Remond in Cosmopolitan Europe*. (University of Massachusetts Press, 2016), chap. 4.

27. "Colored Persons and Passports," *New York Times*, January 24, 1860; "The Case of Miss Sarah P. Remond," *Salem Register*, February 20, 1860.

28. *Boston Traveler*, March 7, 1874; *Newburyport Daily Herald*, April 7, 1868. John Remond was predeceased not only by his wife but also by both of his grown sons, John Lenox Remond and Charles Lenox Remond.

INTERLUDE 6

Mary Spencer

Shipwrecks, Sugar, and Salem

Brad Austin

One of the most fascinating features of Salem's history is the way that important connections appear almost every time we pull on a narrative thread. The story of Mary Spencer, and her son, provides one of the best examples of this. The simplest version of the story (one published in travel guides for decades) goes something like this: Mary Spencer was shipwrecked as she journeyed from England to the United States in the early 1800s. The good people of Salem showed mercy to the widow and gave her a cask of sugar, which she used to make a distinctive form of hard candy called Gibraltars. Soon, Salem sailors were taking Spencer's signature candy (that never spoiled!) to ports around the world, and she became a successful businesswoman who was able to pass along her knowledge and store to her son when she died. Before moving back to Britain, her son sold the company to a friend, John Pepper, who grew and expanded the business. To this day, visitors can buy Gibraltars at Ye Olde Pepper Companie in Salem, across from the House of the Seven Gables.[1]

While that narrative is largely accurate, it is also both far too narrow and incomplete to be satisfactory. Fortunately, a larger, more complete, account of the Spencer family's adventures in Salem is both much more interesting and more illustrative of important themes in Salem's history. Placing the Spencer and Gibraltar story in their larger contexts allows us to understand more fully the complexity of life in Salem in the early nineteenth century.

As Bethany Jay explains in Chapter 3 of this volume, Salem's connections to the sugar islands of the West Indies were strong from the very beginning of

Gibraltar Woman, Salem, 1822. Print. *(Courtesy of Donna A. Seger.)*

Salem's emergence as a British colonial outpost. In fact, the House of the Seven Gables exemplifies these connections quite neatly. When John Turner left England for Salem in the 1640s, his cousin—also named John Turner—migrated to the British West Indies. Both of these John Turners were part of a large migration of Brits to the Americas, and they quickly established themselves in their respective new homes, maintaining family and trading relationships for the following decades. By the 1660s, Salem's John Turner had built his family a home on Salem Harbor. This structure is now the House of the Seven Gables Historic House Museum, with frontage on Turner Street.[2]

Salem's long-standing ties to the Caribbean sugar islands also help us understand the growth of the area's prosperous fishing and merchant fleets, which supplied almost all necessities to the British West Indies, and which brought enslaved Africans, sugar, and molasses back to Massachusetts. Salem counted more than one hundred enslaved people among its residents at the time of the Revolutionary War, and it also had five rum distilleries. The fact that this small city could support five distilleries thousands of nautical miles from the nearest sugar plantation is a clear indication that sugar was a big part of daily life in Salem in the late 1700s and early 1800s. In 1805, the year that Mary Spencer arrived in Salem, the *Salem Gazette* had more than twenty-five hundred mentions of sugar and molasses in advertisements alone, on top of the hundreds of news stories and price guides it published discussing these commodities.[3]

By any measure, Mary Spencer's journey from England was exceptional. It began on the ship *Jupiter*, featured a dramatic longboat rescue and a stop in

Marblehead, and culminated in her Salem residency. Equally as noteworthy was the generosity shown to Spencer and her fellow survivors by the residents of Marblehead and Salem. The surviving *Jupiter* passengers were clearly in need, as the *Salem Gazette* explained in a May 1805 article. The paper noted, "The distressed people saved from the boats of the ship *Jupiter* are now arriving in Marblehead in the different fishing vessels on board which they were distributed; among whom are a number of the female passengers [including Spencer]. As they had no time to take anything from the ship, they were almost destitute of clothing, and of the means of sustaining life. No sooner was their arrival known that the sympathy of benevolent and charitable individuals in this town was awakened, who sent them supplies for their temporary relief; and a subscription is now filling, more effectually to answer their wants, and afford them comfort."[4]

This assistance lasted for months, inspiring one of Spencer's shipmates to print a public statement of gratitude in the *Salem Gazette* in October 1805. As he prepared to leave the region, Henry Merritt wrote "on behalf of himself and his fellow-sufferers" a card to "return his sincere and heartfelt thanks to those friends at Marblehead, Salem and Danvers, whose humanity and Christian love induced them to assist the distressed and supply the wants of the destitute, in the most generous manner."[5]

For Mary Spencer, the most vital part of her assistance came in the form of sugar, the availability of which speaks to Salem's long-standing Caribbean connections. The fact that she was able to transform this sugar into a commodity carried across each of the world's oceans speaks to Salem's prominence in global trade in the beginning of the nineteenth century and to the opportunities that a town accustomed to women living without men (because of absences caused by the sea) could provide to female entrepreneurs.

An essay with less strict length limitations would use Spencer's rise to prominence as a vehicle for explaining the ways that women could find spaces for independence and entrepreneurial activity in the streets of Salem and during the times when they were separated from their "responsible" fathers, brothers, and husbands, who were frequently absent and at sea. Histories written by Robert Booth and Daniel Vickers, among others, highlight the challenges faced by women living in Salem during the early nineteenth century and help us contextualize just how representative and exceptional Mary Spencer's arc was as she advanced from selling candies on the steps of Salem's First Church to being able to leave a prominent and thriving global business to her son when she died.[6]

Her English-born son's life and decisions shine a spotlight on even more ways that the Spencer family's experiences capture the complexities of early nineteenth-century Salem. Thomas appears to have joined his mother in Salem by the early 1820s, where both he and his wife (also named Mary) welcomed two sons to their family and they resided until Thomas inherited enough land to allow him to return to England and to assume his desired life as a farmer. The available evidence, however, suggests that his family's story does more than merely illustrate the long-standing Anglo-centric trans-Atlantic connections that characterized many Salem families. Instead, Thomas's time in Salem also highlights the town's continuing engagement with the worlds of sugar and slavery.[7]

The historian Joanne Pope Melish persuasively argues that the popular understanding of Massachusetts (and the North, generally) as a hotbed of abolitionism in the decades before the Civil War is mistaken. It's an invented tradition that her book, *Disowning Slavery*, dismantles over its 320 pages, but the fact remains that there *were* ardent abolitionists in Massachusetts and Salem by the 1830s, even if some of them owed their prosperity and livelihood to trade based on sugar cultivated by enslaved people (or to the emerging New England textile industry that depended on cotton from the South).[8]

One event, in particular, highlights Thomas Spencer's engagement with the abolitionist movement and the social and physical perils that accompanied this unpopular stance. As one of Salem's practicing Quakers, Thomas would have been exposed to that faith tradition's increasingly vocal opposition to slavery in the 1820s and 1830s, and he worked to translate that conviction into action. Both he and his wife were active abolitionists, and, in 1834, Thomas was a cofounder of the Anti-Slavery Society of Salem and Vicinity.[9] The 1830s witnessed the first real spike in abolitionist sentiment in the United States, and the Spencers attended a wide variety of abolitionist conventions in the region.

The Spencers' conference attendance and society memberships might not have attracted much attention, but their decision to host a fellow British abolitionist, later in 1835 certainly did. George Thompson was an evangelist for abolitionism, traveling throughout the United States, successfully planting hundreds of abolitionist societies along his way in the 1830s. As he neared the end of his barnstorming tour of the United States, he came to Salem to stay with the Spencers in their large home. He was greeted in late October 1835 by signs, calling on the townspeople to drive him away, that stated: "the Citizens of Salem, the friends of order, who are desirous to preserve the quiet of families, and the peace of the town by driving from our society the foreign pest, who is endeavoring to agitate the country with his [abolitionist] doctrines and to destroy the Union of state by his fanaticism."[10]

By the time a mob of four hundred had gathered outside of the Spencer home, Thompson had fled, leaving the entire Spencer clan (Thomas, both Mary Spencers and the Spencer children, including a newborn) to listen to the threats shouted by "Southerners from Boston" and from "some of the *pro-Slavery* men of Salem." The mob hurled rocks and other projectiles at the house, vowing to burn down the Spencer home if they didn't turn over Thompson, while some proclaimed that "one Englishman is as good as another" and "let us have the Quaker" before it became clear that Thompson had fled the area.[11]

About two hours after the siege began, the mob finally dissipated, leaving the Spencer family doubtlessly to wonder if the Salem that had welcomed Mary three decades before was still a hospitable place for their family. When mother Mary died shortly thereafter (she had been "on a bed of lingering sickness" during the threatened assault), and when Thomas inherited a sizable estate in England, the family chose to sell their candy business and return, in 1837, to Britain. The Pepper candy empire of Salem had begun.

Ultimately, the story of Mary Spencer and her sugar candies reminds us that Salem in the early 1800s was a place of complicated connections. It was a place where traditionally masculine activities related to the sea (including daring rescues of shipwrecked passengers) could lead to enhanced economic opportunities for women. It was a place where access to rich fisheries led to centuries-long symbiotic relationships with Caribbean sugar islands. It was a place where English immigrants could feel welcomed, in a new Revolutionary nation, until these same immigrants' commitment to expanding liberty and freedom led them to fear for their lives and return to their homeland across the Atlantic.

NOTES

1. For an example of how this narrative is often presented, see Jeff Swartz and Rinus Oosthoek, eds., *Salem's Cookin': Recipes and Stories from Salem's Best Chefs, Bakers, Brewers and Celebrities* (Salem Chamber of Commerce and Civics, 2021), 68.
2. Nell Porter Brown, "Preserving a Muse: Nathaniel Hawthorne's Debt to Caroline Emerton," *Harvard Magazine* (May–June 2016).
3. 1805 editions of the *Salem Gazette*, American Antiquarian Society, Worcester, Massachusetts.
4. *Salem Gazette*, May 28, 1805.
5. "A Card," *Salem Gazette*, October 1, 1805.
6. See Robert Booth, *Death of an Empire: The Rise and Murderous Fall of Salem, America's Richest City* (Thomas Dunne Books, 2011); Daniel Vickers, *Young Men and the Sea: Yankee Seafarers in the Age of Sail* (Yale University Press, 2005).
7. Donna Seger, "Slavery Siege in Salem," *Streets of Salem* (blog), May 21, 2021, available at https://streetsofsalem.com/2021/05/21/slavery-siege-in-salem/.
8. Joanne Pope Melish, *Disowning Slavery: Gradual Emancipation and "Race" in New England, 1780–1860* (Cornell University Press, 1998), 1–10.
9. The "object" of the society was "the extinction of Slavery in the Nation of which we are citizens." See the Anti-Slavery Society of Salem's *Constitution of the Anti-Slavery Society of Salem and Vicinity* (W. and S. B. Ives, 1834).
10. Broadside cited by Seger, "Slavery Siege in Salem." Earlier in October, Thompson's visit to Boston was the catalyst for the infamous mob rising against William Lloyd Garrison, carrying him through the streets and calling for him to be hanged in the Boston Common.

See Ken Ellingwood, *First to Fall: Elijah Lovejoy and the Fight for a Free Press in the Age of Slavery* (Pegasus Books, 2021), 101.

11. "Thomas Spencer Letter," printed in the Glasgow Ladies' Auxiliary Emancipation Society's, *Three Years' Female Anti-Slavery Effort, in Britain and America: Being a Report of the Proceedings of the Glasgow Ladies' Auxiliary Emancipation Society since Its Formation in January, 1834, Containing a Sketch of the Rise and Progress of the American Anti-Slavery Societies, and Valuable Communications Addressed by Them Both to Societies and Individuals in This Country* (Aird and Russell, 1837), 20–21.

THE THIRD CENTURY

1826–1925

Salem's third century began at a moment of significant changes in the city's, and the nation's, fortunes. In 1826, Americans mourned the July Fourth deaths of both Thomas Jefferson and John Adams, two members of the committee that drafted the Declaration of Independence, which had been approved by the Continental Congress precisely fifty years before. That same year, investors incorporated a nearby town on the Merrimack River, a town they named Lowell. The death of these two Revolutionary leaders, combined with the emergence of industrial and commercial rivals in the region, help us understand some of the growing pains and changes Salem experienced during its third century.

Salem seemed old by 1826, as it celebrated its bicentennial. Many of its most illustrious families were decamping for Boston, and its region was energized by the economic vitality of the emerging industrial economy, sped along by steam engines on ships and trains. Even its most famous son, Nathaniel Hawthorne, unflatteringly (and perhaps unfairly) referred to the city as "Old Salem" and ridiculed "its flat, unvaried surface, covered chiefly with wooden houses, few or none of which pretend to architectural beauty—its irregularity, which is neither picturesque nor quaint, but only tame."[1] Despite the fact that the city's fortunes were literally fading, along with the paint on many of its houses, the city remained vibrant and its history vital for understanding the nation's story.

The U.S. Census Bureau's listing of the largest American cities documents some of the changes Salem experienced during its third century as well as the ways the country was transformed around it. In 1820, as the city neared its bicentennial, Salem was still the nation's tenth-largest city, with 12,731 residents, 97.7 percent of whom were white (the other 2.3 percent of residents identified as Black). One hundred years later, Salem had dropped off the "100 largest cities" list, even though it had more than tripled in size, with 42,529 residents, 99.5 percent of them officially labeled as white by the Census Bureau. Census labels, however, are notoriously broad, and these census statistics conceal almost as much as they reveal about the transformative and important ways that Salem's population changed over these one hundred years.

As Salem officially became a city in 1836 and adopted a new seal and motto that celebrated its (literally) rich maritime history and its links to the "farthest ports of the rich east," rails replaced sails as the most important ways Salem connected with the larger world. Some of Salem's first railway lines, in fact, connected Salem to Lowell, as the new city eclipsed Salem in terms of both size and national economic significance. Lowell grew from 6,000 to 112,000 during this period (it was the eighteenth-largest city in the nation less than twenty years after its founding), and this population growth was fueled by the same immigration that also sparked Salem's smaller expansion.

Even though its regional neighbors, particularly Boston and Lowell, gained in population and prominence between 1826 and 1925, Salem remained an important cultural and economic center. During these years, the city hosted a wide range of social, cultural, political, and intellectual societies and hosted some of the nation's most important authors, speakers, and inventors. Nathaniel Hawthorne lived there and wrote, as we have seen, often unflatteringly, about his hometown. Frederick Douglass and the Grimké sisters called for the abolition of slavery in Salem meetings. Charles Lenox Remond and other speakers recruited for the Massachusetts Fifty-Fourth regiment in the city's streets, and Alexander Graham Bell sent the world's first telephone message from Salem's Lyceum Hall to Boston.

As a community, Salem participated both in the big debates of the age and in the most significant changes. During its third century, Salem was as the historian Gayle Fischer has labeled it a true "society of societies," and a brief list of these some of these organizations provides a hint of the issues that animated life there. Salem was home to numerous temperance and antislavery societies (as well as the Salem Freedman's Aid Society from 1863–1876), and it also saw many residents travel west in the Gold Rush of 1849. Hoping to prevent the type of cataclysmic fire that eventually devastated the city in 1914, Salemites formed and maintained a variety of fire clubs, just as they organized themselves into self-help organizations, ranging from the Charitable Mechanic's Association to the Young Men's Christian Association to the Association for the Relief of Aged and Destitute Women of Salem. During this period, Salem hosted competing women's suffrage and antisuffrage associations. By the early twentieth century, the Russian Immigrant Aid Society was just down Derby Street from the Polish community's St. Joseph's Hall (and also close to the House of the Seven Gables and its settlement house, which aimed to "Americanize" these populations). Salem residents served honorably in each of the wars of this era, and they also made time for cultural pursuits, creating bicycle clubs, the Salem Academy of Music, the city's Lyceum, the Schubert Club, and the Female Book and Tract Society, among dozens of other groups intended to make life in Salem better and more enjoyable.

As the region and the nation grew between 1826 and 1925, Salem was transformed by the changes brought by industrialization, wars, political upheaval, and waves of immigration, each of which helped transform the city. Throughout its third century, Salem was a vibrant and energetic place, full of men and women who both shaped and reflected the national culture in a myriad of significant ways.

NOTE

1. Nathaniel Hawthorne, "The Custom-House—Introductory," in *The Scarlet Letter, A Romance* (Metcalf, 1850), 8.

CHAPTER SEVEN

Salem and the Civil War

ROBERT W. MCMICKEN

On the morning of Thursday, December 20, 1860, Salemites awoke to the last day of a brisk Massachusetts autumn. The ladies of Crombie Street Sabbath School Society anticipated the second day of their sale of "useful and fancy objects."[1] The ladies of the Universalist Society in Danvers prepared for their holiday fair that evening with musical entertainment and charades. The Salem Cadets awaited their weekly drill the following evening at 8:00 P.M. While these events reflected an ordinary Thursday in December, an urgent uneasiness nevertheless stalked Salem—indeed, the entire nation.[2]

Accompanying the mundane notices for Christmas fairs and missing skates in the morning edition of the *Salem Register* was a proclamation issued six days prior from the politically moribund President James Buchanan. Buchanan urged Americans to seek the salvation of the Union through a day of prayer and fasting on January 4. Indeed, the *Salem Register* also noted the emotional tension of the day by printing two poems juxtaposed in the same column: John Greenleaf Whittier's "The Crisis" and Lucy Evelina Akerman's "An Appeal." Whittier's poem reinforced a free-soil message of choosing freedom over slavery, while Akerman's poem makes a human appeal to kindness and shared humanity. The events of the afternoon would lead to five years of testing of the commitment of the United States to both of those sentiments.[3]

As Salemites read the morning edition of the *Salem Register* on December 20, the South Carolina politicians gathered in Charleston were finalizing an Ordinance of Secession formalizing their dubiously legal secession from the

Union. This would begin a period of several months marked by the secession of Mississippi, Florida, Alabama, Georgia, Louisiana, Texas, Virginia, Arkansas, North Carolina, South Carolina, and Tennessee. But on December 20, few, if any, Salemites would have predicted that the next day would begin a winter that would last much longer than one season. As Christmas approached in 1860, not many could guess that for so many men across the nation, in the very beginning of their adult lives, like nineteen-year-old William Hurley from Union Street, and twenty-year-old shoemaker George A. Thompson, the events of the day would set in motion a catastrophic war that would make this their last Christmas. From all cities in Massachusetts, many young men leaving to fight never returned, and many more would never return quite the same as when they left. Salem could not, however, in good faith, completely abjure its own responsibility in this reckoning. While chattel slavery had been effectively abolished in Massachusetts since before the turn of the nineteenth century, the relationship of Salem's Naumkeag Steam Cotton Company with the cotton economy demonstrates the role of Northern industrialists in enabling slavery and the sociopolitical hierarchies of the Southern cotton interests.[4]

The November election of Abraham Lincoln as the sixteenth president of the United States proved to be the spark igniting the sectional tensions that had steadily escalated since the Missouri Compromise in 1820. This sectional blaze grew to an inferno with the Compromise of 1850, which strengthened laws enforcing the capture of formerly enslaved people claimed by their enslavers, and the 1854 Kansas-Nebraska Act, which led to a de facto civil war being fought in the Kansas Territory. Further, the Roger Taney–issued *Dred Scott v. Sandford* (1857) decision ruled not only that the enslaved plaintiff, Dred Scott, was not allowed the right to sue in court but also, and devastatingly so, that the Missouri Compromise—the flimsy guardrails that had kept free-soil and slave interests from open conflict—was effectively nullified.[5]

As talk of disunion grew from a chatter to a clamor and, finally, to a reality, American unionists reacted in a variety of ways. While fire-eating secession commissioners made pilgrimages to Southern legislatures proselytizing and preaching an unholy gospel of "Black Republican" oppression, Northern constituencies reacted with no small degree of ambivalence between disgust and despair. One Salemite observed in December 1860 that "the South Carolina people shout just now for the 'lone' star. They will find secession a very lonely affair in all respects before they get through with it."[6] Meanwhile, prominent politicians were attempting to turn out a "compromise" that would legitimize the institution of slavery with the hopes of a national reconciliation. This effort was made in no small part to avoid the major financial repercussions and economic depression that would accompany dire political instability.[7]

Despite the progressive political schism between Northern free-soilers and abolitionists and the Southern slave power, the Northern and Southern economic interests were often shared and mutually reliant. While industrialized Northern states had more diversified economies than the cotton-dominated Deep South, political adversaries often made for economic bedfellows. Simply put, slave labor enabled much of the industrialization of the 'North. While the institution of chattel slavery in the 1850s is culturally associated with the Deep South, it would be disingenuous to harbor any notion that Northern industrialists did not derive direct benefit from cotton picked by enslaved hands and from the money lent to enslavers from Northern banks and insurance companies. In turn, textiles manufactured in the North—especially "negro cloth," specifically intended to clothe enslaved people—were sold back to Southern merchants and planters. As the textile economy grew in Middlesex and Essex Counties, the cotton woven by the looms into textiles bore the taint of slave labor and enriched Northern industrialists and Southern planters alike.[8]

On May 8, 1845, the *Salem Register* announced the capitalization of the Naumkeag Steam Cotton Company, which had been incorporated in 1839. Massachusetts had long been a center of textile manufacturing, but Salem's Naumkeag Steam Cotton Company was different. Rather than harnessing the power of flowing water to power its Pequot Mills location, David Pingree and the Naumkeag Steam Cotton Company's other directors ventured on another use of water: steam power. In so doing, the directors constructed the first steam-powered textile mill in New England. Innovative, industrial, and inventive, Pequot Mills captured the zeitgeist of the rapidly industrializing Northern states. Nevertheless, a dependence on steam power necessitated a dependence on fuel: whereas mills in Lowell were powered simply by the flow of the Merrimack River, Pequot Mills required a steady supply of coal to power their operations. Still, with steam power, the mill had the opportunity to operate with great output.[9]

By 1857, the Naumkeag Steam Cotton Company operated the four-story Pequot Mills building, located on land with ample frontage on Salem's harbor. It employed six hundred hands collectively working on 641 looms. The mill operated on a four-hundred-horsepower steam engine that was coal powered. In November 1856, the Naumkeag Steam Cotton Company announced a capitalization of $700,000 with a total debt of around $211,000. Naumkeag's venture into steam power had worked, and Pequot Mills featured prominently in Salem. For a city whose maritime trade had been eclipsed by Boston and New York, and whose colonial identity featured as a retort by Southern enslavers directed toward Massachusetts abolitionists for its "witch-burning" past, the success of Pequot Mills offered Salemites a new *industrial* identity.[10]

To perpetuate the prosperity enjoyed by the Naumkeag Steam Cotton Company, Pequot Mills required two fundamental resources that could not be adequately sourced locally, or even regionally: cotton and coal. For the bulk of the early to mid-nineteenth-century, urban Massachusetts sourced its bituminous coal primarily from the eastern Virginia coal mines due to the coastal accessibility. Virginia coal mining was largely reliant on slave labor; mine owners sourced labor from hired slaves to perform the inherently dangerous task of mining. Rock falls and methane fueled explosions posed a consistent danger to the miners. At Virginia's Black Heath Pits in 1839, forty-five enslaved workers died horrifically in a methane explosion.[11]

While railroads eventually allowed more accessibility to Pennsylvania's bituminous coal deposits, thus mitigating the region's extensive reliance on Virginia coal, Pequot Mills remained fundamentally dependent on cotton produced by enslaved labor. Before the Civil War, the prosperity of Northern textile mills and the Naumkeag Steam Cotton Company relied on an abundance of cotton and a Southern economy prepared to supply it. Cotton monocropping enriched the Southern planter class, however much they resented the Northern prosperity based off of imports and industrialization. Packet ships carrying cotton from ports in the Deep South, such as Mobile, Alabama, conveyed huge quantities of cotton bound for the Pequot Mills. Shipping the cotton carried risks, and the purchaser—in this case the Naumkeag Steam Cotton Company—bore the financial responsibility of transportation. Cotton could easily be damaged in transit. However, the cycle proved mutually beneficial to Southern planters and Northern industrialists alike; left out of this equation entirely was the welfare of the enslaved.[12]

As the Civil War approached in Salem, the regional rhetoric of abolition reached a crescendo. Yet still the Pequot Mills relied on enslaved laborers to provide the cotton necessary to continue its operations. What would happen if that source suddenly were removed? How would the mill and company remain profitable? Further, what would happen to the employees reliant on the mills for their livelihood? This uncertainty led to fear of secession and the deep desire to maintain the status quo. The fear of an economic panic driven by Southern secession caused hesitation among the Northern industrialists. Legislative efforts at quelling secession led by Kentucky Senator John Crittenden proved ineffective. A separate effort, led in the House of Representatives, by Maryland Representative Henry Winter Davis and Massachusetts Congressman Charles Francis Adams was targeted at limiting the damage through shaving off border states from the cause of the Deep South. Ultimately, the ideological divide was too great, and, like most cities and towns of the divided nation, Salem too wrestled with ways to do its part during the existential crisis of the American Republic.[13]

The Union army in the secession winter of 1860–1861 offered a woefully inadequate solution for the task of suppressing a nascent rebellion. Most of the sixteen-thousand-man federal army was out west. To make matters worse, the army had a dearth of sufficient staff, an overabundance of inexperience, and, perhaps most embarrassingly, an appalling lack of basic supplies like maps. Inevitably, this dire situation forced Lincoln to call on seventy-five thousand militiamen—the first step of a protracted process of recruitment and conscription.[14]

The emergent problem, Lincoln found, was that the state militias were ill-prepared as effective combat units. Over the course of the nineteenth century, militias had degraded. The result presented an overemphasis on a performative martial identity, which had "transformed the Organized Militia into a gaudily uniformed group of public entertainers."[15] Accordingly, many of these units had no hesitation in bringing a full brass band with them. Certainly, there were fewer means of more effectively generating a "display." Antebellum militia regiments had become social clubs. Their bands aided in recruitment and enticed the formation of further regiments, which then, in turn, employed more bands.[16]

While the social utility of local militias like the Salem Light Infantry and the Salem Cadets was unquestionable as much beloved Salem institutions, the actual military functionality of the organizations was questionable at best and problematic at worst. The furthest that the Salem Light Infantry had ever "campaigned" was to Providence, Rhode Island, in September 1853, as a social function.[17] Future campaigning for many of these men involved mud, privation, and epidemic disease. Once called, as a unit, the Salem Light Infantry was charged with bringing the USS *Constitution* from Washington, DC, to New York City; however, many of the men from the infantry enlisted in other volunteer units once it became clear that mere militia units were not capable of suppressing the rebellion.[18]

On October 12, 1860, William Cogswell prepared to rally Salemites toward Lincoln and rode mounted as an aide to the grand marshal down Lafayette Street as part of a parade of each of Essex County's Wide Awake clubs. The Wide Awakes were composed of youthful Republicans eager to claim their generation's share of political power, often through dramatic paramilitary displays. Cogswell, who practiced law with his partner William Dummer Northend at 214 Essex Street, believed firmly in civic duty, serving as an Essex County justice of the peace. In April 1861, Cogswell raised a company of men

RECRUITS WANTED

FOR
CAPTAIN COGSWELL'S COMPANY
OF THE GALLANT
2D REGIMENT

20 good able-bodied men wanted for Captain Cogswell's Company, the

ANDREW LIGHT GUARD!

This Company won great renown in the Battle at WINCHESTER in covering the Retreat of

GEN. BANKS

Application may be made at once to

CAPT. A. B. UNDERWOOD,
LIEUT. A. D. SAWYER,
At 7 DERBY SQUARE, Salem.

Recruits wanted for Captain Cogswell's Company of the gallant 2d Regiment. 20 good able men wanted for Captain Cogswell's company, the Andrew Light Guard! Poster, 75 × 54 cm, Civil War posters, 1861–1865, PR-055-3-9, ac03009s. *(New York Historical Society.)*

from Salem that eventually mustered in as part of the Second Massachusetts Volunteer Infantry.[19]

The Second Massachusetts saw a tremendous amount of fighting throughout the war, both in the Eastern theater, and, later, in the Western theater. Cogswell survived the Battle of Cedar Mountain, which claimed the lives of Salemites John Corcoran, Franklin Jewell, William Larrabee, and W. D. Williston. Cogswell earned a promotion following the Battle of Antietam, which saw prominent Boston Brahmin officers like Caspar Crowninshield and Robert Gould Shaw wounded and Wilder Dwight killed. At the Battle of Chancellorsville, Cogswell himself was wounded in the arm. Following that engagement, Cogswell was promoted to colonel, and he subsequently fought at Gettysburg. Eventually, Colonel Cogswell became the commander of Atlanta during William Tecumseh Sherman's occupation of the city and was responsible for physically executing much of the planned industrial destruction upon Sherman's departure from Atlanta and ensuing March to the Sea.[20]

On September 27, 1862, the *Salem Observer* heralded with great joy the "moral courage" of Abraham Lincoln's recently issued preliminary Emancipation Proclamation.[21] The Emancipation Proclamation illustrated the increasing understanding in many quarters that the elimination of chattel slavery in rebel states, while not the outright goal of the war, certainly aided its prosecution. Salemites celebrated the Emancipation Proclamation and rallied around Abraham Lincoln. A letter imploring Senator Charles Sumner to speak on the matter was signed by 137 Salemites; on October 20, 1862, "one of the largest political meetings ever held in Salem was gathered in Mechanic Hall . . . to listen to Charles Sumner."[22] Salem, unquestionably, rallied around emancipation and Lincoln.

Despite the increasing popularity of abolitionism in Salem from the 1850s into the 1860s, White Salemites did not generally view free people of color as social equals. Salem had one of the larger free Black populations in Massachusetts, but most Black Salemites were relegated to menial jobs and subjected to cultural inundations of minstrelsy, pernicious racial stereotypes, and derision, even when celebrating Election Day.[23] White Salemites populated the ranks of many Massachusetts volunteer infantry regiments along with volunteer cavalry, and heavy artillery, but Black Salemites were largely excluded from enlistment initially. The first man of color from Salem to join the war effort was George Johnson who joined the First Massachusetts Volunteer Infantry in October 1861, likely "passing as white."[24]

Only after the Emancipation Proclamation would other Black Salemites find the opportunity to fight to preserve the Union and fight for the emancipation of those still enslaved. The Fifty-Fourth Regiment of the Massachusetts

Volunteer Infantry remains the most unique regiment in which Salemites served. Much popular attention has accompanied the Fifty-Fourth Massachusetts since the 1989 Edward Zwick film, *Glory*, but this attention typically ends with the assault on Fort Wagner and the death of Colonel Robert Gould Shaw. Lesser known in popular culture than the "blue-eyed child of fortune," Salemite Luis Emilio served for a time as the commanding officer of the regiment following Fort Wagner.[25] The persistent views of racial inequality in Northern society also infected many African American regiments during the Civil War. While the devastatingly one-sided assault on Fort Wagner cemented the legacy of the Fifty-Fourth Massachusetts and illustrated to skeptics that Black troops would fight bravely and effectively, it did not resolve all issues. One such issue plaguing Black regiments both prior to the assault on Fort Wagner and after was the issue of equal pay.

The Salem clerk Francis H. Fletcher was one of the key figures who helped enlist volunteers for the Fifty-Fourth Massachusetts and was also the only Black Salemite to become a noncommissioned officer in the regiment. Sadly reflective of general sentiments toward African Americans, the *Salem Gazette* published several articles both doubting the benefits Black soldiers would bring and encouraging disproportionate disciplinary measures like "instant death" for infractions that were implied as likely because of the soldiers' race.[26] Meanwhile, Fletcher, along with other white and Black members of the Fifty-Fourth Massachusetts lamented the racial discrimination manifest in pay discrepancies. Despite promising recruits the standard $13 per month, Secretary of War Edwin Stanton ordered that Black regiments be paid only $10 per month. Outraged, Robert Gould Shaw wrote to his father that he would refuse to have the regiment paid at all at that lower rate and that "the [regiment] ought . . . to be mustered out of service, as they were enlisted on the understanding that they were to be on the same footing as other Mass Vols."[27] He reiterated this sentiment in a subsequent letter to Governor John Andrew of Massachusetts. Fletcher, understandably, expressed deeper resentment regarding the pay dispute when it was finally resolved in May 1864: "Just one year ago today our [regiment] was received in Boston with almost an ovation. . . . In that one year no man of our regiment has received a cent of monthly pay all through the flaring perfidy of the U.S. [government]."[28] For Salem's members of the Fifty-Fourth, the fight to be treated as men and as soldiers was just as important as the fight to take Fort Wagner.

The Union war effort in Salem did not restrict itself to the military. For women, and for men unable to serve, there were opportunities at home to contribute and support those campaigning in the field. The U.S. Sanitary Commission originated as a movement to promote field hygiene, but it transformed into a force for medical reform. As early as 1861, Salem women were meeting to contribute as best as they could. On July 25, 1861, the *Salem Register* published a notice calling for women "to make Hospital Garments" and urged "contributions of money or soft unbleached cotton."[29] Cotton, produced by the planter-textile partnership responsible, in part, for opening the wounds of disunion, now served to staunch battlefield wounds and clothe those languishing in general hospitals. The Sanitary Commission called on Salem women to form sewing circles and contribute quilts and blankets. Local branches of the Sanitary Commission also welcomed financial contributions. On January 9, 1863, the Salem musician Manuel Fenollosa—Luis Emilio's brother-in-law—donated $360.25 of his concert proceeds to the New England Women's Auxiliary Sanitary Commission.[30]

By the war's end, over 3,000 Salem men had served in the Union army or navy. Over 230 of these men were killed in battle, died from their wounds, or succumbed to illness. Forty-seven of these men died in Confederate prisons, including Andersonville. Many returned home disabled from wounds or illness. All returned home forever changed.

Salem [who did so] itself was changed. Some of the veterans needed assistance, as seen when the *Salem Register* urged Salemites to help James Frey, a disabled veteran who served in the Second Massachusetts Volunteer Infantry under William Cogswell, find work. Caring for disabled veterans also taxed local charities, as Reverend R. C. Parsons implored in his 1869 annual report:

> [Do not forget the] sick or disabled soldiers going to hospitals, or to visit friends in different parts of the country. . . . And as long as you give me money to buy food for the hungry and clothes for such as are cold, not one of these men . . . shall leave Salem without some substantial assurance, that we have not forgotten the price they paid for our present security.[31]

Often unseen were the mental scars that returning soldiers bore. And for those who did not understand the hardship that returning soldiers had endured, their behavior might be judged as erratic, unreliable, or perhaps even insane. Henry A. Farnum, a Salem carpenter before the war, served in the Thirty-Second Massachusetts Volunteer Infantry during the war, and his service came at a great personal cost. Farnum died at the age of forty in the Worcester Insane Asylum "of sickness caused by hardship and exposure in the army during the late war."[32]

On April 15, 1865, Abraham Lincoln died of the wounds delivered by John Wilkes Booth the previous evening at Ford's Theater. The news was received in Salem with shock and mourning. "The flags were at once placed at half mast, and by order of the Mayor all the bells in the city were tolled, in testimony of the public grief. Many stores and other places were also dressed in mourning," the *Salem Register* reported on April 17, 1865.[33] Days later, "the sorrow [was] all-pervading," and Mayor Joseph Osgood called for the day of Lincoln's funeral to be a day of mourning and worship throughout the city.[34] The war was effectively over. The Naumkeag Steam Cotton Company suffered little from fluctuations in the price of cotton, and Pequot Mills remained a Salem fixture for decades. Brevet Brigadier General William Cogswell of the Second Massachusetts Volunteer Infantry resumed his law practice on Essex Street and was later elected mayor of Salem. In 1886, William Cogswell was elected to Congress.[35]

The Crombie Street Sabbath School celebrated July 4, 1865, by presenting "twelve tastefully decorated carriages containing historic and mythological scenes of great force and beauty."[36] One carriage depicted Justice, Innocence, and Peace. Innocence was depicted as a young child dressed in white. The carriage, according, to the *Salem Observer*, depicted the virtues "for which the Republic was founded."[37] But, this year in America, Innocence could no longer simply shut her eyes when looking at the world around her. Aged, and world weary, Innocence was left to count the dead and hollowed men, women, and children wrought by eighty-nine years of alternating indifference and naivete.

NOTES

1. "Sale Continued," *Salem Register*, December 20, 1860, 2.

2. "Notice," *Salem Register*, December 20, 1860; "Attention Cadets," *Salem Register*, December 20, 1860, 2.

3. James Buchanan, "A Recommendation," *Salem Register*, December 20, 1860; John Greenleaf Whittier, "The Crisis," *Salem Register*, December 20, 1860; Lucy Evelina Akerman, "An Appeal," *Salem Register*, December 20, 1860.

4. T. J. Hutchinson and Ralph Childs, *Patriots of Salem: Role of Honor of the Officers and Enlisted Men, during the Late Civil War, from Salem, Mass.* (Salem Publishing, 1877), 11, 54.

5. Dred Scott v. Sandford, 60 U.S. 393.

6. Charles B. Dew, *Apostles of Disunion: Southern Secession Commissioners and the Causes of the Civil War*, 15th anniversary ed. (University of Virginia Press, 2016), 18–24; "The Secession Spasm," *Salem Observer*, November 17, 1860.

7. James McPherson, *Battle Cry of Freedom: The Civil War Era* (Oxford University Press, 1988), 252–253.

8. Edward E. Baptist, *The Half Has Never Been Told: Slavery and the Making of American Capitalism* (Basic Books, 2014), 322–325; David Brion Davis, *Inhuman Bondage:*

The Rise and Fall of Slavery in the New World (Oxford University Press, 2006), 178–181; Ronald Bailey, "'Those Valuable People, the Africans': The Economic Impact of the Slave(ry) Trade on Textile Industrialization in New England," in *The Meaning of Slavery in the North*, ed. David Roediger and Martin H. Blatt (Garland, 1998), 3–4.

9. George Adams, *The Salem Directory: Containing the City Record, Schools, Churches, Banks, Societies, etc., Names of the Citizens, Business Directory, General Events of the Years 1854 and 1855, an Almanac for 1857, and a Variety of Miscellaneous Matter* (Henry Whipple and Son, 1857), 228; "Steam Factory," *Salem Register*, May 8, 1845; Aviva Chomsky, "Salem as a Global City, 1850–2004," in *Salem: Place, Myth, and Memory*, ed. Dane Anthony Morrison and Nancy Lusignan Schultz, rev. ed. (Northeastern University Press, 2015), 201; Clive Jarvis, *The Story of Pequot* (Naumkeag Steam Cotton, 1934), 28.

10. George Adams, *Salem Directory*, 228; "Naumkeag Steam Cotton Co.," *Salem Register*, January 26, 1857; Gretchen A. Adams, *The Specter of Salem: Remembering the Witch Trials in Nineteenth-Century America* (University of Chicago Press, 2008), 94–95. Gretchen Adams argues that the erroneous accusations of "witch-burning" were used to castigate New England abolitionists as the spiritual inheritors of Cromwellian Puritanism with all of its commensurate excesses.

11. Ronald L. Lewis, "'The Darkest Abode of Man': Black Miners in the First Southern Coal Field, 1780–1865," *Virginia Magazine of History and Biography* 87, no. 2 (April 1979), 190, 196–198.

12. Walter Johnson, *River of Dark Dreams: Slavery and Empire in the Cotton Kingdom* (Belknap, 2013), 288–293; Bulkley v. Naumkeag Steam Cotton Company, 65 U.S. (24 How.) 386.

13. David M. Potter, *The Impending Crisis: America before the Civil War: 1848–1861* (HarperCollins, 1976; repr., Harper Perennial 2011), 530–535.

14. McPherson, *Battle Cry of Freedom*, 313, 322. The president's call for seventy-five thousand militiamen was the first of many calls for military force. These first volunteers were only called for ninety days. Volunteer militia units were different from volunteer infantry units, which were called subsequently to serve for longer periods of time.

15. Kenneth E. Olson, *Music and Musket: Bands and Bandsmen of the American Civil War* (Greenwood, 1981), 17.

16. Olson, *Music and Musket*, 18–20.

17. George M. Whipple, *History of the Salem Light Infantry from 1805 to 1890* (Essex Institute, 1890), 51–52.

18. Whipple, *History of the Salem Light Infantry*, 65–66.

19. "Grand Wide-Awake Demonstration in Salem," *Salem Register*, October 11, 1860; Jon Grinspan, "'Young Men for War': The Wide Awakes and Lincoln's 1860 Presidential Campaign," *Journal of American History* 96, no. 2 (September 2009), 357–360; "Northend and Cogswell," *Salem Register*, November 26, 1860; "Salem and Vicinity," *Salem Observer*, October 27, 1860; "Military," *Salem Observer*, April 20, 1861; "Movements in Town," *Salem Observer*, May 4, 1861; "War Items and Incidents," *Salem Register*, July 11, 1861.

20. Charles F. Morse, *Letters Written during the Civil War: 1861–1865* (privately printed, 1898), 89–90, 138, 196; Hutchinson and Childs, *Patriots of Salem*, 50–51; "From Gen. Hooker's Army," *Salem Register*, May 7, 1863.

21. "The Proclamation of Emancipation," *Salem Observer*, September 27, 1862.

22. McPherson, *Battle Cry of Freedom*, 497–500, 557–559; "Charles Sumner in Salem," *Salem Register*, October 13, 1862; "Senator Sumner in Salem," *Salem Register*, October 23, 1862.

23. Michael Sokolow, "'New Guinea at One End, and a View of the Alms-House at the Other': The Decline of Black Salem, 1850–1920," *New England Quarterly* 71, no. 2 (June 1998), 206, 214–216.

24. Sokolow, "New Guinea at One End," 217.

25. William James in *Exercises at the Dedication of the Monument to Colonel Robert Gould Shaw and the Fifty-Fourth Regiment of Massachusetts Infantry*, May 31, 1897 (Municipal Printing Office, 1897), 41; Luis F. Emilio, *A Brave Black Regiment: History of the Fifty-Fourth Regiment of Massachusetts Volunteer Infantry 1863–1865*, 2nd ed. (Boston Book, 1894), 105.

26. Sokolow, "New Guinea at One End," 218.

27. Robert Gould Shaw to Francis George Shaw, July 1, 1863, in Russell Duncan, ed. *Blue-Eyed Child of Fortune: The Civil War Letters of Robert Gould Shaw* (University of Georgia Press, 1992), 367–369.

28. Emilio, *Brave Black Regiment*, 47–48; Francis H. Fletcher to Jacob C. Safford, May 28, 1864, available at https://www.gilderlehrman.org/sites/default/files/inline-pdfs/t-07345.pdf.

29. Dale C. Smith, "Military Medical History: The American Civil War," *OAH Magazine of History* 19, no. 5 (September 2005), 18; "Notice," *Salem Register*, July 25, 1861.

30. "War Items and Incidents," *Salem Register*, October 7, 1861; "Mr. Fenollosa's Charity," *Salem Register*, January 15, 1863.

31. "Help a Disabled Soldier," *Salem Register*, January 31, 1867; R. C. Parsons, "Annual Report of Rev. R. C. Parson, City Missionary," *Salem Register*, December 30, 1869.

32. George Adams, *Salem Directory*, 89; Hutchinson and Childs, *Patriots of Salem*, 80; "Mortuary Notice," *Salem Register*, January 10, 1867.

33. "The Nation Mourns!" *Salem Register*, April 17, 1865.

34. "The National Grief," *Salem Register*, April 20, 1865.

35. "Advertisement," *Salem Register*, September 17, 1866; "May Training," *Salem Register*, May 28, 1868; "Election Results," *Springfield Republican*, November 3, 1886.

36. "The Fourth in Salem," *Salem Register*, July 6, 1865.

37. "The Great Celebration," *Salem Observer*, July 8, 1865.

INTERLUDE 7

The Civil War Service of Luis Fenollosa Emilio

Brian Valimont

Luis Fenollosa Emilio (1844–1918) grew up amid an energetic and expanding abolitionist community in Salem. The Anti-Slavery Society of Salem and Vicinity and its pioneering sister organization, the Salem Female Anti-Slavery Society, were founded in the 1830s as local chapters of William Lloyd Garrison's American Anti-Slavery Society. Both organizations were integrated and included among their membership representatives of Salem's most prominent African American family, the Remonds, as well as Luis's father Manuel Emilio and uncle Manuel Fenollosa. The two Manuels, who had emigrated to the United States from Spain in 1836, were professional musicians, educators, and composers who merged their art and advocacy often: Emilio's 1852 song *Little Eva: Uncle Tom's Guardian Angel* was "composed and most respectfully dedicated to Mrs. Harriet Beecher Stowe," and Fenollosa's *Emancipation Hymn* (1863) lamented "fettered manhood's moans." This was the environment both in which Luis was raised and in which he developed a persistent sense of equality with and support for African Americans.[1]

When the Civil War began in 1861, Emilio was a mere sixteen, not yet old enough to enlist legally as a soldier in the Union army. Nevertheless, he passed himself off as an eighteen-year-old and enlisted as a private in Company F of the Twenty-Third Massachusetts Volunteer Infantry for a three-year term of service. In February 1862, the Twenty-Third Massachusetts landed on Roanoke Island, North Carolina, and were engaged in battle the very next day, in the Union attempt to capture the multiple forts and batteries on the island. Company F of the Twenty-Third Massachusetts was positioned on the Union right, supporting the Twenty-Fifth Massachusetts during the combat, and, after the Union victory, Private Emilio participated in the escort of some five hundred Confederates to a wharf for transport.[2]

A month later, the Twenty-Third Massachusetts was camped about one thousand feet from the Confederate lines on the outskirts of New Bern, North Carolina. Battle commenced the next day, with Emilio's regiment positioned on the right flank of the front line. Company F engaged in combat until their ammunition was nearly spent. The men then laid down on the ground with fixed bayonets and charged the Confederate works when ordered. During this battle, Private Emilio and others crept along the ground ahead of the regiment's line, using logs and brush as cover, and engaged in combat in the area between the opposing armies. After the Confederate works were captured, Emilio's regiment remained in and near New Bern, which served as a base of Union operations that deterred the Confederates from recapturing coastal North Carolina. Emilio was promoted to corporal on August 23, 1862, and then to sergeant shortly thereafter.[3]

At the end of 1862, Sergeant Emilio and the Twenty-Third Massachusetts were deployed as part of a brigade on a campaign to destroy the railroad between Gouldsboro and Wilmington, North Carolina. The regiment participated in the Battle of Kinston on December 14, functioning as a rear provost guard charged with maintaining the discipline of the ranks. By the time of this battle, Emilio's feet had become badly chafed; he discarded his shoes in favor of three or four pairs of socks, which became worn during the course of the day, leaving him barefoot. He had to scavenge replacement pairs of socks daily while his regiment marched back to New Bern. In late December, the regiment became heavily engaged in battle at the town of Whitehall. Each soldier expended his forty rounds of ammunition during an hour or two at the riverbank. After the battle, Sergeant Emilio and others volunteered to recover their dead and wounded from the battlefield, but Confederate gunfire prevented them from completing their duty. En route back to their camp in New Bern, Emilio and several comrades accepted a ride in a springless army wagon full of muskets, which the soldiers recalled as an extremely uncomfortable ride.[4]

Back in Massachusetts, Governor John Andrew responded quickly to President Abraham Lincoln's call for the raising of African American regiments and began forming the Fifty-Fourth Massachusetts Volunteer Infantry in February 1863. Advocates for the recruitment of African American soldiers wanted to afford them the opportunity to prove that they were capable of engaging in combat. Governor Andrew chose the son of prominent Boston abolitionists, Robert Gould Shaw, to lead the Fifty-Fourth and looked for similar backgrounds and inclinations for its other officers. The majority (forty-eight) of the new regiment's officers were from Massachusetts, including four from Company F of the

Twenty-Third Massachusetts, among them Luis Emilio. With his combat experience and the reputation of Salem's vocal abolitionist community behind him, Emilio was promoted to second lieutenant on March 12, 1863, and he received his captain's commission by the end of the month. He was eighteen years old and assigned to command Company E of the Fifty-Fourth Massachusetts Volunteer Infantry, a unit of one hundred men.[5]

The Fifty-Fourth Massachusetts was recruited "from St. Louis to Boston." During its two and half years of service, it included over 1,350 white and Black men (29 percent of which were from Massachusetts). Their average age was twenty-four. Many of the enlisted African Americans worked as farmers and laborers, as well as barbers, mariners, waiters, boatmen, and teamsters. At least thirty of them were formerly enslaved people, but 25 percent of the recruits were from Southern states, so the total may be much higher.[6]

By July 1, the Fifty-Fourth Massachusetts was on James Island, South Carolina, in preparation for the assault on Battery Wagner on nearby Morris Island. Captain Emilio and Company E served on picket duty the night of July 13, and the steadfastness of the regiment in maintaining their picket line allowed the Tenth Connecticut the ability to retreat safely back. On July 18, the regiment marched to the front near Battery Wagner, where the six hundred soldiers and twenty-two officers laid down in a line with their muskets loaded. Emilio's Company E was positioned on the right of the attack column behind Company B. They charged through the beach water at knee's height. As it became dark, orders were given to approach the works quickly and then storm the works with bayonets. As the width of the island narrowed, the troops on the flanks had to fall behind the advancing troops due to a lack of space. The Confederates unleashed a massive volley of gunfire when the Union troops were at two hundred yards. The Fifty-Fourth responded by charging forward at double quick speed.[7]

Undertaking heavy casualties, the men of the Fifty-Fourth crossed a water-filled ditch, up a slope to the rampart and its parapet above, while engaging in a deadly struggle using bayonets and muskets as clubs. Hand grenades and lit shells were rolled down the parapet onto Union troops still in the ditch. The Union troops were outnumbered, and no reinforcements arrived quickly enough to support the soldiers of the Fifty-Fourth, so they were forced to fall back. As the highest-ranking surviving and unwounded officer, Captain Emilio became the acting commander of the Fifty-Fourth Massachusetts on the battlefield. Emilio and several lieutenants managed to rally the disordered men and place them into line in a rifle trench, after which he marched the two hundred or so men forward to support the Twenty-Fourth Massachusetts. At about 1:00 A.M., the surviving members of the regiment were relieved, marched to the rear, and encamped for the night. The regiment was diminished dramatically by their vanguard role at Fort Wagner: over 250 of its 600 soldiers were killed, wounded, or captured, including Colonel Robert Gould Shaw.[8]

Following the assault on Fort Wagner, the Fifty-Fourth Massachusetts was sent to Florida, where it supplied essential rearguard support for the Union retreat at the Battle of Olustee and was subsequently reassigned back to South Carolina, where Emilio was given command of Companies C, E, and H, which garrisoned the outpost on Black Island. In a brief respite from his regularly active combat service, Emilio was detailed as a judge advocate for court-martial trials held at Hilton Head in May 1864. In July, Confederate forces attempted to recapture James Island, and the Fifty-Fourth Massachusetts participated in its defense. Emilio's companies were engaged in a variety of duties, including guard duty and escorting prisoners to transport, but their role was dedicated largely to manual labor: road construction, hauling supplies from the wharf, moving artillery, and repairing earthworks.[9]

Most of the Fifty-Fourth Massachusetts was transported to Port Royal, South Carolina, in November 1864 and assigned to the Coast Division, a corps of six thousand soldiers tasked with severing the Charleston and Savannah Railroad as part of General William Tecumseh Sherman's "March to the Sea" campaign. But, despite several engagements for the Fifty-Fourth, including the Battle of Honey Hill on November 30, that mission was not fulfilled until Sherman's army took Savannah, Georgia. After the surrender of Savannah, a month later, the Coast Division turned their attention to the capture of Charleston, South Carolina, and arrived at the South Edisto River across from the city on February 24. Company E functioned as the provost guard, with Captain Emilio as the acting assistant provost marshal, keeping order among the soldiers and civilians. The Fifty-Fourth arrived in Charleston on February 27, 1865, began working picket duty, and were transferred to Savannah with the same assigned duty a month later. Emilio mustered out of Civil War service on March 27 when his three-year term of enlistment expired. His regiment had proved its valor: in terms of the highest percentage of soldiers killed and wounded, the Fifty-Fourth Massachusetts ranks among the three hundred (out of two thousand) hardest-fighting regiments in the Union army.[10]

Emilio's experiences serving during the Civil War had a profound impact on him; he returned to civilian status but remained overtly interested in military matters throughout his life. It should be kept in mind that he was a teenager for most of his service, fulfilling great obligations and establishing consequential authority. In the postwar years, Emilio actively participated in numerous veteran organizations, for which he presented papers about Civil War battles and campaigns. He collected military buttons and published a book about his collection and was an effective advocate for the installation of the Twenty-Third Regiment Massachusetts Volunteer Infantry monument in his native city in 1905 (prominently located near Salem Common). Most important, he was a military historian, researching, compiling, and collecting letters, diaries, memoirs, and other materials for his foundational history of the Fifty-Fourth Massachusetts, *A Brave Black Regiment* (1891). Luis Fenollosa Emilio died at age seventy-two on September 16, 1918, and is buried at Harmony Grove Cemetery in Salem.[11]

NOTES

1. Manisha Sinha, *The Slave's Cause: A History of Abolition* (Yale University Press, 2016), 215–223, 269.

2. Luis Emilio, "Roanoke Island, Its Occupation, Defense and Fall," a paper read before the Roanoke Associates, New York City, February 9, 1891; James Emmerton, *A Record of the Twenty-Third Regiment Massachusetts Volunteer Infantry* (William Ware, 1886), 1–52; Herbert Valentine, *Story of Company F, Twenty-Third Massachusetts Volunteers in the War for the Union, 1861–1865* (W. B. Clarke, 1896), v–46.

3. Emmerton, *Record of the Twenty-Third Massachusetts*, 53–97; Valentine, *Story of Company F*, 41–68.

4. Emmerton, *Record of the Twenty-Third Massachusetts*; Valentine, *Story of Company F*, 47–86.

5. Emmerton, *Record of the Twenty-Third Massachusetts*, 98–140; Richard Reid, "Raising the African Brigade: Early Black Recruitment in Civil War North Carolina," *North Carolina Historical Review* 70 (July 1993): 266–301; Luis F. Emilio, *History of the Fifty-Fourth Regiment of the Massachusetts Volunteer Infantry, 1863–1865* [*A Brave Black Regiment*] (Boston Book, 1891), 13–21. (Hereafter *Brave Black Regiment*). While the Fifty-Fourth Massachusetts was the first African American regiment raised in the North, African American regiments were previously raised in Louisiana, South Carolina, North Carolina, and Kansas from free black and runaway enslaved people.

6. Emilio, *Brave Black Regiment*, 22–27; Edwin Redkey, "Brave Black Volunteers: A Profile of the Fifty-Fourth Massachusetts Regiment," in *Hope and Glory: Essays on the Legacy of the 54th Massachusetts Regiment*, ed. Martin Blatt et al. (University of Massachusetts Press, 2001), 21–28.

7. Emilio, *Brave Black Regiment*, 30–48; Luis Emilio, *The Assault on Fort Wagner, July 18, 1863, the Memorable Charge of the Fifty-Fourth Regiment of Massachusetts Volunteers*, written for the "Springfield Republican" (Rand Avery, 1887), 10–16.

8. Emilio, *Brave Black Regiment*, 48–57; Emilio, *Assault on Fort Wagner*, 10–16.

9. Emilio, *Brave Black Regiment*, 102–109.

10. Ibid., 117–130, 148; William Fox, *Regimental Losses in the American Civil War, 1861–1865* (Albany Publishing, 1898), 1–2, 423.

11. *Boston Globe*, Tuesday, September 17, 1918. Luis Emilio, *The Emilio Collection of Military Buttons: American, British, French, and Spanish, with Some of Other Countries, and Non-military, in the Museum of the Essex Institute, Salem, Mass.* (Essex Institute, 1911).

CHAPTER EIGHT

Immigrant Catholicisms

Elizabeth Duclos-Orsello

Just a short walk from the intersection of Salem's well-trod Derby and Lafayette Streets and no more than half a mile from key sites of Puritan-era Salem, sit two buildings that are unremarkable to the casual passerby. The first is a multistory early twenty-first-century mixed-use building: retail space and a meeting room fill the first floor with apartments above. The second, next door, is a three-story historic brick structure with Corinthian columns, beautiful cornices, and large windows evoking a statelier time of formal parlors and refined teas. The shine of the windows, the manicured landscaping, and the gracious porch are enjoyed by the homeowners living in its modernized historic residential spaces. Together, these edifices telegraph Salem's twenty-first-century resurgence: historic buildings repurposed in a gentrifying city alongside modern mixed-use structures serving business and community needs. But a peek into the windows of the first reveals historic photographs of church buildings and worshippers. And a glance above the front door of the second reveals something even more unexpected. Etched in stone are the words "*Presbytère* St. Joseph," French for "St. Joseph's Rectory."

These nods to the past are silent but powerful reminders of what used to grace this corner of Salem: the St. Joseph's Catholic church complex replete with school, rectory, convent, and church. It was an institution that was the spiritual, social, educational, and even economic home to more than sixteen thousand French-speaking Canadian immigrants and their children in the early to mid-twentieth century and to thousands of Spanish-speaking Caribbean immigrants and their children by the end. Until its closure and nearly

Postcard of St. Joseph's Church, n.d. *(Nelson Dionne Salem History Collection, Salem State University Archives and Special Collections.)*

complete razing in the 2010s, St. Joseph's shaped this area of Salem for decades, catering to Salemites who shared not only a faith but a language and a national origin. It catered to Salemites who were not always fully embraced by the city's largely Anglophone and Protestant power brokers. As such, St. Joseph's story is a Salem story.[1]

But St. Joseph's story is not unique. Walk in any direction from the historic site of the St. Joseph complex and you will encounter other such Catholic church sites, even if today many exist only in worn words carved in stone or a roofline suggesting an ecclesiastical purpose. Although most well known as a colonial-era Puritan city and as a site of well-established Protestant New England, Salem's late nineteenth- and early twentieth-century story was shaped significantly by the thousands of Roman Catholic immigrants from Ireland, French-speaking Canada, Italy, and Eastern Europe who settled there.[2] Pulled (at times recruited) by booming low-wage industries, and pushed by economic and political factors around the world, these Catholic residents built robust ethnic communities, organizations, and institutions. They transformed Salem in the process.

Neither the twentieth- nor the twenty-first-century histories of Salem are complete without the varied histories of Catholic immigrants and the institutions they created and nurtured. Together, they reshaped Salem's economy, landscape, and ethnic and linguistic composition; their legacy lives on in obvious and subtle ways everywhere. Salem's economic growth and might over two and a half centuries and its ability to transform itself into the tourist- and service-focused city that it is today cannot be understood apart from the histories of the many different immigrant Catholics and immigrant Catholicisms that shaped it. The individual names and faces, life achievements, struggles, hopes, and losses may be hard to extract from either the public archives or the public narratives currently told in Salem, but there are no parts of the city untouched by the material remains of their rich and expansive worlds. Reminders are everywhere.

Beginning: A Multiethnic Catholic Communion

The early 1800s were a challenging time to be Catholic in the United States, especially in New England. Despite an origin story tied to a quest for religious freedom, for nearly two centuries civic and ecclesiastical authority had been firmly in the hands of mainline Protestants with links to the Anglo-Saxon world. Antagonism toward Catholics was significant. In fact, colonial law had banned Catholic clergy from the colony; Salem fell right in line.[3] Not until 1790 could the handful of lay Catholic residents in Salem begin to imagine a more public faith. In that year, thanks to a combination of Protestant liberalism and Salem's growing global reach, the city's Catholics attracted the interest of the Boston-based Reverend Thayer, a former Protestant minister and Catholic convert turned priest in the fledgling Boston mission church.[4] Thayer contacted Reverend Bentley, Salem's respected minister and resident chronicler-in-chief, and with Bentley's blessing established a small but robust parish made up of multiethnic Catholics.[5] Initially served by a priest from County Kerry, the worshippers were primarily Irish with a few congregants of French extraction.[6] By 1820, what had been a missionary parish grew to more than one hundred members, prompting the construction of St. Mary's, a dedicated 350-seat Catholic church at the corner of Mall and Bridge Streets. Salem was officially on the map as a Catholic city: St. Mary's was only the third Catholic church in Massachusetts and fourth in New England. There was no turning back, especially as tragedy and strife struck nations around the world over the next half century, displacing Catholics at each turn.[7]

The first to arrive in large numbers were the Irish. Fleeing famine and persecution at home, Salem's proximity to Boston was a draw. Soon St. Mary's had reached capacity. The leaders worked hard to keep up with the spiritual and communal needs of the new arrivals by enlarging the church in 1842, but the congregation kept growing and new immigrants arrived at an even greater pace. By 1850, Salem's population topped twenty thousand thanks to its industrial and manufacturing base. Jobs could be found with the railroad, in the tanning industries, and in the Naumkeag Steam Cotton Company's new mill. Soon Salem's Catholics could not be ignored: they now made up fully one-fifth of the population.[8] This momentous shift to an observable immigrant-majority Catholic population in the city of peace mirrored mid-nineteenth-century patterns across the nation as Irish, German, and some French-Canadian Catholics began to remake American Catholicism as a specifically *immigrant* church marked by distinct Catholic churches divided by communicants' ethnic identity and place of origin.[9]

The Mid-nineteenth Century: The Irish Predominate

In Salem, the first of these ethnic churches was St. James on Federal Street. It catered to Irish immigrants who were increasingly living nearby and adjacent to the tanneries. Still officially part of St. Mary's parish, the first mass was said at St. James on Christmas Day 1850, and as the Irish Catholic community grew over the subsequent decades, so too did the building. By 1900, the renovated structure was formally dedicated, its Gothic Revival architecture and soaring two-hundred-foot steeple boldly proclaiming its parishioners' presence in Hawthorne's city.[10]

But St. James was just one among many Catholic churches being constructed and populated at this moment. To serve Salem's ballooning Catholic community, a second new church was necessary. Immaculate Conception was erected on Walnut Street (present-day Hawthorne Boulevard), its central location and striking architecture commanding the attention of all residents, Catholic or not. Dedicated in 1858 (along with St. James), it replaced the "old St. Mary's" in the same relative area of the city. Its Romanesque style and brick facade were imposing; inside, it could seat up to thirteen hundred. By 1880, it had donned a soaring tower and a belfry housing the city's largest bell. Most important, for Salem's Catholic history, this new church soon began to serve newer immigrant Catholic arrivals. Over the next half century, it would help launch ethnic parishes across the city.[11]

The Know-Nothing Party and Nativism: Mid-nineteenth Century Style

The Catholic population growth brought conflict. Catholic immigration and the dramatic demographic shifts it represented in Salem and elsewhere in the 1850s fueled a backlash from native-born Protestant residents, a backlash fed by both rampant anti-Catholic and anti-Irish sentiment. Massachusetts emerged as particularly fertile ground for the Know-Nothing Party, a group that actively resisted and lobbied against immigration, immigrants, and immigrant voting rights in the 1840s and 1850s. Party leaders and their supporters consistently cited Catholics and their purported allegiance to Rome as a central threat to American democracy and life.[12] By the middle of the 1850s, as two new Catholic churches were constructed in Salem, the Know-Nothings took control of the Massachusetts legislature and, in 1858, they swept Salem's elections.[13] The impact of this leadership change on Salem's lay Catholics is not particularly well documented, but anti-"papist" sentiment was enough to surface in the words locals used to describe Catholics, including "poor [and] superstitious," and it led to harassment of the Sisters of Notre Dame who arrived in Salem in 1855 to educate girls. During the first few weeks of their tenure, these women religious were accosted verbally in public and three men attempted to break in to their residence under the cloak of darkness.[14]

But times changed, and, by the late nineteenth century, Irish Catholics, once feared and excluded from power, had begun to find their way into the ranks of both economic and civic leadership in Salem. Assisted greatly by the fact that they were Anglophone, members of the Irish Catholic community were able to retain a robust Catholic identity and spiritual practice alongside flexibility in their public practices. Additionally, the classical and commercial education provided by the Catholic nuns[15] who taught at Immaculate Conception and St. James helped ease the way for Irish American graduates to enter a wide swath of economic activities and positions in Salem.

Anglophone Catholics were now part of the city's mainstream. So much so that by 1890, Salem merchants, recognizing the economic role this constituency played, took out advertisements in *The Sacred Heart Review* (a Catholic weekly) as soon as it began distribution in Salem. Some merchants even had their names and goods printed in the shape of a cross. Just ten years later, Salem had elected its first (Irish) Catholic mayor and the police and fire forces began integrating Irish Catholic members; their numbers would grow significantly in the following decades.[16]

Without dismissing the efforts of Irish Catholics themselves, understanding their assimilation into Protestant Salem at the end of the nineteenth century also owes a great deal to the arrival of *new* Catholic immigrants at that precise moment. These non-Anglophone Catholic arrivals became a new "other" in the still predominantly Protestant and Anglophone city. In turn, this othering, in Salem as across the nation, fed the immigrants' drive to become architects of dozens of new parishes, schools, fraternal organizations, and immigrant Catholic networks. Together, these efforts fueled and enhanced life in Salem for the next half century.

1880–1920: Immigration Changes and Salem's Catholic Ethnic Enclaves

The combined forces of urbanization, industrialization, and immigration that reshaped the United States between 1880 and 1920 also reshaped Salem, with Catholics at the center of it all. The fledgling industrial base of the mid-nineteenth century had, a few decades later, become a flourishing one with more tanneries, a greater capacity textile mill, and all their attendant businesses demanding a significant influx of workers willing to work long hours for low wages. Immigrants from heavily Catholic Southern and Eastern Europe and French-speaking Canada (Quebec) were the answer. Pushed by political struggle, famine, war, and the inability of industrial systems to absorb rural populations, these migrants sought refuge and new beginnings in the United States, where industrialists recruited men, women, and children to work long hours for limited pay. The era's race-based immigration restrictions barred Asian migrants from the United States. The result was that immigration became a largely white, non-Anglophone, Jewish and Catholic endeavor, with Catholics predominating in overall numbers.[17]

The changes wrought in Salem were dramatic: the city's population increased 50 percent between 1875 and 1915, and, on the eve of World War I, nearly one-third of Salem residents were foreign born with French Canadians and Polish immigrants predominating. New Catholic parishes were organized in short order, and new churches emerged in different areas of the city, each anchoring a particular set of new immigrant communicants not only spiritually but linguistically, culturally, and socially as they navigated their new lives. These churches and parishes served as mediating institutions, operating not only within the distinctive traditions of their congregants' respective homelands but within the pressures of Salem's secular society, and mandates of the Boston diocese, U.S.-based ethnic Catholic leadership, and the broader American Catholic church. Each immigrant group faced hardship and isolation even as they rewrote Salem's history as one of religious and ethnic diversity, while transforming its institutions and landscape in ways the founders could not have imagined.

St. Joseph's (French Canadian: 1873)

French Canadians were the first significant non-English-speaking Catholic group in Salem. As Mark Richard and others have documented, between 1840 and 1930, close to one million French-speaking Canadians (mostly rural residents and farmers) left the Catholic environs of Quebec province to find work in New England's mill towns.¹⁸ Salem was a key destination point, and, by the early twentieth century, these immigrants and their U.S.-born children made up over 20 percent of the city's population, with two parishes around which a thriving communal life revolved.

After navigating the Irish Catholic world of Salem for some years, a group finally heard mass in French in 1872, and thanks to a French-speaking priest at Immaculate Conception, began worshipping regularly in French in the basement of that church. By this time, there were ninety French-speaking Catholic families in Salem and the archbishop was as keen on establishing a parish for them as they were on having a parish and church of their own.¹⁹ In only months, these immigrants raised the necessary funds, the Seaman's Bethel on Herbert Street was purchased, and, by the close of 1873, St. Joseph's parish was established in that location.²⁰ This new parish flourished thanks to an increased flow of immigrants. By 1884, land had been purchased and a new wooden church built on Lafayette Street, close to the Naumkeag mill. Four years later, the parish boasted three thousand parishioners and, in 1893, the first St. Joseph's parish school opened.

Over the next two decades, the neighborhood between St. Joseph's and the Naumkeag mill became home to hundreds of mill workers and their families with businesses, services, and support by and for one another. This was a fully functioning city within a city in many ways. French was the language, and the smell of pork was ever present. The historic Stage Point had become "La Pointe," Salem's Little Canada (Petit Canada), and St. Joseph's anchored it—and its residents. The degree to which St. Joseph's was the center of the neighborhood's spiritual, social, and cultural life was underscored in account after account. As one resident recounted: "St. Joseph's church was really sort of the glue that kept the whole French-Canadian population together."²¹ It also provided for the economic well-being of its parishioners, founding St. Joseph's Credit Union in 1908 to provide banking services to French Canadians who often struggled to gain access to banking services elsewhere.²²

The relative insularity of St. Joseph's communicants (especially, first-generation immigrants and their children) was also encouraged by the church itself. French-speaking priests from Boston were replaced by Quebec-born or -trained priests who understood and promoted *la survivance*, an ideology asserting the need to preserve French-Canadian Catholic culture in the United States and ward off assimilation. Preservation of faith, family ties, and the French language were essential to this effort.²³

Parish growth continued, and, in 1911, the wooden church on Lafayette Street was replaced by a grand brick one, marking, in three dimensions, the significance of faith and the parish to this, the city's largest Catholic immigrant group. Tragically, the Salem Fire of 1914 destroyed nearly the entirety of La Pointe. The brand-new church was gone, leaving the sixteen thousand parishioners without a spiritual home. The congregants regrouped and redoubled their efforts to maintain an ethnic parish, worshipping for decades in the basement chapel of the burned out church, and reconstructing schools and residences for priests and nuns. They finally secured enough money by the 1940s to build a new church, which made waves for its cruciform shape and international style.

Ste. Anne's (French Canadian: 1901)

As had been the case with Irish Catholics, the French-Canadian population of the city continued to grow, and, by the 1890s, a second French-Canadian ethnic enclave had been established. Across town from St. Joseph's, the Castle Hill neighborhood sat on the city's southwest corner, in a more sparsely settled area with small houses and more open space.[24] The difficulty of navigating harsh winters and poor public transportation made worship at St. Joseph's a hardship for residents, and, in November 1900, construction began on a new church in Castle Hill. Ste. Anne's opened in June of the following year, replete with a grand bell in the steeple and an altar that was an exact replica of one in Quebec.[25] Within a year, Ste. Anne's became independent of St. Joseph's. The city now had two very dynamic French-Canadian Catholic parishes, both of which were shaped by sojourner migration (regular return migration to a home country) and would hold tight to the French language and Quebecois ecclesiastical practices for decades.[26]

St. John the Baptist (Polish: 1903)

While Quebecois immigrants were establishing themselves, so too were Polish Catholic immigrants. Ethnic Poles fled from what is now part of Germany, Austria, and Russia after occupying powers divided a once-thriving Polish nation-state. Out-migration increased exponentially as the nineteenth century wore on and Salem became home to more and more of these cultural, political, and economic migrants between 1890 and 1914.[27] In 1890, the waterfront area of Derby Street (close to the Turner Ingersoll mansion) was a mixed ethnic neighborhood, with some Irish and French Canadians, but was fast becoming a predominantly Polish enclave thanks to a pattern of immigration and residency that connected newcomers to more established families from a shared homeland who often took in boarders and connected them with employers.[28] Many of the Polish immigrants found jobs in the tanneries, leather factories, and cotton mill where long hours and meager compensation were the norm.

But this growing community had no dedicated place to worship. By 1899, Polish immigrants had organized the St. Joseph Society, which, as a mutual aid society, brokered links between and among the various groups of Poles in the city and secured a space for society activities at 160 Derby Street.[29] The leaders of the society were aware of the spiritual needs of their Polish community and worked to address this issue. Initially, Immaculate Conception was (as it had been for French Canadians) a welcoming location for the small congregation to hold mass in Polish, and a Polish priest from Boston journeyed to Salem for this purpose.[30] But over time, as the numbers of Polish-speaking Catholics grew and unity among the various Polish groups increased so too did the need and desire for a Polish parish proper. St. Joseph Society leaders understood that their own communal space, while a critical social, civic, and educational hub, was neither a parish nor a church. Soon, they turned their attention to the task of founding and funding both.

They succeeded, and, by 1903, the parish of St. John the Baptist had been formed, fundraising efforts had met their goal, and a structure suitable for a church had been purchased on Herbert Street in Nathaniel Hawthorne's boyhood neighborhood. Shortly thereafter, buildings were purchased for a school and convent and the parish thrived. But immigration continued and soon the congregation had outgrown the church.[31] Fundraising began in earnest again, and, in 1906, the parish purchased a shuttered Baptist church on St. Peter Street which, after three years of renovations, was reopened as St. John the Baptist. The Herbert Street church was repurposed as much needed additional classrooms as the Polish population continued to expand. By 1911, Polish immigrants and their children numbered thirty-five hundred (8 percent of Salem's population).[32]

The outbreak of World War II effectively ended Polish immigration to Salem, but it did not curb the dynamism of St. John the Baptist, which remained a driving force in the lives of Polish and Polish-American Salemites. For the founding members and for generations to come St. John the Baptist was a rock, offering parishioners social, civic, educational, and mutual aid services for decades.[33]

St. Mary's (Italian: 1925)

In 1914—just as Polish immigration to Salem slowed dramatically—Salem's small Italian immigrant community began worshipping together in a room above a fish market on Front Street. Italian immigrants who did not speak English heard mass in Italian by Rev. Pietro Piemonte, an Italian priest living in the neighboring town of Swampscott. At this point, there were about thirteen hundred Italians in Salem (3 percent of the population), all largely settled in the areas around High, Endicott, Margin, and Prescott Streets near the city center.[34] For four years, the worshippers gathered as a mission before being named an official parish in 1918, at which time, they, like their fellow immigrant Catholic neighbors, began dreaming of a church building to call their own and set out to do just that. Sacrificing portions of their meager incomes for the cause, the congregants purchased a plot of land rendered vacant by the devastation of the 1914 Salem Fire. Funding the church's construction proved a more challenging task. The parishioners' earnings could not cover the $60,000 cost.[35] Instead, many worshippers donated their manual labor to the cause, while others were said to have donated gold jewelry to be melted into the bell. The resulting St. Mary's church, modeled on Santa Chiara in Assisi, Italy, was dedicated on Thanksgiving 1925 with enough pomp that the "excitement of the day" remained fixed in one parishioner's mind some seven decades later.[36] Over the next thirty years, St. Mary's was the centerpiece of Italian life in Salem, anchoring Salem's Little Italy, which was rich with markets, services, and community spaces.[37]

Each of these immigrant-serving parishes was established at a critical time in the history of the American Catholic church. By the turn of the twentieth century, Roman Catholics were established as the single-largest religious denomination in the United States. At the same time, the American Catholic church writ large was in a state of flux, with some leaders pushing for an embrace of the American ideals of democracy, individualism, and modernization to ensure the survival of the faith in a new century. Others encouraged a conservative approach, maintaining the traditions and practices dictated from Rome.[38] In Salem, these debates do not seem to have been well known to the average parishioners. Records suggest that the immigrant congregants and their children most significantly adhered to the specific guidance of each parish's priest(s) and other parish leaders, who created distinctive Catholic experiences at each parish based on the ancestral language, faith traditions from a homeland, and ethnic group mores. The sights, sounds, smells, and rhythms of worship at each congregation were distinct, as were the shape of annual parish events, feast days, and celebrations. At St. Joseph's, the midnight mass was the norm at Christmas, followed later by réveillon, a middle of the night feast featuring tourtière (a pork pie), after walking home in the cold and dark. Public demonstrations of faith were common. There were regular Italian and Polish Catholic processions through the city streets on feast days, while the congregants of Saint Anne's illuminated their homes and erected an arch of evergreens in the street with "Bienvenue" (Welcome) spelled out in light when their new bell was installed. Not to be outdone, St. Mary's bell dedication ceremony brought more than one thousand participants to downtown Salem.[39]

While each parish reinforced connections to and traditions from ancestral places, they also emerged as crucial sites of cultural assimilation by the second decade of the twentieth century.[40] For the French Canadians, the formal presence of a banking institution connected with St. Joseph's eased access into property ownership as well as the business community. Across the city, parish-based mutual aid societies provided networks for job seeking and family support and created physical spaces for communal gatherings and sharing information about the city at large. They were dynamic "third spaces" in the parlance of today. For women, participation in women's sodalities (lay religious societies) offered some access to spaces and roles beyond, home, wife, mother, or laborer, and connected women to one another.

The city of Salem benefited immensely from the presence of so many Catholic churches, Catholic leadership, and their organized support for their own members. In an era of limited public services or any social safety net immigrant Catholics in Salem created and sustained such institutions for themselves. Parishes were welcome centers, providing relocation/assimilation support for the newly arrived immigrants, grounding them in place, language, and tradition. Parishes attended to the poor and needy among their congregants, and their affiliated mutual aid societies buttressed these efforts. In addition, more general care for orphaned children, the city's sick, and the care for victims of the 1914 fire, regardless of faith, were all made possible by institutions and hospitals established, managed, and/or staffed by well-trained Catholic women religious.[41] Catholics and Catholic institutions eased the stress on secular Salem.

But perhaps no parish-linked institutions shaped the lives and legacies of immigrant Catholics—or on Salem itself—more than the city's Catholic schools, which educated tens of thousands of immigrant Catholics, their children, and their grandchildren. These schools accomplished a tremendous task: preparing children for the rigors and requirements of life in Salem and the United States, while simultaneously helping keep both faith and ancestral languages alive. Schools helped ensure a significant degree of in-group solidarity even as they facilitated assimilation.

Schools

Salem's first Catholic school opened in 1831 thanks to Boston's Bishop Fenwick and his successors whose grand vision was to establish parochial schools throughout the diocese.[42] In due course, nearly every new parish in Salem set about to help fulfill Fenwick's goal. For many of the specific immigrant Catholic communities in the city, retaining the language and particular customs of a homeland was foundational to their religious identity. As such, the children of immigrant parents often attended Catholic schools affiliated with the ethnic Catholic parish to which they belonged, a pattern that reflected the level of ethnic and linguistic insularity that shaped so much of immigrant Catholic Salem. Such a pattern can be read in two ways: as a retreat from civic life in Salem, or as an attempt to bridge the old and the new, to develop a new form of American experience, one that did not see Catholicism as at odds with American culture. It is the second reading that emerges from the historical record. And the success of this bridging is largely thanks to women.

While individual parishes can be heralded for funding and supporting the schools, it is the often overlooked women religious who ran and taught in them whose work was most impactful.[43] Starting in the 1850s, many different orders of women religious—most often immigrants themselves—were responsible for the education of Salem's immigrant children and their descendants and, ultimately, for their ability to navigate at ease in American society writ large. Instruction at these schools combined religious and secular subjects (with a classical bent), with coursework in both English and a home language. For more than three quarters of a century, this sort of quality education was commonplace for the Salem born and raised children and grandchildren of industrial laborers from around the world.[44] In this way, parish schools contributed significantly to the ability of future generations of immigrant/ethnic Catholics to navigate a new world without leaving the old one, or its Catholicism, behind.

Anti-Catholicism and Anti-immigrant Forces at Play in the Early Twentieth Century: The Klan and Immigration Laws

But, no matter the goals of immigrant Catholics or their efforts to bridge the past, present, and future worlds, they were far from universally welcomed or accepted. In Salem, there was enough anti-immigrant and "Americanization" sentiment that it was noted publicly. One early twentieth-century resident wrote to the *Salem Evening News* complaining about the growth of immigrant enclaves in the city and pronounced that immigrants "already hold the balance of power in city politics, and if they are not . . . assimilated and inspired with respect for American ideals and American institutions, they will . . . swell the columns of socialism, militant laborism, and other isms."[45] Across the region, the revived Ku Klux Klan (active in New England by the late 1910s) had Catholic immigrants in its sights. Anti-Catholicism combined with nativism fueled its activities with loud and public laments about the changing demographics, particularly the increase in Catholic immigrants and their children.[46] In Massachusetts, Klan leaders sought to push back. In the Klan's own words, the state's "problem" was that it now was home to "a conglomerate mass of diverse . . . inheritances." Their goal: to recruit to their ranks people who were "American, native-born citizen . . . white, Protestant, Gentile. . . ." In short: citizens whom they believed would have no allegiances to any foreign government or leader—including, and especially, the Pope.[47]

No doubt Salem's immigrant Catholics were concerned, but, by this point, the Irish Catholics had ascended to positions of prominence and influence in the city, and, in 1923, the city council took a bold step, adopting an Irish-led resolution to ban Klan parades and meetings in the city.[48] Just the following year, the Klan burned crosses in two cities bordering Salem, but it seems that the ascendency of the Irish Catholics in Salem had served as a protective shield for the city's more recently arrived Catholics.[49] However, as David Vermette and others have demonstrated, both in new England and across the nation as a whole, anti-immigrant sentiment had taken hold with a vengeance, fueling the 1921 Emergency Quota Act and the Immigration Act of 1924.[50] Combined, these effectively ended immigration from the very nations and regions that had made up the flow of immigrants since 1880.

The Interwar Years

For Salem's immigrant Catholic communities, the abrupt stop to new immigrant arrivals seems to have strengthened in-group identity and fueled a recommitment to maintaining ties to and practices from an ancestral homeland, and, in the interwar years, the city's Catholic parishes proved critical sites of personal and communal support as well as a connection to places and cultural identities that had been cut off. Distinct immigrant churches focused on ways to secure and maintain their unique ethnic Catholic identities in an American setting without the benefit of new arrivals, even as they helped prepare a new generation to exist in both Catholic and non-Catholic Salem. In addition to the work of Catholic schools, many parishes organized groups to provide specific ethnic, faith-based versions of secular society. At most parishes, athletic clubs, children's scouting troops, and women's and men's societies were common.[51] Across the city, such efforts served to both inculcate ethnic and religious group cohesion and expose young people to "American" cultural practices, thereby encouraging patriotism alongside religious, familial, and ethnic identities.[52]

Other sites, affiliated with, but not formally, parish spaces, like St. Joseph's Hall (affiliated with the Polish St. John the Baptist church), the Christopher Columbus Society (St. Mary's), or the Klondike Club (St. Joseph's) provided comfortable and accessible gathering spaces for residents who sought companionship and opportunities for social engagement/celebration with their neighbors and fellow worshippers outside religious services. Together, they ensured that, on the eve of World War II, there was no way to understand Salem without understanding the immigrant Catholic Salem. And, together, these institutions, and the residents who imagined, led, and supported them, worked to simultaneously shore up distinct ethnic Catholic sensibilities and ease the tension between being American and Catholic in Salem.[53]

Coda: The Success of Immigrant Catholic Salem

Salem's immigrant Catholic communities and institutions succeeded in their efforts. So much so that, by the end of the twentieth century, the children and grandchildren of the white ethnic immigrant Catholics, who transformed both the demographics and the physical landscape of Salem, were assimilated. They had held the city's highest offices, led some of its major institutions, and guided its reincarnation as a tourism hub and self-proclaimed city of inclusion. Hard-won inclusion was more common than not, and the once uniquely Catholic worlds of Salem began to fade. Over time, economic and professional assimilation, combined with major changes to the Catholic liturgy in the 1960s and more regular intermarriage between members of white ethnic groups, weakened the rigid lines that separated parish from parish and one set of Catholics from another. The fallout of the early twenty-first-century Catholic clergy sexual abuse scandal dealt another blow to the diversity and public presence of Catholicism in Salem, with many Catholics leaving the church and diocesan-led church closures to ward off financial ruin.[54] Today, a walk around Salem will rarely include the sounds of Irish, French, Italian, or Polish. And Catholic churches are no longer regularly filled with congregants who share the same ethnic or national origin, or language (other than English).[55]

Yet, the material, cultural, economic, and personal legacies of the rich, complex, and distinct worlds of nineteenth- and early twentieth-century immigrant Catholicisms can still be found across Salem if we know where to look. Many buildings that once opened their doors to immigrant laborers on Sunday mornings and holy days, or welcomed children into their classrooms, or served the social and economic needs of parishioners, are finding new occupants and new uses, just as the Catholic communities who erected them had often repurposed existing Salem sites and buildings. And, in many cases, these current uses pay homage to the spirit of service, education, support, and hope that marked early immigrant Catholic efforts in the city.

St. Anne's continues its role as an active parish on Jefferson Avenue; St. John the Baptist now operates as St. John Paul II Shrine of Divine Mercy, offering a place for prayer and veneration as well as a weekly mass in both English and Polish.[56] On Federal Street, sharing a boulevard with eighteenth-century architecture, St. James Church has retained its identity as a place of Catholic worship as part of Mary Queen of the Apostles parish, which also includes Immaculate Conception on Hawthorne Boulevard. On weekends, parish masses are offered in English and Spanish, reflecting the religious, linguistic, and cultural demands of both new Catholic immigrants and the almost exclusively Anglophone descendants of immigrants past. Salem's multiethnic Catholic world continues in a new form.

Other important immigrant Catholic spaces and structures also remain, standing often as silent sentinels holding the stories and legacies of the laypeople, clergy, and women religious whose faith made Salem what it is today, demographically, religiously, and physically. Near to the grand downtown post office is the former St. Mary's church, its Grotto of Our Lady of Lourdes removed but facade intact; it now serves as home to another Christian community. On Hawthorne Boulevard and Federal Street, old church complex buildings are being reimagined as affordable housing.[57] The neighborhood now known as "The Point" was named a National Historic District in 2015, in significant part because of the history of the French-Canadian immigrant Catholics who once called it home.

In these buildings and neighborhoods, and in their new uses, can be found the stories of Catholics who arrived in Salem from around the world, seeking both new opportunities and the spiritual and cultural support provided by specific Catholic identities and practices. In so doing, immigrant Catholics and their Catholicisms laid much of the groundwork for Salem's twentieth- and twenty-first-century reinventions as an economically vibrant and culturally and philanthropically active, pluralistic, multiethnic, and multireligious city. And now another new wave of Catholic immigrants from different areas of the world, with new linguistic, liturgical, and communal emphases continue to write the next chapters of this history.

NOTES

1. Many thanks to Susan Edwards, the archivist at the Salem State University Archives and Special Collections (SSU Archives) for her assistance. A note on terminology: "Church" refers to the structure where worship takes place. "Parish" refers to the formal organization of a group of worshippers. I maintain this distinction throughout, with only a few deviations when context is clear. On the building of affordable housing and commercial space on the former site of St. Joseph's parish campus from the perspective of the Catholic Archdiocese of Boston, see "Dedicating New Affordable Housing for Salem," Cardinal Sean's Blog, October 3, 2014, available at https://cardinalseansblog.org/2014/10/03/dedicating-new-affordable-housing-for-salem/, accessed August 16, 2023.

2. Due to brevity, this chapter focuses on the Roman Catholic parishes in Salem that were established in the late nineteenth and early twentieth centuries predominantly for and/or by immigrants. As a result, it excludes the Ukrainian Catholic church and St. Thomas. The former because it is not Roman Catholic, and the latter because when established on the Salem/Peabody line in 1927, it was not specifically serving an immigrant community.

3. William B. Sullivan, *The Early Catholic Church in Massachusetts* (Fort Hill, 1907), 3–4.

4. Louis S. Walsh, *Origin of the Catholic Church in Salem and Its Growth* (Cashman, Keating, 1890), vii–xi.

5. Walsh, *Origin of the Catholic Church*; Sullivan, *Early Catholic Church*, vii–xi.

6. This was only the second parish to be established in Massachusetts. See Jerome Curley, "A Look Back—Salem's Irish History," *Salem Patch*, March 10, 2012, available at https://patch.com/massachusetts/salem/green-salem, accessed April 15, 2024. On the makeup of the parish, see Walsh, *Origin of the Catholic Church*, and Rev. P. J. Hally, pastor, "Catholicity in Salem," *Sacred Heart Review*, vol. 3, no. 24, May 10, 1890.

7. St. Mary's was the third Catholic church in Massachusetts and the fourth in New England. On October 1821, the bishop himself celebrated mass there. See Sullivan, *Early Catholic Church*, 16; Walsh, *Origin of the Catholic Church*, generally; *St. James Church: 150 Years of Faith in Salem, Massachusetts* (St. James Church, 2002), 22–23, in the SSU Archives; "Mass to Mark the Anniversary of the Archdiocese's Oldest Parish Church," available at BostonPilot.com, September 5, 2008; Cathy Stanton and Jane Becker, *In the Heart of Polish Salem: An Ethnohistorical Study of St. Joseph Hall and Its Neighborhood* (National Park Service, Northeast Region Ethnohistory Program, 2009), 29.

8. The mill opened in 1847. Over time, the company referred to their Salem mill as the "Pequot Mill." See Stanton and Becker, *Heart of Polish Salem*, 35.

9. Julie Byrne, "Roman Catholics and Immigration in Nineteenth-Century America," National Humanities Center, 2000, available at https://nationalhumanitiescenter.org/tserve/nineteen/nkeyinfo/nromcath.htm, accessed July 10, 2023.

10. St. James was the tallest building in Salem for many years. *St. James Church*, 29; "Immaculate Conception Parish, Hawthorne Boulevard, Salem, Massachusetts: 175th Anniversary, 1826–2001," in the SSU Archives.

11. Although Immaculate Conception's parishioners and leadership were consistently Irish and Irish American, and it remained an Anglophone parish, it played a critical

church-planting role for other ethnic Catholics. See Sullivan, *Early Catholic Church*, 11; Walsh, *Origin of the Catholic Church*, 83. On dedication, see *St. James Church*, 25.

12. For an overview of the Know-Nothing Party (officially, the American Party) in Massachusetts and elections in the 1850s, see John Mulkern, *The Know-Nothing Party in Massachusetts: The Rise and Fall of a People's Party* (Northeastern University Press, 1990).

13. Curley, "Salem's Irish History."

14. Walsh, *Origin of the Catholic Church*, 106. In 1834, under the cover of darkness, nativists had burned an Ursuline convent and girl's school in Charlestown, MA, only twenty miles away.

15. The Sisters of Notre Dame de Namur and the Sisters of Charity.

16. *Immaculate Conception 150th Anniversary, 1976*, Salem Collection, Salem Public Library.

17. John Bodnar's *The Transplanted* (Indiana University Press, 1987) remains an excellent starting point for an overview of the patterns and experiences of transatlantic migrations/immigration in this era as well as the lived experience of these immigrants. Note that Jewish and Orthodox Christians as well as some Hindus, Buddhists, and Muslims made up part of this flow of immigrants in Salem (and nationally), but, statistically, Roman Catholics predominated. In 1875, foreign-born residents accounted for only 25 percent of the city's population. That percentage increased to nearly one-third on the eve of World War I.

18. For French-speaking Canadian migration, immigration, and the anti-Catholic sentiment that massive French-Canadian immigration wrought in New England, see Gerard J. Brault, *The French-Canadian Heritage in New England* (University Press of New England, 1986); Yves Roby, *The Franco-Americans of New England: Dreams and Realities*, trans. Mark Ricard (Septentrion, 2004); esp., David Vermette, *A Distinct Alien Race: The Untold Story of Franco Americans* (Baraka Books, 2018).

19. Loraine St. Pierre, "A Brief, Informal History of St. Joseph Parish," *St. Joseph Parish, Salem, MA: Anniversary,1873–1973*, 2, Salem Collection, Salem Public Library; Laurier Association, *A History of Saint Joseph's Parish in Salem, Massachusetts: 1873–1948*, trans. Elizabeth Blood, ed. Elizabeth Duclos-Orsello (2019), *Franco American Heritage Collection*, in the SSU Archives, available at https://digitalcommons.salemstate.edu/fchc/1.

20. Laurier Association, *History of Saint Joseph's Parish*.

21. See L. St. Pierre, "Brief History of St. Joseph Parish"; Elizabeth Blood and Elizabeth Duclos-Orsello, "The Point: A Franco-American Heritage Site in Salem, Massachusetts," in *Encyclopedia of French Cultural Heritage in North America* (2018), available at http://www.ameriquefrancaise.org/en/article-739/The%20Point:%20a%20Franco-American%20Heritage%20Site%20in%20Salem,%20Massachusetts; Franco American Salem Oral Histories, Franco American Heritage Collection, in the SSU Archives; quotation from Franco-American Salem Oral History: Robert St. Pierre, available at https://digitalrepository.salemstate.edu/handle/20.500.13013/478.

22. Elizabeth Blood and Elizabeth Duclos-Orsello, "A Brief History of French-Canadians and Franco-Americans in Salem, Massachusetts," French-Canadian and Franco-American Heritage in Salem, MA, 2011, available at https://frenchcanadiansalem.org/brief-history, accessed August 25, 2023; Laurier Association, *History of Saint Joseph's Parish*, 17n.

23. L. St. Pierre, "Brief History of St. Joseph Parish"; Ronald Arthur Petrin, *French Canadians in Massachusetts Politics, 1885–1915: Ethnicity and Political Pragmatism* (Balch Institute, 1990), 17–18; Brault, *French-Canadian Heritage*.

24. This area is where the first house built by a Canadian in Salem was erected in 1881.

25. *Diamond Jubilee of Sainte Anne's Church, Salem, Massachusetts, 1901–1976*. The Church, 1976; *25ieme Anniversaire de la Paroisse Sainte Anne Salem, Mass., Programme Souvenir, 1901–1926* (J. N. Gagnon, 1926), Salem Collection, Salem Public Library; *Cinquantieme Anniversaire de la Paroisse Sainte-Anne de* Salem, Mass., November 11, 1951, Salem State University Archives and Special Collections; *Dedication Sainte Anne's Church, August 23, 1986*, Salem Collection, Salem Public Library. For more on the Polish and Polish-American community in the Derby Street neighborhood, see Stanton and Becker, *Heart of Polish Salem*.

26. Sojourner migration was practiced by other immigrant groups as well but was particularly frequent among French Canadians due to the geographic proximity. Figures for various periods show about one-third eventually returning home, according to Roger Daniels, *Coming to America: A History of Immigration and Ethnicity in American Life* (Harper Collins, 2002), 215; Helena Znaniecka Lopata, *Polish Americans* (Transaction, 1994), 28.

27. Nearly two million Poles arrived in the United States between 1900 and 1914. On Polish/Polish-American emigration and immigration patterns, see Stanton and Becker, *Heart of Polish Salem*, 7, 36, 68, 69; John Radzilowski, *The Eagle and the Cross: A History of the Polish Roman Catholic Union in America, 1873–2000* (East European Monographs, 2003); Jerzy Lukowski and Hubert Zawadski, *A Concise History of Poland*, 2nd ed. (Cambridge University Press, 2006).

28. See the 1910 census enumeration sheets for the streets in this section of Salem. One resident, whose childhood paralleled the opening decade of the twentieth century, summed up the pattern of Polish immigration this way: "That area at that time was just beginning to get settled by Polish people. When I was growing up, my playmates were all Irish. . . . There were very few Irish [Polish?] people. But then they kept coming in in the 1900s, the immigration started to come in more from Germany and Russia and Austria and there was more and more of them coming in. And they'd live with the people that were there—and my mother said many times that she didn't want anybody, but they'd be begging her, just if they could have a place to sleep, even on the floor, just so they could be with their own people, just until they got settled," in Stanton and Becker, *Heart of Polish Salem*, 69.

29. Ibid., 54, 55. By 1912, the St. Joseph Society was officially linked to the Polish Roman Catholic Union of America.

30. Minutes of the St. Joseph Society, 1899–1909, trans. Ewa Newman, Salem Maritime National Historic Park Collections, Salem, MA. Per Stanton and Becker, starting in 1899 a priest came from Boston quarterly to hear confessions in Polish (*Heart of Polish Salem*, 70–71).

31. Stanton and Becker, *Heart of Polish Salem*, 76; Minutes of the St. Joseph Society, 1899–1909.

32. Stanton and Becker, *Heart of Polish Salem*, 68–77; "Remarkable Progress of Poles in Salem," *Salem Evening News*, [1911?], House of Seven Gables News Clippings 1909–

April 1950, box 1, News Clippings Scrapbook 1910–1916, as quoted in Stanton and Becker, 146.

33. Stanton and Becker, *Heart of Polish Salem*, 77.

34. Data based on 1910 decennial census.

35. In 1948, the church's mortgage was paid off in a public ceremony. "St. Mary's Italian Church Burns $29,000 Mortgage," *Salem Evening News*, February 7, 1948, 1, 8.

36. "Church Marks 75th Year," *Salem Evening News*, September 11, 1993, 6.

37. Kristin D'Agostino, "Salem's Little Italy," *Salem Gazette*, September 12, 2008, 15, 22–23; Jen Ratliff, "Salem's Little Italy," Salem State University Archives and Special Collections blog, April 25, 2023, available at https://libguides.salemstate.edu/home/archives/blog/Salems-Little-Italy, accessed August 15, 2023.

38. Neil T. Storch, "John Ireland's Americanism after 1899: An Argument from History," *Church History*, vol. 51, no. 4, December 1982, 434–444; Byrne, "Roman Catholics and Immigration"; Michael F. Lombardo, *Founding Father: John J. Wynne, S.J. and the Inculturation of American Catholicism in the Progressive Era* (Brill, 2017).

39. "Cast Bell on Church Site," *Lynn Daily Item*, December 6, 1924; *Diamond Jubilee of Sainte Anne's Church*; Stanton and Becker, *Heart of Polish Salem*, 77.

40. In "Roman Catholics and Immigration," Byrne points out that "as new generations were born Catholics became quite 'Americanized' . . . as aspects of the Old World devotional culture and theology were gradually left behind and shades of a new, more individualistic and democratic Catholicism appeared."

41. For how this played out during the 1918 influenza pandemic, see Donna Seger, "Sisters in Service, 1918," *Streets of Salem*, available at https://streetsofsalem.com/2020/03/28/sisters-in-service-salem-1918/, accessed August 8, 2023. The Sisters of Charity of Montreal (The Grey Nuns) served at the Salem City Orphan Asylum beginning in 1892. More is available at https://sgm.qc.ca/en/the-grey-nuns/the-sisters-in-america/lexington/, accessed August 12, 2023; Elizabeth Blood and Elizabeth Duclos-Orsello, various resources and publications at French-Canadian and Franco-American Salem, available at https://frenchcanadiansalem.org, accessed August 10, 2023.

42. Walsh devoted an entire chapter of his 1890 history of Catholic Salem (*Origin of the Catholic Church*) to schools (private, free, and Sunday School), citing the historic call of the apostolic church to "teach all nations" and do so in a way that linked knowledge of the world with that of the faith.

43. There were a few informal short-lived schools established between 1831 and 1855 (for both girls and boys), but it was not until 1855 that a school with any notable longevity was established.

44. For accounts by former pupils attesting to the ways parish schools shaped them, see various interviews within the Franco-American Oral History Project, available in transcribed forms in the SSU Archives; see also Stanton and Becker, *Heart of Polish Salem*, chap. 6.

45. Quoted in Joseph Conforti, *Imagining New England: Explorations of Regional Identity from the Pilgrims to the Mid-20th Century* (University of North Carolina Press, 2001), 254.

46. The most comprehensive look at nativism in this era remains John Higham, *Strangers in the Land: Patterns of American Nativism, 1860–1925* (Rutgers University Press, 1955). In 1920, first- and second-generation white ethnic immigrants made up two-thirds of Massachusetts's population. Over one million (28.3 percent) were foreign born.

Mark Paul Richard, *Not a Catholic Nation: The Ku Klux Klan Confronts New England in the 1920s* (University of Massachusetts Press, 2015), 12–13, 91. By 1926 the state's Roman Catholic population stood at 1.6 million; more than five times greater than the combined number of the next two closest denominations, Richard, 13.

47. KKK pamphlet, *A Mobilization of Americans!* as quoted in Richard, 92.

48. Richard, 102–103.

49. These were Lynn and Swampscott; Richard, 101–102, 104.

50. Vermette, *Distinct Alien Race.*

51. *Diamond Jubilee of Sainte Anne's Church*; Stanton and Becker, *Heart of Polish Salem*, 111n20; Laurier Association, *History of Saint Joseph's Parish*, 17n8.

52. *Diamond Jubilee of Sainte Anne's Church*; *75th Anniversary Booklet*, 4.

53. Stanton and Becker, *Heart of Polish Salem*; Blood and Duclos-Orsello, *A Brief History*.

54. See the records in the SSU Archives for details of church closures and the clergy sex abuse crisis.

55. The distinct ethnic identities of Catholic churches a century ago had begun to wane significantly by the 1980s. On this, see the church bulletins and directories from the late twentieth and early twenty-first centuries in the Sainte Anne's folder, in the SSU Archives, and in the final chapters of Stanton and Becker, *Heart of Polish Salem*. Tracing surnames in parishes over time speaks to intermarriage.

56. Offering both a place for prayer and veneration and a weekly mass in both English and Polish, available at https://jpiidivinemercyshrine.org/, accessed July 13, 2023.

57. John Laidler, "Plan to convert two former Catholic schools into affordable housing advances in Salem," *Boston Globe*, January 1, 2023, available at https://www.bostonglobe.com/2023/01/06/metro/plan-convert-two-former-catholic-schools-into-affordable-housing-advances-salem, accessed August 21, 2023.

INTERLUDE 8

Salem's Black Picnic

An American Tradition

Donna A. Seger

African American residents of Salem and its region have sought out forms of association, recognition, and celebration for centuries, from the "Negro Election Days" held annually in the colonial era to the "Black Picnics" held at Salem Willows from the 1870s to the present. Referenced in two notable Salem diaries of the eighteenth century, Negro Election Day was a world-turned-upside-down celebration observed by African Americans throughout New England on the last Wednesday in May. Kings, governors, and other leaders were elected by their peers, and processions, dinners, and dances would follow during a day (or several) of ephemeral liberation. The first reference to this "hallowday" is a 1741 entry in Judge Benjamin Lynde's diary, but it was clearly an established tradition two decades later, when several Salem inhabitants petitioned their selectmen to regulate the festivities, as "great disorder usually happens among us on Election Days, by Negroes assembling together, beating drums and using powder to fire guns etc. etc. Some have appeared with swords and all which we think of bad tendency." Not all Salem residents were so disturbed: William Pynchon returned from a day trip to Danvers "to election at Primus's flag, and take ale and pies, and see the dances" in 1788.[1]

References to Negro Election Day are sparse after 1800, but other celebrations emerged. William Williams, a prominent member of Salem's small African American community in the early nineteenth century, represents a link between three emerging celebratory occasions. As an officer in the Sons of African Society in Salem, he organized several events in the first decade of the century, generally consisting of a procession, a sermon, and a dinner, which he hosted at his own house on Fish Street. A decade later, Williams participated in the "African Jubilee" events held in Boston between 1819 and 1825: these July celebrations also featured processions and religious exercises, though the former was eliminated in 1824 for fear of violence by "a number of blackguard men and boys of the white-race."[2] Following the Slavery Abolition Act of 1833, which abolished slavery throughout the British Empire, Williams became an organizer and advocate for Emancipation Day festivities, which generally took the form of outdoor celebrations—picnics—on August 1. In an 1841 letter to William Lloyd Garrison, Williams asked that Garrison publish a notice of the upcoming emancipation celebration in *The Liberator* so that "all the Boston friends [may] participate with the friends of Salem." His hopes for a unified and "consistent" celebration are expressed in the letter, as is his intent to involve "teachers and scholars of the colored Sunday school," who were prominent participants of African American picnics later in the century.[3] A notice in the *Emancipator and Weekly Chronicle* three years later seems to indicate that Williams' vision was fulfilled: "Our friends at Salem are making very large calculations for the Essex mass meeting on *Emancipation day*. Liberal provisions are made—railroad tickets half price—good speakers, singers, ladies, fugitives from slavery, zealous friends, &c. Come from all quarters and let us have a mass meeting indeed."[4]

This notice implies that Emancipation Day events evolved quickly from celebrations to "mass meetings" with "zealous friends": the mixed-race antislavery picnic of the antebellum era, fueled by the expanding abolitionist movement, was the forerunner of the church-organized picnics of the late nineteenth century. These were more rallies than picnics, but they were very popular celebrations for African Americans prior to the end of the Civil War, when emancipation became associated with the passage of the Thirteenth Amendment. The Massachusetts Anti-Slavery Society held an annual picnic on July Fourth at Harmony Grove in Framingham from 1846 to 1865, and Emancipation Day offered another opportunity to draw crowds. Because so many antislavery events were large and located some distance from urban centers, they necessitated the logistical planning referenced: special trains, speakers, and musical arrangements, all setting the standard for later events.

Following the Civil War, the African Methodist Episcopal churches of greater Boston were the principal organizers of summer picnics for their congregations in general and their Sunday or Sabbath Schools in particular. These were July and August events, held in picturesque groves around the region: Centennial Grove in Essex, Shawsheen Grove in Andover, Idlewood Grove in Hamilton, Smith's Grove in Ipswich, Howard's Grove in Saugus, and Echo Grove in Lynn. A comparatively early and apparently nondenominational gathering occurred in 1875: "The colored people of Beverly and Salem hold a second picnic at

Idlewood Grove, Hamilton, on Thursday, September 9th, under the direction of Messrs. George Stevens and J.H.A. Defreace, when a good time may be expected. Music by Burnham's Quadrille Band."[5] No emancipation, no commemoration, just a "good time."

It seems like every town and city had a grove, except Salem, but Salem had the Willows, an illuminated (from 1881) seaside park with attractions beyond compare, easily accessible by electric streetcar or steamship or barge. Salem Willows began to crowd out all the groves as the destination for parties and picnics from the 1870s on, as Sunday schools and spiritualists, veterans and unions, and various clubmen and clubwomen descended upon its "pleasure grounds" for their annual retreats. The Willows was not an exclusive location for African American picnics in the late nineteenth century: depending on the congregation, other sites were chosen. The African Methodist Episcopal Church in nearby Lynn, however, increasingly chose Salem Willows as the location of its annual picnic and invited local congregations to attend: in 1878 and 1879, the Lynn church held its annual "basket picnic" at the Willows and invited delegations not only from Lynn but also from Salem, Chelsea, and Boston to participate. In the next decade, congregations from the African Methodist Episcopal Churches in Malden and Everett also attended.[6]

The Lynn sponsorship was important as Salem had no African Methodist Episcopal Church of its own. Its African American population had dwindled over the nineteenth century, so there were insufficient numbers to support a formal congregation, though a Salem Mission of sixty-five members under the spiritual leadership of the formerly enslaved Jacob Stroyer did meet regularly and is likely the Salem delegation to which invitations were offered.[7] The audience for African American picnics at Salem Willows was always regional in the final decades of the nineteenth century: notices of travel to and from these events in area newspapers testify to their increasing size and reputation. A succession of railway companies provided regular service to the Willows, and, by the 1890s, the Lynn & Boston Railway Company had replaced horsecars with electrified trolleys and built a network encompassing eighteen towns.[8] The association of the "Colored Picnic" or "Colored Peoples Picnic" with Salem Willows seems so close in this era that at least one organizer took advantage: a "colored convention" featuring an array of tributes, speakers, and "performances" (stunts) sponsored by the Our Father Free Christian Association drew thousands to Salem on August 2, 1894, for a crowded and chaotic gathering that frustrated the white attendees and "disgusted" the much smaller group of African Americans in attendance.[9]

Church sponsorship of the August picnic, along with its regional draw and a more exclusive association with Salem Willows, continued into the twentieth

PICNIC

THERE WILL BE

A UNION S. S. PICNIC

OF THE THREE

African M. E. Churches

Of Chelsea, Lynn & Salem.

AT

THE WILLOWS, SALEM,

ON

Thursday, Aug. 15, 1878.

A Handsome Map for the use of the S. S. will be given to the School who shall sing in the best style.

One of the Salem Brass Bands will be in attendance at the Willows on that day.

The Churches will unite and form at Harbor Street, corner of Lafayette St., and start for the Willows at 10 A. M.

Picnic: there will be a Union S.S. Picnic of the Three African M.E. Churches of Chelsea, Lynn & Salem at the Willows, Salem on Thursday, August 15, 1878. (Phillips Library, Peabody Essex Museum.)

century. In the second half of the century, the event was moved from August to the third Saturday in July, and its name was changed from the "Colored Picnic" to the "Black Picnic" and, occasionally, the "Black Family Picnic," reflecting the observation of one recent attendee that "for our grandparents, it was more about slavery, being free, the Baptist Church. For us, it's about family."[10] The gathering also fulfilled William Williams's goal of uniting "friends" from Boston and Salem, as it was also referred to as a "unity picnic" of Greater Boston's Black churches as late as 1982.[11] From that time, the Black Picnic has been sponsored by secular organizations, including the North Shore branch of the NAACP and its present sponsor, Salem United Inc., but the emphasis on free association, family, and tradition endures. The advocacy efforts of Salem United, an organization dedicated to "preserving, protecting, and building black history," resulted in the designation of the third Saturday in July as "Negro Election Day," by the Massachusetts Legislature in 2022, and the formal association of the Black Picnic and Negro Election Day.[12]

NOTES

1. *The Diaries of Benjamin Lynde and of Benjamin Lynde, Jr.* (Riverside, 1879): "Negro's Hallowday Here in Salem," May 27, 1741, 109; Peter Frye, petition, "Negroes Create Great Disorder" on Election Day, May 5, 1768, Salem State University Archives and Special Collections, City of Salem Archives Collection; *The Diary of William Pynchon of Salem: A Picture of Salem Life, Social and Political, a Century Ago* (Houghton Mifflin, 1890), 308. The 1741 date referencing a "Negro's Hallowday" in Lynde Sr.'s diary has been conjoined in public memory with a gathering of twenty-six enslaved persons on the Saugus River in Lynn at the invitation of King Pompey, a formerly enslaved African man reputed to be of royal lineage and their elected leader, but as yet no documentary connection has been found: see William Dillon Piersen, *Black Yankees: The Development of an Afro-American Subculture in Eighteenth-Century New England* (University of Massachusetts Press, 1988), 117–118.

2. *Boston Gazette*, July 16, 1824.

3. "Letter from William Williams, Salem, to William Lloyd Garrison, 1841 July 12," Boston Public Library, Anti-Slavery Collection.

4. "First of August at Salem," *Emancipator and Weekly Chronicle*, July 31, 1844.

5. *Salem Register*, August 30, 1875.

6. *Picnic: There Will Be a Union S. S. Picnic of the Three African M. E. Churches of Chelsea, Lynn and Salem, at the Willows, Salem, on Thursday, Aug. 15, 1878*, Phillips Library Broadside, Peabody Essex Museum; *The Daily Item*, August 11, 1879: the latter picnic was held on a Wednesday, traditionally the Negro Election Day, though in August rather than May.

7. Jacob Stroyer (1849–1908), a South Carolina native who was freed as a teenager during the Civil War, was an ordained Methodist Episcopal minister who led the Salem Mission from 1876 until his death in 1908. In 1879, he published *Sketches of My Life in the South, Part One* (Salem Press), a memoir of his enslavement and liberation.

8. Salem Evening News, *Illustrated History of Salem and Environs* (1897).

9. "Colored Convention," *Boston Globe*, July 27, 1894: a "national gathering at Salem Willows," Thursday, August 2; "It Was A Picnic Of White Folk," *Boston Evening Transcript*, August 3, 1894: "More Than 10,000 Persons Went to the Salem Willows to See about 100 Colored Persons and Could Not Find Them in a Crowd"; "Sold Again," *Boston Globe*, August 3, 1894: "15,000 Assemble at Salem Willows / Program was not Carried Out as Scheduled / Fake Poster that Caught the Multitude."

10. Camille Caldera, "A Special Day in Black History: Hundreds Gather in Salem to Celebrate with Parade," *Boston Globe*, July 17, 2022, B1.

11. Diane Lewis, "Black Churches Hold Annual Picnic," *Boston Globe*, July 18, 1982, 1.

12. Bill S.2083 192nd (2021–2022), "An Act to Establish the Third Saturday in July as Negro Election Day," Massachusetts Legislature, available at https://malegislature.gov/Bills/192/S2083.

CHAPTER NINE

A Salem Scholar Abroad

The Worldview of Walter G. Whitman

MICHELE LOURO AND ELIZABETH MCKEIGUE

Introduction

Buried in the archives at Salem State University just north of Boston, the Walter George Whitman Collection has attracted little scholarly attention.[1] Professor Whitman (1874–1952), no relation to the poet, joined the faculty of the State Normal School in Massachusetts, in 1909, and went on to teach science to hundreds of Salem-area students for the next thirty-five years. A committed scholar-teacher, Whitman published widely on the connections between everyday life and scientific knowledge. His most popular works included *Household Physics* (1924) and his coauthored *Civic Science in the Home* (1921), *Civic Science in the Community* (1922), and *Civic Science in Home and Community* (1923). While these works form part of his archival record, the most abundant materials consist of hundreds of postcards and lantern slides, which are photographs printed on glass and viewed through a "magic lantern," the forerunner to the slide projector. The content of the postcards and slides, however, includes no materials on physics or civic science but, rather, offers rare glimpses of China and India on the eve of revolutions across Asia.

This chapter brings to light for the first time the Whitman collection on Asia and reveals a neglected dimension of Salem's engagement with the wider world. Whitman, along with his wife and two young children, arrived in China in September 1925, where Professor Whitman taught science at the University of Nanking (present-day Nanjing) until their departure via India and Egypt in the fall of 1926. The family lived in Nanjing at the height of imperialist and missionary expansion in China. Since the mid-nineteenth century, American and European investors aggressively asserted control over ports and commerce flowing in and out of China. A series of military conflicts beginning in the 1840s led to both the forced opening of Chinese trade with the West and the several unequal treaties that empowered foreigners to special rights, open trade, and settlement. Cities like Shanghai and Nanjing fell under these agreements as treaty ports, and a robust and growing population of Western businessmen and missionaries arrived to spread commerce and Christianity. Along with their settlement, these Americans and Europeans carried with them a set of beliefs that their epistemological ideas, education, and religion were superior to Chinese "tradition," leading to aggressive efforts to convert and educate the local populations to "civilize" them.[2]

The Whitman Collection provides one of many examples of the interplay between Salem's local history and global and transnational connections of the early twentieth century. Salem's historical connections to China, India, and the "Far East" run deep, although most scholarship concentrates on the city's maritime history in the eighteenth and nineteenth centuries.[3] The first New England vessel to trade with China was Elias Hasket Derby's converted privateer ship *Grand Turk*, which returned to Salem from Canton (present-day Guangzhou) in 1787 stocked with porcelain, tea, silk, and spices. Yet, by the mid-nineteenth century, Salem's status as a major American seaport was in decline, as it could not compete with the deep harbors and robust inland transportation networks of Boston and New York. Some Salem ships continued to travel to Africa and South America, but, by the 1890s, the last commercial trading ship had left Derby Wharf. With the diminishing place of Salem in global trade, the histories of Salem's engagement with the wider world also disappear to an extent.[4]

Whitman's collection on Asia extends our understanding of the extraterritorial experiences of Salem's citizens with the wider world, while also offering a rare glimpse of a pivotal moment in global history as India's anticolonial movement gained momentum and China's civil war and revolution dramatically altered the landscape of twentieth-century world history. The Whitman material about China and India offers clear evidence that American expatriates and scholars in the age of empire shared with their European counterparts a strong commitment to cultural imperialism and the civilizing mission despite evidence of local resistance. In his letters, memoirs, and lecture notes, along with his photographic and postcard collections, Whitman represents the East as a traditional and primitive "other" to Western religion, politics, and knowledge.

Historians have long argued that the construction of knowledge about the colonial world was a crucial tool in empowering American and European stakeholders over their counterparts in Asia and Africa.[5] As the economic and political power of empires extended in the nineteenth and twentieth centuries, scholars of science, history, art, geography, and philology accompanied politicians, civil servants, and soldiers. With the intentional and unintentional aid of scholars as producers of knowledge, the imperialist powers supported and circulated images of the "east" as essentially different and, therefore, inferior to the "west."[6] While China was not a formal colony of any empire, cultural imperialism was rampant and bolstered the military, economic, and missionary dominance of treaty ports like Nanjing, Shanghai, and Canton. As Whitman's historical record demonstrates, American scholars played a significant role in producing the "orientalist" knowledge of Asia and bolstered cultural imperialist perceptions of the East.

Knowledge of China and the world arrived in Salem through Walter Whitman and his family. Their archived letters, photographs, postcards, and general impressions provide rich materials for thinking about the lens in which 1920s Salem encountered the world. A close reading of Whitman's published letters on China, lantern lectures, and postcards that he shared with the public offer a case study for thinking about Salem's encounter with American representations of the East in the early twentieth century. Linking his ideas to imperialist ones, the Whitman archive demonstrates the power of Orientalism in shaping Salem's worldview in the age of empire.

The Orientalist Gaze and Whitman's East

In December 1925, readers of the *Salem Evening News* learned of the Whitman family's sojourn to China and the turbulent events engulfing Nanjing. Running the headline, "Salem Normal School Teacher 'Under Fire' in the Chinese War," the article reprinted two letters Whitman sent home to the head of the school, J. A. Pitman. The letters detail the military conflict between rivaling warlords over the sovereignty of Nanjing in October 1925. This event served as a critical precursor foreshadowing the escalation of civil war across China and the importance of Nanjing in the power struggle for dominance of the country. The Whitmans were witnessing historic events that shaped Nanjing, China, and the twentieth-century world.

Whitman was a man of his times as a scientist who published and coauthored books that subscribed to the ideas of social Darwinism and scientific racism, both ubiquitous in the Western canon and academy in the age of imperialism. Appropriating Darwin's theory of evolution, scientific racism promoted the theory that skin color and physical characteristics were the primary indicator of mental capacity, intelligence, civilization, and inner character.

Scientific racism further proposed that these inner and physical characteristics were fixed in "races," and imperialist powers imagined the world as a set of racial hierarchies to justify empires and their political, economic, and cultural control over Asian and African peoples.[7] For example, *Civic Science in the Community* includes a chapter, "How the Human Race Progressed," which explores hierarchies of civilization and eugenics as a progressive force for mankind.[8] In one illustration, an indigenous Australian from the twentieth century kindles a fire, a practice that Whitman and his coauthor liken to "remote ancestors" of the human race.[9] Whitman's coauthor, George William Hunter of Scopes Trial fame, described the top of the human hierarchy in his book *A Civic Biology* as "Caucasians" who were "the civilized white inhabitants of Europe and America."[10]

Professor Whitman was an ideal candidate to join Nanjing University and amplify the civilizing mission of missionaries and academics in China. He and his family assimilated into a community of foreign missionaries, academics, and business interests based in Nanjing at the apex of imperialist expansion in China. Whitman shared with this community a desire to change the world by teaching the Chinese people Western science and contributing to evangelical efforts to proselytize locals. His time in China crystallized his preexisting assumptions about the differences between East and West and the racial hierarchies of the civilizing mission.

Whitman bequeathed his knowledge about the East in publications and public lectures in New England just as avidly as he sought to enlighten students and teachers in the fundamentals of applied science. His letters published in the *Salem Evening News* detail the "bloodless capture" of Nanjing by Sun Chuan-Fang, a warlord who ruled until 1927. Whitman describes this military conflict in rather lighthearted descriptions, given the gravity of events unfolding outside their window. On October 17, according to Whitman, Mrs. Whitman asked him if he heard firecrackers at 2:00 A.M. The professor and his wife at first dismissed the commotion, noting that the "Chinese have no regard for one's slumber" as strange noises could often be heard each night.[11] He simply turned over and was "soon asleep" until the frequency of the "popping" escalated around 5:00 A.M. and the Whitmans realized that the noise, only one hundred meters from the house, was not firecrackers but rather machine guns. Only three days prior, Shanghai fell to a new warlord, and the railways and communication lines, including letters and newspapers, between the coastal port and Nanjing had been severed. The old regime, a warlord contingency from the North, had been in full retreat. In most cases, according to Whitman, soldiers either returned home or simply changed allegiances to the other side and continued their military service for a new warlord. In the days leading up October 17 and with growing concerns about Nanjing as the next site of capture, Whitman took to the streets with a camera, an amateur photographer seeking to snap a few photos of the conflict.[12]

Yet, when warfare arrived in Nanjing on October 17, Whitman's response to the events revealed a disinterest in the struggles of the Chinese. As the streets filled with soldiers and shots were fired across their yard, Whitman wrote that his Chinese neighbors climbed the six-foot stone fence to hide on their lawn for "protection."[13] This did little to encourage Whitman to shelter his neighbors, instead noting that he and his wife "didn't think it worthwhile to dress and tried to get a little more sleep."[14] When the sun rose over Nanjing, the children—George, age thirteen, and Mary, age eleven—dressed quickly and left to explore the streets and witness the conflict. Whitman writes that they collected war "trophies," including soldiers' helmets and cartridge shells from the overnight blasts. Rather casually, Whitman adds that George encountered a soldier who drew his sword and threatened the young boy. When little George offered a salute to the soldier, he was able to pass and return home with his "trophies."[15]

Much of the letters reveal the turbulent events as a source of inconvenience for the foreign population. From disrupting their sleep to the looting of foreign banks and businesses, the Chinese encountered in Whitman's letters are not seen as political actors but rather dismissed as opportunists at best. Their conflict, according to Whitman, seemed more about whether the retreating soldiers could keep their weapons and ammunition as they evacuated. Whitman notes that only one soldier had been killed, run over by a bullock cart rather than shot. Tongue in cheek, Whitman adds that it was "almost against the principles of the Chinese to shoot anyone in their wars."[16] Instead, according to Whitman, the disbanded soldiers either joined the opposite side or wandered the countryside pillaging and looting for personal gain. Only the coolies and poor farmers were subject to Whitman's sympathies, adding that it "makes one sick and disgusted but with pity" that the common people endure the looting and political turbulence as warlords fight over sovereignty of Nanjing and its contiguous areas.

The letters offered one representation of China for Salem, while Whitman's lantern slides provided another. Created in 1850, just ten years after photography was invented, lantern slides were widely used in the late nineteenth and early twentieth century yet rarely studied by historians. Martyn Jolly and Elisa deCourcy have argued, "every magic lantern show was a virtual passage to a physical and temporal reality" often very distant from the audience and speaker.[17] A close reading of a variety of magic lantern lectures affords nuanced ways of examining these rare materials. It reveals transnational connections between local audiences who were "witnesses" to very distant events and places. Likewise, Jolly and Courcy conclude that the "collective experience" of the lantern show enabled audiences to feel "connected to others."[18] Moreover, attention to the lantern lecturer's sequencing and textual scripts provides evidence of the performative element of persuasion associated with the slides.

Whitman's lantern lectures offer a glimpse of how Salem "witnessed" distant lands. The collection of slides includes one hundred and fifty-four images, of which one hundred and four were taken by Whitman personally. He purchased the remaining slides from several manufacturers, all based in Shanghai and connected to the missionary work of Europeans and Americans in China. Most of the missionary slides emphasized the backwardness of China.[19] The missionaries' selection of subjects for the slides reveals a larger purpose: to represent China's great and ancient past as corrupted through time by the failure of the Chinese to "modernize" through religious conversion and the appropriation of Western knowledge and technologies. In one color slide, a street vendor sells medicine in the form of "bone powder" taken from decaying skulls on display in the image.[20] Another represents a young girl, no older than twelve, holding a baby and seated next to an elderly man with the handwritten caption: "Caring for little sister. Man's toes bare. Straw sandals."[21]

Walter G. Whitman Lantern Slides, slide MS2010.1.PB1.2. *(Walter G. Whitman Papers, Salem State University Archives and Special Collections.)*

The lion's share of the lantern slide collection comes from the camera lens of Whitman. As a budding amateur photographer, Whitman's images of China formed the basis of his lifelong passion for photography. Once he returned to Salem in 1926, he joined and eventually led the Salem Camera Club. His photographs turned slides reveal in his own words "some of the things, places, and people I have seen."[22] Like all historical sources, however, the selection of subjects and curation of slides are informed by his assumptions about China and present a worldview that Whitman held and later publicly presented back at home in Salem. His Chinese subjects fished with rudimentary rods or bare hands, while manual labor, rather than steam engines, fueled the local economy. Although he also snapped photos of his family and dwellings in Nanjing, along with images from the university and student life, among these images were encounters with local militias and soldiers who occupied Nanjing, a rare photographic glimpse of the political turbulence engulfing the city and the country.[23] The visually rich images in the form of lantern lectures combined with the modality of performative narration offered a powerful tool for Whitman to disseminate knowledge of the East.

One lecture, "A Year in China," revealed much about Whitman and, more broadly, American perceptions of the East.[24] The lecture opens by characterizing China as a "land of contradictions": whereas it is home to some of the "world's best thinkers," most of the population cannot read or write. In the past, China introduced gunpowder and made silk for the first time, yet today it lagged "behind the rest of the world in scientific development and invention." Although politically a republic, the "country is governed in small sections by half a dozen different militarists."[25] This opening image is consistent with Orientalist ideas about Asia as a timeless land, rich in history and tradition but lacking and, indeed, backward in the "development" of literacy, innovation, and politics.

While Whitman's lantern lectures do not identify specific slides that accompanied his presentation, it is not difficult to imagine what images he could call on from the collection to visually represent China as "behind the rest of the world" in various aspects of life. In one image, Whitman snaps a photo of a mother and son standing by the walls encircling Nanjing. The child is naked and has a bloated, protruding belly, reflective of severe malnutrition, while the mother's clothes appear ragged and dirty. She stares intensely into the lens.[26] In other photographs, Whitman captures donkeys carrying hay, three fisherman shirtless and catching fish with bare hands, and street scenes where men, women, and children eat and labor in unsanitary conditions. Images of affluent or elite Chinese are nearly absent in his collection, although there would be no dearth of such subjects in Shanghai, Nanjing, or among his university community.

Another lecture narrates the sojourn from disembarkation in Shanghai to the family's settlement in Nanjing. Whitman juxtaposed the foreign-controlled Shanghai with an authentic China in Nanjing, where the population is five hundred thousand with only four hundred foreigners in residence. Whitman felt "quite at home" in Shanghai, where the waterfront was lined with banks, hotels, a customs building, and foreign legations, alongside the domineering Baptist college as the most prominent building on the Bund.[27] The city is flanked by American, British, and Japanese warships, a sign of the uncertain political milieu of China in 1925. The "ever present coolies" and signs in Chinese script were the only indications that one was in China.[28] Otherwise, they could have mistaken Shanghai for an "American or European port." Whitman casually describes "a nice park" on the waterfront within the boundaries of the British concession and a sign that read, "no Chinese or dogs are allowed."[29]

Whitman's journey from Shanghai to Nanjing provides a segue into spaces where one saw the "Chinese in their native element."[30] The train passed rural villages with mud huts and traditionally dressed natives, and Whitman embeds these scenes into his lantern lectures. Halfway between Shanghai and Nanjing, the train stopped at Soochow (present-day Suzhou), representing for Whitman the "real native China" far from and absent of foreign influence.[31] Suzhou is best known for "beautiful women," according to Whitman, who captured a photograph of a young woman at the station.[32] She was wearing a long silk dress that is vibrant even in the black and white image, her hair long and pulled back into a neat ponytail. A young girl stood beside the woman and stared inquisitively into Whitman's lens, perhaps wondering why he had decided to snap their photo. The choice and emphasis in the lecture and lantern slide of a "beautiful" and feminine woman as the representation of the "real native China" provides evidence of a gendered construction of China that echoed Orientalism. The East, in this case China, came to be constructed as passive and feminine, and the West, as masculine and dominant.

Much like Orientalist representations of the East, Nanjing for Whitman was a place of intrigue, danger, and superstition. In his lectures, he attempts to recount the history of the city from ancient times to the present, offering vague, and at times inaccurate, sketches of emperors who plotted for power, murdered their rivals, and wrought havoc on the city over hundreds of years. In his view, the Chinese people in Nanjing were superstitious, paying tribute and worshipping idols of various sorts. In one case, as Whitman displayed Nanjing's bell tower dating from the fourteenth century, his lecture recounts a

Walter G. Whitman Lantern Slides, slide MS2010.1.PB1.27. *(Walter G. Whitman Papers, Salem State University Archives and Special Collections.)*

tale in which a Ming emperor demanded a local bell maker cast three large bells for the city. After many failed attempts, as the bells mysteriously cracked or the molds broke, his three beautiful daughters sacrificed themselves to the God of Bells to save their father and the city. The bells were cast successfully because of the sacrifice of the daughters. Consequently, a shrine was constructed and placed in the bell tower with life-size likenesses of the three daughters wearing "beautiful garments" and having "real hair, flowers, and gold ornaments."[33] On the new and full moons each month, a caretaker combed, oiled, and perfumed their hair. Whitman also elaborated on superstitions associated with the other iconic site in Nanjing, the drum tower. Large stone elephants and turtle statues at the drum tower warded off evil spirits and brought health to local children. The elephants, in particular, were significant in indicating whether an expecting mother is to have a boy or girl.[34]

In another lecture, "Disposal of the Dead," Whitman extended his gaze beyond Nanjing and explored the rituals and burial practices of India and Egypt alongside China.[35] Whitman began one of the lengthiest lantern lectures in the collection with a story about encountering the decomposing body of a young child in China, which had been half eaten by dogs. Seeking assistance from locals to acquire the body and bury it, Whitman soon learned from a foreigner that this is a common practice for locals who leave wildlife to dispose of their dead. Even formal burial disturbed Whitman, who noted that priests left decaying bodies in temples for weeks and added: "I had at that time become quite acclimated to the ordinary street smells, but that was no adequate preparation for one to nose around among these coffins which had been in storage surely more than one month."[36]

As Whitman turns his gaze from China to India and Egypt, he strengthens his criticism of Eastern practices in relation to the West. In observing the cremation of Hindus along the Ganges River, Whitman describes a "ghastly sight" of "roasting flesh," while priests demonstrated a "harshness" and "lack of any sentiment."[37] In one case, a son arranged his father's body on a funeral pyre in an "indifferent way" before lighting his body with a "cigarette."[38] Whitman adds that young children of Hindus were simply flung into the river, where it was "fairly common" to see dead bodies floating down the Ganges. Whitman also considers several burning ghats in Benares and Cawnpore, where "in former days, widows would jump into the fire and burn alive with their dead husbands."[39] The burning of widows in their husband's funeral pyre, or sati, was among the first religious practices banned in the aggressive social reforms led by the British in 1829.[40]

Whitman also comments on the burial practices of the Parsi community in India. Parsis were descendants of Zoroastrians who fled the Persian Empire in the aftermath of the Arab conquest in the seventh century. Fearing religious persecution, a small community of Parsis settled in early modern India and continued to practice their faith. Parsis neither cremated nor buried the dead but, rather, placed bodies outside in the "Tower of Silence" for natural elements and vultures to dispose of the corpse. On Whitman's travel itinerary was a visit to the Tower of Silence in Bombay, where he described the disposal of bodies as "disturbing" for Americans although Parsis entered the grounds with a "sense of peace."[41] He could see, "perched on the rim of one of the towers, twelve vultures which were waiting for the next body to be brought in. . . .

For, two hours after a body is put inside of a tower, the vultures have picked it clean. There is nothing but the bone remaining."[42]

Although few lantern slides depicting India exist in the collection, Whitman returned with an extensive postcard collection from India, which may have been used for his lectures. The postcards overall share with the Chinese lantern slides a depiction of Indian society as traditional, primitive, and superstitious. In certain instances, the strong resemblance in images of Chinese and Indian subjects engaged in manual labor with primitive tools rather than machinery is striking.[43] The scholarship on photography as a tool of cultural imperialism and colonial power is abundant. Colonial administrators sought to know and, therefore, control the diverse peoples of India, photographing and classifying (often inaccurately) Indian society as a form of cultural imperialism and a means to "divide and rule."[44]

Whitman's postcards from India offer reprints of iconic images produced by the British, representing Indians as timeless, traditional, and backward in relation to the West. Among these images was the "Madras Hunt," a widely circulated print of five Indians seated in a line, picking head lice from one another's hair much like similar photographs of monkeys doing the same.[45] The message is clear: Indian society is more closely linked to monkeys than humans, echoing the hierarchies in scientific racism. In relation to the disposal of the dead, Whitman's collection includes "Hindu Funeral Pile," a troubling print capturing a large heap of decomposing corpses on a shabby pile of wood, demonstrating effectively the "ghastly sight" Whitman describes in his lantern lectures.[46] Such images reinforced the colonial constructions of India

"Madras Hunt." *(Walter G. Whitman Postcards, Walter G. Whitman Papers, Salem State University Archives and Special Collections.)*

that empowered the British over the colonized, while also bolstering Whitman's representations of burial practices in Asia as "uncivilized" in relation to Western ones.

When thinking about the wider implications of Whitman's representations of Asia, and China in particular, it is important to consider the dissemination of his ideas at home in Salem. Whitman was not simply compiling observations but rather constructing an image of the East for Salem audiences that he shared in the local newspapers and his public lectures. This wider dissemination reinforced and amplified the Orientalist stereotypes of the East as backward and primitive rather than modern like the West.

Conclusion

A close reading of Walter G. Whitman's archive reveals a history of Salem's views of Asia at the height of European imperialism. From his lantern lectures and slides to his collection of postcards, Whitman's views of the "East" appropriated and amplified for local audiences in Salem an Orientalist interpretation of China and India. The images from China, in particular, offer a rare glimpse of a country in turmoil, largely a consequence of foreign expansion and cultural imperialism. Whitman's understanding of Asia was informed and shaped by many of the missionary and foreign interests that he encountered on the ground in Nanjing. He also arrived in China with an understanding of the world that emerged from the most prevalent and widely circulated ideas of his time about scientific racism and eugenics. This changed only with the waning of empires in Asia and a new and more critical generation of expatriates and travelers, including Whitman's globe-trotting son, George, whose early life in China fueled his desire to leave Salem, travel the world, and settle abroad in Paris for the rest of his life.[47] Although beyond the scope of this chapter, the younger Whitman's experiences were shaped by a deep distrust of imperialism and capitalism, overturning within the family the long-standing ideas about racial hierarchies and civilization that were held by his father and have been archived in Walter Whitman's lantern slides and lectures.

NOTES

1. Walter G. Whitman Papers, Archives and Special Collections, Salem State University, Berry Library, Salem, MA. (Hereafter WGW Papers.)

2. There is an abundant scholarship on modern empires and the civilizing mission. For an introduction, see Heather Salter and Trevor Getz, *Empires and Colonies in the Modern World* (Oxford University Press, 2015).

3. See, e.g., Dane Morrison, *True Yankees: The South Seas and the Discovery of American Identity, 1784–1844* (Johns Hopkins University Press, 2014).

4. Exceptions appear in this volume. See also, Aviva Chomsky, "Salem as Global City, 1850–2004," in *Salem: Place, Myth, and Memory*, ed. Dane Anthony Morrison and Nancy Lusignan Schultz (Northeastern University Press, 2004), 219–247.

5. Bernard Cohn, *Colonialism and Its Forms of Knowledge* (Princeton University Press, 1996).

6. See seminal texts by Edward Said: *Orientalism* (Vintage Books, 1979) and *Culture and Imperialism* (Vintage Books, 1994).

7. See introduction to Salter and Getz, *Empires and Colonies*.

8. Walter G. Whitman and George William Hunter, *Civic Science in the Community* (American Book, 1922).

9. Ibid., 412.

10. George William Hunter, *A Civic Biology: Presented in Problems* (American Book, 1914), 196.

11. "Salem Normal School Teacher 'Under Fire' in the Chinese War," *Salem Evening News*, December 17, 1925, 9.

12. There are several images of Chinese soldiers in Whitman's lantern slide collection. See WGW Lantern Slides, WGW Papers. (Hereafter WGW Slides.)

13. "Salem Normal School Teacher 'Under Fire,'" *Salem Evening News*.

14. Ibid.

15. Ibid.

16. Ibid.

17. *The Magic Lantern Slide at Work: Witnessing, Persuading, Experiencing, and Connecting*, ed. Martyn Jolly and Elisa deCourcy (Routledge, 2020), 12–13.

18. Ibid., 13.

19. WGW Slides, Slide MS2010.1.PB1.133, Mission Photo Bureau, Shanghai, Slide no. 7167.

20. WGW Slides, Slide MS2010.1.PB1.2 (color), Credit: Mission Photo Bureau, Shanghai, 2 June 1924, Col. J., Slide E60, Neg. 3978. Handwritten inscription on front: "Street Medicine Vendor, Bone Powders." Inscription on back: "Slide E60 Neg. 3948."

21. WGW Slides, Slide MS2010.1.PB1.34 (color), Credit: Mission Photo Bureau, Shanghai, Slide no. C105 Lect. no. MPB Neg. no. 5464.

22. Walter G. Whitman, Lantern Lectures, "A Year in China," Box: Observations on Life in China, 1925–1926, Folder 4, WGW Papers. (Hereafter WGW Lectures.)

23. See note 12.

24. WGW Lectures, "Year in China."

25. Ibid.

26. WGW Slides, Slide MS2010.1.PB1.65.

27. WGW Lectures, "Year in China."

28. Ibid.

29. Ibid.

30. Ibid.

31. Ibid.

32. WGW Slides, Slide MS2010.1.PB1.27.

33. WGW Lectures, "Year in China."

34. WGW Slides, Slide MS2010.1.PB1.25, Credit: Educational Department, National Committee YMCA's of China.

35. WGW Lectures, "The Disposal of the Dead," Box: Observations on Life in China, 1925–1926, Folder 2, WGW Papers.
36. Ibid.
37. Ibid.
38. Ibid.
39. Ibid.
40. For a history of colonialism and reforms that specifically targeted Sati, see Lata Mani, *Contentious Traditions: The Debate on Sati in Colonial India* (University of California Press, 1998). On the politics of the disposal of the dead, see Kelsey J. Utne, *Corpse Politics: Disposal and Commemoration of the Indian Interwar Dead, 1919–1939* (Ph.D. diss., Cornell University, 2022).
41. WGW Lectures, "Disposal of the Dead."
42. Ibid.
43. WGW Slides, Slide MS2010.1.PB1.56; "Sawing Timber," Walter G. Whitman Postcards (hereafter WGW Postcards).
44. For scholarship on knowledge production, see, e.g., Nicholas Dirks, *Casts of Mind: Colonialism and the Making of Modern India* (Princeton University Press, 2001).
45. "Madras Hunt," WGW Postcards.
46. "Hindu Funeral Pile," WGW Postcards.
47. For a less academic but fascinating tale of George Whitman's ownership of the Shakespeare and Company bookshop, see *Shakespeare and Company, Paris: A History of the Rag and Bone Shop of the Heart* (Shakespeare and Company, 2016).

INTERLUDE 9

Salem Willows

Playground of the North Shore

Brad Austin

In a 1941 *Woman's Day* article about Salem's stature as a "Mecca for all true devotees of fried fish and chowder," Sallie Belle Cox observed that "there is nothing sensational in the appearance of Salem Willows. It is just another smallish summer resort on the ocean with an amusement area and a cottage colony. It seems hard to believe that before the turn of the century it was *the* outstanding gathering spot on Boston's north shore." Now, she continued, "it is a little old lady with a past."[1] That characterization would have surprised the hundreds of thousands of New Englanders who traveled to Salem in the late 1800s and early 1900s to explore and enjoy the unique city park that both juts into Salem Harbor and provides views of Cape Ann from Beverly to Gloucester.

To understand the appeal of the Salem Willows amusement park, back before she had aged gracefully into "little old lady" status, one must understand first the city it neighbored and the amusement park it rivaled. In many ways, Salem was a typical New England city in the late 1800s and early 1900s. The seventh-largest city in the nation in 1790, Salem had slipped to being the seventy-second-largest in 1880, twenty-four spots ahead of San Antonio, and housing only ten thousand fewer residents than Atlanta. The 1890 census would be the last time that Salem ranked among the nation's one-hundred-largest cities (it was no. 100), but, as other chapters in this volume explain, Salem experienced all of the cultural and logistical disruptions that industrial cities faced as their growing factories brought newcomers to their streets and shops, many from Southern and Eastern Europe.[2]

In its development, Salem was representative, not unique, but the city's recreational response to these changes was. The cultural historian John Kasson has argued that Brooklyn's Coney Island—with its roller coasters, night lights, exotic architecture, and opportunities for New Yorkers to flee their crowded neighborhoods for cheap, frivolous fun—became, in his words, "the unofficial capital of the new mass culture." Commercial amusement parks, such as Coney Island, gave their nearby urban residents physical and psychological releases from the familiar streets of their neighborhoods and workplaces by offering them artificially exotic escapes from their usual surroundings and routines.[3]

The Wonderland Park at Revere Beach served this purpose for Boston, and Salem Willows emerged as an ideological and experiential counterpoint to Wonderland. Located on the seaside, just north of Boston, Wonderland Park was accessible from the Hub for just ten cents by 1875. By 1881, there were more than sixty trains a day bringing visitors to mingle with those who arrived by ferries that delivered them to Wonderland's seventeen-hundred-foot pier. Wonderland offered these visitors a wide range of experiences, spanning from mechanical rides to nighttime swimming under the lights to beer shanties to mock Civil War and War of 1812 battles to scores of firefighters extinguishing fires daily in front of stands seating thousands.[4] In short, Wonderland was designed to excite and stimulate, as this song from 1906 suggests:

Wonderland
Any night in the week
if for pleasure you seek
Take a trip to Wonderland Park;
On the peaceful Lagoon
in a boat you can spoon
It's the only place for a lark;
When they're "Fighting the Flames"
then my girl will say "James!
It's as good as the St. Louis Fair";
I'll be down at the Park
just as soon as its dark.
Ev'ry night you'll find me there.[5]

As the historian Joseph Garland has noted, another verse suggests more explicitly the appeals of Wonderland Park. It concludes:

> Wonderland, Wonderland, that's the place to be!
> Each night when I call on my sweetie, she says to me:
> "Let's take a trolley ride to the oceanside
> Where the shining lights are grand."
> If you want to make good as a true lover should,
> Just take her to Wonderland!

Created at the same time as Wonderland Park, Salem Willows purposefully offered a sober and shaded alternative to Wonderland's more chaotic and less reputable offerings. Very quickly, thanks to the prevalence of cheap trolley rides from Salem and abundant ferry options for travelers escaping Boston, the Willows became an enticing option for those who wanted "respectable" escapes from industrial life and work in the greater Boston area. In its 1880s announcement of the creation of a "charming resort, about a mile and a half from Salem proper," the *Boston Globe* informed readers that the Willows would always provide visitors with "cool breezes and refreshing shade." Additionally, they would find a "first-class theater" that would soon "equal in all respects most of our metropolitan theaters."[6] By the 1890s, the Willows offered a wide range of active amusements (bandstands, dance halls, restaurants, shooting galleries, a giant Shoot the Chutes water ride, and an Edison movie house) to the thousands who took trains and ferries there. Some of these attractions

Postcard of Salem Willows. *(Nelson Dionne Salem History Collection, Salem State University Archives and Special Collections.)*

might have felt familiar to those who frequented nearby Revere Beach, but the Willows differentiated itself in several significant ways.

Modern visitors to the Willows will notice that it still has only a small crescent-shaped beach, not suitable for mass bathing, and this was also true a century ago. Additionally, as a city park that boasted numerous promenade paths, the Willows banned the sale of alcohol, appealing to a less rowdy crowd than its Revere rival. While one local entrepreneur advertised seventeen types of "temperance drinks" to visitors, the Juniper House sated the thirst of patrons wanting different options by taking advantage of the fact that only half of its building was on park property. This inn cleverly sold alcoholic drinks in the half that lay outside the park boundary.[7]

Half of the Juniper House notwithstanding, the Willows' family and business friendly atmosphere paid off, literally, for the restaurateurs, arcade owners, carrousel operators, and other business owners, as the park attracted an astonishing array of family gatherings, military reunions, and business association outings in the late nineteenth and early twentieth centuries. The park's appeal was clear, as an 1896 description explained, "What a relief it must be to those who, after a hard week's work, are tired in mind and body, who have patiently borne the torrid weather of the past week, today seek the quiet and historic shore of Salem."[8] Instead of mechanical roller coasters and other loud colorful rides that must

Perspective View [*of the Salem Willows Pavilion*]. Watercolor, ca. 1878. *(Courtesy of Historic New England.)*

have reminded laborers of the industrial workplaces they were seeking to escape, the quiet of the Willows appealed to many.

We can witness the regional appeal of the Willows by noting the distances people would travel to relax there. Visitors came from all over New England, and they came representing a wide variety of groups, choosing to travel to Salem for the scenery and the sanity (relative to Revere Beach) that the Willows offered. Some of the very first publicized gatherings at the Willows were of Civil War veterans, with newspapers sharing accounts of "Battlefield Comrades" reunions there in the 1880s. Over the ensuing decades, the descriptions of "grizzled veterans" reunions came to include the dwindling numbers of survivors. By the time of its 1921 Willows reunion, only six members of the Fourth Massachusetts Battery survived, including Salem's former mayor John Hurley and "his chum of 60 years," Woburn's Frank Smith.[9]

While the Willows was hosting the last of the Civil War reunions in the 1920s, it was also serving as a gathering ground for a different type of political gathering, those for women voters. Throughout the decade, female voters congregated by the thousands to hear from politicians and to have politicians hear from them. In 1921, in the "first [rally] of its kind in the history of the district," the League of Women Voters gave "all candidates for Congress [the] opportunity to define their positions on public welfare measures." Four years later, the G.O.P. Women of Essex and Middlesex County had a lengthy discussion of "divorce and jury service" with more than one thousand attending.[10]

Other groups came for more lighthearted reasons, and they represented a wide variety of regional associations. For example, in 1902, the National Association of Cemetery Superintendents visited the Willows, and, in 1909, eight hundred New England Dry Goods Men held their business meeting in the Willow's casino.

The "Smile and Work Club" gathered at the Willows in 1925, where men competed in wheelbarrow and two-legged races, and women competed in ball throwing and needle threading contests. As Interlude 8 in this volume discusses, the Willows also hosted some of the largest gatherings of African Americans in New England during the early 1900s. Their welcome at the Willows doesn't mean, however, that life for these New Englanders was always comfortable, as is revealed by a quick glance at a 1924 *Salem Evening News* page juxtaposing an article titled, "Colored Folks Picnic, Attended by 900" with, only one column away, an article describing the rapid growth of the Ku Klux Klan in Salem and Lynn, as "Imperial Empire" members detailed their ability to elude police and to hold their meetings in neighboring Swampscott.[11]

Ultimately, unlike many competing amusement options in Revere and up the coast in New Hampshire, the Salem Willows provided generations of New

Englanders with a place where they could swim, dance, eat, and promenade alongside the ocean in a relatively tame and family friendly environment. There, they could gather with family members, fellow veterans, or other like-minded people to see bands, bonfires, lantern parades, political speakers, submarines, explosions, and other novelties. This contemporaneous poem captures both the charm and the allure of the Willows.

> You don't mind the trolley because you can jolly
> The nice little girls by your side.
> On moonlit nights, Gee! It is dandy,
> And on Sundays it's simply divine.
> You can have all your "Coneys,"
> To me they're all phoneys,
> But Salem Willows for mine—it's mine[12]

NOTES

1. Sallie Belle Cox, "Shore Dinners," *Woman's Day*, July 1941.
2. See U.S. Census Bureau, "Population of the 100 Largest Cities and Other Urban Places in the United States: 1790 to 1990," 1998, available at https://www.census.gov/library/working-papers/1998/demo/POP-twps0027.html, accessed January 25, 2024. See also Elizabeth Duclos-Orsello's essay in this volume (Chapter Eight) to learn more about the growth of immigrant communities and their contributions to Salem's life and culture.
3. John Kasson, *Amusing the Million: Coney Island at the Turn of the Century* (Hill and Wang, 1978).
4. Joseph E. Garland, *Boston's Gold Coast: The North Shore, 1890–1929* (Little, Brown, 1981), 18.
5. Lyrics to "Wonderland" is available at https://lost-wonderland.com/wonderland-music/, accessed February 15, 2023.
6. "Salem Willows," *Boston Globe*, June 13, 1880, 9.
7. Garland, *Boston's Gold Coast*, 24; Jim McAllister, "Salem Willows Still a 'Favorite Picnic Ground' for Many," *Salem Evening News*, September 23, 2010, 5; Postcard of Salem Willows, Nelson Dionne Salem History Collection, Salem State University Archives and Special Collections, Salem, Massachusetts.
8. "Attractions at Salem Willows," *Boston Daily Globe*, August 16, 1896, 18.
9. "Grizzled Veterans: Reunion at Salem Willows of 5th Regiment," *Boston Daily Globe*, June 27, 1891, 11; "Old Civil War Comrades Meet at Salem Willows," *Boston Daily Globe*, August 25, 1921, 14.
10. "Women Voters Hear Candidates' Views," *Boston Daily Globe*, August 25, 1921, 3; "G.O.P. Women Have Outing," *Boston Daily Globe*, August 26, 1925, 1.
11. "Bank Officers Take 1200 on Outing: Rough Sea Trip to Salem Willows Forgotten When Festivities Begin—Sports and Dancing Attract Many," *Boston Daily Globe*, June 16, 1912, 13. "Colored Folks Picnic, Willows Attended by 900" and "Claim 150 Salem Members in Lynn Ku Klux Klan," *Salem Evening News*, August 8, 1924, 8. To learn more about the larger context of the Klan's presence and activities in Massachusetts and throughout New England, see Mark Paul Richard, *Not a Catholic Nation: The Ku Klux Klan Confronts New England in the 1920s* (University of Massachusetts Press, 2018).
12. Garland, *Boston's Gold Coast*, 24.

CHAPTER TEN

From Shrine to Source

Salem and the Colonial Revival, 1876–1934

Donna A. Seger

A succession of notable visitors made their way to Salem in the late nineteenth and early twentieth centuries, often using the word "pilgrimage" to describe their trip. The journalist Edwin Bacon's *Historical Pilgrimages in New England* devoted two chapters to Salem and its "mansion houses of old-time grandeur, and ancient dwellings close pressed by modern." The authoritative trade periodical *The American Architect* recommended an "architectural pilgrimage" to Salem to both students and midcareer professionals alike. On his pilgrimage to see the House of the Seven Gables in 1904, Henry James found a busier and more "polyglot" city than he expected to see but still noted the "spacious, courteous doorways of the houses, expansively columned, fluted, framed; their large honest windows, in ample tiers, only here and there dishonoured by the modern pane." Daniel Low, the owner of one of Salem's largest retail stores and a mail-order entrepreneur, included copies of a pamphlet titled, *The Salem Pilgrim: His Book*, with every order after 1903. Low's namesake store was located in Salem's most historic square, which was presented as *sacred* soil and "the focus and centre of Puritan New England, on the spot where was planted one of the twin shoots of American Democracy, and from which there went forth not a few of the great forces that have shaped American history."[1]

While the word pilgrimage implies spirituality, these references were exclusively secular. As scholars of Colonial Revival culture have long noted, there were many colonial *revivals*, and Salem's was distinctly urban and characteristically entrepreneurial. In a densely settled city, where neighborhoods of colonial cottages and Federal mansions were situated mere blocks from coal wharves, factories, and immigrant quarters, the older buildings inspired an enthusiastic and evangelical devotion among both residents and visitors. Behind this enthusiasm, there was also an evident concern that the old city might be overwhelmed by the new: the instinct in Salem was not just to appreciate and emulate but also to preserve and defend. For Salem "pastkeepers" and past purveyors, there were also linkages between the material and the dramatic narrative of the city's history: there was quite a story to tell *and* sell.[2]

Building on the foundation of the continuous lure of the 1692 witch trials, the national appeal of Nathaniel Hawthorne, and the romanticized memory of diminished maritime dominance, a group of Salem antiquarian advocates intensified the draw of Salem in general, and colonial Salem in particular: Low (1842–1911), a purveyor of Salem wares to a national market, Mary Harrod Northend (1850–1926), a late-blooming and extraordinarily prolific author of books and articles on architecture and interior design as well as a major publisher of architectural prints and photographs, Frank Cousins (1851–1925), a retailer who evolved into a successful photographer, publisher, and author of architectural images and texts, Caroline Emmerton (1866–1942), philanthropist, preservationist, and founder of the House of the Seven Gables Settlement Association, and, finally, George Francis Dow (1868–1926), historian, author, and secretary (essentially, director/curator) of the Essex Institute, Salem's regional historical museum, from 1898 to 1918. All but Dow were Salem natives, and all viewed Salem's long "colonial period" (which they extended conveniently to 1820) as its material and cultural apex, a golden era in both the city's and the nation's history, which must be broadcast to as wide an audience as possible. They were a generation of Salem antiquarian advocates, recognized as such by Dow's much later successor at the Essex Institute, Anne Farnam, who identified "a lively, buzzing network of collectors, writers, researchers, photographers and artists, antiquarians all" present in Salem in the years just before and after 1900 "engaged in a busy pursuit of the past and things old. New England was the logical center of focus for all this activity, and Salem was one of the chief 'shrines.'"[3]

As busy as this generation was, it was building on a solid foundation. A generation before, a succession of architects had made their way to Salem to sketch and measure its venerable structures, from Arthur Little and the founding members of McKim, Mead, and White in the 1870s to William Rotch Ware's MIT architecture students in the 1890s, whose "Summer School" drawings were featured in the volumes of his *Georgian Period* series, published from 1898 to 1902.[4] Salem civic and cultural leaders had engaged energetically with the Massachusetts commissioners and managers of the Centennial Exhibition in 1876 and the Columbian Exposition in Chicago in 1893–1894, two major opportunities for national exposure. *The Report of the Massachusetts Commissioner to the Centennial Exhibition at Philadelphia* notes that only two municipalities, Salem and Nantucket, responded to its request for representative exhibits: the former sent a "large quarto album illustrating the history of Salem by a series of photographs, cabinet-sized, 208 in number and giving in print the principal events in the history of Salem from its settlement, also statistics of its industries, public works, societies, charities, city officers, school system, etc., etc." as well as an entire exhibit of historical portraits and colonial "relics" from the collection of the Essex Institute to Philadelphia, an effort underwritten by the Ladies Centennial Committee of Salem. Prior to their departure for Philadelphia, an exhibition of the items, including witch trial judge Jonathan Corwin's baby clothes, revolutionary pistols, and a wine glass used by President George Washington on his visit to Salem in 1789, was held at the Institute's Plummer Hall and featured in *Frank Leslie's Illustrated Newspaper*.[5]

The Columbian Exposition presented another opportunity for "Old Salem" to shine. Great effort and expense were expended on the Massachusetts state building and an enlarged reproduction of John Hancock's lost Boston house, but interior exhibits were scarce as many of the state's venerable anti-

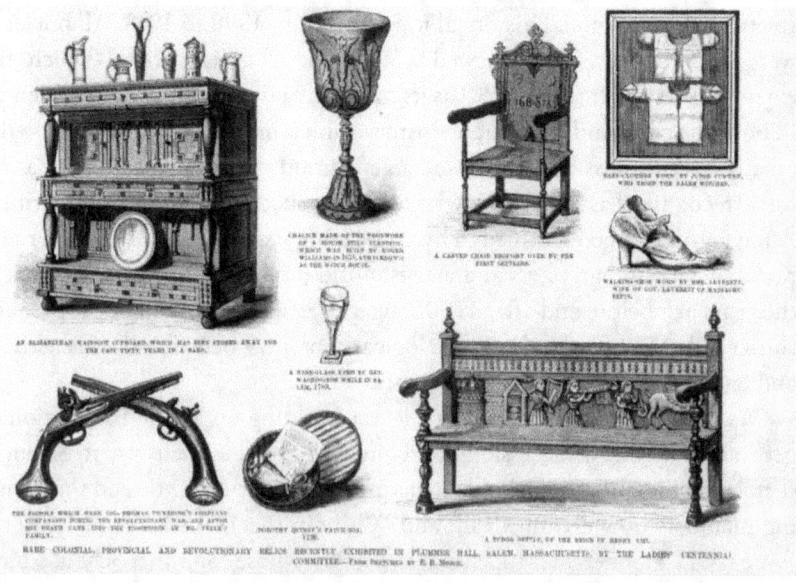

Rare Colonial Provincial and Revolutionary Relics Recently Exhibited in Plummer Hall, Salem, Massachusetts, by the Ladies Centennial Committee; From sketches by E. R. Morse. (Frank Leslie's Illustrated Newspaper, *January 22, 1876.*)

quarian societies were unable or reluctant to send their collections west. The field was left largely to Salem and the Essex Institute, which took full advantage of the opportunity with the installation of what would become an award-winning exhibition in the main reception room of the building. This room contained "no piece of furniture less than a hundred years old," making it a distinctly colonial presentation, and "was interesting and instructive beyond imagination." There were portraits of Salem dignitaries on the walls as well as photographs and paintings of Salem houses, recognized as "relics" as much as the encased objects, texts, and furnishings in the room, and all were "collected through the industry of the citizens of Salem, and, through their liberality, courtesy, and public spirit, placed within the keeping of the Massachusetts Board of World's Fair Managers, as the contribution of Essex County to the State Building at the World's Columbian Exposition."[6]

The photographs were the work of Frank Cousins, a Salem shopkeeper who first picked up a camera only five years before. Cousins reprinted images from his series "Art Views of Historic Salem" for the faux Hancock House: this was one of the first times the term "historic" was linked with Salem in such a formal way, and it remained a form of urban identification along (and often in competition) with Salem's other moniker, "Witch City." Historical branding in Salem had a banner year in 1892, as it was not only the Columbian anniversary but also the witch trials bicentennial. Cousins was able to take advantage of both events, offering witch wares and postcards from his Essex Street store (Frank Cousins's Bee-Hive) at the same time as he was publishing artistic views of Salem's stately mansions. Daniel Low focused more exclusively on the commercial opportunities provided by the witch trial bicentennial, as he debuted his first mail-order catalog, featuring the already popular souvenir witch spoons. Cousins was also entrepreneurial, but the major spotlight on his new avocation both in Chicago and Salem shifted his focus from dry goods to photography. Throughout the 1890s, he advertised his repeatedly "new" series of photographs of Salem and its environs in both national and local periodicals, offering "the architectural beauties of old colonial doorways, stairways, fireplaces and interiors, for which Salem is so noted" as well as "nearly every house or object connected with witchcraft times."[7] Cousins was focused on documenting and disseminating not only Salem's existing colonial architecture but also that which was lost; he also advertised his views of "sketches made years ago of buildings long since destroyed," a hint of a preservation concern that would become increasingly central to his photographic work.

Cousins and his contemporaries, who were engaged in highlighting a glorious past through one means or another, were motivated by national forces as well as those discreet to Salem, a dynamic city that was losing historical fabric with each passing year. Their pride in Old Salem was partially an expression of their concerns about the city in which they lived: no longer a romantic seaport inhabited almost exclusively by Protestant Anglo-Americans but, rather, a bustling and noisy manufacturing center with an increasingly "foreign" population. In one of the most comprehensive local histories and surveys of the era, the Reverend George Batchelor expressed this perception of old versus new not only quite dramatically but also with a lack of sentimentality that characterized the observations of some of his fellow Salem observers. For Batchelor, the "Old Salem is gone. The men, the commerce, the Puritan spirit, the high-bred courtesy, the stately ways, the great men and women with strong local attachments—these are gone" but "a new Salem is rising. . . . The shores are now deserted by commerce, and the shaded lanes of the old time are now the paved and lighted highways through which begins to move, with increasing energy, the business which is to repair and rebuild the fallen fortunes of the city. Home industries, domestic commerce, manufactures, science, literature, music, art and education are now restoring the vanishing wealth, renewing the ancient renown, and making the city a center of enterprises which are already enriching the national life." Look to the future, urged Batchelor, while remembering the past and engaging with the present: "The people of Salem are proud of their ancestry and history, and a diligent band of local antiquarians is working out the story of the past, with results of more than local fame. But the city is entering upon a new career and may become as notable for its achievements in the years to come as it was justly famous in the past."[8]

Batchelor was a bit of a Salem outsider: he was not a native and presided over the Barton Square Unitarian Church for a mere sixteen years before moving on to another appointment. This explains his perspective and ability to push the "old time" and its families slightly off the center stage. Though he was born in Salem, Cousins did not descend from one of those old mercantile families who sent their third-generation sons to Harvard quite religiously. Instead, he came from another sort of trade altogether and did not attend university at all. His photographic and antiquarian activities enhanced his national and local reputations simultaneously, over the 1890s, and he appears more frequently in the *Bulletins* of the Essex Institute, giving talks and "imaginary" walking tours in the company of the scions of all those Old Salem families. At the same time, he needed to make his new occupation profitable, so he established the Frank Cousins Art Company to publish, copyright, and market his photographs and began to cultivate his reputation in both trade and preservation circles. The transition from general retailer to photographer, publisher, and, eventually, author was not a smooth one: Cousins experienced both financial and legal difficulties but still managed to expand his presence in both architectural and preservation circles.[9]

In 1912, Doubleday Page and Company published *Colonial Architecture Series 1: Fifty Salem Doorways*, a portfolio of Cousins's prints of Salem doorways with an introduction by Glenn Brown, Secretary of the American Institute of Architects. The book received glowing reviews from every contemporary periodical, general or trade, with the *Journal of the American Institute of Architects* opining that "there could be no more valuable work on Colonial Architecture for an architect to have on his shelves."[10] In the following year, Cousins was commissioned by the Art Commission of the City of New York to photograph fifty endangered buildings of historical and architectural interest in a notable illustration of what the *New York Times* called "preservation by camera."[11] Thereafter, he extended his range to other cities and towns with significant inventories of colonial architecture, including Philadelphia, Baltimore, and Annapolis.

A month after Cousins's work was highlighted in the *New York Times*, his native city very nearly burned to the ground: the Great Salem Fire of June 25, 1914, destroyed about a third of the urban center, engulfing 253 acres, 3,150 houses, and 50 factories. Over eighteen thousand people were displaced, and at least half of that number lost their jobs. The Salem fire was one of the last of the great urban fires that devastated downtowns in the second half of the nineteenth and first few decades of the twentieth centuries, including Portland, Maine (1866), Chicago (1871), Boston (1872), Baltimore (1904), San Francisco (1906), Chelsea, Massachusetts (1908), and Atlanta (1917), all ample evidence that the perceived vulnerability (and consequential increased value) of surviving colonial structures was a result of more than intentional urban growth.[12]

Salem made national headlines for weeks in the summer of 1914 due to the extensive damage and displacement, some rather exuberant "disaster tourism" (the *Boston Globe*'s day-after headline was "Sightseers Stampede to Stricken City"), and its status as a shrine of antiquity. While some of the initial stories reported that landmarks like Hawthorne's birthplace and the newly restored House of the Seven Gables were burned, later reports correctly identified the fire's path as jumping from industrial section to industrial section via Lafayette Street, Salem's major southern thoroughfare, the site of much residential construction in the late nineteenth century. With a few notable exceptions, the fire skirted the older colonial sections of the city in the east, west, and center and took out quarters of "modern" (Victorian) homes as well as the "tinderbox tenements" adjacent to the factory of Salem's largest employer, the Naumkeag Steam Cotton Company. Over the summer of 1914, there emerged a striking divergence in the coverage of the fire's aftermath, with newspapers focused on the refugee camp, relief efforts, and rebuilding plans and architectural, household, and arts publications reassuring their readers that much of the colonial city survived. *The Bulletin of the Society for the Preservation of New England Antiquities* opined that "from an antiquarian point of view, the fire could scarcely have behaved better if it had tried. It may even be that the fire will inadvertently protect the remainder of the town, for if the burned district is rebuilt of less combustible material, as now seems likely, Salem will be much less of a fire risk in the future than it was in the past."[13]

The fire focused attention on what survived in Salem, its remains and relics, as well as on its rebuilding, thus linking the colonial and the Colonial Revival explicitly. This was very much the approach of Frank Cousins's fellow antiquarian author-photographer, Mary Harrod Northend. Cousins and Northend were exact contemporaries who built their careers on showcasing Salem, before and after the fire. Northend published her first book, *Colonial Homes and Their Furnishings*, in 1912, the same year as Cousins's *Fifty Salem Doorways* appeared, but she had been publishing articles in household and women's magazines for a decade. Over her career, she published twelve books and hundreds of magazine articles, on everything from andirons to breadcrumbs to wallpaper. In 1914 alone, she sold over 150 articles and employed a stenographer, several file clerks, and a full-time photographer, enabling her to illustrate her own works as well as those of other authors. She had started out ten years earlier, with her own camera and a few sporadic submissions to random publications: now she was almost an industry unto herself. While Cousins restricted himself to the realm of architecture, with publications on colonial buildings in Salem and Philadelphia and the first work on Samuel McIntire written in collaboration with fellow photographer Phil M. Riley, Northend expanded her range into the popular field of "domestic advice," incorporating interior design, entertaining, and household management.

Despite their national exposure, both Northend and Cousins remained tethered to Salem, and clearly inspired by their mutual mission to preserve, highlight, and revive the colonial style in the postfire landscape of their native city. Cousins and Riley concluded their *Colonial Architecture of Salem* (1919) with a chapter on "Salem Architecture To-Day," surveying the rebuilding efforts and observing optimistically that "it is of the utmost significance that most of the new buildings display colonial motives and that nearly all of the residences of the moment are purely colonial in design. Not since 1818 and the advent of the illogical Greek Revival have colonial houses to any considerable number and worthy of the name been erected in Salem, and the present general reversion to them after an interval of a century indicates conclusively the power of persistence of the colonial tradition."[14] Northend expressed similar sentiments in her important article "Worthwhile Houses in Salem Built Since the Conflagration of June 1914," published the following year in *The House Beautiful*, but her conceptions of "colonial" were a bit more flexible than Cousins's, adapted by and for her larger audience.[15]

While both were identified as colonial "experts" in myriad periodicals, Cousins and Northend represent two strands of the traditional aesthetic: one focused primarily on architecture, another on its broader commercial appeal. Cousins's major postfire project was the first comprehensive and illustrated book on Salem's major Federal architect, *The Wood-Carver of Salem: Samuel McIntire, His Life and Work*, published in 1916.[16] It introduced McIntire to a larger audience of architects and (particularly) collectors than existed before, with major consequences for Salem. There could never be enough McIntire to go around, however, and Northend's colonial advocacy was more accessible and egalitarian. Her whole career was based on accessibility, that is, access granted to her by friends and family, in Salem and beyond, to their houses, gardens, and collections. She acknowledged this accessibility in each of her books and clearly wanted to share her access with her readers, exposing them to the comfortable and tasteful atmosphere created by the architecture and furnishings from the past. How fortunate the reader was to see and learn about "family bits, wonderful old Lowestoft, and other treasures. . . . All brought over in the holds of cumbersome ships, at the time when the commerce of Salem was at high tide."[17] This was a common characterization: the treasures of the seaport towns, with their ladies getting first dibs on everything that came from the exotic East. Her predecessor in cultivating and collecting the requisite objects for the colonial home, Alice Morse Earle, envisioned it in detail, but, as Mary descended from two old maritime families in Salem and Newburyport, she could speak from experience.

Northend's approach to architecture and interior design was personal, instructive, and inviting. As the title of one of her most popular books, *We Visit Old Inns*, indicates, the reader is along for the ride everywhere Miss Northend goes, entering and observing with her. As her audience expanded, Northend became more flexible with her advice, both in her books and, especially, in her many magazine articles: colonial was still the standard, but accommodations had to be made for radiators, bathrooms, comfortable furniture, and glass doors. The automobile made a countless number of New England farmhouses perfect candidates for remodeling as summer homes, which became the entire premise of her 1915 book *Remodeled Farmhouses*. Although there was as much emphasis on interiors and objects as in architecture, there were more options for Northend's copyrighted photographs than those of Cousins, and she expanded her product line by offering wistful hand-painted Wallace

Nutting–esque prints as well. Northend photographs appear in building trade catalogs from the teens and twenties as well as the occasional quote from the expert herself. The 1920s woodwork catalogs published by the Curtis Companies featured excerpts from Northend's 1920 pamphlet titled, *Door Lore*, also published by Curtis. Such a partnership benefited both parties and reflected an era in which, in Northend's words, "we are constantly coming across new ideas through a careful study of both old and new architecture or the combining of the two."[18]

Cousins and Northend were projecting images of Salem outward, while other antiquarian advocates were drawing people to Old Salem (rather than to the "Witch City"). For Caroline Osgood Emmerton, who founded the House of the Seven Gables Settlement Association, in 1908, with a dual mission of preservation and assimilation of Salem's émigré communities, and George Francis Dow, the Essex Institute curator and a pioneer in historical interpretation through "living history," the medium was wood and the material, rather than paper and the visual. Inspired by the enduring appeal of Hawthorne and, perhaps, some disappointment in the fact that Concord stole away some of Salem's limelight during the centennial of his birth in 1904, Emmerton purchased the Turner-Ingersoll mansion, generally believed to be the inspiration for Hawthorne's novel, and commissioned its restoration under the direction of Boston preservation architect Joseph Everett Chandler. Architectural historians remain frustrated by Chandler's lack of documentation of the process, which he later called a "picturesque adaptation": essentially the existing house was transformed into the novel house, with the addition of four gables and a Cent Shop and the rebuilding of a central chimney along with an adjacent "secret staircase," which proved immensely popular once the house was opened as a museum in 1910. Emmerton's dual mission of showcasing Hawthorne/Old Salem and establishing a continuous revenue stream to support her settlement work in the (then largely Polish) neighborhood appeared successful, and, over the next decades, she created a new/old Gables neighborhood by purchasing two additional endangered seventeenth-century houses in Salem, the Hooper-Hathaway House on Washington Street and the Retire Becket House on Becket Street, moving them to the Gables's vicinity, and commissioning Chandler to return them to their postmedieval appearance. Looking back on her ongoing efforts from the vantage point of 1935, it was clear to Emmerton that "the historical and literary associations of the old houses must surely help in making American citizens of our boys and girls."[19]

The House of the Seven Gables received an *American* response when it opened in 1910, and it became clear that it had established landmark status on a national level only four years later at the time of the Salem fire, when newspapers across the country reported that it might be lost and then that it was saved. The same was true for the Essex Institute, long known to be a treasure house but more recently as the home of Dow's innovative 1907 "period rooms": three glass-encased rooms, a colonial kitchen and ca. 1800 parlor and bedroom, furnished with antique furniture and "objects of the everyday" to enhance their projection of daily life in Old Salem. These rooms were open on one side, so museum visitors could get close and almost touch their material representation of the past. Dow went further, anticipating and no doubt influencing Caroline Emmerton's museum neighborhood at the House of the Seven Gables: he removed a vulnerable seventeenth-century house a block away to the rear of the Essex Institute and restored it to a semblance of its original appearance, installed period and deemed-appropriate furnishings, and opened it to the public as the nation's first museum house, complete with costumed tour guides. Over the next decade, Northend's photograph of the John Ward House and its attendant guides appeared in an array of publications, both trade and general.

Salem's colonial revival was literal, material, and commercial, all at the same time. Both the House of the Seven Gables and the Essex Institute published postcards of their period rooms and grounds as soon as they were completed and relied on the antiquarian infrastructure of Salem to disseminate the images and narratives as well. A synergy developed before the Salem fire and intensified afterward. Dow's impact on the museum world was manifest in succeeding decades as the Metropolitan Museum of Art installed fifteen period rooms in its new American Wing in 1924, and the Philadelphia Museum of Art (1928), Museum of Fine Arts, Boston (1928), Brooklyn Museum of Art (1929) and St. Louis Museum of Art (1930–1931) followed suit. He expanded his range from restoration to re-creation, fueled by a primary interest in traditional craftsmanship, when he planned and oversaw the construction of an entire "Pioneers' Village" in Salem's Forest River Park for the Massachusetts Tercentenary in 1930. The Village, "a reproduction of the settlement in the wilderness that was Salem in 1630," was supposed to be a temporary commemorative installation, but it endured as a seasonal attraction into the late twentieth century, among the first of a succession of outdoor "living history" museums opened up across the country from Henry Ford's Greenfield Village in 1929 to Colonial Williamsburg in 1932 and Plimoth Plantation in 1957. The impact of Dow's work both on the interior and on the exterior curated spaces "lies in the fact that at the Essex Institute the two new methods of architectural display, period room and outdoor museum, were introduced into the mainstream of American museology at the same time."[20]

Dow, in conjunction with Emmerton, Northend, and Cousins, had an impact on the commercial production of "colonial" material culture as well.

The John Ward House in Mary Harrod Northend's *Historic Doorways of Old Salem* (1926). *(Photograph by Mary Harrod Northend.)*

Before period rooms were installed in museums up and down the Eastern Seaboard and beyond, they appeared in the Daniel Low and Company store in Salem: a New England kitchen and living room and a colonial dining room, all designed to display their reproduction wares. Low died in 1911, and his son Seth, perhaps an even more passionate aficionado of the colonial style and spirit, succeeded him. The period rooms were intended to draw people to the Low store (especially, the well-heeled families who maintained summer cottages on the North Shore), but the company was expanding its national mail-order business continually, and many of the objects therein could be shipped across the country, along with all those witch spoons. This was an age in which the colonial could be commodified in myriad ways: even Dow approved of reproductions to facilitate the aesthetic of his curated spaces.

The projected images of Cousins and Northend combined with the physical manifestation of Nathaniel Hawthorne's romantic vision in the restored House of the Seven Gables created a demand for Salem *things* and the market responded: in the twenties and thirties a steady supply of Salem rockers, Salem chests, and Salem mantels, moldings, and doors were reproduced by national wood manufacturers, Pittsburgh paints featured a "Salem yellow" and entire lines of furniture could be purchased in an "Old Salem" maple stain. At least two major furniture manufacturers, Karpen and Danersk, produced Salem collections: the former advertised its pieces in national periodicals in a beautiful vignette illustration of the "Salem Room" by artist Edgar W. Jenney in 1928, the same year that Salem period rooms were being installed in the Museum of Fine Arts, Boston, and the Philadelphia Museum of Art.

The commodification of material culture can be a form of emulation, but it can also lead to loss and dislocation. The progression of period rooms was at odds with another movement in the second quarter of the twentieth century: historic preservation. The Metropolitan Museum of Art was particularly voracious in its quest for material for its new American Wing and clashed with the Society for the Preservation of New England Antiquities over its purchase of the Wentworth-Gardner House in Portsmouth, New Hampshire, from Wallace Nutting and plans to dismantle the entire structure for installation in the museum, prompting the Society for the Preservation of New England Antiquities founder William Sumner Appleton to sound the alarm. Appleton asserted that period rooms "brought a new element of danger to our finest houses." While he could approve removing details from an endangered house, "where museum trustees are open to criticism, is in their efforts, sometimes unfortunately successful, to take from buildings still standing intact, and capable of being preserved."[21] The Metropolitan backed off, claiming only two rooms of the Wentworth-Gardner House, but as Appleton feared, this was just the beginning of a "tendency." A decade later, at the Boston auction house, Benjamin Flayderman held an unrestricted auction that included "a complete Samuel McIntire room removed from the Putnam-Hanson House in Salem. Paneling, mantel, doors, windows, etc. are included," in what was proclaimed to be "one of the most important pieces of its kind ever offered at public sale."[22] This McIntire room in what was commonly known as "Frye's Tavern," a structure that was not endangered and still stands, became the "Salem Room" of the City Art Museum in St. Louis, now the St. Louis Art Museum.

By 1930, Salem's association with the colonial "spirit" seems well established, so much so that a visit to Old Salem was not even necessary. The Pequot House, yet another seventeenth-century re-creation for the Massachusetts Tercentenary that year, evoked the colonial past "in spirit, if not in actual construction" in the opinion of Samuel Chamberlain, Frank Cousins's successor in capturing Salem on camera. Those who were intent on living in a Salem colonial could reproduce this reproduction: for the George Washington Bicentennial of 1932, the *Ladies Home Journal* adapted the Pequot House plans for purchase, advertising it as a "revival of the fittest" and the New York department store Arnold Constable installed a Samuel McIntire room as the highlight of its "Colonial Exhibition." In the following year, Chicago's "Century of Progress" Exposition opened, with a theme of technological innovation and a grand exhibit of "Homes of Tomorrow." An estimated thirty-nine million people visited the Chicago exposition over its duration, in the midst of the Great Depression, to see visions of the future but also structures from the past in a "Colonial Village" of reproduction landmarks from the thirteen colonies. In the midst of this Chicago setting was not *the* but rather *a* House of the Seven Gables, appropriately situated right next to a Paul Revere House and liberated from its original location's views of "a great textile mill visible off the starboard bow and a coal bunker to port."[23]

Postcard of the Reproduction of the House of the Seven Gables in the Colonial Village of the Chicago Century of Progress Exposition, 1933–1934. *(Curt Teich Postcard Archives Digital Collection, Newberry Library.)*

NOTES

1. Edwin M. Bacon, *Historic Pilgrimages in New England: Among Landmarks of Pilgrim and Puritan Days and of the Provincial and Revolutionary Periods* (Silver, Burdett, 1898); Claude Fayette Bragdon, "Six Hours in Salem," *American Architect* 39 (January 21, 1893), 41–43; Henry James, *The American Scene* (Harper Brothers, 1907), 257–258.

2. Karal Ann Marling first utilized the term "revivals" in *George Washington Slept Here: Colonial Revivals in American Culture, 1876–1986* (Harvard University Press, 1988); for more on pastoral expressions of colonial revival culture in New England, see Sarah L. Giffen and Kevin D. Murphy, eds., *"A Noble and Dignified Stream": The Piscataqua Region in the Colonial Revival, 1860–1930* (Old York Historical Society, 1992) and Michael C. Batinski, *Pastkeepers in a Small Place: Five Centuries in Deerfield, Massachusetts* (University of Massachusetts Press, 2004).

3. Anne Farnam, "George Francis Dow: A Career of Bringing the 'Picturesque Traditions of Sleeping Generations' to Life in the Early Twentieth Century," *Essex Institute Historical Collections* 121, no. 2 (April 1985), 58.

4. Arthur Little, *Early New England Interiors: Sketches in Salem, Marblehead, Portsmouth and Kittery* (A. Williams, 1878); Donald Albrecht, *The American Style: Colonial Revival and the Modern Metropolis* (Museum of the City of New York, 2011); William Rotch Ware, *The Georgian Period: A Collection of Papers Dealing with "Colonial" or 18 Century Architecture in the United States, Together with References to Earlier Provincial and True Colonial Work* in *American Architect*, 1898–1902.

5. *Report of the Massachusetts Commissioner to the Centennial Exhibition at Philadelphia* (A. J. Wright, 1877), 31; *Frank Leslie's Illustrated Newspaper*, January 22, 1876, 325. The centennial album was made up of photographs taken by J. W. Moulton and J. S. Moulton, photographers of Salem.

6. *Report of the Massachusetts Board of World's Fair Managers* (Wright and Potter Printing Co., State Printers, 1893), 24.

7. *Putnam's Monthly Historical Magazine* 2 (September 1893–August 1894), n194, n280, n384.

8. Duane Hamilton Hurd, ed., *History of Essex County, Massachusetts, with Biographical Sketches of Many of Its Pioneers and Prominent Men* (J. W. Lewis, 1888), 11.

9. Cousins had serious financial difficulties after 1900, including the failure of his dry goods store, the Bee-Hive, after which he declared bankruptcy. Frank Cousins Art Co. appears to have been reasonably successful, but he initiated another publishing venture that led to financial losses and was compelled to take a job with the Post Office in Boston as a stamp agent. In July 1907, he was arrested for embezzlement of $4,725 of Post Office funds. He confessed to five counts of embezzlement and made restitution. *Boston Globe*, July 27, 1907.

10. Frank Cousins, *Colonial Architecture: Series I—Fifty Salem Doorways* (Doubleday Page & Co., 1912); *Journal of the American Institute of Architects* 1, no. 2 (1918), 107.

11. "The Camera to Preserve New York's Old Buildings," *New York Times*, May 10, 1914.

12. For numbers, context, and consequences of the Great Salem Fire, see Jacob Remes, *Disaster Citizenship: Survivors, Solidarity, and Power in the Progressive Era* (University of Illinois Press, 2015).

13. *The Bulletin of the Society for the Preservation of New England Antiquities* 5, no. 2 (December 1914), 16.

14. Frank Cousins and Phil. M. Riley, *The Colonial Architecture of Salem* (Little, Brown, 1919), 237.

15. Mary Harrod Northend, "Worthwhile Houses in Salem Built Since the Conflagration of 1914," *The House Beautiful* 48, no. 111 (September 1920), 193–196.

16. Frank Cousins and Phil M. Riley, *The Wood-Carver of Salem. Samuel McIntire, His Life and Work* (Little, Brown & Company, 1916). While *The Wood-Carver of Salem* met with success, Cousins's fellow antiquarians at the Essex Institute desired a more academic study of Salem's great architect and commissioned the pioneering architectural historian and museum director Fiske Kimball to research and write *Mr. Samuel McIntire, Carver: The Architect of Salem*, which was published in 1940 by the Southworth-Anthoenson Press for the Institute. See Hugh Howard, *Dr. Kimball and Mr. Jefferson: Rediscovering the Founding Fathers of American Architecture* (Bloomsbury USA, 2006).

17. Mary Harrod Northend, *Colonial Homes and Their Furnishings* (Little, Brown, 1912), vii.

18. Mary Harrod Northend, *We Visit Old Inns* (Small, Maynard & Co., 1925); *Remodeled Farmhouses* (Little, Brown & Co., 1915); *Door Lore* (Curtis Services Bureau, 1920), 15.

19. Caroline O. Emmerton, *The Chronicles of Three Old Houses* (Thomas Todd Company, Printers,1935).

20. Edward N. Kaufman, "The Architectural Museum from World's Fair to Restoration Village," *Assemblage* 9 (June 1989), 29.

21. William Sumner Appleton, "Destruction and Preservation of Old Buildings in New England," *Art and Archaeology* 13, no. 3 (May–June 1919), 170–171.

22. *Art News* 29, no. 27 (April 4, 1931), 26.

23. Samuel Chamberlain, *Open House in New England* (Stephen Daye, 1937), 17–18; *Ladies' Home Journal House Pattern Service* (1932); Thomas E. Tallmadge, *The Colonial Village: A Reproduction of Early American Life in the Thirteen Colonies—A Guide to the Buildings of Historical Interest* (Century of Progress International Exposition, 1934); "Pilgrimage," *New York Times*, August 16, 1937.

INTERLUDE 10

Suffrage Success

The Election of 1879

Donna A. Seger

As was the case in many communities in Massachusetts and elsewhere, the movement for women's suffrage in Salem emerged before the Civil War but picked up considerable steam afterward. The suffrage struggle was intertwined with antislavery and anti-segregation initiatives prior to 1861 and characterized by an equality of gender participation. Charles Lenox Remond, the scion of Salem's most prominent African American family and agent of the American Anti-Slavery Society, famously protested the exclusion of women at the 1840 World Anti-Slavery Convention in London, and an 1850 petition "to confer upon women the Elective Franchise on Equal Terms with men" to the Massachusetts legislature features the signatures of Salem men ("legal voters") and women ("non-voters") in equal number.[1] That same year, Salem sent several representatives to the National Woman's Rights Convention in Worcester, an event that was organized by Lucy Stone and other associates of the Anti-Slavery Society with both Sojourner Truth and Frederick Douglass in attendance.[2]

Similar conventions were held until after the Civil War and the division of the suffrage movement over the enfranchisement of African American men by the Fifteenth Amendment in 1869–1870. The National Woman Suffrage Association, under the leadership of Susan B. Anthony and Elizabeth Cady Stanton, opposed the enfranchisement of Black men before women had achieved the vote while the American Woman Suffrage Association, formed by Lucy Stone, Julia Ward Howe, and others, favored a more incremental approach to suffrage with the enfranchisement of Black men as a first step.[3] Supporters of suffrage in Salem, both women and men, were firmly in the camp of the American Woman

Suffrage Association, which also influenced the formation of regional, state, and local associations. No records for the Salem Woman Suffrage Club exist, but both its meetings and the annual conventions of the Massachusetts Woman Suffrage Association are recorded in Stone's weekly newspaper, the *Woman's Journal*. In its coverage of an 1874 meeting by the former at the Salem Lyceum, with Stone in attendance and fabulous food and flowers on the tables, the *Woman's Journal* opined that "Other Clubs may take a lesson from this of Salem, which draws members by pleasant means—clergymen, lawyers, judges, editors, and not least in evidence, women. What remains to do now is the steady and continuous circulation of tracts, as a means of enlightenment, and with the light will come the end."[4]

One path toward the "light" was provided by the "school suffrage" initiatives implemented in many states, beginning with Kentucky in 1838. In 1879, the Massachusetts legislature passed a school suffrage bill, granting women in the commonwealth the right to run and vote in local school committee elections.[5] What seems like a progressive development was more likely an expression of the traditional "separate sphere" belief that education matters were safely within the realm of female expertise more than any desire to move toward universal suffrage on the part of Massachusetts legislators.[6] Nevertheless, Salem women offered up four female candidates and really turned out at the polls in December 1879, resulting in all four women being elected to the Salem School Board, the highest number in Massachusetts. With the headline of "Women on the School Committee in Salem," the *Boston Globe* observed that "the school board, with its lady members, seems to be in a good position to manage matters judiciously."[7]

Salem's election might have featured new voters, but these voters elected women who were experienced leaders. The four new "lady members" of the committee were Mrs. Mary G. Ward of Federal Street, a noted advocate for suffrage and temperance in the city, Dr. Sarah E. Sherman, Salem's first female physician, Emma B. Lowd, who was very active in veterans' affairs as an officer in the National Woman's Relief Corps Committee, and Mrs. Lurana Bigelow Almy, the wife and business partner of James. F. Almy, the founder of Salem's famed department store Almy, Bigelow, and Washburn. Unfortunately, Lurana Almy died before she could take up her seat on the committee, but the other three women served for several years, paving the way for more committee women.

Salem's first female school committee members do not represent a broad spectrum of society certainly, but their lives and endeavors (and, indeed, election) do illustrate how the cause of suffrage continued to be intertwined with other reform and social movements. Temperance had been a popular cause in Salem for decades (a statue of the famed "apostle of abstinence," the Irish priest Father Theobold Mathew, was erected after his visit to Salem in 1849, and it still occupies a prominent space in the downtown) with considerable connections to the suffrage cause. Mary Ward must have benefited from her regular attendance at "Prohibitory" conventions, and she was also active in state and national Baptist associations. Dr. Sherman was active in both public health committees and the women's club movement on the North Shore, and Emma Lowd's work for veterans was focused as much on advocating for local soldiers' homes as serving on national committees. They were all busy women, committed to multiple causes at the same time.[8]

The election of 1879 seems inspirational, but appearances can be deceiving. It prompted Massachusetts suffragists to begin advocating for an extension of school suffrage to *municipal* suffrage and a committee of Salem suffragists to submit a petition to the U.S. Congress in support of a constitutional amendment then pending.[9] As with the earlier state petition, there were two columns of signatures: those of male legal voters in one and disenfranchised women in another. Many of the names, of both women and men, seem familiar: they were citizens active in myriad movements. Their petition that "the right of citizens of the United States to vote shall not be denied or abridged by the United States or by any state on account of sex, or for any reason not equally applicable to all citizens of the United States" was not successful in 1880 (or for forty years afterward), and the cause of suffrage in Massachusetts seemed not only to stall after that date but actually to regress. During this time, the suffrage movement experienced a generational shift of leadership, most dramatically realized by the death of Lucy Stone in 1893, and Salem suffragists eventually reorganized their Woman Suffrage Club into the Salem Equal Suffrage League. Most significantly, two major suffrage referenda defeats occurred in 1895 and 1915, accompanied by the rise of a countermovement in the form of the Massachusetts Association Opposed to the Further Extension of Suffrage to Women, with a Salem branch headed by Anna L. Warner and Ellen B. Laight.[10] The 1895 referendum was nonbinding and restricted to municipal suffrage, but nevertheless there was robust campaigning by both sides. With universal suffrage on the ballot in 1915, the stakes were much higher and the advocacy even more intense.

Massachusetts antisuffragists were committed to the cause of the "separate sphere," and they disseminated their views in a variety of publications, including *The Remonstrance*, titled for their mission of supporting remonstrances or protests against "the imposition of any further political duties upon women." They grounded their opposition to worldly suffrage in the defense of the home, which was "more than a dwelling; it was inviolable, immune from the evils of the world, and infused with feminine virtues."[11] In Salem, contention between the "antis" and the "suffs" did not generate many headlines, and genteel ladies on both sides were neighbors on Chestnut Street. Boston and Cambridge were more competitive settings, with antisuffragists "shops" for the dissemination of leaflets, pamphlets, posters, and red roses (the symbol of the movement, or countermovement) as well as (very planned and orderly) lectures and rallies. While the Massachusetts Anti-Suffrage Association claimed that it had branch organizations in all but thirty towns in the state on the eve of the vote on the 1915 amendment, the Boston-area ladies led the charge and made the headlines. They organized a "silent protest" to the long-planned and well-attended suffragist parade on October 16 in Boston, colored by the sale of red roses to offset suffragist yellow, which the *Boston Daily Globe* deemed "effectively pictorial."[12]

Both the Salem Equal Justice League and its rival organization were active in the weeks before the election on November 7. Each group canvassed the city with the suffragists claiming a "large number" for their cause and the antisuffragists identifying the more precise number of 450 women in their camp.[13] Apparently the antis were "less aggressive" in their endeavors, or at least less public, while the Salem suffragists held open-air rallies and raised considerable funds for the statewide campaign in support of the referendum. Despite their efforts, they faced the headline "Suffrage Badly Beaten" the next day as both Massachusetts and Salem men voted against universal suffrage by a wide margin.[14] Later that month, Massachusetts suffragist leaders announced their intentions to forsake further state campaigns in favor of a national effort to amend the U.S. Constitution, which was successful just five years later. Massachusetts became the eighth state to ratify the Nineteenth Amendment on June 25, 1919, and it became law in the summer of 1920. When women started registering for the vote shortly thereafter, one "new" Salem voter made national headlines: Almira C. Griswold, a ninety-two-year-old woman who was "easily the oldest woman registered among the nearly 1000 woman who had their names placed on the voting lists" in early September 1920.[15]

NOTES

1. For more on Remond's actions here, see Dorothy Burnett Porter, "The Remonds of Salem, Massachusetts: A Nineteenth-Century Family Revisited," *Proceedings of the American Antiquarian Society* 85 (1985), 276; Digital Archive of Massachusetts Anti-Slavery and Anti-Segregation Petitions, Massachusetts Archives, Boston, MA, 2015, "House Unpassed Legislation 1850, Docket 2577, SC1/series 230, Petition of Eliza J. Kenny," Harvard Dataverse, V5, available at https://doi.org/10.7910/DVN/FNFVV, accessed January 29, 2024.

2. *Proceedings of the Woman's Rights Convention, Held at Worcester, October 23d and 24th, 1850* (Prentiss and Sawyer, 1851), NAWSA Collection, Rare Book and Special Collections Division, Library of Congress, Washington, DC.

3. Ellen Carol Dubois's classic work remains essential for understanding these different organizations: see *Feminism and Suffrage: The Emergence of an Independent Women's Movement in America, 1848–1869* (Cornell University Press, 1978). For more on the suffrage

movement in general, see "Interchange: Women's Suffrage, the Nineteenth Amendment, and the Right to Vote," *Journal of American History* 106, no. 3 (December 2019), 662–694.

4. *Woman's Journal* 5, no. 16 (April 18, 1874), 128.

5. Seventeen states had passed school suffrage laws by 1880. For more context, see Carolyn M. Moehling and Melissa A. Thomasson, "Votes for Women: and Economic Perspective on Women's Enfranchisement," *Journal of Economic Perspectives* 34, no. 2 (Spring 2020), 3–23.

6. Glenda Elizabeth Gilmore, *Who Were the Progressives?* (Bedford/St. Martin's, 2002), 13–14.

7. *Boston Daily Globe*, December 14, 1879, 8.

8. Dr. Sarah E. Sherman became the first female president of a professional medical association, the Massachusetts Surgical and Gynecological Society, in 1893, and the first female trustee of Boston University in the same decade.

9. Petition from the Citizens of Massachusetts in Support of Woman's Suffrage, May 26, 1880: petitions and memorials, resolutions of state legislatures, and related documents that were referred to the committee on the judiciary during the Forty-Sixth Congress (SEN46A-H11.2), Committee Papers, 1816–2011, Records of the U.S. Senate, Record Group 46, National Archives Building, Washington, DC, online version available at https://www.docsteach.org/documents/document/petition-massachusetts-suffrage, accessed January 29, 2024.

10. An earlier Massachusetts antisuffrage committee had formed in 1882, in response to the 1879 election. The association eventually changed its name to the Women's Anti-Suffrage Association of Massachusetts.

11. Louise L. Stevenson, "Woman Anti-Suffragists in the 1915 Massachusetts Campaign," *New England Quarterly* 52, no. 1 (March 1979), 5.

12. *Boston Daily Globe*, October 31, 1915.

13. *Boston Daily Globe*, October 12, 1915.

14. *Boston Daily Globe*, November 3, 1915.

15. *Boston Daily Globe*, September 11, 1920.

THE FOURTH CENTURY

1926–2026

Salem's residents at the dawn of this fourth century clearly recognized that the city had experienced a jarring series of transformations, and they used the city's tercentenary celebrations to reflect on many of those changes and to welcome visitors (a new ceremonial arch originally "greeted" guests, but it was remodeled to "welcome" them, instead). In ways that both hearkened back to the city's past and foreshadowed its future, Salemites celebrated their city's three hundred years of history with a host of events between July 3 and July 10, 1926: from a one-hundred-foot-high bonfire on July 4 and a tremendous fireworks display launched from Gallows Hill to a "Grotesque, Antiques, and Horribles" parade of costumed schoolchildren, a "great" parade (attended by the vice president), as well as a "Floral and Historical" parade to historic house tours and history lectures. Many gatherings of different groups, representing the full diversity of Salem's community, celebrated the tercentenary. This celebration's combination of history, scary costumes, and spectacle would characterize much of the city's fourth century.[1]

After 1920, Salem was no longer one of the nation's largest cities, and it might have seemed fated to fade into relative oblivion as just another small city defined by its subordinate relationship to a larger city that dominated the region's media market and economy. To be honest, in many ways, that *is* an accurate description of contemporary Salem. The region's pro sports teams, after all, are all located in Salem's one-time rival, Boston (or Foxboro), and Salem's train station's platforms fill each morning with lawyers, businesspeople, students, and service industry workers ready for their twenty-five-minute commute to

Boston's North Station. Salem, however, has never been defined primarily by its proximity to Boston. It still isn't.

Much of the contemporary city itself might not be recognizable to Salem's residents of a century ago. The thriving downtown of 1926, complete with anchor department stores, multiple haberdasheries, and a wide variety of other merchants who provided the essentials for daily life is now dominated by a world-class art museum (Peabody Essex Museum), the country's first national historic site (Salem Maritime National Historic Site), restaurants offering a wide range of ethnic cuisines, and shops that cater to seasonal tourists with an interest in witches, pirates, ghosts, and the macabre. The Pequot Mills that dominated the French-Canadian La Pointe neighborhood and employed thousands now houses a charter school and some city offices and is surrounded by Spanish-speaking residents with connections to the Dominican Republic and Puerto Rico. The site once occupied by an armory for the National Guard now hosts a National Parks Service visitor center. The structure that once served as the home base for a national mail-order business is currently a high-end seafood place.

Salem has always drawn its power from its proximity to the sea. Its location has helped its residents accrue financial power, which, in turn, contributed to the city's cultural and political significance. The city's harbor has also, however, provided *actual* power. First, the sea (and its winds) carried Salem's people and goods across the world. Its enormous textile mill was a world leader in adopting first steam and then electric power. This electricity came from the enormous coal-fueled power plant that dominated the harbor for decades, transforming Columbian coal into Essex County's energy. That hulking coal power plant has now been replaced by a sleek natural gas facility. In the extra available space, Salem workers will assemble four-hundred-foot-high wind turbines to harvest the power in coastal winds and use it to fuel the next century of Salem's life and culture.

NOTE

1. Donna Seger, "The Salem Tercentenary, 1926," *Streets of Salem* (blog), January 7, 2024, available at https://streetsofsalem.com/2024/01/07/the-salem-tercentenary-1926/.

CHAPTER ELEVEN

From Fire to Wind

The Development and Redevelopment of Salem, 1914–2026

Donna A. Seger and Brad Austin

The twentieth century brought dynamic changes to Salem's land- and streetscapes, which continued into the twenty-first century. Salem Harbor provides a useful preview of these changes: no longer a global gateway at the turn of the twentieth century, reduced to a silted-up afterthought by train and car, it regained its importance over the century through the successive forces of tourism, environmentalism, and the search for alternative energy sources. The harbor cannot tell the whole story, however, as Salem did not simply transition from seaport to wind port; the nineteenth-century trends were all about the land and the challenges and opportunities brought on by industrialization, immigration, and new forms of transportation. Salem's residents also had to decide what they wanted to retain of their "old" city: a question that became more pressing after so much of it was swept away (or threatened) by the Great Salem Fire of 1914 and by urban renewal initiatives later in the century. Balancing the preservation of *what remained* with improvements and developments necessary to navigate the needs of Salem's changing population and economy was the challenge of the century.

Even before the rebuilding efforts after the fire mandated a more systematic approach to city planning, Salem's first Plans Commission had demanded it in its 1912 report. This is a very representative document of the Progressive Era, assertively calling for a master plan, or what the commissioners called an "Official City Plan," for Salem. To obtain their objective, they emphasized how dire the current situation was: Salem had no "tolerable entrance or exit," its traffic and housing congestion was "a growing menace to the health and welfare of the community," its major arteries were too narrow, its "decayed" waterfront was in need of "redemption" by a shoreline drive, its North River was a "stinking open sewer," it lacked a proper "zone system," and its outlying regions—such as the "Great Pastures" in South Salem—needed to be developed for residential use. Even when calling for dramatic changes, however, the report emphasized the importance of preserving Salem's "individuality": its crooked (*secondary*) streets, historic houses, old burying grounds, and fine old (but "fast-disappearing") trees "all have a charm and interest that is ever increasing and give to Salem an attraction that brings thousands in annual pilgrimage to our gates."[1]

The Great Fire of 1914

Before there could be any initiatives, much less immersion, in master planning, the Great Salem Fire of June 25, 1914, destroyed about a third of built Salem, encompassing 251 acres and more than thirty-two hundred structures along the western and southern thoroughfares of the city, including Broad and Lafayette Streets, the only two arteries that the plans commissioners actually admired. The fire wreaked havoc on the community and economy of Salem, "leaving 18,380 individuals homeless, jobless or both."[2]

As one of the last of the great urban fires of the era, the fire could have been predicted—and it was. When seeking to rebuild, Salem benefited from the experiences of recovery and rebuilding in other devastated cities as well as its own historical reputation. Widespread campaigns funded the recovery for what was seen as a city of national landmark status, and sighs of relief were expressed in print when it was revealed that the rumors of the destruction of Chestnut Street and the House of the Seven Gables were incorrect. Much of "Old Salem" was still standing, and now the "New Salem" would be built to more exacting standards and codes: no wooden roof shingles, no triple-deckers, the introduction of green spaces in La Pointe (present-day "the Point"), the destroyed neighborhood that served as the residential neighborhood for workers in Salem's adjacent textile mills and shoe factories. The architect Walter Kilham, who would later receive some significant rebuilding commissions, envisioned a new industrial city "more unique than ever" rising above the old harbor, constructed with careful planning, but he also issued Salem residents a directive: as their "quaint streets and ancient buildings, now doubly precious [and] the property of the nation" had been spared by a shift in the wind, they should safeguard them against a greater danger, namely, rampant and indistinct modernization.[3] There was an immediate mandate for planning and preservation, which impacted the redevelopment of the city for the next century.

The Rebuilding Commission, composed of five members appointed to three-year terms by the governor of Massachusetts in July 1914, promptly went about its business, and rebuilding began in the "burnt district" only weeks after the smoke cleared, under a new building code devised by the advisory architect Charles H. Blackhall. The commission's final report, issued in July 1917, described the fire as "a clean sweep but a chance for a fresh start" and disclosed that 828 residential structures had been rebuilt according to the new code, which was extended to the rest of the city. A new Saltonstall School on Lafayette Street replaced two lost grammar schools, and two new firehouses arose in the rebuilt district. Reflecting an understanding that "Salem was only one city and not two" as well as an appreciation for the 1912 Plans Commission recommendations, citywide improvements were also included in the report, including new sidewalks, widened streets, more green spaces, and the planting of more than a thousand trees.[4]

The rebuilding initiatives were "progressive" in terms of building and housing ordinances, but the zoning measures were limited by the necessity of bringing people back to Salem and putting them to work. The city's population was forty-seven thousand before the fire and dropped to thirty-seven thousand in the weeks afterward; by the time the commission's report was issued in 1917, the population had risen to forty-three thousand, in large part due to the rebuilding efforts of manufacturing facilities, with the largest employer in the area, the pioneering Naumkeag Steam Cotton Company, pledging to replace its twenty lost mill and storage buildings with an enlarged and electrified complex. It was back up and running by 1916, the same year that a new company, the Hygrade Incandescent Lamp Company (later GTE Sylvania) opened its headquarters in South Salem. And then there were all the tanneries and shoe factories, one of which was the site of the spark that lit the Great Salem Fire, and twenty of which were destroyed in the conflagration. In a special issue of the *Shoe and Leather Reporter* focusing on "the Great Leather and Shoe City" of Salem, issued in July 1917, these surviving and rebuilt establishments announced that they were back in business.[5] Salem *was* back in business, with improved thoroughfares but little delineation between residential and industrial districts, a feature of its twentieth-century landscape that would become more problematic as deindustrialization set in halfway through the century.

Federal funds were both not immediately forthcoming and limited in scope in the wake of the fire; recovery and rebuilding were funded primarily from state, private, and insurance sources. This would be the last time that the City would engage in substantive development without federal funds and/or mandates. From the onset of the Depression to that of urban renewal, an escalation of federal funds for public buildings, recreation facilities, and infrastructure altered the city center significantly. Salem's two largest federal projects of the 1930s—the construction of a new Salem Post Office in 1932 and the Salem Maritime National Historic Site in 1938—had significant but distinct impacts on their surrounding neighborhoods. While the post office project necessitated the destruction of more than fifty historic structures in one of Salem's oldest sections, Salem Maritime was "the first area of its type established under the important and far-reaching national policy for historic preservation embodied in an act of August 21, 1935 (49 Stat. 666)," and its process was focused more on restoration and relocation than removal.[6]

Salem's status as a commercial and retail center for its surrounding communities was untouched by fire, Depression, and war, but, by 1950, there were concerns that its continuous congestion was driving regional customers elsewhere. In this age of the encroaching car, the answer was to bury the train that still ran right down the city's key north-south avenue, Washington Street. The City had been gearing up for this project for some time, and Works Progress Administration (WPA) funds had been designated for a comprehensive plan, including the construction of a new tunnel and station to replace the pioneering 1839 tunnel and 1847 Gothic Revival depot, referred to as the "Old Castle." Despite this fond moniker, the gargantuan train station was not as beloved in its declining years as it would become, in hindsight, after it was gone.

Work on these projects was delayed until the early 1950s and continued for most of the decade, during which those in the downtown area experienced mud, dust, noise, rats, rickety crosswalks, and a rank odor due to the diversion of sewage into the North River. Between twenty-five and forty merchants shut their doors for good during the years of construction, and, because of delays, Salem's tunnel was completed at about the same time as the new Northshore Shopping Center next door in Peabody, a key factor in the continued decline of Salem's commercial reign. This decline was not the focus in 1959, however, when the dust cleared to reveal so much more room for cars, both in motion and parked, and only optimism was in the air. The *Boston Globe* declared, "Salem Business Booms Again," in an article that predicted even more modernization for the old city, and, indeed, that was the plan.[7]

The Battle over Renewal

The word "battle" is often utilized in narratives of Salem's experience with urban renewal, both when it was enjoined and afterward. Certainly, conflict was the case in other cities confronted by such comprehensive change, but, as the editor of the *Sunday Herald Traveler* magazine observed in his preview of one of several battle articles issued in the late 1960s, "Nowhere has the struggle been so prolonged and bitter or the stakes so high as in Salem."[8] In retrospect, it is easy to see how a plan focused on "clearance" would have seemed to be workable: there had been no notable resistance to the sweeping away of either fifty houses to make way for the new post office or the Gothic Revival depot to make way for a plaza/parking lot. Salem's first renewal plan, created after several studies and overseen by the new Salem Redevelopment Authority (SRA), did provoke a strong resistance, however, both local and national. The SRA was given sweeping jurisdictional powers over 38.5 acres of downtown Salem, which was both renamed the Heritage Plaza-East Urban Renewal Area and identified as both "decadent" and "blighted," rationalizing the agency's primary mission to "restore the Area to a well-planned, economically stable central business district."[9] Clearly, the great train tunnel project had not resulted in a stronger Salem, capable of withstanding not only the Northshore Shopping Center but also Route 128, a bypass for greater Boston that drew traffic away from the original seaport settlements of Massachusetts.[10]

To achieve its mission, the SRA possessed a tool kit that included the powers of conservation, rehabilitation, development, and demolition. When the detailed plan was rolled out in 1965–1966, however, it was clear that the overwhelming focus was on demolition. The SRA Executive Director John Barrett furnished Historic Salem Inc., a preservation organization founded twenty years before to save the seventeenth-century Jonathan Corwin House (or "Witch House") from a street-widening project, with a "Do-It-Yourself Walking Tour" of all the buildings in the area. This tour divided the area's structures into categories, including an ominous *to be razed* category. A total of 151 structures were referenced in his "tour," with 119 designated to be demolished and 32 slotted to remain. The infill would be new retail or office buildings, a shopping "arcade," and much parking and plantings. The SRA plan gave no thought to replacing the downtown area's lost residential space apart from new housing for the elderly. Space was needed for at least one major road reconfiguration as well: the transformation of what was once a colonial lane, St. Peter Street, into a four-lane "highway" intersecting with Essex Street, Salem's main street.[11]

Historic Salem Inc. organized the primary local opposition to the Heritage Plaza-East preliminary plan, in collaboration with Salem's two major museums, the Essex Institute and the Peabody Museum. The director of the latter, Ernest S. Dodge, issued a dire warning (with particularly striking graphics illustrating the effect of the plan on the museum's grounds) in the museum's quarterly newsletter in June 1965, while the Essex Institute Council voted to oppose the plan in October, "due to the widespread destruction of significant old buildings, to the vast changes of old streets, and to the resulting loss of identity of a significant portion of Salem." That same month, Ada Louis Huxtable, the eminent architectural critic for the *New York Times*, published a front-page article titled, "Foes Fear Plans Will Mar Old New England Heritage: Urban Renewal Plan Threatens Historic Sites in Salem, Mass," drawing national concern and scrutiny.[12] After surveying the plan and sentiments of local officials and preservationists, Huxtable concluded that "it will take some potent modern witchcraft to save Salem's historic past." Witchcraft was not forthcoming, but neither were the necessary federal funds to initiate the implementation of the Heritage Plaza-East plan until several years after its approval by the necessary authorities: bulldozers began rolling through the streets of downtown Salem in 1969, demolishing fifty-six buildings in that year alone, with more to come.[13]

Salem's early experience of urban renewal coincided with a contrary trend in national preservation initiatives. While the City was presenting its Heritage Plaza-East plan in 1966, Congress passed the National Historic Preservation Act, and the Salem Historic District Study Committee was surveying neighborhoods for local and federal districts. Eventually, the forces of "progress" and preservation would converge. Strong preservation voices emerged both before and, especially, after the bulldozing began, including Historic Salem's presidents Elizabeth Reardon and Donald Koleman, who utilized legal challenges and led by example, buying and restoring seven houses in the Charter Street endangered area. Another important figure was, as the eminent architectural historian, Abbott Lowell Cummings, who served on both the Historic District Committee and the SRA's Design Review Board, the sole means by which preservationists could work *within* the renewal process. Koleman's consistent message was on economic renewal through restoration rather than demolition, as "Salem's greatest economic resource is tourism—and you can be sure that the present plan doesn't have any relation to that." Cummings's concerns were less pragmatic but just as focused; his tenure on the Design Review Board lasted mere months before he submitted his letter of resignation in December 1970, stating that "it is virtually incomprehensible to me why such an historically important city as Salem continues to endorse a program dedicated to the consistent erosion of her historic street patterns and individual early buildings."[14]

Ultimately, it was the practices of both preservation and politics that shifted Salem's course away from clearance toward rehabilitation. The wasteland impact of the demolition, which encompassed eighty-seven historic buildings by 1970, combined with the inability of the SRA to attract sufficient private capital, resulted in shifting public opinion about the sheer scale and longevity of urban renewal. As explained earlier, some of the resistance was philosophical, some practical. Salem's downtown had been under construction since the tunnel project of the 1950s, and people were tired of the disruptions and mess.

The incumbent Mayor Francis X. Collins, in office during all of this development and dislocation, retired in 1969 and was succeeded by Samuel E. Zoll, who was more sympathetic to preservation arguments. Zoll reorganized the membership and mission of the SRA in 1971, appointing members with similar preservationist sentiments. The new SRA proceeded without a master plan but with its own architect and engineer and a commitment "that there would be no more demolition unless there was a firm prospect for something better on the site," in the words of the new Vice-Chair William Tinti, an attorney, member of Historic Salem Inc., and legislative aide to the Massachusetts's U.S. Representative Michael Harrington.[15]

Over the next year, considerable progress was evident, including a refurbished Derby Square around Old Town Hall and the beginning of an innovative facade easement program, through which the SRA purchased the right to restore the exteriors of a dozen significant buildings downtown, leaving their owners responsible for interior renovations. The facade easement program was innovative in terms of both design and financing, as it marked an early diversion of the Department of Housing and Urban Development funds to substantive restoration. Federal funds were also used for an extensive pedestrian infrastructure designed by the landscape architect John Collins of Philadelphia, who transformed Salem's original streetscape through brick and cobblestone, site-specific lighting, benches, bollards, fountains, and trees rather than by simply wiping the slate clean. A renewed emphasis on housing for the downtown, combined with increasing opportunities for Salem residents to weigh in on the ongoing redevelopment, expanded public support and enthusiasm according to Mayor Zoll, who characterized his vision of urban renewal as "not so much bricks and mortar as it is a renewal of the community spirit."[16] What was still called Heritage Plaza-East (but representing an entirely different vision than the original plan) won a Department of Housing and Urban Development "urban design concept" award in 1972, the first of several honors it would receive over the decade. Another imprimatur came in the form of a follow-up story in the *New York Times* by Huxtable, who heralded Salem's course correction as representing "a progressive change of policy and practice, not just in this one city but in many cities, in terms of economic, environmental and human values and goals."[17]

By 1980, the narrative of Salem as a city that had altered the course and financing of urban renewal to suit its own developmental needs and create an exemplary blend of past and present was well established. Three large buildings, very much of the present, filled out the downtown: the new Ernest Dodge wing of the Peabody Museum (1975) and the East India Mall and Parking Garage (1975), built on opposite sides of the Essex Street pedestrian mall, and the First District Court building on Washington Street (1977). These buildings were assertively modern, and none lasted long in its original form: the East India Mall was stripped of its distinct arched colonnade in the 1990s as it became Museum Place Mall. The Dodge wing was demolished to make way for a new entrance atrium and addition for the Peabody Essex Museum in 2003, and the First District Court building was replaced by a multistory condominium building after the construction of a new Judicial Center on Federal Street in 2017.[18] The fate and fortune of Salem's venerable main street, Essex Street, was increasingly tied to that of just two entities: the struggling mall, which lost its anchor when the century-old Almy's department store was shuttered in 1985, and the expanding Peabody Essex Museum, formed by a merger of the Essex Institute and the Peabody Museum of Salem in 1992.

Residential Shifts and a "Redeemed" Harbor

The downtown developments distracted from another major postwar development in Salem: the expansion of settlement to the city's boundaries, away from the central core. Even while the city was pursuing urban renewal, it was also seeking to establish itself as a bedroom community for Boston through a policy of "creeping expansion": yet another "battle" article concludes with a reference to "Witchcraft Heights," a new development of 140 homes on Gallows Hill in the western part of the city.[19] The suburbanization of Salem continued with development on both sides of Highland Avenue, where another nonprofit institution, the Salem Hospital, was also expanding.

There had been considerable residential development in both north and south Salem prior to World War II, but, as late as 1979, the city's master plan indicated that open space comprised twenty-five hundred acres, or half of its land area.[20] From the perspective of both the city and the potential developers, the west and southwest sectors were ripe for both residential and commercial development in the latter decades of the twentieth century. At the same time, infill opportunities arose closer to the city center, with the closure of the GTE Sylvania and Parker Brothers plants in the 1990s, with the former plant accommodating the expansion of Salem State University in south Salem.

The 1912 Plans Commission report focused intently on Salem's waterfront and the importance of its "redemption," and, a century later, it is, indeed, in a very different state. The closing of the Naumkeag Steam Cotton Company's Pequot Mills, in 1953, ended industrial production on the shoreline, but its large facilities remain. Proceeding eastward, a coal and oil storage facility along Salem Harbor was replaced, in 1979, by the Pickering Wharf development, a six-acre "commercial and residential village" with its own marina and later a hotel. The development and stewardship of the Salem Maritime National Historic Site and the House of the Seven Gables Settlement Association has both preserved and enhanced public access to the waterfront.

On land that was previously coal wharves and mudflats, two major utilities, the Salem Harbor Power Station and South Essex Sewage District treatment facility, have dominated the shoreline along Derby Street leading to Winter Island and Salem Willows from the 1950s. The original coal-fired station was replaced by a natural gas plant in 2020, reducing the size of its footprint and thus making way for the new wind farm facilities. Winter Island was long the site of military fortifications and stations, from the construction of Fort Pickering in the seventeenth century to the Coast Guard Air Station of the twentieth century. Its ownership was transferred to the city of Salem by the federal government in 1972, after the Air Station was closed and Mayor Sam Zoll "invaded" the island, citing a Civil War agreement by which the city ceded it to the federal government only for as long as it might be needed "for defense of the harbor."[21]

The ruins of the shoreline's seventeenth- and twentieth-century installations remain as Winter Island operates as a municipal seaside park. The adjacent Salem Willows evolved as one of the North Shore's chief summer attractions in the decades after its opening in 1858, with an amusement park, arcades, restaurants, and a ferry and streetcar service. The popularity of the Willows ensured its connection to the center of Salem by streetcars before and after the 1912 Plans Commission report, but still its authors recommended that it and all of Salem's coastline, from Forest River Park near the Marblehead line to Collins Cove and the Beverly Bridge, be linked together by a "Shore Line Drive," which would "redeem practically all of Salem's waterfront for walking and driving" and accelerate the transformation of the mudflats into playgrounds and parks. A century later, this coastal road to redemption is not visible everywhere in the city, but it is in parts and places, along with seawalls, bike paths, and even a restored salt marsh along Collins Cove. This planned shoreline parkway serves as a fitting metaphor for much of Salem's development over the past one hundred years. It has its roots in the prefire Progressive Era, and it sought to connect previously prominent towns and cities and to revitalize all the involved communities. The infusion of federal funds into other projects, most important, Route 128, changed the entire context for these plans, and, while the original plans (much like the SRA's plans for downtown Salem) were incompletely and imperfectly implemented, they still left an important and lasting impact on the ways that residents and visitors experience Salem to this day.

NOTES

1. *First Annual Report, Salem Plans Commission: City of Salem, Massachusetts, December 26, 1912* (Newcomb and Gauss, 1912), 17.

2. Jacob Remes, *Disaster Citizenship: Survivors, Solidarity, and Power in the Progressive Era* (University of Illinois Press, 2015), chap. 2, n. 1.

3. Walter Kilham, "The Salem Fire from an Architect's Point of View," *The Brickbuilder* 23, no. 7 (July 1914), 170–171.

4. *Report of Salem Rebuilding Commission* (Newcomb and Gauss, 1917).

5. "Industrial Section of Salem: The Great Leather and Shoe City," *Shoe and Leather Reporter*, July 19, 1917.

6. U.S. Department of the Interior, National Park Service, National Register of Historic Places, Inventory Nomination Form, "Salem Main Post Office," April 30, 1986; U.S. Department of the Interior, *Annual Report of the Secretary of the Interior*, 1938, 28.

7. Robert Glynn, "Witch City's Wrinkles Ironed Out, Salem's Business Booms Again," *Boston Globe*, July 15, 1959.

8. Alta Maloney, "The Battle for Salem," magazine of the *Sunday Herald Traveler*, April 4, 1971.

9. SRA, Documents Relating to Heritage Plaza-East Project No Mass R.-95 (1966), Phillips Library, Peabody Essex Museum, Rowley, MA.

10. Lizabeth Cohen's *A Consumer's Republic* offers the best discussion of the role that new suburban shopping centers played in luring consumers away from urban centers, such as Salem's, in this period. She provides context for Salem's situation by noting that "by 1957, 940 shopping centers had already been built. That number more than doubled by 1960 and doubled again by 1963; by 1976 the 17,520 shopping centers in the nation would represent an almost nineteen-fold increase across twenty years." Cohen also explains that "traffic congestion and parking problems discouraged commercial developers from expanding in central business districts of major cities and smaller market towns [such as Salem], already hindered by a short supply of developable space. Rather, retailers preferred catering to suburbanites on the open land where they now lived and drove." Lizabeth Cohen, *A Consumers' Republic: The Politics of Mass Consumption in Postwar America* (Vintage Books, 2003), 258. All of Cohen's chap. 6, "Commerce: Reconfiguring Community Marketplaces," is useful for understanding Salem's situation in the 1950s and 1960s. For a discussion of the creation of Route 128, see Susan Rosegrant and David R. Lampe, *Route 128: Lessons from Boston's High-Tech Community* (Basic Books, 1992), 106–109. Originally derided as "the road to nowhere," Route 128 was so heavily trafficked that workers were busy expanding it from six to eight lanes only seven years after construction started.

11. SRA Design Review Board Records, 1960–1984, Phillips Library, MSS 120; The number of buildings targeted for demolition by the SRA expanded from 119 to 139 to 141 over 1965–1966.

12. SRA Design Review Board Records, Phillips Library, MSS 120; *New York Times*, October 13, 1965.

13. Maloney, "Battle for Salem."

14. John Herefort, "Salem: Can City Retain Old Flavor and Improve Economic Base through Urban Renewal?" *Boston Globe*, July 30, 1967; "Letter of Resignation from Design Review Board by Abbott Lowell Cummings, December 4, 1970," SRA Design Review Board Records, Phillips Library, MSS 120.

15. Massachusetts Office of Local Assistance, *Built to Last: A Handbook on Recycling Old Buildings* (Preservation, 1977), 112.

16. Jim Tagalakis, "A Workable Urban Renewal," *Lynn Daily Item*, January 30, 1975.

17. Ada Louise Huxtable, "How Salem Saved Itself from Urban Renewal," *New York Times*, September 29, 1974.

18. "Salem's Mall Loses That Fortress Look," *Salem Evening News*, December 16, 1996.

19. Russell P. Burbank, "Salem Battles Geography," *Boston Globe*, October 3, 1965.

20. Massachusetts Historical Commission, *Reconnaissance Survey Town Report* for Salem, 1985, 39.

21. Anthony Pearson, "Salem Mayor Invades CG Island Site," *Boston Globe*, July 20, 1972.

INTERLUDE 11

Salem's Labor History

The Naumkeag Steam Cotton Company and the 1933 Strike

Aviva Chomsky

Nestled among the "3 L" aging manufacturing cities of Lynn, Lowell, and Lawrence, Salem is not known for its industrial past. The history of Salem's textile mill is generally overshadowed by the city's famed witch trials and maritime history, yet it is significant in numerous ways. Salem's Naumkeag Steam Cotton Company was remarkable (1) as the first coal- and steam-powered mill in the region, (2) as, for several decades, one of the country's largest mills, (3) as a national pioneer in labor-management collaboration in the 1920s, when many of New England's mills shuttered to seek cheaper operating conditions in the South, and (4) as the site of a radical wildcat strike in 1933 that brought communist organizers and Roosevelt administration officials to the city. The strike contributed to shaping the New Deal's National Industrial Recovery Act's 1933 Cotton Textile Code, which set national standards for the industry.

The Naumkeag Steam Cotton Company, incorporated in 1839, was a latecomer to the New England textile industry. Samuel Slater established the first New England mill in Pawtucket, Rhode Island, in 1793; others followed in the region with both Lowell and Lawrence, Massachusetts, emerging as major centers of cotton textile production. Salem merchants shipped Lowell cloth (*merekani* or American) to a burgeoning Indian Ocean and East African market and soon moved to establish their own mill, becoming a node linking the plantations of the U.S. South and the coal fields of Pennsylvania and West Virginia, through the port of Zanzibar and by a dense caravan trade, to consumers throughout East Africa—some of whose kin could have been laboring, enslaved, on the plantations growing the cotton.[1] The Naumkeag was one of the first to transcend the industry's reliance on water power—and the need to locate near a river—with its use of the new coal-fired steam power, and it quickly became one of the region's, and the world's, largest mills.

The Naumkeag's late entry into the industry gave it a technological advantage over other New England mills in the 1800s; the destruction it suffered in Salem's 1914 catastrophic fire paradoxically gave it another advantage, as it rebuilt in the newer expansive "Southern" style to accommodate the latest innovations in automatic looms. When depression struck the textile industry in the 1920s, many of New England's cotton mills fled to the South lured by proximity to the sources of cotton, state and local incentives, lower labor costs, a non-union environment, and the chance to rebuild cheaply from the ground up with the new looms. The Naumkeag, which had already adopted the automatic loom, was one of the few that stayed in New England.

Still, the mill had to compete with those that moved South, and one of its strategies was to draw its workers' union into collaborating on "research" to speed up the work process and lower costs. United Textile Workers Local 33 represented the workers since a series of strikes in the 1910s, but, over time, its male Irish American leadership had grown increasingly distant from its mostly female French-Canadian and Polish immigrant workforce. Even as worker resentment at the speedup simmered, the Naumkeag was lauded in both the business world and the press as a paragon of labor-management collaboration. The muckraking journalist Ida Tarbell penned "Notes on Salem Cotton Undertaking" lauding the "sportsmanship" of the industry and its workers for recognizing their mutual interest in keeping the industry running by lowering costs.[2]

By 1933, what workers derided as "research"—the joint labor-management strategy—had come to mean reduced hours, lower pay, and layoffs as well as increasingly stressful and dangerous working conditions. "I guess it's me, I'm not quite automatic!" one young worker mourned.[3] Another, reported the *Salem Evening News*, explained that "the work was to be doubled and more than doubled and that the workers had reached the limit. She told about workers going home nights with their fingers and hands cut, blistered and burned." Others protested "that girls lose weight because of research demands; many are injured by machines, the mill disregards the human side."[4]

Workers directed much of their rage against their own union's leadership, who appeared more interested in cozying up to management and accusing their members of being "radical" or "red" when workers tried to make their voices heard in opposition to another round of "research," speedups, and layoffs. In the weeks leading up to the strike, observers noted that "the workers became increasingly bitter in their disparagement of the Union and contemptuous of the ability of its officials to represent them and protect their interests. Many of the workers now openly accused the union officials of 'selling out' to the management."[5] When the workers defied their union and went out on strike in May 1933, the United Textile Workers international office ordered them to return to work and froze the local's funds. Salem's mayor denounced the strikers, and the *Salem Evening News* editorialized against them, urging local businesses and social service agencies to refuse any aid and workers to "be thankful you have a job and stick to it, not letting any radicals stir you up."[6]

In contrast, workers found strong allies in the local community and even businesses, as well as from the socialist mayor of neighboring Peabody and from the communist National Textile Workers Union. (Remember that this was the 1930s, a heyday of Communist Party labor organizing in the United States.) While these latter connections provoked hysteria about "radicals" and "reds" from the mill, union leaders, and city officials, the National Textile Workers Union provided crucial moral and material support that helped sustain the strikers and their families during the eleven-week wildcat strike.

The National Textile Workers Union, based in Rhode Island, sent its young national secretary, Anne Burlak, to Salem to help organize community support. "Union meetings and social events regularly attracted hundreds of workers; songs, cheering, and spirited picket lines remained characteristic of the strike

Naumkeag Steam Cotton Co., Pequot Mills, 1930s. *(Nelson Dionne Salem History Collection, Salem State University Archives and Special Collections.)*

week after week, and workers speaking different languages and adhering to different political beliefs, sometimes even attending competing rallies, continued to collaborate and concentrate on their concrete demands." The *Salem Evening News*, despite editorializing against the strike, reported in great detail on the large and enthusiastic meetings, rallies, marches, and fundraisers around Salem attended by thousands, where workers' speeches were greeted with "cheers and stamping of feet." Hundreds of community members mobilized to donate and prepare food and organize fundraising events, including a tag sale, a "benefit show" with youth boxing and wrestling, and a baseball match, and set up "relief stores" throughout the city. A fundraising picnic ten weeks into the strike attracted some six-hundred to seven-hundred locals with "games, sports, music and entertainment."[7]

In the midst of the strike, on June 16, 1933, President Roosevelt signed the National Industrial Recovery Act, a key component of his administration's New Deal legislation. On June 20, two federal conciliators arrived in Salem to mediate talks between Naumkeag's management and the strikers. After several days of lengthy meetings, the mill conceded to all of the workers' demands: an end to "research" and the stretch-out, accepting seniority rules for layoffs, and recognition of their new independent union. The first code adopted under the National Industrial Recovery Act, through an agreement between industry leaders and the federal government, was the Cotton Textile Act, which went into effect in July. The code regulated many aspects of the industry, mandating minimum wages and maximum hours and placing strict limits on the stretch-out, thus undercutting some of the industry's key strategies of pitting workers in one mill, or one region, against others.[8]

The *Boston Globe* called the agreement "an almost complete victory" for the strikers. The mill, which had repeatedly threatened to relocate to counter workers' demands, in fact stayed in Salem until the 1950s. When it did finally close, relocating to Spartanburg, South Carolina, it was in the face of repeated concessions from a much more conciliatory union. After numerous mergers and acquisitions, the Spartanburg mill also closed, in 1996, as the new owners shifted production to Mexico. In Salem, the mill buildings were converted into offices and warehouses, while the immigrant workers' housing in the Point neighborhood came to welcome new generations of immigrants, mostly from the Dominican Republic and Puerto Rico.[9] Salem's history of industrialization, workers' struggles, deindustrialization, and immigration parallels that of many U.S. cities and constitutes a rich counterpart to the city's better-known colonial and maritime histories. It remains to be seen how the kinds of challenges and opportunities of the new postindustrial economy will compare to those experienced by the past century's immigrants.

NOTES

1. Philip Northway, "Salem and the Zanzibar-East African Trade, 1825–1845," *Essex Institute Historical Collections* 90 (1954); Norman Bennett, "Americans in Zanzibar: 1845–1865," *Essex Institute Historical Collections* 97 (1961); Jeremy Prestholdt, "On the Global Repercussions of East African Consumerism," *American Historical Review* 109, no. 3 (June 2004), 755–781, available at https://doi.org/10.1086/ahr/109.3.755; Anna Arabindan-Kesson, "From Salem to Zanzibar: Cotton and Cultures of Commerce, 1820–1861," in *Global Trade and Visual Arts in Federal New England*, ed. Patricia Johnston and Caroline Frank (University Press of New England, 2014), 288–303; Joshua Sidney Chamberlin Morrison, "Cut from the Same Cloth: Salem, Zanzibar, and the Consolidation of the Indo-Atlantic World, 1790–1875" (Ph.D. diss., University of Virginia, 2021), available at https://libraetd.lib.virginia.edu/downloads/b5644s46x?filename=1_Morrison_Joshua_2021_PHD.pdf.

2. See Aviva Chomsky, *Linked Labor Histories: New England, Colombia, and the Making of a Global Working Class* (Duke University Press, 2008), 57, citing Richmond C. Nyman and Elliott Dunlap Smith, *Union-Management Cooperation in the "Stretch Out": Labor Extension at the Pequot Mills* (Institute of Human Relations, Yale University Press, 1934), 78–79; Ida M. Tarbell, "Note: [Naumkeag] An Experiment in Industrial Civilization," December 1, 1932, Allegheny College Special Collections, "The Documents of Ida M. Tarbell," available at https://dspace.allegheny.edu/handle/10456/39858 and https://dspace.allegheny.edu/bitstream/handle/10456/39858/09.2678.0051.pdf?sequence=1&isAllowed=y.

3. Chomsky, *Linked Labor Histories*, 83.
4. Chomsky, 64–65.
5. Chomsky, 58.
6. Chomsky, 61.
7. Chomsky, 62–63, 71, 72.
8. See U.S. National Archives, "National Industrial Recovery Act (1933)," available at https://www.archives.gov/milestone-documents/national-industrial-recovery-act; "Code of Fair Competition for the Cotton-Textile Industry," *Monthly Labor Review* 37, no. 2 (August 1933), 265–272.
9. Chomsky, *Linked Labor Histories*, 76, 78.

CHAPTER TWELVE

Salem and World War II

BRAD AUSTIN AND SUSAN EDWARDS

Matthew Guinta could vividly picture the scale and scope of the carnage when he first learned about the December 7, 1941, Japanese attack on the U.S. naval base in Pearl Harbor, Hawaii. After all, only a few months before he had worked there. On that December night, as he exited a Cab Calloway concert in Boston, he learned that the trajectories of his country, his city, and his own life all had changed.

A Salem High School graduate, Guinta had followed the lead of his buddy, Dennis Mullanski, and had taken a qualifying exam at the Salem Post Office to go work on the battleships in the Pearl Harbor Naval Yard in 1940. By mid-1941, however, Guinta had left his home next to Hawaii's Waikiki Beach and had returned to Salem to work at the United Shoe factory in Beverly. After he and his Salem friend learned about the attack, according to Guinta, "All the young fellas, anyone with the age of sixteen years and up wanted to go to war," sharing the desire to "go get the Japanese now!" Guinta enlisted in the navy, and his brother joined the army.[1]

Guinta spent much of the next four years in harm's way, many of them serving as a machinist on the USS *Massachusetts*, passing through the Panama Canal to get from the Boston Navy Yard to join the fight in the Pacific. Once there, he spent up to eighteen months at a time at sea as the *Massachusetts* helped protect aircraft carriers and shelled island targets, firing up to eight hundred shells in a single day. Meanwhile, his brother was engaged in brutal land combat in Europe after the D-Day invasion, including the Battle of the Bulge. When the war ended, Guinta was situated just off the coast of Japan, and he vividly recalled the way the U.S. military performed one last show of force that day, flying thousands of planes over Japan, just to remind the Japanese that they had lost. Ultimately, Guinta recalled his war years fondly, remembering that life on a battleship "was the good life" but allowing that serving on a destroyer wasn't as great, "because they had no ice cream parlors."[2]

Irene Norton experienced those same years very differently. Another product of Salem public schools (who later completed graduate work in Boston and Chicago), Norton had been enjoying an afternoon New Hampshire picnic and was returning to Salem when her car radio reported the news of the Pearl Harbor attack. She remembered that "it took two or three days for it to sink in" and that while "war wasn't declared that day . . . that was the day" it began.[3]

Her experience differed sharply from Guinta's over the ensuing years. As a young mother of an infant at the beginning of the war, Norton spent most of the war years in Salem and witnessed a surge of patriotic actions, with Red Cross volunteers rolling bandages at their headquarters on Essex Street and the ornate iron fence from the enormous Frick estate in Beverly Farms being scrapped to make war material. Norton described both how Salem residents stuck together and how seriously they took their air raid drills, but she also noted that when it came to rationing ("the thing that caused the most trouble") "some people weren't too patriotic." Many Salemites circumvented ration limits and participated in black markets that allowed them to purchase desired goods "under the carpet," while others used their surplus funds to hoard hundreds of pounds of sugar and loads of other commodities.[4]

As these two very brief accounts suggest, Salem residents' World War II experiences differed as widely as their circumstances. A young mother's story of a community collecting animal fat and coordinating blackout drills contrasts sharply with the story of a navy mechanic's preparation for the possible invasion of Japan. Ultimately, the city's World War II experience was shaped by its proximity to a vulnerable shoreline, by its residents' service, by the general anxiety the war created, by the specific anxiety that service created for those left behind, and by the innumerable disruptions to ordinary life that the war caused.

While there are many ways to tell the story of Salem at war, we have chosen to use this essay to highlight the voices of the men, women, and children who lived through these years in Salem or who entered military service, corresponding with those who remained at home. We can utilize this approach because we have access to two remarkable collections housed in local archives. In 1981, the Salem Youth Commission conducted a series of oral history interviews as part of a "Salem: The Home Front, 1941–1945" project, and the Peabody Essex Museum currently preserves the records at its Phillips Library in Rowley, Massachusetts. The second invaluable collection is the Dr. Edna McGlynn Collection of World War II letters, preserved in the Salem State University Archives. We have drawn from these collections, and other archival sources, to illustrate some of the ways that World War II came to Salem and how Salem residents went to war.

The Home Front: World War II Comes to Salem

As other essays in this volume have suggested, to understand Salem, one must always consider how the sea has shaped its history. While this is most obvious in Salem's colonial, Revolutionary, and Early National eras, it remained true during World War II, when the threat of submarine and air attacks loomed large in the imagination of residents and prompted a wide range of responses. Although the United States had resisted entering the war for its first two years, its residents were certainly well aware of the danger the conflict posed. The future Salem mayor, Samuel Zoll, for example, later recalled his Jewish family discussing how "the Germans were practicing a lot of antisemitic and harmful things against the Jewish people and the Jewish people [being] very concerned so that it just brought this thing a little closer to home." Zoll was only seven when the United States entered the war, yet these discussions clearly made an impression.[5] Similarly, Norton remembered how Edward Murrow's broadcasts from London gave her "the feeling of what people were going through" and that "before Pearl Harbor we realized that if all of Europe went we were next, and we were just going to have to go in so we started getting ready."[6]

These individual memories of the perceived need for Salem to prepare for war are reinforced by official government statements and actions. As early as April 1941, the Commonwealth of Massachusetts had distributed an Air Warden's Manual (collated by the Massachusetts Work Projects Administration [WPA] Writers' Project) that reminded readers of the fact that "the destruction and suffering caused by insufficient preparation and lack of foresight in other parts of the world during the past two years is a lesson not to be overlooked." This section concluded with the ominous warning, "'Total war' includes civilians as well as soldiers."[7] This manual called on Massachusetts to prepare for attacks, and Salem spent the next several years doing exactly that.

While this call to action occurred in April 1941, the plan was not fully activated until after the Pearl Harbor attacks, even if the infrastructure was already largely in place. After that infamous December day's attack, the chair of the Salem Defense Committee, Michael Reardon, called for his subordinates and Salem's ward wardens to recruit almost one thousand volunteers, men and women, to enroll in an Air Raid Warden's School, with classes beginning in early January 1942. There, the volunteers practiced their reporting mechanisms and learned about the "extreme importance of making correct, complete and brief incident reports." In their drills, the air raid wardens received scenarios and rehearsed how they would report to very specific situations. This was vital because, as one document explains, "if a high explosive bomb fell in the middle of a street, water mains, sewer pipes, gas pipes and other public utility equipment would surely be affected." Similarly, "if a plane (particularly an enemy plane) fell there would probably be bombs, there would obviously be destruction of property and there would surely be fire."[8] The threats were tangible and real.

They were also local. Salem's air raid wardens needed to be prepared to give precise instructions to first responders, as this Salem-centric explanation lays out. "If you report a high explosive bomb has fallen at the corner of Essex and Summer Streets, the Report Center will not know what to do about it unless you tell them the nature and extent of the damage. At that particular place, obviously, water, gas, sewer, electricity, telephone, and possibly fire alarm and police alarm will be damaged. There will be casualties, probably. Possibly people trapped. The whole intersection would be blocked. . . . Ammonia fumes from the Mohican Market might cause local trouble." Salem's preparations were specific, intense, ongoing, and carried out by the city's residents and leaders.[9]

The Salem plumber Kenneth Barry served as an air raid warden during the war. He recalled that it involved a lot of nighttime foot patrols and pain from banging his knees against fire hydrants in the dark of the night. When wardens happened upon a house emitting light, the process was straightforward. In Barry's words, "We would warn them right away. Bang on the window. Our language wasn't too good sometimes. Close the window, block the light." He remembered that "there wasn't too much of that, though. People were really scared. They were scared."[10]

Mrs. Ty Riordon's perspective of the blackouts was from the other side of those windows. She remembered her father installing blackout shades and taping them shut every night. Because they couldn't use electric lights, Riordon's family "had candles situated all over the house so that during the time of the blackout [they] could at least move around the inside of the house." If light escaped one's house, and if the wardens noticed, then a fine followed. This meant that whenever Riordon did leave at night, "it was just complete blackness."[11] Norton's oral history explains that Salem schools served as the headquarters for the air raid wardens and that the "fright over air raids," especially during the "two or three times [they] were told there were submarines off the coast" made for a "very unpleasant time, especially at Christmas" when festive lights were, of course, prohibited.¹² The fear of interior lights providing targeting and navigation landmarks to enemy submarines was especially pronounced at the Plummer Home for Boys, situated right alongside Salem Harbor and along the channel leading to many of Salem's industries.¹³

While the acute fears of an enemy attack (and the corresponding blackouts) were concentrated in the early years of the war, Salem residents participated in other war-related activities that were both less dramatic and longer lasting. The most significant and pervasive of these activities was the ration program, which involved collecting and using stamps and attempting, through authorized and unauthorized methods, to supplement a family's stocks.

The wartime deprivations were not altogether new to Salem's residents, as one oral history reminds us, explaining that rationing "was hard to live with in one way; in another way it wasn't because people in the 1930s were used to doing without." Fortunately, in at least this very specific context, the experience of the Depression had prepared Salem's residents to manage supply shortages. For this resident, the most difficult items to procure were stockings. She recalled joining a women's sewing club in an effort "to make things last a little longer instead of going to the store and buying them. Even if you had the money, you couldn't buy them."¹⁴

In Salem, one had to register for ration stamps in the former home of WPA soup kitchens, a now-demolished building known as the Flat Iron Building next to "the Italian church." Stamps were free and were distributed to families based on the number of family members and their circumstances (newborn, sick, elderly, etc.). The stamps covered much of the most essential commodities, including coffee, sugar, butter, and meat.¹⁵ While it seems that most of these remained available to families, if not in unlimited or unrestricted quantities, Salem residents noticed at least three significant challenges. Preteen Samuel Zoll decried his family's inability to acquire "much ice cream" and also noticed the severe shortage of new bicycles available for holiday gifts, due to the changing manufacturing priorities during wartime, while Ruth Carlin recalled that Salem residents "could not get bananas because the boats could not risk the trip from South America" so that "very few bananas got through to families in these parts."¹⁶ Banana splits, it seems, were largely off the menu during Salem's war years.

As noted earlier, while Salemites dealt with a scarcity of cigarettes, nylons, bananas, and bicycles, some circumvented the ration rules by hoarding commodities and participating in a black market. There were other solutions to the problem of mismatched supply and demand. One of these solutions was the creation of individual and collective Victory Gardens. One resident explained that "Salem Common was full of victory gardens," as was Forest River Park.[17]

Ultimately, though these years were "always anxious moments . . . the worry of it was tremendous," the residents of Salem did all that they could do to make it through the war and to preserve their sanity and their personal relationships. While that sometimes involved joining clubs, collecting scrap metal, and other collective actions on the home front, it also involved corresponding with Salem residents who were serving in the military around the globe, often in dangerous conditions. As one young woman recalled, "Everyone was conscious of what could happen, and a lot of my friends got those telegrams."[18]

Salem's Students Go to War

In the late 1930s and early 1940s, the Salem Teachers College educated around five hundred young men and women, the group most likely to have friends called into military service or to serve themselves. Unsurprisingly, the wars in Europe and Asia were on the minds of students and faculty. The International Relations Club took the lead in sponsoring speakers and panel discussions. In these years, Dr. Anton de Haas of Harvard University was a frequent lecturer on the crises in Europe and the Sino-Japanese war, and the Pitman Debating Society faced off against colleges such as Holy Cross, Harvard, and Boston College on war-related topics, including isolationism and whether the Roosevelt administration policies were leading the country to war. A student newspaper (*The Log*) survey in October 1940 provided a snapshot of students' feelings about the war. This was thirteen months after Germany had invaded Poland, and a mere 40 percent of Salem Teachers College students believed that democracy would survive worldwide. The figures were worse for some areas of the world: 30 percent of respondents believed that democracy in Europe had almost no chance for survival, and 80 percent of students believed that Salem men should be drafted.[19]

The last query was not an abstract question for Salem's students. Detailed information about the draft appeared in the same issue of *The Log*. The Selective Training and Service Act of 1940 required that all men between the ages of twenty-one and forty-five register for the draft. Sixteen men at Salem Teachers College were conscription eligible, but the government "assured students who are twenty-one years of age or older that not until July will they be among those effected by the draft."[20] Deferment was important to the seniors as it would allow them to finish their degrees.

Joseph Sullivan, class of 1940, was one of the first Salem graduates to be drafted. Sullivan wrote a letter to the editor of *The Log* about "the adventures of a rookie under the new draft system." The letter was lighthearted, and he spoke of "chuckling at the comments and innuendos sprinkled here and there by the older men in the group" during the enlistment process.[21] William Fine, a fellow member of the class of 1940, also wrote to *The Log*. Unlike Sullivan, Fine had volunteered for the army in February 1941. He was sent to train as a medical and surgical technician. Fine was awarded a senior surgical rating and wrote that "the army has opened my eyes to many conditions that I had always taken for granted." He was pleased to be doing "useful work" and hoped to use what he learned in his postwar teaching career.[22] He never got that chance. Fine was killed in action in France in 1944. After the attack on Pearl Harbor, these two would soon be joined in military service by many other Salem Teachers College students and alumni.

After the declaration of war on December 8, 1941, the faculty and students quickly became involved in the war effort. Salem Teachers College President Edward Sullivan formed a faculty defense committee, invited civilian defense speakers, and declared that "within two weeks every student in the college will be engaged in some defense work."[23] The defense school, which offered classes in first aid and air raid precautions, enrolled over three hundred people. Eventually, it was necessary to add an extra hour to the school day for "defense period." There were also courses in first aid, air raid drills, and blood drives.[24]

Perhaps the most important initiative was the Collegiate Defense Committee. The committee's main mission was to send care packages and letters to the alumni, students, and faculty who joined the service. The committee, and all of its work, was supervised by Dr. Edna McGlynn, who had joined the college in 1936 and was one of the younger and most popular members of the faculty. The committee began by sending out baked goods and raising money to buy copies of the yearbook and subscriptions to *Reader's Digest* for the servicepeople.

Starting in the summer of 1942, the committee also started collecting the names of volunteers to correspond with Salem draftees. The letters quickly became more popular than the baked goods. As Robert Sheehan wrote in 1942, "The kids have been swell about writing and I have received quite a few letters. Mail means a lot to a soldier. If anyone could see the expressions of the fellows while waiting for mail, I'm certain that they would write more often."[25]

Photos from the Salem Teachers College "Roll of Honor," 1945. *The Clipper*, Salem Teachers College yearbook. (Salem State University Archives and Special Collections.)

In addition to the volunteer correspondents, McGlynn wrote to every Salemite on the committee's list of students and alumni in service. Some of the correspondence was voluminous and, as more students and alumni entered service, it became necessary to find a new way to disseminate the news. Thus, the *Salem Newsletter* was born as "the most effective way of letting everybody hear the latest in the shortest possible time."[26] It mixed news from the home front with updates on Salemites in service.

The early newsletter editions concentrated on the happenings at home. In the first issue, McGlynn described her experience with rationing in Salem: "You should see the lines of people trying to get butter. The *Salem News* referred to it jokingly as the 'V' line for butter because it extends from Kennedys (next to Woolworth's) down to Liggetts and around the corner up to the bus terminal. No standing in line for me, though."[27] As McGlynn explained, rationing also led to a growth in the number of gardeners. McGlynn was always an avid gardener but said of others: "For the first time in their lives, a great many people, because of the threatened food shortage, try to raise a garden, and a combination of lack of plows, lack of labor, lack of seed, and bad weather keep them from it."[28]

She tried to put their service in the context of greater sacrifices being made by so many Salem families. "Being in camp shows you one side of the picture, staying at home another. Remember the French Church on Lafayette St. with the tall tower? They have just constructed a role [sic] of honor out front. And on it at present there are 1005 names. You begin to get some general idea of the depopulation of our cities, when one church alone lists a thousand of its members as being in the active service."[29]

The newsletter also contained updated addresses for those in service. This became a valuable resource for people trying to find their fellow Salemites. In the early years of the war, most people were stationed stateside, and their addresses were straightforward. Once units started shipping out to different areas of conflict, the servicepeople could often discern location from the APO or FPO number. Many wrote of finding others through the addresses and having reunions in Italy, London, or closer to home in New York City. Others, like Bill Dalton, preferred more roundabout ways to find folks from home: "Bill D. has his own procedure for digging up Salem friends. When a trainload of recruits arrives where Bill is stationed, he starts asking 'Any of you rookies from Devens?' There's sure to be a Salem man in any Devens crowd."[30]

Salemites served in all theaters of war; some worked in clerical or administrative positions and never left the United States. The letters were a mix of excitement, boredom, and longing for home. Ray Barbarick, who would later serve in the South Pacific, wrote from New Orleans that "every time I get near a music box, I play the tune called 'Massachusetts' so that I won't forget that such a place exists and that's where I belong."[31]

Female students and alumnae also joined the armed forces as members of the Women's Army Corps, the Navy Women's Reserve, the Marine Corps Women's Reserve, and the Coast Guard Women's Reserve. Women often described having different experiences than the men. Mary Lovett, a member of the Women's Army Corps, wrote in 1943 about her experiences at Fort Stevens in Oregon: "If we bowl in slacks, word gets back that we look too sexy and divert the men. When we wear too long utility coats, the men officers send word that we look too dumpy, that they like our clothes short. Very inconsistent. If a button is unbuttoned, news of it gets back to our orderly room in no time. Two of our girls ran home from mess at noon. They were stopped by a man officer who told them ladies did not run! The Post Commander says that stopping to talk to a boy even for a moment out of doors is loitering."[32]

The newsletters weren't all just synopses of letters; they were also conversations. In a May 1945 newsletter, McGlynn mentioned a letter from Maurice Chornesky in which he noted that the student newspaper seems unconcerned with the war. In reply, she wrote, "It must seem to all of you that civilians, judged by such, just don't care. It is the opposite that is true. So many people are under such terrible strain, that it is better to keep normal whatever we can. The war is all around us. It has gotten so that I hate to ask a student about an absence, because the answer is so often 'My brother was killed in action. I didn't feel like coming to school.'" While this was a response to a particular letter, McGlynn also wanted to reassure the readers that those at home were heavily invested in war efforts. In later newsletters she made sure to highlight home front activities such as the college's successful war bond auction: "The students bought altogether $1800 dollars worth. The item that drew the largest bid was a portable radio, donated by Mr. Woods, which went as I remember for $320. The Presidency of the college for a day went for $270. And that meant for an interesting day at the college—with student president and teachers in charge. It was fun for the students, but even more so for the faculty, for we had the chance of a lifetime to do to the students what they do to us. And were they amazed!"[33]

The end of the war was a time of celebration both at home and at service. While V-E Day was "quiet and solemn" because "the boys in Europe were to be sent to the Pacific and the war was not over," V-J Day was a different story. McGlynn described cashing in her remaining A gas coupon and driving through Beverly, Salem, and Boston: "I never saw such spontaneous enthusiasm, and never expect to again—crowds pouring into church, the Chinese laundryman dashing around madly ringing a big dinner bell, grandmothers unaffectedly jumping around banging tin pots together, jalopies with 20 or 30 boys hanging onto all parts of them, horns tooting, trucks with hastily constructed effigies of Hirohito hanging from a gallows, the air-raid wardens and auxiliary police hurriedly performing their duties on the one real occasion the war afforded."[34] Christopher Eliopolous, who was trained as a Japanese interpreter, shared the perspective of someone serving in the Pacific theater: "We heard the great news this morning at about 0830 hours. There were no church bells ringing—simply because there aren't any—but the ships in the bay were blasting away with their fog horns with all the steam they had. The announcement itself was greeted with mixed boos and cheers. The boos being reserved for that party which said 'we must now work harder and harder.'"[35]

While the war was officially over, it would take some time for all the service members to come home. As their time in the service came to an end, many reflected on their experiences and the future. John Pineault, who served in the navy, wrote, "When some semblance of normal life is restored, and I get back to civilian life, it will be a most helpful experience—when I get back and into teaching. These experiences make me realize how small and how incomplete a formal education is. You, of course, can understand and will readily agree with me. There is much in life that most people do not realize exists—customs and traditions of new and different people, life in the various countries, the beauty of the world."[36] Like John, many alumni went back to the teaching ranks.

By the fall of 1945, veterans, or as *The Log* called them "Ex–G.I. Joes," had returned to campus. Veterans quickly became influential on campus; by 1948, they held all the officer positions on the Cooperative Council, the most important student organization on campus. Those who served, including those who had died, were not forgotten. The Collegiate Defense Committee and the Men's Athletic Association "joined forces in an effort to honor all the Salem students who served in the armed forces during the recent war." Many of the people who served contributed to a fund to create the memorial. These organizations also sponsored a drawing, with a pair of stockings as the main prize.[37]

Enrollment at the college had plummeted over the war years, going from a high of around five hundred to under three hundred. The G.I. Bill, officially known as the Servicemen's Readjustment Act of 1944, provided a range of benefits to help those who served readjust to civilian life. One of the most significant benefits was expanded access to higher education, and the college experienced rapid growth in the decades to come. By the time that the college became Salem State College in 1960, enrollment had more than tripled, and growth was hindered only by the lack of facilities. World War II had had a profound effect on both the life of students, faculty, and alumni of Salem Teachers College and its future as an academic institution.

Obviously, no one source can capture completely the wide range of ways that World War II affected Salem, but the August 16, 1945, edition of the *Salem Evening News* comes close. It shares the efforts of an eleven-year-old Jane Pearl who had "canvassed the Juniper neighborhood" and had raised almost $35 to help pay for that town's fireworks display. Jane's motivation almost certainly came, in part, from a desire to honor her brother, C. Dexter Groves, who had been killed at the age of eighteen in the fighting at Guadalcanal. Another article highlights how "Defense Plants Remain Closed" in celebration of the end of the war, as local factories, including the Pequot Mills, Sylvania plant, and Hytron Radio and Electronic Corporation, gave their workers a much-needed break from war production. Many of those workers were among the twenty-thousand spectators who attended Salem's Peace Parade, enjoying the "gaily decorated thoroughfares" and cheering "as military units, fraternal groups, veterans' organization and representatives of mercantile and industrial concerns marched past." The parade reflected not only the labor of different groups but also their backgrounds, with "the stirring music of bands and the brilliant costumes and uniforms of the French, Polish, Italian, Greek, and Hebrew delegations" enlivening the event. Though joyous, the spectators never lost sight of the sacrifices that had led to the day's celebration with "spontaneous applause" greeting veterans and Gold Star mothers along the parade path. For the first time in Salem's history, a parade had a woman as the honorary grand marshal, with Mrs. Blandine Vaillancourt, the city's first Gold Star mother—who lost her son in the Philippines in 1942, leading the way. This multiethnic celebration, one that put the contributions of women, veterans, and workers in the foreground, concluded in the prototypical Salem way, with a "mammoth fireworks display" launched from the Revolutionary-era Fort Lee and enjoyed by tens of thousands gathered at Salem Willows.[38]

NOTES

1. "Oral History Records, Matthew Guinta, 1981," Interviewed by Joe Lopez, ACC 81023, Phillips Library, Peabody Essex Museum, 1.

2. "Oral History Records, Matthew Guinta, 1981," 1.

3. "Oral History Records, Irene Norton, 1981," Interviewed by Randolph Moisan, ACC 81023, Phillips Library, Peabody Essex Museum, 1.

4. "Oral History Records, Irene Norton, 1981," 5–7.

5. "Oral History Records, Chief Justice Samuel E. Zoll, 1981," Interviewed by Randolph Moisan, ACC 81023, Phillips Library, Peabody Essex Museum, 3.

6. "Oral History Records, Irene Norton, 1981," 11–12.

7. Massachusetts Committee on Public Safety, *Air Raid Wardens' Manual*, Boston (April 1941), found in "Howard Corning Collection of Air Raid Materials, 1941–1945," MSS 0.1401, Phillips Library, Peabody Essex Museum.

8. "Seek 1000 for Air Raid Duty" and "Ward 3 Practices" (May 7, 1942), found in "Howard Corning Collection of Air Raid Materials, 1941–1945," MSS 0.1401, Phillips Library, Peabody Essex Museum.

9. "Ward 3 Practices."

10. "Oral History Records, Kenneth Barry, 1981," Interviewed by Randolph Moisan, ACC 81023, Phillips Library, Peabody Essex Museum, 4–5.

11. "Oral History Records, Paula Turner, 1981," Interviewed by Paula Turner, ACC 81023, Phillips Library, Peabody Essex Museum, 8. It seems this file was miscataloged, and the actual interview subject was Mrs. Ty Riordon.

12. "Oral History Records, Irene Norton, 1981," 2.

13. "Oral History Records, Ruth B. Carlin, 1981," Interviewed by Allyson Swiniuch, ACC 81023, Phillips Library, Peabody Essex Museum, 2.

14. "Oral History Records, Paula Turner, 1981," 3–4.

15. "Oral History Records, Paula Turner, 1981," 4.

16. "Oral History Records, Chief Justice Samuel E. Zoll, 1981," 8; "Oral History Records, Ruth B. Carlin, 1981," 1.

17. "Oral History Records, Paula Turner, 1981," 9.

18. "Oral History Records, Paula Turner, 1981," 10–11.

19. "Salem Favors Draft," *The Log*, October 30, 1940, 2.

20. "Sixteen Men Deferred from Draft Service," *The Log*, October 30, 1940, 4.

21. "Rookie 'Joe' Sullivan Relates Experiences as One of First Salem Graduates Drafted," *The Log*, March 26, 1941, 2.

22. "Private Brags for Fort Bragg," *The Log*, October 29, 1941, 2.

23. "Students to Begin Defense Measures," *The Log*, December 19, 1941, 1.

24. "362 Students Study A.R.P. and First Aid in Defense School," *The Log*, February 26, 1942, 1.

25. Robert Sheehan to Edna McGlynn, December 29, 1942, MSS 8, Box 5, Folder 101, Edna McGlynn World War II Letters Collection, Salem State University Archives and Special Collections, Salem, MA.

26. "Salem Newsletter," no. 1, n.d. [ca. early 1943], 1, MSS 8, Box 6, Folder 125, Edna McGlynn World War II Letters Collection.

27. "Salem Newsletter," no. 1, n.d. [ca. early 1943].

28. "Salem Newsletter," no. 10, n.d. [ca. late May/early June 1943], 1. MSS 8, Box 6, Folder 125, Edna McGlynn World War II Letters Collection.

29. "Salem Newsletter," no. 5, n.d. [ca. mid-April 1943], MSS 8, Box 6, Folder 125, Edna McGlynn World War II Letters Collection.

30. "Tidbits and Tidings from Servicemen," *The Log*, October 30, 1942, 4.

31. Ray Barbarick to Edna McGlynn, April 16, 1943, MSS 8, Box 1, Folder 5, Edna McGlynn World War II Letters Collection.

32. Mary Lovett to Edna McGlynn, September 20, 1943, MSS 8, Box 4, Folder 62, Edna McGlynn World War II Letters Collection.

33. "Salem Newsletter," no. 28, May 1945, MSS 8, Box 6, Folder 125, Edna McGlynn World War II Letters Collection.

34. "Salem Newsletter," no. 31, September 1945, MSS 8, Box 6, Folder 125, Edna McGlynn World War II Letters Collection.

35. Christopher Eliopolous to Edna McGlynn, August 15, 1945, MSS 8, Box 1, Folder 26, Edna McGlynn World War II Letters Collection.

36. John Pineault to Edna McGlynn, January 18, 1944, MSS 8, Box 4, Folder 82, Edna McGlynn World War II Letters Collection.

37. "CDC, MAA Plan Service Memorial," *The Log*, February 28, 1946, 4.

38. See the following articles, all from the *Salem News*, August 16, 1945: "Jane Pearl Led Fund Raising for Fireworks," 5; "Defense Plants Remain Closed," 2; "20,000 Viewed Great Salem Peace Parade," 1; "Fireworks at Willows to End Two-Day Celebration," 1.

INTERLUDE 12

The Sixties Come to Salem State

Brad Austin and Elizabeth Duclos-Orsello

Students often think they are being tricked when their professors ask them questions with seemingly obvious answers, such as "When did the sixties begin?" To them, January 1, 1960, is the clear answer, and, if historians felt strictly constrained by the Gregorian calendar, then it would also be the correct one. The reality is that historical trends and developments rarely coincide directly with calendar years or decades (or centuries, as this book's contents illustrate), and historians have recently made referring to "long" decades and centuries something of a cottage industry. Bruce Schulman's masterful *The Seventies: The Great Shift in American Culture, Society, and Politics*, for example, starts with the events of 1969 and concludes with Ronald Reagan's reelection in 1984. The seventies, in Schulman's convincing interpretation, neither began nor ended in years containing a "seven," and the decade lasted sixteen years.[1]

Most people associate "the sixties" with a wide variety of cultural and political shifts and conflicts. They might think immediately of the overlapping groups of people protesting the Vietnam War, a vast array of intersecting rights- and consciousness-raising movements, and a general antiauthoritarian attitude—as well as a considerable backlash to all of these. Although these trends and developments were certainly present throughout the 1960s, they did not all surface when the calendar turned from 1959 to 1960. Some of the conversations that would dominate campus life in the late-1960s actually began during the 1950s, but most gained prominence in the latter half of the decade and extended into the early 1970s as students gained experience and enhanced perspectives in some movements and applied the lessons they learned to others.[2]

We can see how Salem State students, faculty, and staff participated in the tumult of the era by looking closely at the most important campus debates of the era, focusing on the conflicts surrounding the Vietnam War while also giving a brief overview of different student groups' demands for rights and respect in the same era. In significant ways, the Salem State College experience of the 1960s and early 1970s offers an important lens for understanding the wider Salem experience of this turbulent time.

Vietnam

Probably the first time that a public speaker addressed the United States' role in Vietnam at Salem State was in 1955 when then-Senator John F. Kennedy warned a gathering of students, as almost a throwaway line in a speech about the Cold War in Europe, that they needed to pay attention to Vietnam and encroaching communism in Southeast Asia.[3] Almost a decade later, after the 1963 assassination of President Kennedy and while his successor, Lyndon B. Johnson, was escalating American military spending and troop levels in Vietnam, Senator Ted Kennedy also spoke to a large Salem State audience. In late 1965, Senator Kennedy identified Vietnam as "singularly the most important problem" the nation faced and contrasted the American desire for peace with the enemy's tactics of "infiltration, subversion, murder, [and] kidnap." Kennedy advocated for a dollar-to-dollar match of spending on military and civilian/infrastructure spending, warning that the failure to improve "civil matters" would lead to a "hollow or vain victory." While Kennedy's prepared remarks might interest historians of the war and domestic politics, the question and answer period immediately following them gives us greater insight into Salem State's campus concerns. According to the student newspaper's coverage of the event, questions "ranged from negotiated peace settlements, blood donations to the Viet Cong, through the refugee problem to the teach-ins."[4]

This wide range of questions might have caught Senator Kennedy off guard, but it shouldn't have surprised the members of the Salem State community who had gotten used to seeing news about draft procedures, notices of Vietnam-related campus activities, and all sides of the related debates shared in virtually every edition of the student newspaper, *The Log*. In fact, in the same issue that detailed Ted Kennedy's visit to campus, readers could learn about how the Salem Jewish Association was preparing to host a campus debate around the question: "Viet Nam: Are We Morally Right or Wrong?"[5]

During that debate, Salem State professors aired perspectives that will certainly be familiar to anyone who lived through, or who has studied, the conflict. One English professor blamed the press for minimizing the moral questions involved in resisting communist expansion and "for the failure of the American people to accept the Vietnam situation as 'something more than a back page war.'" His fellow English professor countered that the American "policy in Vietnam is morally wrong and politically stupid." After a lengthy debate, the chairperson of the Geography Department, according to *The Log*, "observed that even though it is improbable that we will win the war in Vietnam, [Americans] have a moral obligation to put pressure on the enemy so that we can get a satisfactory settlement at the negotiation table."[6] In 1965, long before tens of thousands of Americans and millions of Vietnamese, Cambodians, and Laotians lost their lives, even Salem State geographers could predict the conflict's eventual outcome.

Over the next several years, Salem State's community remained engaged around the topic of the Vietnam War, with outside speakers (and singers), dueling editorials, continuous debates, and protests revealing the passions and the principles people felt and held. The sixties came to Salem State in the late 1960s and early 1970s in the form of the Lovin' Spoonful, William Kuntsler, Saul Alinsky, Barry Goldwater, Dick Gregory (identified in one visit as a "comedian" and, in a later one, as racial tensions heated up on campus, as a "preacher of black power and activism"), and Students for a Democratic Society volunteers, as *The Log* gave regular updates about how current draft policies would affect its readers.[7] While the stereotypical view is that universities in the sixties were incubators of liberalism, conservative students clearly had a voice on the Salem campus. In one 1966 editorial, two students argued that "the point of disagreement between the conservative and the liberal is how the war is being conducted. The conservative feels that our policy in Vietnam is not enough. We must strike harder and do more to win the war because half-measures will do nothing more than hinder the Communists, not defeat them, and time and population are on their side."[8]

While campus conservatives got a regular column in the student paper and opportunities to share their perspectives during the numerous public debates, those who opposed the war often drove the debate. On April 20, 1967, Salem State College had its first official antiwar protest as seventy-eight community members (including ten faculty members) gathered in silent protest of the United States' policies toward Vietnam. The protest's organizers recognized the complexity of the nation's, and the campus's, antiwar coalition and asked protesters not to bring any signs, because, as they explained it, "The person next to you may have different reasons for protesting."[9]

The twenty students who staged a counterprotest suffered no such limitations. Their stated objective was "to make noise," and a crowd of about four hundred watched as the silent antiwarriors were confronted by students holding signs proclaiming, "I Protest against Phony People," "Support Our Men in Vietnam," "Bomb Hanoi," and "My Country Tis of Sheep," while listening to chants of "We Hate Commies" and "Let's Bomb Hanoi."[10] When asked for comment, the Salem State College president was quick to say the antiwar protesters had a right to share their views, but he also made it clear both that he was "not in sympathy with the protestors" and that he thought they were giving "aid and comfort to the enemy."[11] As at many other colleges across the United States in the 1960s and early 1970s, Salem State's students continued to agitate around the Vietnam War, even as other issues and topics roiled their campuses.

A close examination of the Salem State College student newspaper illustrates how a host of issues emerged as hot topics and catalysts for change during the late 1960s and 1970s. Some of these topics were specific to Salem State, but most of the protests and challenges were related to larger discussions prevalent during the era and highlight the ways that this campus both reflected and shaped activist culture in the region and nation and how students' exposure to, and experience in, one movement prepared and emboldened them to participate and lead others.

The early 1970s brought a greater awareness of other concerns that especially affected women, including birth control and sexual assault. In a virtually unprecedented move, in 1970, the editors of *The Log* devoted almost three full pages to an essay that was "researched and prepared" by the newly formed Women's Center, titled, "North Shore Women Face Increasing Rape Threat." The article began by detailing two recent assaults in the region, positioning the article both in local circumstances and in the national conversation, and the women student leaders explained its purpose in this way: "We at the Salem State's Women's Center are concerned by this recent outbreak of rapes in our neighborhoods. During the past few years, the subject of rape has been very prominent in feminist literature. This article will discuss rape as myth and rape as reality; what the victim can expect after the crime; and suggestions for women to protect themselves."[12]

This essay is a stark reminder of the type of toxic climate that prevailed in the early 1970s and the work that young women across the nation were doing to fight back. Some of the shocking myths that the authors hoped to disprove included: "women really want to be raped," "a woman who is raped gets what she deserves," and "a healthy woman cannot be raped by one man alone." The essay featured advice for victims, including where to kick an attacker, suggestions that victims yell "fire" instead of "help" if they wanted people to respond, and how to use keys to strike the assailant's eyes and face. The authors had this very specific advice for those assaulted in public: "If . . . you do make it

Student Strike, 1970, Cover of *The Log*, Salem State College student newspaper, May 1, 1970. *(Salem State University Archives and Special Collections.)*

up to a porch of a lighted house, remember: you are **not** dropping in for a visit; if no one comes to the door immediately—do not stand there and politely ring the bell again—BREAK THE GLASS."[13] Drawing on the scholarship and activist strategies of the wider women's movement emerging at the time, this was an era when Salem State's female students vocally sought to claim control of their clothes (by fighting dress codes), their dorm rooms (by protesting dorm visitation rules), and their bodies. Claiming space and receiving student government funding for the Women's Center itself was a telling indicator of how students and student leaders were shaping campus culture and forcing the institution to face and grapple with contemporary social discontent.

The early 1970s also witnessed two other groups of students demand the college's respect for their culture and contributions. Both demands had identifiable catalysts, and both resulted in complete shutdowns of the entire campus so that student voices could be heard. While these protests were both perfectly in line with other examples of student activism across the nation, both had very specific Salem State sparks.

In the first instance, language students rose in protest against the chairman of the Foreign Languages Department, Professor Edwin Francis, criticizing the dismissal of four professors and, vitally, what they perceived as widespread disrespect of the French spoken by students of French-Canadian ancestry, who made up a significant proportion of the college's enrollment, thanks to Salem's history as a major destination for French-Canadian immigrants through the 1920s. More specifically, student teachers with French-Canadian accents were afraid that Francis would not let them pass their student teaching practicum because the Quebec-origin French they spoke was not the French spoken in Europe or in the academy. One student asked, in a letter to the editor in *The Log*, "How would you feel if you were told repeatedly that your ancestry and the language spoken by your ancestors is inferior?" Pointing to a pattern of intimidation, she further explained, "The French-Canadian students were afraid to speak, afraid to admit that they were French-Canadian because they were afraid of being ridiculed and humiliated."[14] The students met with the college president, had the faculty senate vote to support them, hosted forums with almost one-thousand attending, and circulated petitions before they, ultimately, concluded, "WE HAVE LEARNED THAT PROPER CHANNELS DO NOT WORK. The important question now is 'WHY?' The only answer is that proper channels are open when the administration wants them open and closed when they want them closed. This is done to maintain the level of intimidation that presently exists at Salem State College."[15] In late April and May 1970, students executed a general strike against the administration and its perceived disinterest in their experiences and frustrations.

Several years later, an even deeper campus schism was publicly revealed when the Afro-American Society used a residence hall's "slave auction" to draw attention to Black students' experiences on campus and to call for immediate and dramatic changes. In 1970, when the large number of French-Canadian students were demanding respect for their culture and contributions to campus, there were only twenty-one Black students on campus, with only four (total) juniors and seniors. By 1973, that number had quadrupled to eighty-eight Black students, with most of them (fifty-two) freshmen.[16] They joined a predominantly white working-class campus in a region that had been recently confronted with its racial inequities, most vividly in the controversy and violence of Boston's experience with court-ordered busing and racial integration.

Supported by the handful of Black faculty and staff at the college, the Afro-American Society grew out of student frustrations with not only racism in the United States, at large, but also experiences of isolation and discrimination at Salem State, in particular. In February 1970, a "slave auction" fundraiser in Salem State's Bowditch Hall made public what had been largely overlooked and prompted the society to issue a "Valentine's Day Manifesto," a searing document that outlines the society's demands and that begins with the simple declaration: "We are angry!" While the manifesto lists ten demands, including the hiring of more Black faculty, the offering of more courses that recognized the contributions of Black men and women to history and culture, and the active recruitment of more Black students, the separate lists of things the Afro-American Society was *for* and *against* are even more direct and telling. The "We Are Against" list includes ten items, beginning with "public institutional consent to racially degrading activities" and including "personal affronts to minority individuals," "false promises made in good faith, never kept," and a "priority system that puts economy before humanity."[17]

Much like it is possible to read *The Log* essay about rape to get a fuller sense of what life was like for women at Salem State, one can read the Afro-American Society's heartbreaking list of items and actions "We Are For" to understand the campus culture they were confronting. Among other things, the society was for "equal education for minority students," "a social awareness of Black students as a valuable part of the College community," the "correction of false images of Black students as a sub-element within Salem State College," and a "major commitment of the administration to the plight of the minorities not only on this campus, but in predominantly minority communities (East Lynn, Roxbury)."[18]

What followed was an emotional and tension-filled three days of meetings, memos, and negotiations, highlighted by an "emergency meeting of the entire campus," called by John Tierney, then the president of the Student Government

Association and later the representative for Salem's district to Congress. Tierney acknowledged that "racism exists on this campus, whether [people] want to believe it or not," and called on the community to listen to, and learn from, each other, before turning the stage over to the four representatives of the Afro-American Society.[19] According to one account of the meeting, after a few tense exchanges and accusations by white students that "somebody's trying to make me feel guilty," the tone of the meeting changed when the Music Department's Carolyn Jordan "moved virtually everybody with a lucid and forceful appeal to them to imagine what it means to be owned by another person."[20] Her comments prompted most of the crowd to rise and deliver a standing ovation, for the first time uniting both Black and white students in that type of response.[21] Work to shift campus culture was just beginning; over the next decade, Black students, Black faculty, and community partners worked hard to remake the college to serve a more diverse population.[22]

These brief accounts of Salem State's campus upheaval and student unrest are both characteristic of the late 1960s and early 1970s and uniquely Salem stories. They call our attention to the national trends of students protesting against the Vietnam War and for greater rights and representation, while they also must be understood within the specific circumstances of Salem's public university, one that educated people on both sides of the debate about Vietnam, people proud of their immigrant ancestry, women who wanted more control over their clothes, free time, and bodies, and Black students who wanted to be able to learn and live in a place that respected them as people and as full members of the community.

NOTES

1. Bruce J. Schulman, *The Seventies: The Great Shift in American Culture, Society, and Politics* (Da Capo, 2002).

2. Terry Anderson's book addresses these topics, explains how "the sixties" actually stretch into the early 1970s, and argues that the debates of the sixties dominated for decades afterward. See Terry H. Anderson, *The Sixties*, 2nd ed. (Pearson Longman, 2004), vii.

3. Roger Hardy, "Notes on Senator John F. Kennedy's Speech Given at Salem Teacher's College, 11 November, 1955," Roger Hardy Papers, Salem State University Archives, Salem, MA.

4. "Nature of Vietnam War: Infiltration and Murder," *The Log*, November 24, 1965, 1.

5. "S. J. A. Viet Nam Debate," *The Log*, November 24, 1965, 5.

6. "S. J. A. Viet Nam Debate Sparks Controversy," *The Log*, December 15, 1965, 1.

7. For an example of the draft updates, see "The Draft—Don't Panic Yet Boys," *The Log*, February 18, 1966, 2. *The Log* reported that the Students for a Democratic Society volunteers from Brandeis University "had been met with no special reaction. They anticipated this because there have been no demonstrations here at Salem." "SDS Questions Fairness of 'Beat-the-Draft' Exams," *The Log*, May 19, 1966, 7.

8. Robert Vogler and Loren Smith, "Conservative," *The Log*, November 18, 1966, 6.

9. "War Protested: Faculty and Students Protest U.S. Policy in Vietnam," *The Log*, April 28, 1967, 1. Melvin Small highlights the complexities and contradictions of the antiwar movement in his book, *Antiwarriors: The Vietnam War and the Battle for America's Hearts and Minds*, Vietnam: America in the War Years (Rowman and Littlefield, 2002).

10. "War Protested," 1.

11. Chris Kent, "Demonstration's Aftermath," *The Log*, May 5, 1967, 3.

12. Women's Center, "North Shore Women Face Increasing Rape Threat," *The Log* [1970], 1.

13. Women's Center, "North Shore Women," 7.

14. See, e.g., Nancy Hodge, "Ten Years Change People," *The Log*, April 10, 1970, 3. Elizabeth Duclos-Orsello's and Avi Chomsky's essays in this volume provide greater context for this episode.

15. "Editorially . . . ," *The Log*, April 10, 1970, 2.

16. "Black Enrollment," Arthur Gerald Records, Afro-American Society, 1969–1979, "Afro-American Society, 1972–1973" folder, Salem State University Archives, Salem, MA.

17. Afro-American Society, "The Valentine's Day Black Manifesto of Salem State College," Arthur Gerald Records, Afro-American Society, 1969–1979, "Afro-American Society, 1972–1973 (2)" folder; Afro-American Society, "We Are Against," Arthur Gerald Records, Afro-American Society, 1969–1979, "Afro-American Society, 1972–1973 (2)" folder.

18. Afro-American Society, "We Are For," Arthur Gerald Records, Afro-American Society, 1969–1979, "Afro-American Society, 1972–1973 (2)" folder.

19. Terry Sheenhan, "Valentine's Day Revisited," *The Log*, February 20, 1973, 1; "Uncle Frank's Cabin," *The Log*, February 20, 1973, 4.

20. "Uncle Frank's Cabin."

21. Terry Sheenhan, "Valentine's Day Concluded," *The Log*, February 20, 1973, 4.

22. For a better understanding of the full scope of these students' and staff members' activism and work to make Salem State a better place, see the Arthur Gerald Collection in the Salem State University Archives.

CHAPTER THIRTEEN

Situating the Self in Salem

Identity, Social Justice, and the Descendants of 1692

ANDREW DARIEN

> I was talking with one of my nieces on the West Coast. She was probably six or seven years old, and she asked me whether I had anything that belonged to Rebecca Nurse or if I knew whether there was a spell book anywhere. I started looking at the phone and said, "What has my brother taught her?" I had to politely explain to her [that] I don't have anything that belongs to her. Yes, I live near her house, and when you visit me, I'll show you her house. No, I'm very sure that there's no spell book and that there was never any spell book. I really don't think she was that kind of a witch. [Sighs]. That myth of Rebecca Nurse as a witch who casts spells. They come up with these fictions and encourage the spread of these fictions, I guess for the entertainment value.
>
> —ROBERT CORCORAN, Rebecca Nurse Descendant,
> Oral History, November 16, 2017

Salem is a curious place. This city's diverse architectural, cultural, and economic heritage built on the East India and China Trade is dwarfed by its popular identity as the locale of the 1692 witch trials. The branding of "Witch City" largely has been a twentieth-century affair, heightened and commercialized by "Haunted Happenings," an October festival started in 1982 in which hundreds of thousands of tourists, many costumed, descend on the city to partake in witch kitsch, ghost tours, psychic readings, magic expositions, games, rides, and, perhaps, a nominal homage to the twenty victims executed in 1692.[1] Visitors might take in the grandeur of Salem's Federal and Colonial architecture, explore the remarkable collection of Asian art at the Peabody Essex Museum, stroll the manicured grounds of the House of the Seven Gables, or take a reverential pause at the witch trials memorial, but most come to be spellbound. Historical accuracy and social justice take a back seat to enchantment.

Salem residents tolerate the October craze for the tourist dollars it brings to the city, but the descendants of the victims lament the ahistorical stain on their ancestors. This issue was brought to the fore during a one-day academic conference, Salem's Trials: Lessons and Legacies, at Salem State University in 2017, honoring the Trials' 325th anniversary. Historians, archivists, and educators grappled with the significance of the trials, their place in public memory, and the gulf between popular and scholarly knowledge. Descendants of both victims and accusers traveled from across the country to Salem to learn more about the trials, connect with fellow descendants, and, in some cases, provide testimonials. As the History Department's resident oral historian, I set up a recording booth where descendants discussed their specific ancestors, the significance of genealogy, and the trials' contemporary lessons. At least one descendant was a professional historian, but most testimonials came from people who viewed their ancestry as the essential credential that authorized their voices in the proceedings.

The descendants were an eclectic bunch with varied views of Salem's history. Still, something that emerged from these informal interviews was a sense of ancestral responsibility as guardians of Salem's past. Descendants identified personal and societal lessons about intolerance, mob mentality, shame, fear, and the fallibility of the justice system. It was not uncommon for speakers to have ancestors among the accusers and victims. Accuser descendants, though in some cases saddled with shame, were no less compelled to set the historical record straight and glean lessons from the trials. Jeff Folger, whose ancestor Bathsheba Pope falsely accused Martha Corey, John Proctor, and Rebecca Nurse of witchcraft, explained simply: "I can't change history, but the best we can do is learn from it and try not to repeat it."[2]

But what, exactly, might one learn from the descendants about this episode, and how might one apply that to contemporary life? Descendants offered no uniformity of sentiment about what transpired during the witchcraft hysteria, the specific lessons that ought to be drawn from it, or how that might serve as a guide to modern law, society, or politics. The testimonials came from people of varied backgrounds with unique pockets of knowledge whose ancestors had different experiences during the trials. Two other limitations of these testimonials were their brevity and the fact that the speakers had yet to be vetted. The narrators answered three questions and were restricted to fifteen minutes. Although there was little reason to doubt the narrators' ancestral claims, it is worth noting that they self-identified with no screening process to confirm authenticity.

Even if the testimonials included more extensive recordings with a uniform group of vetted ancestors, they would not constitute an oral history of the trials. Oral historians gather, preserve, and interpret the voices and memories of people and communities who were participants in or can provide first-person accounts of past events.[3] If one were seeking an oral history of the witch hysteria of 1692, the records of court testimony from the trials would be most apt.[4] No matter how well informed, descendants provide no first-person accounts of the trials. And yet, the family stories passed on among generations constitute an oral tradition that illuminates how a portion of the community has guarded these narratives over the years. The stories they have told one another, finessed over time and imparted to the larger public, tell us a good deal about how this group has derived meaning from the episode and folded their version into the historical record.[5]

The Towne Family Association

The intrigue of their testimony led me to reach out to the Towne Family Association (TFA), a genealogical organization for the descendants of William and Joanna Towne. The Townes migrated in the seventeenth century from Great Yarmouth, England, to Salem, Massachusetts, and had eight children. In 1692, two of their daughters, Rebecca Nurse and Mary Eastey,[6] were charged and hanged for witchcraft. Nurse, a revered community elder at the time of her execution, held steadfast in defense of her innocence. Generations of Salemites would later come to see her as the saintly martyr who proclaimed, "I can say before my Eternal Father I am innocent, & God will clear my innocency."[7] A third daughter, Sarah Cloyce, was also among the accused, though never indicted. With three ancestors, particularly the beloved and martyred Rebecca Nurse, at the center of the witchcraft hysteria, Towne descendants see themselves as caretakers of a fragile historical legacy. Like the descendants at the Salem's Trials conference, they had family stories to share and historical lessons to impart. In the fall of 2017, I worked with a team of graduate students to record a dozen of their oral histories.[8]

TFA members interviewed for this project were registered descendants of an established genealogical association for some of the most prominent victims of the trials. However, one still needs to consider the challenge of representativeness.[9] The TFA is a relatively small group of about five hundred self-selecting members, a tiny fraction of the Towne family descendants. Given that Rebecca Nurse alone had nine children and fifty-seven grandchildren, the Towne family descendants could number in the tens, perhaps hundreds, of thousands. It is entirely possible that a vast number of these descendants do not know their connection to these prominent historical figures. Moreover, Nurse, Eastey, and Cloyce were only three of the more than two hundred people accused of witchcraft. The TFA oral histories represent a select group of perspectives that cannot stand-alone as the sentiments of all accused descendants. And yet, the life histories of the most vibrant and publicly engaged genealogical organization associated with the Salem witch trials reveal a good deal about group identity, ancestry, living memory, and the commodification of the past.

"Injustice: Buried and Exhumed"

Nurse family lore and most historians agree that her sons and sons-in-law retrieved Rebecca's body from the gallows and reburied her in the grove of pines west of the house where the cemetery is located today.[10] This private burial allowed a degree of closure for the Nurse family, but the Nurse legacy was centuries in the making. If anything, Salem residents wanted to forget the misery wrought upon their city, particularly after a general amnesty in 1711 exonerated most of the victims. The Towne family worked tirelessly to erase their ancestors' ex-communication and, through oral tradition, kept alive stories of their valor. Still, most Salemites preferred to move on from the stain on their city. The historian William P. Upham noted in his 1886 *Account of the Rebecca Nurse Monument*, "This general desire to obliterate the memory of the calamity has nearly extinguished tradition. It is more scantly and less reliable than on any other event at an equal distance in the past. A subject on which men avoid to speak soon dies out of knowledge."[11]

Late nineteenth-century immigration, industrialization, economic development, and social division kindled a new interest in genealogy and progressivism. By 1875, Nurse's descendants formed the Nourse Monument Association, and a memorial was dedicated in 1885. To honor the legacy of her supporters, the Nurse family constructed a second memorial engraved in stone with the names of neighbors who signed a petition claiming her innocence. For nearly a century, Nurse was the only victim of 1692 to have a memorial erected in her memory.[12] In 1907, Nurse descendants and Danvers (formerly Salem Village) residents purchased the family home and farm. Descendants lobbied assiduously to clear her name and elevate her as the martyr of 1692. Inscribed on the monument was a poem by John Greenleaf Whittier: "O Christian martyr, who for Truth could die. When all about thee owned the hideous lie. The World redeemed from Superstitions sway. Is breathing freer for thy sake today."[13] Reverend C. B. Rice, the pastor of the First Church of Salem, delivered an address in front of four hundred descendants.

> The children of any of those that have suffered grievous wrong in the former generations may properly take redress from mankind in the following ages. The inheritance in families of personal character and remembrance is in itself of value to be reclaimed and kept. There is also a public interest with every many, demanding that public errors of the past should stand in the light and be reproved.[14]

By 1926, the Nurse Memorial Association purchased and ceded control of the Nurse property to the Society for the Preservation of New England Antiquities.[15] The Rebecca Nurse Homestead became the only home of the witch hunt preserved and open to the public. A testament to Nurse's legacy was the hundreds of descendants, historians, and other interested parties present at the witch trials' 300th anniversary.[16] At the 325th anniversary of Nurse's execution, Massachusetts Governor Charlie Baker declared July 19 "Rebecca Nurse Day," and the Danvers Alarm List Company, the owners and stewards of the property since the mid-1980s, held a solemn and respectful commemoration.

Haunting Tourism

The City of Salem honored the victims of the trials with similar reverence, but, since the 1970s, Salem's history has come under the spell of popular culture, marketing, and tourism. Take, for example, the Samantha Stephens statue in downtown Salem's center, which was dedicated in 2005. That statue commemorates the 1970 "Salem Saga" episode from the popular television show *Bewitched*. Having the most popular television witch in American history come to Salem helped the city start the process of branding itself for mass consumption. Around the same time, Salem institutions, such as the local paper, the chamber of commerce, and the police department, adopted Witch City as their logos. Then, in 1971, Laurie Cabot, a Wiccan and California transplant, declared herself the city's official witch and opened a downtown shop selling witchcraft paraphernalia. In 1972, an old church used as an auto museum was reopened as the Witch Museum, and the city had a new means of telling its story and selling it to tourists. By 1982, the Salem Chamber of Commerce saw the potential to draw on the connection between Halloween and the witch trials and officially established Haunted Happenings.[17]

The witchcraft industry proved lucrative, and tourism spared Salem from the economic misfortunes plaguing other postindustrial cities. Salem revitalized its economy and became a magnet for Wiccans, Goths, alternative musicians, unconventional healing therapies, vegan cuisine, and a little bit of colonial and maritime history thrown in for good measure. What troubles historians of the witch trials is the great gulf between the serious questions they pose in their works and what they see as Haunted Happenings' vulgar celebration of and ignorance about the execution of innocent victims. For academics, the tragic events of 1692 demand reverence rather than celebration.

"A Disgrace to the History"

If the witch trials hold a special place of reverence for Salem's residents, victim descendants guard the integrity of the narrative with singular protectiveness. Take, for example, the case of Geoffrey Esty Woodward, a descendant of both Mary Eastey and the nineteenth-century historian of the trials, William Elliot Woodward.[18] A Harvard graduate and scientist whose father was a lifetime member of the New England Historic Genealogical Society, Woodward possesses vast knowledge about the witch trials. Woodward's family impressed on him at an early age that Mary Eastey's execution had nothing to do with actual witches but rather the persecution of a "devout evangelical Christian falsely accused due to a land and property dispute with the Putnam family."[19] Especially galling to Woodward was the public ignorance about the trials and ways in which Salem has become a mecca for modern-day Wiccans, Pagans, Goths, and alternative musicians and artists. He recounts a recent visit to the Salem Witch Trials Memorial, a commemorative space in the heart of downtown, constituted of granite benches surrounded by a low stone wall and adorned by locust trees. The area was built in 1992 next to the Old Burying Point Cemetery for the three hundredth anniversary and was dedicated by Holocaust survivor and Nobel Peace Prize recipient Elie Wiesel. Woodward notes the disconnect between the intention the creators had for the space and its public uses:

> I went around to where the stones are behind the Peabody Essex Museum, and there was a line of people going around looking at them, but I just got this feeling that a lot of this history, that these people know nothing about, do you know what I'm saying? They have not been schooled in it. I've seen people dressed up in costumes, and they were traveling to Salem. And it's sort of like, literally, I have been told thousands of people, and they are sort of edgy people with nose rings and tattoos and they sort of, I think, do a disgrace to the history.[20]

Other descendants echoed Woodward's critique of the trials' commercialization. Barbara Hanno, a Rebecca Nurse descendant from Petersham, Massachusetts, expressed frustration with the popular notion that the executed were indeed witches. "Salem seems to have turned their [the accused] personal life stories into a fantasy based on their tragic stories, with the Halloween onslaught and the [*Bewitched*] Samantha statue[21] and the witchy stores," Hanno observed. "It's sacrilegious, almost. And it's hurtful to their memory. I've tried to justify it by thinking, well, you know Salem needs their income to keep their place going, and if they didn't, they wouldn't be able to memorialize and have the nice parks. But I find the commercialization difficult. It offends me."[22]

Pat Wilson, a Mary Eastey descendant from West Hartford, Connecticut, likewise laments the commercialization of Salem as being demeaning to her ancestors. "Salem has made lots of money," Wilson observed, "by making this [Haunted Happenings] a spectacle." Like Woodward, Hanno, and Corcoran, Wilson abhors how, in the popular imagination, the victims who were falsely accused of witchcraft seamlessly morph into witches: "I say to people that she [Mary Eastey] was a woman *accused* of witchcraft and she was executed, but she was not a witch!"[23]

TFA descendants irked by Haunted Happenings and the witch kitsch tempered their remarks with expressions of gratitude for Salem's recent efforts to venerate the victims. They conveyed particular appreciation for the Salem Witch Trials Memorial and the newly constructed Proctor's Ledge memorial. Researchers had surmised for years that Gallows Hill was a rocky ledge between Pope and Proctor streets, just less than a mile outside downtown Salem.[24] In 2016, a team of historians, geologists, archaeologists, and archivists confirmed the site.[25] The following year, a Community Preservation Act funded the construction of a semicircular granite wall with nineteen stones engraved with the names and execution dates of the victims.[26] "I like the newest memorial," noted Wilson. "There is more dignity now and a little less excitement about the whole tourist thing. I don't mind whatever Salem wants to do about their economy. Good for them. But personally, I'm for giving them a lot of dignity and a lot of respect for what happened."[27]

For some TFA descendants, the commercial success of Salem's tourism and its efforts to educate the public about the "true lessons" of the trials are inseparable. John Keenan, lifetime Salem resident, Rebecca Nurse descendant, attorney, former state legislator, and current president of Salem State University, sees the revival of Salem's economy as inextricably linked with an agenda to enshrine the social justice lessons of the trials. A multigenerational understanding of Salem industry informs his perspective. "I grew up in Salem. I've been here my entire life. My father and grandfather worked in the leather factories," Keenan explained. "When I grew up here, we had the tanneries. We had Parker Brothers. We had Osram Sylvania [light bulb production]. We had all these manufacturing jobs. My aunt worked at Parker Brothers. My dad worked at Flynntan [tannery]. The manufacturing jobs are gone, one way or another, for the most part."[28] As a witness to the city's declining manufacturing base, Keenan served on the tourism committee of the Massachusetts legislature so that he could help reinvigorate Salem's economy. The group was able to keep the Peabody Essex Museum in Salem by expanding its space and creating a pedestrian mall that would become the basis for future tourism. A self-described pragmatist, Keenan views Haunted Happenings as essential to the lifeblood of the local economy.

Keenan acknowledges that some museums may muddle the history of the trials or sensationalize events for profit. Still, he defends the October festivities for getting people to Salem so that they can engage in discussion about the meaning of its history. Keenan cites by way of example the House of the Seven Gables, a national historic landmark and setting of Nathaniel Hawthorne's classic 1851 novel. Keenan's wife, Kara McLaughlin, was the Gables director and reported that 30 to 40 percent of the institution's revenue is generated during the Halloween season. "They wouldn't be able to function if they didn't have the revenue they generated in October. Lots of businesses are relying on that[,] that September, October revenue to carry them through the difficult months of January." Omitting the issue of *what exactly* is taught to visitors to Salem, Keenan concluded, "Overall, tourism has been good for Salem because it also allows bringing more people here and educat[ing] them as to what really happened."[29]

Robert Corcoron, though dismayed by the fictions perpetrated about the witches of 1692, also took a more measured view of tourism. "I'm encouraged to see people who show an interest in history. Any aspect of history, whatever that is," Corcoran explained. "I am encouraged to see what I think is some incremental interest in some aspects of the historical story being told out there. If someone were to tell me that the historical story being told at these events isn't a hundred percent accurate, I'd believe you. I'd still be ok with that. On the margin, I think there is some incremental history learning go[ing] on."[30]

Past and Present Lessons

For over three centuries, Americans have embraced a multitude of lessons from the trials. Every generation has inherited the teachings of previous generations and reinterpreted them in the context of the contemporary political, social, and cultural landscape. Some universal themes include the dangers of group mentality, the subjective nature of evidence, the imperfection of the legal system, the vulnerability of women, religious intolerance, petty neighbor rivalries, and the fear of outsiders. The TFA members interviewed for the project articulated many of these lessons by pulling strands from professional and popular history and filtering them through the lens of the present. Although some narrators communicated a sophisticated understanding of the scholarly work on the Salem witch trials, the long shadow of Arthur Miller's play *The Crucible* and the tense political atmosphere of late 2017 informed many of their comments.

One would be hard-pressed to find a more credentialed expert on the trials than Rebecca Nurse's tenth great-granddaughter, Margo Burns, linguist, historian, and educator. A native of Manchester, New Hampshire, with deep New England roots going back to the Mayflower, Burns only came to learn of her connection to Rebecca Nurse through a serendipitous meeting:

> One day, one of my students [when I was teaching at Manchester Central High School] came in saying he was going to be cast as Francis Nurse in the school's play of *The Crucible*. And I had just received a whole bunch of stuff. My dad had given me his mother's genealogy research, and I'd been going through some of that. And I said, "You know, I think that's a name in my family." I went home and dug through my grandmother's things, and there on the page [was] the Nurse family. This little asterisk at the bottom of the page said, "Nurse hanged for witchcraft in Salem, 19th July 1692." And I went. "Oh. I guess they are real."[31]

The family silence around Rebecca Nurse is telling. "I never heard about it within my family even though my grandmother clearly knew about it," Burns explained. "I mean, she was into the Mayflower Society and the DAR [Daughters of the American Revolution], but she didn't talk about that one." Burns regretted that her grandmother had died shortly before her own Rebecca Nurse discovery, because she never had the opportunity to inquire about why the information had been hidden. When she asked her father's brother the question, he said explicitly that he did not want to discuss it. "For [my uncle and grandmother], the Mayflower was everything." In the Burns family, a Mayflower ancestor was a source of pride, a claim to an authentic American connection, whereas an ancestor executed of witchcraft, however erroneously, was an indignity.

Burns got to work on her family's genealogical research, became consumed by the surviving legal primary sources, and became a renowned scholar of the trials. She worked with a team of scholars as the project manager and associate editor for *The Records of the Salem Witch-Hunt*.[32] The thousand-page tome was published in 2009 as the first comprehensive collection of chronologically arranged legal documents about the Salem witch trials. This meticulous collection of primary sources is a tremendous resource for scholars, to whom it leaves interpretation and analysis.

Burns's archivist sensibility about painstaking documentation and verification left her exasperated with how Arthur Miller's 1953 play *The Crucible* has jumbled the popular understanding of the trials. Among the many historical inaccuracies and fabrications perpetrated through Miller's creative license are the scene of wild dancing girls in the woods, the love affair and ages of John Proctor and Abigail Williams, the deep sleep of Betty Parris and Abigail Williams, and the scripting of Tituba as black or African rather than Native American. "It may not matter if one's sole interest in Miller's work is as literature or theater," Burns writes, but "what happens when people *only* know history through creative works of art and not from primary sources and facts, letting someone else pick and choose between which facts to include and which to alter for their purposes and political arguments?"[33]

Burns seeks to hold citizens accountable for historical truth, and she believes historical knowledge has aplace in contemporary politics. Indeed, the bewildering nature of truth in the administration of President Donald J. Trump got at the heart of what Burns viewed as wrong with the political culture. She was especially vexed by the notion of "alternative facts" as first articulated by Counsel to the President Kellyanne Conway:[34]

> There are facts, and there are lies. And I think trying to separate truth from fiction is even more critical right now. There have been so many fictions written and repeated about the Salem Witchcraft Trials. So when somebody says something, I want to know where that came from. And that informs a lot of my political [beliefs]. Take the 45th President of the United States—who shall remain nameless—claiming that the biggest witch-hunt is against him is just totally ridiculous. How dare he! Then again, the politicians in Salem tweeted against him. Do you know your history? I really think we need to figure out what facts are, and what we agree upon is how we determine facts. Then, can you have interpretations? But if you mess with what you think is the truth? That really causes a lot of problems. So I always want to know: What are

the facts? How do you know? That's the other thing. How do we know what we know? Facts shouldn't be debatable.[35]

The TFA oral histories reflected Burns's commentary on truth's unstable and murky nature. Each descendant was drawn to unique political causes and conclusions: opposition to the death penalty, the necessity of due process, the protection of women, and the defense of religious freedom. Not all descendants were religious, but each embraced Nurse's resolve as a model for an ethical life.

Richard Nelson was raised in Southern California by a transplanted New England family with deep ties to their Mayflower and Towne family ancestors. Nelson first came to Salem while he was a graduate student at MIT. While visiting the Salem Witch Museum, he came across Rebecca Nurse's name and remembered her from his mother's pedigree charts. This began Nelson's lifelong fascination with the history of the trials and the reckoning of the executions with his modern sensibility about science, faith, and rational thought:

> In my mind, there's this grandmother, a great-grandmother, a 77-year-old lady who has done her best to live a god-fearing life. Very religious. I am very religious. She was very religious—I can relate. And she's put on trial for something—maybe she understood better because she lived in that age than I would about how the superstitions affected the accusers and the judges and the jury, but when I heard the story about how she was on the stand and testified and the jury was going to let her go. They couldn't find anything wrong with her, and then when the verdict was read and the increasing agitation on the part of the accusers, the judge said, "Well, maybe we should reconsider and ask her some more questions." They ask her some questions, and then she's just tuckered out and tired. And she doesn't hear the questions right or whatever. On that basis, they want to convict her; they convict her to appease the accusers. I thought, "I'm proud of her." At least for standing up for what she believed. She was doing her best, to the end, to live a god-fearing life.[36]

Robert Corcoran of Wenham, Massachusetts, a vice president of marketing, Nurse descendant, and amateur genealogist, shares the descendants' frustration with the misuse of history and the commercialization of the trials. Like Nelson, he holds a spiritual, though not necessarily religious, connection to his ancestor. His proximity to the Rebecca Nurse Homestead allows him to pass it several times weekly, a reminder of his ancestral resolve. Like many descendants, Corcoran sees Nurse as a source of social justice, personal determination, and self-acceptance:

I'm gay, and I came out of the closet in 1986, coincidentally, right around the time when I was taking an interest in researching this Betty Nurse character. Could she possibly be connected to Rebecca Nurse? And so it's a coincidence that I discovered this descent from Rebecca Nurse while I was going through the process of coming out of the closet. And certainly, once I'd done the genealogy to find a connection to Rebecca Nurse, it was in and of itself exciting to find a connection with a historical figure. It was inspirational. To read her testimony during her trial, which, from my reading of it, was, "I haven't done anything wrong, and why are you coming after me? I haven't done anything wrong." That was a wonderful message to read and have someone feel some connection as I went through this coming-out process. And there are many times during the spring and summer, probably a six-month period, that I think of as my coming out period when I would turn to her, her testimony every few days to read again. It's only a few pages, but it was just wonderful to have a connection to someone who has gone through this horrible experience where her message was, "I haven't done anything wrong." So that was wonderful and something of a gift.[37]

The Democratization of 1692

For descendants of the Towne family, such as Corcoran, Burns, and Nelson, Rebecca Nurse is an enduring symbol of liberty, independent thought, and unwavering personal resolve. Like numerous generations before them, these descendants actively preserve and pay homage to her legacy as the revered martyr of Salem. This virtuous and morally upright version of Rebecca Nurse is consistently depicted in scholarly accounts of the trials.[38] Ancestors can see this dignified legacy at prominent sites like the Salem Witch Trials Memorial, the Rebecca Nurse Homestead, Proctors Ledge, and the Danvers Witchcraft Victims Memorial.

Despite this sanctification, ancestors remain steadfast in combating the commercialization of tragedy, the branding of Salem as Witch City, and the political misuses of popular history. Yet, genealogical organizations like the TFA that represent a tiny fraction of descendants may lose their authority to control family stories. With the increasing accessibility of DNA testing through platforms like 23andMe and AncestryDNA, tens of thousands of potential new descendants may emerge, each interpreting Nurse for their own personal or political agenda. The "heritage dynamics" of the trials will evolve on the various individuals or groups who value, use, or do heritage work in Salem. As the witchcraft industry shows no signs of abating, the democratization of genealogy will bring new voices, interpretations, and claims to the legacy of 1692.[39] Professional, popular, and family accounts of the trials will remain contested terrain, as will the membership of the genealogical societies like the TFA. An ideal future history will allow for a collaborative approach in which scholars can facilitate an open dialogue among descendant communities, the tourist industry, civic leaders, and other interested parties.[40]

NOTES

1. There is no historical link between Halloween and Salem. The journey from the witch trials town to "Witch City" was the result of confusion, ahistorical accident, and economic pressure. See Frances Hill, "Salem as Witch City," in Dane Anthony Morrison and Nancy Lusignan Schultz, *Salem: Place, Myth, and Memory* (Northeastern University Press, 2004), 283–298.

2. Jeff Folger, Interview with the author, June 10, 2017.

3. "Oral History: Defined," *Oral History Association*, available at https://www.oralhistory.org/about/do-oral-history, accessed May 21, 2019.

4. Paul Boyer and Stephen Nissenbaum, *The Salem Witchcraft Papers: Verbatim Transcripts of the Legal Documents of the Salem Witchcraft Outbreak of 1692* (Da Capo, 1977).

5. For more on the ways in which American genealogy defined and reinforced individual and collective identities, see François Weil, *Family Trees: A History of Genealogy in America* (Harvard University Press, 2013).

6. The Eastey name is also written as Esty, Easty, Estie, Easstie, and Estye.

7. Rebecca Nurse testimony from Reverend Parris's account of the examination at Salem Meeting House, March 24, 1692. See *Salem Witch Trials Documentary Archives and Transcription Project*, University of Virginia Library, available at http://salem.lib.virginia.edu/Commemoration.html.

8. Special thanks to Jessica Analoro, Laura Cleary, Kendra Czernicki, Ashley Dettore, Nicki Girourd, Gregory James, Courtney Klapman, Thomas Landers, Danielle Luman, Mark Pappas, Brendan Powers, Keith Van Hook, Ana Maria Weddey, Thomas Wright, and Dan Zinna.

9. The TFA facilitates genealogical research for its members but does not make this a prerequisite for admission. Many members engaged in DNA testing before and after joining the organization. "Interview with TFA President Gail Garda" and "'Testing' the Towne Family Association," available at http://townefolk.com/testing/TFA_ABOUT.php, accessed May 28, 2019.

10. Daniel A. Gagnon, *A Salem Witch: The Trial, Execution, and Exoneration of Rebecca Nurse* (Westholme, 2021), 260.

11. William P. Upham, *Account of the Rebecca Nurse Monument* (Salem Press, 1886).

12. Gagnon, *Salem Witch*, 260. Some members of the family used the Nourse spelling of the name in the late nineteenth century.

13. *Rebecca Nurse Memorial*, erected 1885, Rebecca Nurse Homestead Cemetery, Danvers, MA.

14. "Rebecca Nourse, Hanged as a Witch Two Hundred Years Ago, Honored Yesterday by Hundreds of Her Descendants," *Boston Globe*, July 31, 1885, 5.

15. Danvers Alarm List Company, "Miscellaneous Clippings, Brochures, and Announcements," Peabody Essex Museum Archives.

16. Gagnon, *Salem Witch*, xix.

17. Frances Hill, "Salem as Witch City," in Dane Anthony Morrison and Nancy Lusignan Schultz, *Salem: Place, Myth, and Memory* (Northeastern University Press, 2004), 283–298.

18. W. Elliot Woodward, *Records of Salem Witchcraft: Copied from the Original Documents* (Privately Printed, 1864).

19. Biographical information form, Geoffrey Esty Woodward, November 20, 2017.

20. Geoffrey Esty Woodward, Interviewed by Nicki Girourd, Salem State University, November 30, 2017, Towne Family Oral History Project.

21. Hanno is referring to Samantha Stephens from the television program *Bewitched*, for whom the city of Salem in 2005 dedicated a statue in the heart of downtown. The statue was a tribute to the actress Elizabeth Montgomery, who, along with the cast of the popular television comedy *Bewitched*, came to Salem in 1970 to film several "Salem Saga" episodes. See "'Bewitched' Statue Charms Salem Fans," *Boston Globe*, June 16, 2005.

22. Barbara Hanno, Interviewed by Ashley D'Ettorre, Salem State University, November 28, 2017, Towne Family Oral History Project.

23. Pat Wilson, Interviewed by Kendra Czernicki, Salem State University, November 16, 2017, Towne Family Oral History Project.

24. For the original scholarly identification of Gallows Hill, see Sidney Perley, "Where Witches Were Hanged," *Historical Collections of the Essex Institute* 55, no. 1 (1921), 1–18.

25. Members of the Gallows Hill Project Team include Emerson Baker, professor of history, Salem State University; Shelby Hypes, Salem Award Foundation; Elizabeth Peterson, director, Corwin Witch House; Tom Phillips, producer and director of *Salem Witch Trials: Examine the Evidence*; Benjamin Ray, professor of religion, University of Virginia; Marilynne Roach, Salem witch trials historian and author; and Peter Sablock, emeritus professor of geology, Salem State University.

26. Christine Woodside, "The Site of the Salem Witch Trial Hangings Finally Has a Memorial," Smithsonian.com, July 13, 2017, available at https://www.smithsonianmag.com/history/site-salem-witch-trial-hangings-finally-has-memorial-180964049/#84q11w5vDYR1QeeQ.99.

27. Ibid.

28. By the 1970s, manufacturing companies such as the Naumkeag Steam Cotton Company, Hygrade Sylvania, and Parker Brothers no longer provide the industrial base that the city so desperately needed. John D. Keenan, Interviewed by Thomas Landers, Salem State University, November 30, 2017.

29. Ibid.

30. Robert Corcoran, Interviewed by Thomas Wright, Salem State University, November 1, 2017, Towne Family Oral History Project.

31. Margo Burns, Interviewed by Courtney Klapman, Salem State University, November 21, 2017, Towne Family Oral History Project.

32. Bernard Rosenthal, General Editor, *The Records of the Salem Witch-Hunt* (Cambridge University Press, 2009).

33. Margo Burns, "Arthur Miller's *The Crucible: Fact and Fiction*," *17th Century Colonial New England with Emphasis on the Essex Country Witch-Hunt of 1692*, October 30, 2015, available at http://www.17thc.us/docs/fact-fiction.shtml.

34. Conway first used the term "alternative facts" to refer to Press Secretary Sean Spicer's exaggerated claims of crowd size at the presidential inauguration. Conway interview with Chuck Todd, NBC Television Program, *Meet the Press*, Transcript, January 22, 2017, available at https://www.nbcnews.com/meet-the-press/meet-press-transcripts-n51976.

35. Margo Burns Interview. Burns refers to the Representative Seth Moulton's response to President Donald Trump claiming that the Russia investigation was "the single greatest witch hunt of a politician in American history." Moulton replied, "As the Representative of Salem, MA, I can confirm this is false." Seth Moulton, Twitter Post, May 18, 2017, 9:13 A.M., available at https://twitter.com/sethmoulton/status/865238855800279040?lang=en.

36. Danielle Luman, interview with Richard Nelson, November 20, 2017, Salem, Massachusetts, Towne Family Oral History Project.

37. Robert Corcoran Interview.

38. See, e.g., Charles Sutherland Taplev, *Rebecca Nurse: Saint but Witch Victim* (Marshall Jones, 1930); Gagnon, *Salem Witch*.

39. See Kalliopi Fouseki, *Heritage Dynamics: Understanding and Adapting to Change in Diverse Heritage Contexts* (University College London Press, 2022).

40. On descendant communities, see Chip Colwell-Chanthaphonh and T. J. Ferguson, eds., *Collaboration in Archaeological Practice: Engaging Descendant Communities* (AltaMira, 2008).

INTERLUDE 13

Salem's Changing Demographics

Aviva Chomsky

Visitors to Salem are greeted with rainbow-painted crosswalks, and candidates for public office vie with each other to tout their commitment to affordable housing and environmental sustainability. But underneath the liberal veneer, twenty-first-century Salem is a deeply divided city. Its shiny new condos, thriving arts scene, destination restaurants and vibrant nightlife coexist uneasily with the city's demographic realities. The visibility of a young white liberal and upwardly mobile Salem can obscure the struggles both of the older and working-class residents, faced with spiraling rent, housing prices, and property taxes, and of the large immigrant population, mostly from the Dominican Republic, faced with the same issues, who have increasingly filled the narrow streets and decaying mill workers' housing of the city's "The Point" neighborhood in recent decades.

The arrival of Puerto Ricans, Dominicans, and others in Salem, which started in the 1960s, increased in the 1980s in response to local, national, and global events. Economic and political trends, including U.S. interventions, dictatorships and revolutions, and modernization schemes that fostered U.S. investment in export processing, agribusiness, and tourism, uprooted rural people in Latin America and the Caribbean without enabling urban infrastructure and services to sustain migrants. They also created new connections that made the United States a realistic destination. Immigration from Latin America grew rapidly after 1965.

The last comparable wave of immigration started in the mid-nineteenth century. Then, the migrants were primarily European (since most non-Europeans were banned until the mid-twentieth century), and newcomers entered a booming industrial economy. Working and living conditions were often dire, and Irish, Italian, Jewish, and other immigrants faced discrimination and prejudice. But, as legally "white," they had easy access to citizenship, and, by the midcentury, through a combination of political and labor mobilization, favorable legislation, and the economic boom of World War II and beyond, many achieved substantial upward mobility.

Things were different in the late twentieth century. Deindustrialization—including the closure of Salem's mill in the 1950s—shifted production out of the United States to places like Latin America, where labor, tax, and environmental regulations resembled those of the nineteenth-century United States. Unionization rates in the United States dropped from over a third of the workforce to a tenth. One labor historian called the 1970s "the last days of the working class" as stable employment gave way to increasing precarity.[1] While the shift to a service sector economy did create jobs at the higher end, most immigrants in the late twentieth century took jobs in poorly regulated and informal sectors like landscaping, cleaning, child- and eldercare, food services, and subcontracted work in formerly unionized sectors like construction and manufacturing. The public investments that had enabled upward mobility for the earlier wave of immigrants were cut back.

Puerto Rico and the Dominican Republic offer clear examples of how U.S. intervention and investment spurred emigration. The United States invaded Puerto Rico in 1898, ruled the island as a colony until 1952, and, in its Cold War attempts to showcase the benefits of capitalism, implemented "Operation Bootstrap" to help U.S. manufacturers relocate there and take advantage of the island's exceptional status that kept Puerto Ricans as nonvoting citizens and the island free from federal income taxes (a big plus for U.S. corporations), and, in addition to that, it is only partially subject to U.S. laws. While Operation Bootstrap brought significant advantages for certain industries (and played a big role in the trend toward government-financed development of export processing zones, runaway plants, and U.S. deindustrialization in subsequent decades), it also spurred a huge out-migration. By 2020, over 60 percent of Puerto Ricans lived in the continental United States.[2]

In the Dominican Republic, the United States invaded in 1916 and occupied the country until 1924 in a bid to take control of its foreign trade, customs revenues, and debts, to create a U.S.-dependent military force to maintain social control, and to establish a U.S.-controlled sugar plantation economy there. The United States warmly supported the dictator Rafael Trujillo, until his repression became a Cold War liability and it then switched to trying to orchestrate his assassination. When popular elections brought the socialist Juan Bosch to the presidency in the early 1960s, the U.S. Marines invaded again. The political turmoil of the 1960s brought the first waves of migration; the export processing zones and neoliberal austerity reforms of the 1980s drove more Dominicans from their homeland.

As late twentieth-century Latin American migrants sought a better life in the United States, many flocked to declining industrial cities like Salem. Cheap housing and downwardly mobile jobs in the remaining industries and in expanding service sectors were one draw. Some declining industries actively recruited skilled Latin American workers. Once the first families came, chain migration (a neutral term describing a pattern that historians and sociologists have observed in virtually all studies of domestic and international migration over time) brought their relatives and acquaintances. From old New England textile towns to the Rust Belt, immigrants revitalized decaying industrial centers.[3]

Salem's recent immigration history reflects this larger trend. The 2020 census found 8,785 Latinos in the city, some 22 percent of the population.[4] The numbers represented a 36 percent increase from the 2010 census, just under the state average increase of 41 percent. (Salem's white population decreased slightly, by 3 percent, over the same decade.)[5] Of Salem's Latinos, 40 percent were foreign-born.[6] Most (4,523) were Dominican, followed by Puerto Ricans (1,719), Mexicans (403), Hondurans (256), and Salvadorans (193).[7]

Contradictions between Salem's self-image as a trendy "destination" and its realities of entrenched poverty and racism played out on a daily basis in its upscale downtown, in the crumbling housing of The Point's narrow streets, and in the city's always-contested schools. The city's median income of $66,428 put it well below the state median of $84,385 (in 2020). Latinos were by far the city's poorest residents, with a median income of $30,486—even lower than the state median for Latinos of $48,450.[8] Of the white population, 60 percent owned their own homes, compared to only 15 percent of Latinos.[9] Of Salem's white population, 49 percent had a college degree, while only 25 percent of the city's Latinos did. Meanwhile, 26 percent of the city's Latino adults lacked a high school diploma, compared to only 5 percent of the white population. (These figures are comparable to what is found statewide.)[10]

A 2022 study of the El Punto community identified deteriorating roads, sidewalks, sewers, and rain-catching systems; infestations of pests, including rats and cockroaches; and lack of decent work opportunities as issues of significant concern to The Point residents.[11] While the intent of the research was to investigate community engagement with climate change resilience, most of their informants felt that this was simply not a priority. As one informant explained, "When we're talking about people who are experiencing poverty, I think they maybe, well, aware that climate change [is an issue] like globally, but I think when they think of their day-to-day lives and they're thinking about where their next paycheck's going to come from, where their next meal is going to come from, maintaining a roof over their family's heads. . . . I think their goals are focused on economic security and basic needs."[12]

These structural issues played out in the city's public schools in ways that for many immigrants reflected their invisibility and abandonment. As of 2022, 60.3 percent of the city's student population of 3,709 were classified as low income, 45.3 percent were Latino, 30.4 percent spoke a language other than English at home, and 17.6 percent were English Language Learners.[13]

On state standardized tests, the city's Latino students scored considerably lower than its white students, which mirrored state and national patterns. Yet, Salem's Latino students scored lower than did Latino students statewide.[14] Only 27 percent of Latino students achieved a "proficient" score on the third-grade reading test in 2014, as compared to 58 percent of white students, a figure that had remained stubbornly consistent over the previous ten years. The gap between Latino and white students shrank slightly over the decade, only because white students in Salem saw their scores decline.[15] (Reading scores were significantly better for tenth graders, though math scores did not show the same improvement.)

Salem immigrants' struggles for educational, economic, and political justice constitute one local manifestation of fights for immigrants' rights going on in gateway cities in Massachusetts, around the country, in Congress, at the border, and worldwide in the twenty-first century. While Salem's tourist industry touts the town's progressive credentials and its unique maritime and witch histories, visitors often miss the grittier realities lived by the city's residents.

NOTES

1. Jefferson Cowie, *Stayin' Alive: The 1970s and the Last Days of the Working Class* (New Press, 2010).

2. The number has increased rapidly since the mid-twentieth century, crossing the 50 percent mark in 2006. César J. Ayala, "Puerto Rico and Its Diaspora," UCLA, available at https://www.sscnet.ucla.edu/soc/faculty/ayala/prdiaspora/index-english.html#:~:text=Puerto%20Rico%20and%20its%20Diaspora&text=In%202018%2C%2064%20percent%20of,the%20Puerto%20Rican%20population%20stateside.

3. See A. K. Sandoval-Strausz, *Barrio America: How Latino Immigrants Saved the American City* (Basic Books, 2019).

4. Granberry, Phillip, and Agarwal, Vishakha, "Latinos in Massachusetts Selected Areas: Salem," *Gastón Institute Publications*, 287 (August 2022), 3, available at https://scholarworks.umb.edu/gaston_pubs/287.

5. Granberry and Agarwal, "Latinos in Selected Areas: Salem," 3.

6. Granberry and Agarwal, 4.

7. Granberry and Agarwal, 5.

8. Granberry and Agarwal, 12, citing the 2016–2020 American Community Survey.

9. Granberry and Agarwal, 13, citing the 2016–2020 American Community Survey.

10. Granberry and Agarwal, 8.

11. Sweet, Elizabeth, Torres-Ardila, Fabián, Bravo, Daniela, and Jara, Leandra, "Reimagining Community Engagement to Increase Resilience to Climate Change in El Punto Neighborhood, Salem, Massachusetts," *Gastón Institute Publications*, 290 (September 2022), 8, available at https://scholarworks.umb.edu/gaston_pubs/290.

12. Sweet et al., "Reimagining Community Engagement," 19.

13. Massachusetts Department of Education, School and District Profiles, Salem, 2022–2023, available at https://profiles.doe.mass.edu/general/general.aspx?topNavID=1&leftNavId=100&orgcode=02580000&orgtypecode=5. For comparison with 2015, see Michael Berardino, "Latinos in Massachusetts Public Schools: Salem," *Gastón Institute Publications*, 202 (April 2015), available at http://scholarworks.umb.edu/gaston_pubs/202.

14. Berardino, "Latinos in Public Schools: Salem," 4.

15. Berardino, 5.

CHAPTER FOURTEEN

Salem

Allowing the Past to Haunt Us on Our Terms

MARGO SHEA AND THERESA GIARD

Welcome to Salem

Salem welcomes almost one million tourists every October, about twenty times the city's population. It is big business, generating more than $140 million in local spending. The city's October festival, Haunted Happenings, which features a parade and a "haunted" street fair and other Halloween-inspired festivities, began as a weekend event forty years ago. Today, tourists flock to Salem all year long, with their numbers increasing over the summer months and reaching a crescendo in October. According to one blogger, people come to indulge their interests in everything from "early American history, to ancient sorcery, to modern witchcraft, to pop culture touchstones like Harry Potter and Hocus Pocus."[1] Like many "dark tourism" hubs, Salem has also become known as a welcoming space for anyone curious about the things that cannot be easily described through reason or rationality. This peaks at Halloween, itself a celebration in which "we remember the dead and conjure up spirits, ghosts and other supernatural ephemera."[2]

While the Peabody Essex Museum, the city-operated Witch House and Charter Street Cemetery Welcome Center, as well as the National Park Service's Visitor Center, all interpret the history of witch hysteria to varying degrees, not all who come to Salem want to engage with museum spaces. Many scholars have noted that museums and other heritage institutions may be experienced as distancing and alienating, and traditional heritage spaces have often been seen to be unwelcoming and inaccessible.[3] In addition, part of the allure of the city is its vibrant street culture. Described as everything from a bachelorette party to a pub crawl to a frat-house rager to cosplay paradise to a monthlong festival, the atmosphere in Salem in the autumn often strikes a tone that is dissonant with its history. Both historical and contemporary factors draw people to the city.

The cityscape plays a significant role in drawing people to Salem. Visitors often reflect on the presence of the past in the canopies of trees, the brick sidewalks of the McIntire District, the carefully maintained Federal-era houses, and the echoes of the city's seafaring connections along Derby Wharf and the Salem Maritime National Historic Site's buildings and ship replicas. As Colin Sterling explains, the built environment plays an important role as the echo and shadow of the past: "The past co-mingle(s) with the present in unexpected ways, with certain places and objects emphasizing a powerful if shadow-like co-existence."[4] Since James Howard Kunstler's warning that the United States was in danger of becoming a "geography of nowhere" has largely been realized, for many visitors, Salem's footprint is itself something of a ghost—an artifact of a distant past to which they normally have little access.[5]

In Salem, historical landmarks and commemorative memorial spaces are often the stage on which stories of ghosts and curses, spells and shadows are told. For many visitors, a haunted walking tour rises to the top of the bucket list. Nighttime tours of Salem have emerged as one of the most popular pastimes for visitors to the city. "Dark History and Murder," "History and Hauntings," "Haunted Footsteps of Salem," "Ghostly Night Tour," "Voodoo, Vampires, and Ghosts," and others offer a mix of history, lore, and spooky tales. Beginning with the assertion that ghost stories are "culturally meaningful, rational, and still very much a part of our modern and technological world," this chapter explores the interests, preoccupations, and anxieties people bring to ghost tours in Salem.[6] As public historians, we (the authors) have endeavored to examine the enthusiasm for all things haunted, from a variety of perspectives, drawing on Theresa Giard's firsthand experience leading nighttime walking tours of Salem and Margo Shea's expertise in the different ways ghost stories and other forms of folk belief have been put to use culturally and socially. If hauntings are said to be "predicated on social and historical discontinuities that imbue the past with a sense of mystery and strange possibility . . . products of present need and desire," we argue here that the layered histories are exposed like a palimpsest through the ghost tour.[7] Fundamental to our perspective is the notion that ghost tours are well worth our attention. Following Colin Sterling, heritage should include "the unsorted and unruly legacies passed on," legacies with which we coexist whether we acknowledge them or not.[8]

At one major tour company's meeting spot, attendees line up along a wrought iron fence that borders the grounds to a Federal-era mansion. As more tour goers cross the street to join the group, easily reaching the maximum of forty people, their tour guide leads them away immediately, so another guide can take her spot and begin the process again. The never-ending flow of tours, often led by people with graduate degrees in history, brings to mind an assembly line and reminds us of scholar Amy Tyson's observation that heritage workers are "replaceable cogs in the machine of the cultural economy."[9] Tour guides tend to be loquacious, warm, and relatable—another difference from perceptions people have of docents and museum interpreters. While guides are often knowledgeable about Salem's history, the currencies of exchange on a tour are democratic. For visitors, the difference between being told a story and being offered a lecture often means that ghost tours allow them to show up comfortably as a participant to be engaged, not as a vessel to be filled with information.

Tour groups in October normally reach capacity for this particular company, with three to four guides leading groups of forty people per time slot. While each group is different, you may see attendees from as young as a few months in a stroller to those advanced in age in motorized wheelchairs. There are friends and families who have traveled across the country for a bucket list trip to Salem and local folks who are visiting from the surrounding New England states. International travelers from Latin America join Canadians, Brits, Irish, and Germans. A Salem tour guide will likely have met tourists from six of the seven continents after one weekend in October. The tour takers, overwhelmingly white and of European descent, often experience Salem as part of their own historical legacy regardless of their knowledge of the history of the events of 1692.

The Ghosts of Our Ancestors

Dark tourism, also known as thanatourism or grief tourism, often involves visiting places that are associated with death, suffering, or tragedy. In Salem, exposure to the uncanny can hold space for individuals to grapple with mysterious aspects of life and death that are difficult or even impossible to explain. As Tiya Miles explains, ghosts and ghost stories help us connect to the past in important ways:

> We interpret our lives through the lens of the past, sometimes for better, sometimes for worse. But in this epic quest for history we encounter a fundamental challenge: the past exists on another plane of time, far

away from us. We cannot fully access the past because it is no longer present. It is distant, shrouded, mysterious. To visit the past we require a sort of mental time machine, such as the feeling of transcendence that can be invoked by standing at an atmospheric historic site, viewing rare objects in a museum, reading a gripping historical study, or, perhaps, encountering a ghost. And, of all the possible means of transport into the past, a ghostly encounter is arguably the most immediate, the most personal, and, for some people, the most "real."[10]

Ghost stories, understood this way, are more than attempts to touch the past. Tales of ghosts and hauntings tend to reveal or reinforce cultural values or, alternatively, to focus on cultural stressors and fears, often homing in on societal conflicts and tensions. For example, ghost tours highlighting paranormal presences often provide important opportunities to talk about the body—its vulnerabilities, traumas, and pain—in ways that are socially acceptable.[11] In Salem, the gruesome public executions in the wake of accusations that often invoked the body as a medium for malevolent spirits to work their will are a backdrop, in their own way haunting October, even as they offer the foundation for the city's ghost tourism.

"Our DNA makes us, in part, the ghosts of our ancestors," Jeannie Farrell asserts, "We embody scraps, fragments, and glimmers of our forebears. We are shadows of who they were."[12] The Salem witch trials of 1692–1693 were by far the largest and most lethal outbreak of witchcraft hysteria in American history. With at least twenty-five million people able to claim descendancy from either an accuser or someone accused of witchcraft in Salem in 1692, those shadows loom large over our collective consciousness. Further, the witch hysteria targeted women and immediate family members of Christian ministers; it makes sense that in an era of the #metoo movement and a mass exodus from organized faith traditions, people might be haunted by that which Salem symbolizes.

Haunted by Its History

The conception of Salem as a place haunted by its history is not a new phenomenon. In the nineteenth century, the idea captivated Nathaniel Hawthorne when he returned from Bowdoin College in Maine to Salem and endeavored to become a writer. "The quaint air, the eerie atmosphere that pervaded Salem with its lingering ghosts of the persecuted witches in whose maltreatment his ancestors took an active part, captured his imagination," wrote one early biographer. Hawthorne was convinced that his bedroom in Salem was a paranormal site and talked often of his "haunted chamber." Indeed, one of his most famous literary characters, Colonel Pyncheon, was based on Hawthorne's own great-great-grandfather, the Salem witch trials judge John Hathorne. In *House of the Seven Gables*, Pyncheon is cursed due to the persecutions of alleged witches. Hawthorne saw Salem itself as cursed by its history and wrote of the city, "I am enduring my banishment here as best I may, (and) methinks, all enormous sinners should be sent on a pilgrimage to Salem, and compelled to spend a length of time there, proportioned to the enormity of their offenses. Such punishment would be suited to crimes that do not quite deserve hanging, yet are too aggravated for the State's Prison."[13]

Hawthorne certainly understood the world historically, but the same might not be said for all those who flock to Salem. There is a tenuous line of correlation between the public's knowledge of the events in seventeenth-century Essex County and the city's modern reputation. Based on anecdotal and informal ethnographic research as a tour guide, it seems that most visitors know that there was a group of people in the late 1600s who were accused of witchcraft and eventually executed for that supposed crime. Very few people, however, have a deeper understanding of any of the other details of the panic outside of this short synopsis. A good portion of visitors may believe that the accused were, indeed, practicing some sort of witchcraft, either in the form of herbalism, midwifery, or pagan rituals associated with the "Old World."[14]

Perhaps these perceptions are rooted in pop culture representations of the time period or maybe shaped by an interest in magic and the supernatural. In either case, tour goers are invested in learning about the lives of the victims and their accusers and about the dynamics that led to the witch hunt in Salem. Historians have demonstrated that, to study the trials, one must consider generations of interpersonal conflict, decades-long reputations of specific community members, intercultural violence between colonizers and indigenous people, the political climate and legal turmoil of the period, and the religious, political, and economic strife between Puritan communities as well as deeply gendered expressions of guilt and anxiety in Puritan culture. Most visitors do not have the time to dedicate to studying early New England history, but they can engage in discovery by visiting the physical place of the events and sharing in the storytelling with their tour guide.

The fun and frivolity associated with ghost tours, witch tours, or other forms of tourism seem so at odds with the city's history, but time and again those who research these areas point to the fact that tourists are playing out broadly experienced contemporary anxieties about everything from climate change to social unrest to financial collapse to the United States' diminishing power in the world. Cultural preoccupations with death, doom, and the afterlife play out in different ways, omnipresent in Salem, as does the pervading sense that society abandoned vulnerable people. At the same time, the motif of ghosts and hauntings has long been used to explain historical significance to visitors in historic places and to promote a sense of place.[15] As Judith Richardson observes, "Ghosts operate as a particular, and peculiar, kind of social memory, an alternate form of history-making in which things usually forgotten, discarded, or repressed become foregrounded, whether as items of fear, regret, explanation, or desire."[16]

How can we represent history when our culture cannot think historically? The answer, is, in Salem at any rate, through letting it haunt us.[17] Erica Feldmann, the owner and proprietress of Haus Witch, "a metaphysical supply store" organized around radical intersectional feminist values, in downtown Salem, has referred to the city as a heterotopia.[18] It is an apt description. In the Foucauldian tradition, heterotopias reflect cultural norms as well as anxieties about space and how it functions. According to Foucault, heterotopias are places, including cemeteries and brothels, that exist specifically so that activities and practices central to human experience—but that, at the same time, make us feel uncomfortable—can be partitioned and separated from other cultural and social spaces. Sanctioning activity in one specific place effectively prohibits the same activities from happening elsewhere. Simultaneously "here" and "not here," constricting and liberating, heterotopias "have the curious property of being in relation with all other sites, but in such a way as to suspend, neutralize, or invent the set of relations that they happen to designate, mirror, or reflect."[19] In Salem, if the whole city is to be seen as a heterotopia, then those partitions that are meant to give us comfort have collapsed—the dead mingle with the living, the holy with the profane, and public activities impinge on private ones.

The collapse of the distinction between public and private space is especially fraught in a city like Salem (and other places, too—Charleston, South Carolina, and Savannah, Georgia, encounter this), where tourists are so prevalent. Reverend Nathan Ives, minister at St. Peter's Episcopal Church in downtown Salem, for example, points out that many people seem to have no understanding of the purpose and function of a church building. He has noted that sometimes travelers wander in off the street while he is preaching: "Lots of folks come in and stand in the back to look, as if they're watching some odd thing take place. It's a church service, and I've had some people walk right down the aisle like they're in a museum. I'm in the middle of a sermon or something, and they're walking around like, 'Oh, I'm just taking pictures.'"

The notion of "the sacred" is a fraught one in contemporary society. Foucault goes on to argue that while we tend to create categories to make sense of and police spaces (public/private, family/social, for example) virtually all spaces are "nurtured by the hidden presence of the sacred."[20] In this liminal space between the sacred and the profane, the figure of the ghost takes on a role of one who disturbs or subverts, often bringing to the surface "involuntary memories from suppressed or forgotten pasts, whereby something that had been deemed overcome and gone reappears to announce some unfinished business that needs to be addressed."[21]

With this in mind, it comes as no surprise that stories of ghosts have become a gateway to grappling with histories of atrocity and contemporary anxieties simultaneously. This is particularly evident at Turners Seafood, a restaurant that sits on the former site of Bridget Bishop's apple orchard and a popular stop on many Salem ghost tours. Bishop was not the first accused during the trials, but she was the first person executed. You might hear many different (and often exaggerated) interpretations of her behavior and physical appearance if you were to walk by the restaurant on any given night. Her story is engaging for visitors, particularly because it traces a connection from her difficult lived experiences to her neighbors' perceptions of her to the specific witchcraft accusations she faced—including spectral and physical evidence against her—to the horrific story of her death. It is a unique chance for them to piece together information about a real woman living in the seventeenth century. When the story transitions to Bishop's ghost haunting modern-day Salem residents and visitors, it is almost as if her agency is restored. Tour goers revel in her ability to taunt and create disturbances in the physical space around them.

In contemporary Salem, arguably the most sacred space is the somber and reflective memorial erected in 1992 to mark the three hundredth anniversary of the witch hysteria. The memorial's designers intended that the memorial space respond to the injustices of 1692, to create a solemn and reflective space. The artist Maggie Smith and architect Jim Cutler defined injustice in relation to the events in Salem as *silence, deafness, persecution*, and *memory*. The Salem witch trials memorial sits on a plot of land next to the Old Burying Point cemetery—where many Salem residents who witnessed the events of 1692 and said or did nothing to prevent or hold in check the unfolding hysteria—are buried. Another unsettling design element can be found in the inscriptions at the memorial's entrance. To enter into the space, we literally have to step on the pleading words of the dead: "My life now lies in your hands"; "On my dying day, I am no witch"; and "Oh Lord—help me."

It is common to spot an individual or a small group slowly making their way through the space, stopping at each bench, their lips moving as they read the names of the executed. Some couples also say their wedding vows there. In the busy Halloween season, jostling tourists take selfies in the space. People munching on fried food, a mom changing their child's diaper, teenagers scrolling on their phones while draped over the stone walls—it can seem like the memory of 1692 gets lost somewhere between the votive candles and the crushed empties. The memorial is, at the exact same time, a sacred space and a public place. It is tempting to decry uses of the memorial that seem inappropriate given the solemnity and gravity of the history it marks.

Many ghost tours culminate at the Witch Trials Memorial. There are misconceptions that the victims were actually executed at the memorial site; once people learn that this is not the case, they want to know where the executions actually happened. Guides share info about Proctor's Ledge, often offering clear instructions for getting directions via Google Maps. For some, the actual space of execution matters—they want to connect with the site of trauma. They may tune out when they realize the memorial is not a killing ground. Others become fascinated by the flowers, coins, and other mementos left on the stones. They want to understand how other people engage with the space. Still others are fascinated with the adjacent graveyard.

We want to suggest that the dissonance found at the memorial reflects the complexity of tourists' engagements with Salem's history. Certainly, people are drawn to the space without a clear understanding of why it matters or what lesson it offers. It is possible that visitors (often with long "to-do" and "to-see" and "to-eat" lists) find it very challenging to slow down and reflect on the meaning of the site. This is something for us to learn from. Maybe the color and noise are necessary so that we may seek and invite the silence. Maybe a worshipful solemnity is not the only or best way to remember those who were executed here in Salem over three hundred years ago. The messy, uneven, even jarring dissonance can be unnerving.

Ghost tours, especially those that are well executed, function as a way for people to be included, to make a space for themselves in the historical narrative. Tours do much more than highlight the "ghostliness" of Salem. Tour goers are invited to do the work, to inform and be informed by a process of discovery instead of passively receiving historical information. Physical movement, a community in the form of the group, attention to the senses, and a relationship between place and story all contribute to an embodied experience.

In "The Ghosts of Place," Michael Mayerfeld Bell suggests that the *"sense(s) of presence of those who are not physically there"* are simultaneously obvious fabrications and uniquely powerful conduits for the "social aliveness" of a place:

> Ghosts help constitute the specificity of historical sites, of the places where we feel we belong and do not belong, of the boundaries of pos-

session by which we assign ownership and nativeness. Ghosts of the living and dead alike, of both individual and collective spirits, of both other selves and our own selves, haunt the places of our lives.[22]

If the victims of the Salem witch hysteria are the ghosts in our cultural attic, ghost tours may be understood as more than cheap money grabs or fantastical performances that dishonor those who were killed in 1692. They may be both of those things. At the same time, ghost tours dramatically highlight the "sense of presence of those who are not physically there" and invite tour goers to participate actively in understanding the past through their movements through the cityscape, interactions with the past, and difficult to answer questions about the meanings and consequences of victimization and violence in our historical narrative.

NOTES

1. "Salem Massachusetts Travel Guide," With Wonder and Whimsy, 10/4/22, available at https://withwonderandwhimsy.com/2022/10/04/salem-massachusetts-travel-guide/, accessed 9/20/2023.

2. Andy Ober, "Experts Explain Our Love of Fear and Fascination with the Supernatural," University of Arizona News, available at https://news.arizona.edu/story/experts-explain-our-love-fear-and-fascination-supernatural, accessed 9/20/2023.

3. See, e.g., Elizabeth Crooke, "An Exploration of the Connections among Museums, Community and Heritage," in *The Ashgate Research Companion to Heritage and Identity*, ed. B. Graham and P. Howard (Ashgate, 2008), 415–424.

4. Colin Sterling, "Spectral Anatomies: Heritage, Hauntology and the 'Ghosts' of Varosha," *Present Pasts* 6, no. 1 (2014): 1.

5. James Howard Kunstler, *The Geography of Nowhere* (Touchstone, 1993).

6. Diane Goldstein, Sylvia Grider, and Jeannie Thomas, *Haunting Experiences: Ghosts in Contemporary Folklore* (Utah State University Press, 2007), 18.

7. *Possessions: The History and Uses of Haunting in the Hudson Valley* (Harvard University Press, 2005), 6.

8. Sterling, "Spectral Anatomies."

9. Amy Tyson, *The Wages of History: Emotional Labor on Public History's Front Lines* (University of Massachusetts Press, 2014), 3.

10. Tiya Miles, *Tales of the Haunted South: Dark History and Memories of Slavery from the Civil War Era* (University of North Carolina Press, 2017), 14.

11. Goldstein, Grider, and Thomas, *Haunting Experiences*, 31.

12. Ibid., 25.

13. Julian Hawthorne, *Nathaniel Hawthorne and His Wife* (Jazzybee, 2013).

14. Nathaniel Hawthorne's *The House of the Seven Gables* drew its inspiration from the Turner-Ingersoll house. Both historical and contemporary oral tradition maintain that the house is haunted. William O. Thompson says, "Nathaniel Hawthorne, who made the house famous, thought the property was haunted and so do many of the guides who

work there today. . . . It sends out strange sounds; guides have reported strange events. Toilets flush when no one has been near a bathroom. Door latches have been lifted up (not down). . . . Guides confirm that such experiences and stories are part of the site's ongoing oral tradition." Cited in Goldstein, Grider, and Thomas, *Haunting Experiences*, 34–35.

15. For more on this, see Alena Pirok, *The Spirit of Colonial Williamsburg: Ghosts and Interpreting the Recreated Past* (University of Massachusetts Press, 2022).

16. Judith Richardson, *The Uses and History of Hauntings in the Hudson Valley* (Harvard University Press, 2005), 3.

17. This is a paraphrase of Catherine Emma Green's reflection in "Spectral Afterlife: Hauntology, Historical Memory, and Inheritance in Postmodernist Fiction," Thesis, 2017, available at https://scholar.google.com/citations?view_op=view_citation&hl=en&user=oyYFBKoAAAAJ&citation_for_view=oyYFBKoAAAAJ:u5HHmVD_uO8C, accessed 11/12/2023.

18. Erica Feldmann, quoted in "Witch Trials and Salem: Then and Now," 10/23/2020, available at https://www.youtube.com/watch?v=TA2Fcv6NQBE, accessed 10/1/2023.

19. Michel Foucault, "Of Other Spaces: Utopias and Heterotopias," *Architecture /Mouvement/ Continuité*, October 1984, 46–49.

20. Ibid.

21. Bjornar Julius Olsen, "Living with Ghosts? Soviet Heritage in the Russian North," *Journal of Contemporary Archaeology* 9, no. 1 (2022): 15.

22. Michael Mayerfeld Bell, "The Ghosts of Place," *Theory and Society* 26, no. 6 (December 1997): 813.

Epilogue

It Happened in Town House Square

Donna A. Seger

A crowd filled Town House Square on an overcast day in June 2005, cheering and jeering the unveiling of a bronze statue of the actress Elizabeth Montgomery in character as Samantha Stephens of the television series *Bewitched*. The rationale for the statue was the filming of several episodes of the series in Salem in 1970, commencing a successful intensification of witchcraft-focused tourism in the view of those who cheered, while the less enthusiastic attendees noted the impropriety of installing a fictitious witch within view of the sites where the victims of 1692 were accused and tried. The Reverend Jeffrey Barz-Snell, the thirty-first pastor of the First Church of Salem, which stood across the street for centuries, was among those who had urged the Salem Redevelopment Authority to reject the statue weeks before "in due deference to our history" and its *location*: "We must object to this statue being sponsored by the city of Salem, less than twenty yards away from [the] site where we committed, arguably, one of the worst . . . crimes in the history of this city."[1] This argument was countered by the majority opinion, expressed succinctly by Salem City Councilor Thomas Furey: "Salem is the Witch City. I think we all need to lighten up, take a breath, and let Salem have fun." This moment in time and place is representative of the continuous significance of a small parcel of land, more of an intersection than a square, over Salem's centuries. The crowd, the expression of civic identity, the representations of church, state, and commerce: all have had their role to play in Town House Square.

In the seventeenth century, Salem developed in a linear fashion dictated by the relatively narrow peninsula on which its first English settlements were established. A central east-west artery, later called Essex Street, was intersected by a series of lanes and ways, with one particular path, now called Washington Street, connecting the North and South Rivers. The intersection of Essex and Washington was the site of Salem's first meetinghouse, built in 1629 as a one-story frame building and replaced on the same site by larger buildings in 1636, 1670, 1718, and 1826. While this intersection was not designated Town House Square officially until 1891, it was named for these sequential meetinghouses and the adjacent "Town House" located on the site from 1718 to 1785, the scene of much official business and agitation in pre-Revolutionary Salem. It was named for buildings that were no longer there, rather, for the memory of these buildings, an acknowledgment of the importance of this space in Salem's founding and development. The first seventeenth-century meetinghouse was recognized as "proper" and foundational to the settlement of Salem, the center of an emerging streetscape of residential and civic buildings. Its situation, adjoining these buildings rather than being separated from them by a green or common, along with the Puritan preference for integrated spiritual and secular places, ensured that the successive meetinghouses would be an integral part of Salem's urban evolution, a reference point, and often a stage or backdrop to important events in local, regional, and national history. Even after the last meetinghouse ceased to function in that capacity in the nineteenth century, that stage endured.

Division, more than communal unity, amplified the stagelike role of Town House Square in the seventeenth century. More than thirty years before the witch trials, a small but impassioned Society of Friends challenged the Puritan hegemony by holding their own meetings in a house adjacent to the 1634 Meeting House, and, in a more radical and public form of protest, the Quaker Deborah Buffum Wilson, accompanied by her mother and half sister, walked "naked for a sign" down Washington Street in imitation of the Old Testament prophet Isaiah.[2] In 1664, Major William Hathorne, almost as zealous in his defense of Massachusetts liberties as he was a persecutor of Quakers, attacked the royal commissioners present in the colony in an impassioned speech before his assembled and armed militia in the square. He was consequently summoned to England to answer to the charge of refusing to submit to royal authority.[3] Decades later, the judicial process of the Salem witch trials played out in this same location, illustrating the intimacy of communal conflict in the seventeenth-century Salem Town. The accused were examined in the courthouse built from the timbers of the 1634 Meeting House, located just north of the meetinghouse toward the North River. On either side of this structure was the property of the trials' first victim, Bridget Bishop, and the court chaplain, the Reverend Nicholas Noyes. The "mansion house" of the trials' judge John

Hathorne, stood just across from the meetinghouse (where the *Bewitched* statue now stands), and further to the south was the house of the High Sheriff George Corwin, who attended to Bishop's execution on June 20, 1692.

The third meetinghouse constructed on the square represented a more distinct separation of the sacred and the secular, especially as it was paired with a new royal town house. This was the first time that a spire loomed over central Salem, and the adjacent town/colony/courthouse became the scene of both celebrations and, increasingly, contentious meetings as the century progressed. Both buildings confirmed and continued the square's role as the center of spiritual, civic, and social life in Salem, especially as more houses and shops lined the surrounding streets. Town House meetings were held to denounce the Stamp Act in 1765 and to choose, in defiance of the royal governor General Thomas Gage, delegates to the first Continental Congress in 1774. That same year, a small chest of tea was seized from a Salem man whose servants had (by his testimony, unknowingly) transported it from Boston, and, in the presence of "several hundred spectators," it was burned in the middle of Washington Street. In February 1775, another crowd assembled in Town House Square to taunt the British soldiers marching through Salem to confiscate a rumored store of cannons and force their commander, Colonel Alexander Leslie, to order a retreat. After the Revolution, Salem welcomed President George Washington with a parade down the street that would soon bear his name. By that

Postcard of Town House Square looking toward the Boston & Maine Railroad Station, Curt Teich Co. (Nelson Dionne Salem History Collection, Salem State University Archives and Special Collections.)

time, the royal Town House was gone, but the First Church remained in its colonial form until it was replaced by "an elegant brick church, with a stone basement . . . of larger dimensions."[4]

Residential buildings had lined the streets around Town House Square from the beginning of Salem's settlement, but they were crowded out increasingly over the nineteenth century. That century produced a succession of Salem historians who began their narratives locating the residences of the First Church's founding pastors in the vicinity, including those of Francis Higginson, Roger Williams, and Hugh Peter, but the colonial settlement was no more. Stone was replacing wood, and commercial blocks were replacing freestanding buildings. One notable new building hearkening back to the height of Salem's dynamic global trade at the beginning of the century, while creating a capital foundation for the future industrial city, was the Asiatic Building, built in 1856, adjacent to the First Church building and the highlight of a *Ballou's Pictorial* story that same year noting all the banks conducting business within (the Asiatic Bank, of course, along with the Salem Savings Bank, Merchant's Bank, Loan and Fund Association, and the Oriental Office and Post Office), along with the observation that "from the cupola of this building a fine and extensive panoramic view of the city and its environs is obtained."[5]

The voices that echo out from Town House Square in the nineteenth century do not reference the decline as often as contemporary assessors do, but there is a definite sense of adjustment as Salem began to focus more on its inland connections than overseas trade from the mid-nineteenth century. Plans to build a railroad from Boston to Salem received a mixed reaction in the 1830s: while some observers saw the railroad as an engine of regional growth, others were afraid it would hasten Salem's increasing dependency on Boston. One letter writer to the *Salem Gazette* was suspect of out-of-town financiers and in favor of Old Salem self-sufficiency: "Let us establish our *own* railroads (if we want any) to the east and to the north, but let us not, if we value our prosperity at all, rest it upon the presumption that a railroad to Boston will contribute in any degree to the interest and welfare of Salem." There was insufficient capital to fund this proposal, especially once the challenging (in terms of financing, engineering, and politics) Salem tunnel was added to the plan, a necessity for its expansion northward to Newburyport and New Hampshire.[6] And so, in late August 1838, the Eastern Railroad trains from Boston roared into the Salem depot just south of Town House Square, and, a year later, under it. While James Duncan Phillips would describe the square as "merely a roof for the tunnel open at both ends" a century later, it was actually transforming into a commercial and transportation hub for Salem, from which horsecar and later trolley lines would branch out in all directions.[7]

Given these developments, it seems fitting that the newest First Church building would become the site of a destination department store, which also operated a pioneering mail-order business until well into the twentieth century: Daniel Low and Company, the purveyors of witch spoons and publishers of annual yearbooks selling Salem goods and Salem history to a national audience. A pamphlet titled *The Salem Pilgrim: His Book* was enclosed in every mail order from 1903, opening with the entreaty that "if the Pilgrim to Salem wishes to stand at the focus and centre of Puritan New England, on the spot where was planted one of the twin shoots of American Democracy, and from which there went forth not a few of the great forces that have shaped American history, let him go to Town House Square."[8] Daniel Low prospered for more than a century, in large part due to its innovative advertising, which often conjured up images of "Old Salem," but other nineteenth- and twentieth-century observers did not find the modern Town House Square so inspiring. While Nathaniel Hawthorne had romanticized the square as the place where Governor Endicott slashed the "profane" cross of St. George out of the English flag and the "old town pump" stood, his granddaughter Hildegarde Hawthorne observed that it was "entirely commonplace and uninteresting" in her time (1916), with "nothing of its old grandeur or beauty remaining."[9]

Hildegarde did note that the square was also the "heart of Salem's business life," but that was not what the tourists for whom she wrote her book sought at that time: they were looking for the material culture of the colonial settlement, still present in other sections of the city but not at its dynamic center. Salem residents, however, clearly recognized Town House Square as both the civic and commercial center of their city, with the "new" city hall (completed in 1838, the same year as the Boston-Salem railroad line and two years after Salem became a city) located mere steps from Daniel Low and Company on the other side of Essex Street: the pillars of covenant and church had been transformed into those of city and commerce. The Greek Revival City Hall, captured in all of its austerity by Walker Evans in 1931, was the location of the municipal offices and the site of all city business, from regular meetings of the city council and school committee to special meetings like those of the Committee on Ancient Memorials in 1891 and the Salem Rebuilding Commission in 1914. It was also the site of crowded receptions welcoming both dignitaries to town and heroes home from the Civil War, the Spanish-American War, and World Wars I and II: a huge crowd turned out for Lieutenant Colonel Frank S. Perkins, the commander of the 2nd Battalion, 101st Field Artillery, and recipient of the Croix de Guerre among other honors for distinguished service over the entire duration of the war, when he returned home to Salem in the spring of 1919 and again just two years later, when his body lay in state in city

Old Home Week in Town House Square, 1909. (Nelson Dionne Salem History Collection, Salem State University Archives and Special Collections.)

hall following his death from appendicitis. Other Salem sons (seldom daughters) were welcomed back through elaborate Old Home Week festivities centered on city hall and Town House Square in the opening decades of the twentieth century.[10]

As it was from almost the beginning of Salem's founding, Town House Square was also the site of political *expression*: election and war bond rallies, strikes by the "Forgotten Men" of the 1920s and Pequot Mills workers in the 1930s, even a large group of Salem High School students protesting disciplinary measures in a "wild riot" during which they burned their unpopular *acting* principal in effigy.[11] Illumination had increased activities in the square nearly a half-century earlier, as Salem commenced its electric street-lighting initiative in the city center. A Republican rally in October 1896 drew crowds from near and far to a city that was "fairly ablaze," its "streets as light as day." Special colored lights outlined the buildings of Town House Square in an illumination that was "far and away the most beautiful ever seen in . . . Essex County."[12] The stage was set for evermore spectacular election and nonpartisan events like the Liberty Loan drives of World War I and the Salem Tercentenary festivities of 1926. Salem's monumental (and illuminated) war chest was located in the square, as was the "Victory Cottage" where one could purchase war bonds, both surrounded by unfurled flags for the duration of World War I, and as soon as the armistice was declared, crowds converged on city hall.[13]

Just as the World War I Victory Cottage was located in Town House Square, so too was the Red Cross station during World War II, and the Salem Tercentenary information booth in between; a century later, the Haunted Happenings information booth inhabits the same space. This is a testament to the longevity of this location, as between 1926 and 2026, there were decades of building and burying, construction and reconstruction. Town House Square was torn apart in the 1950s for a new railroad tunnel project that dominated that decade, just as the Boston beltway Route 128 was drawing drivers and consumers away from old seaports and downtown commercial centers like Salem. There were claims of recovery once the dust cleared from the new train tunnel and the demolition of the old Boston and Maine depot, a clearance for plaza parking that would set a precedent for more of the same. These claims were premature: urban renewal initiatives began in the next decade, causing more construction and placing Town House Square right in the middle of Salem's two designated redevelopment districts, Heritage Plaza East and West. After Salem committed to a redevelopment process more focused on sympathetic restoration than exclusive demolition, a manicured Town House Square, along with Derby Square a block east, became the showcase for the city's award-winning compromise design in the 1970s. A prominent feature of this design was the transformation of the central part of ancient Essex Street into a pedestrian mall, thereby removing the automobile intersection of the square, and, in a way, restoring its nature back to the nineteenth century, or even earlier.

But it was not the nineteenth century, and Salem's regional economy hegemony was fading fast, or even gone, with the closure of heritage businesses all around the square. The combination of decades-long construction in Salem and the opening of the Northshore Shopping Center (1958) and Liberty Tree Mall (1970) displaced many stores from Salem, with Almy's and Daniel Low among the longest to hold out, until 1985 and 1994, respectively. Just across the street from Daniel Low, on that storied site upon which once stood the Hathorne homestead, was Gerber's Restaurant, which rivaled Low's as a social center of Town House Square from 1938 until the retirement of its owner, Louis Gerber, in 1970. Commonly known as "Little City Hall," as it was a favorite of Salem's court and city employees, the restaurant and its building were destroyed by fire in 1971, creating a gap in the tight-knit square, which eventually became the site of the *Bewitched* statue in 2005.

While the Reverend Jeffrey Barz-Snell referenced the power of place in his objections to the statue, his civic counterpart, the Salem Mayor Stanley J. Usovicz, was not inspired similarly in his support. The mayor asserted that both the commercial and the commemorative could coexist in Salem, where the seasonal Halloween traffic sustained the new businesses that emerged in the post urban-renewal environment. The victims of 1692 were honored in an "appropriate way" at the 1992 Witch Trials Memorial adjacent to the Charter Street Cemetery downtown, but the Town House Square was a different space and place, one in which the City could showcase its annual Halloween festivities and emerging status as the "Halloween Capital of the World."[14] Mayor Usovicz's support for the statue included an additional reassurance to the public, an insistence that "the statue be placed away from sites associated with the witch trials," not recognizing Salem's ever-evolving center as the site of the accused witches' indictments, trials, interrogations and judgments.[15]

NOTES

1. Kathy McCabe, "Few Have Seen Bewitched Statue," *Boston Globe*, May 15, 2005.
2. Carla Gadina Pestana, *Quakers and Baptists in Colonial Massachusetts* (Cambridge University Press, 1991), 36–43.
3. Richard Gildrie, *Salem, Massachusetts, 1626–1683: A Covenant Community* (University Press of Virginia, 1975), 130–139.
4. *Salem Observer*, March 18, 1826.
5. *Ballou's Pictorial Drawing-Room Companion*, vol. 11, no. 1 (July 5, 1856), 56.
6. *Salem Gazette*, June 5, 1835. For more discussion of the politics behind the construction of the Eastern Railroad's Boston-Salem line and the location and construction of the Salem tunnel, see Michael J. Connolly, *Capitalism, Politics, and Railroads in Jacksonian New England* (University of Missouri Press, 2003), 119–133.
7. James Duncan Phillips, *Salem and the Indies: The Story of the Great Commercial Era of the City* (Houghton Mifflin, 1947), 19.
8. John Buckham, *The Salem Pilgrim: His Book* (Irving K. Annabale, 1903), 1.
9. Hildegard Hawthorne, *Old Seaport Towns of New England* (Dodd, Mead, 1916), 96.
10. *Boston Daily Journal*, August 1, 1891; *Boston Herald*, September 23, 1891; *Boston Herald*, April 1, 1919; *Boston Herald*, June 12, 1921; *Boston Daily Journal*, July 28, 1902.
11. *Boston Herald*, October 11, 1939.
12. *Boston Herald*, October 29, 1896.
13. *Boston Herald*, August 31, 1918; *Boston Herald*, May 5, 1918; *Boston Herald*, November 18, 1918. Liberty Loan activities in May 1918 included a staged "invasion" of "Germans" who took refuge in an office building on Washington Street from where they shouted German propaganda to the assembling crowd in Town House Square. They were captured by two companies of the Massachusetts Militia and escorted to the Victory

Cottage to purchase Liberty bonds. The *Boston Herald* reported that the five "alien enemies" were really "patriotic Americans" and that Salem expected to reach the $2 million mark in bond sales by the end of the day.

14. Kathy McCabe, "The Saga of the Salem Statue: Witch Way Will They Go?" *Boston Globe*, May 5, 2005.

15. Kathy McCabe, "Bewitched Statue Bothers, Bewilders," *Boston Globe*, April 28, 2005.

Salem

J. D. Scrimgeour

Here there is no hiding
from what we've always been
neither flame nor flood can erase
the city's red streak

Here where we sit
on our diminished loot
living in our sentences
our feet stirring the ocean

Contributors

Dr. Kimberly S. Alexander is director of museum studies and senior lecturer in the History Department at the University of New Hampshire. She is author of *Treasures Afoot: Shoe Stories from the Georgian Era* and *Fashioning the New England Family*.

Dr. Brad Austin is professor and chair of the History Department at Salem State University. He is the author of *Democratic Sports: Men's and Women's College Sports during the Great Depression* and the coeditor of *Understanding and Teaching the Vietnam War* and *Teaching U.S. History through Sports*. He serves as a coeditor for the University of Wisconsin Press's Harvey Goldberg Series for Understanding and Teaching History.

Dr. Emerson W. Baker is a professor of history at Salem State University. He is the author or coauthor of six books including *A Storm of Witchcraft: The Salem Trials and the American Experience*.

Dr. Aviva Chomsky is professor of history at Salem State University and author of numerous books on transnational labor history, immigration, climate justice, Central America, Colombia, and Cuba.

Dr. Andrew Darien is professor of history at Salem State University and interim associate dean of the College of Arts and Sciences. He is the author of *Becoming New York's Finest: Race, Gender, and the Integration of the New York Police Department, 1935–1980* and the creator and coordinator of "Student, Citizen, Soldier: The Veterans' Oral History Project" at Salem State.

Dr. Elizabeth Duclos-Orsello is professor and chair of the Interdisciplinary Studies Department at Salem State University. She is the author of *Modern Bonds: Redefining*

Community in Early Twentieth Century St. Paul, coauthor of *African Americans in Essex County: An Annotated Guide*, and coeditor of *Teaching American Studies: State of the Classroom as State of the Field*.

Susan Edwards earned a bachelor of arts in English from Hamilton College and a master of library and information science from the University at Albany. Since 1996, she has overseen the growth and development of the university's archives and special collections as its first professional archivist.

Theresa Giard is a graduate student in the History MA program at Salem State University. She is database project manager at New England Historic Genealogical Society and has been a tour guide in Salem, Massachusetts, since October 2022.

Marilyn Hayward is a former managing director at an investment bank and current genealogist who wrote her Salem State University MA thesis on Salem merchant John Higginson.

Dr. Bethany Jay is professor of history and graduate coordinator at Salem State University. She is the coeditor of *Understanding and Teaching American Slavery*, which won the 2018 James Harvey Robinson prize for the "teaching aid that has made the most outstanding contribution to the teaching and learning of history in any field for public or educational purposes" from the American Historical Association.

Dr. Michele Louro is professor of history at Salem State University. She is the author of *Comrades against Imperialism: Nehru, India and Interwar Internationalism* and *The League against Imperialism: Lives and Afterlives* and the former managing editor of the *Journal of World History*.

Elizabeth McKeigue is dean of the library at Salem State University. She is the author of several articles on librarianship and has held library leadership positions at Harvard University and Santa Clara University.

Robert W. McMicken is a Ph.D. candidate studying nineteenth-century American history and cultural identities in the American West. Robert received his MA in history from Salem State University.

Dr. Dane A. Morrison is professor emeritus of history at Salem State University. His publications include *A Praying People: Massachusett Acculturation and the Failure of the Puritan Mission, 1600–1690*, *True Yankees: The South Seas and the Discovery of American Identity*, and *Eastward of Good Hope: Early America in a Dangerous World*.

Dr. Maria Pride received her MA in history from Salem State University and her Ph.D. from the University of Stirling for her dissertation on revolutionary privateering in the northeast American ports.

Dr. Hans Schwartz received his MA in history from Salem State University and his Ph.D. in Atlantic and early American history from Clark University. He has taught at Endicott College and Northeastern University, and he is the author of *Freemasonry in the Revolutionary Atlantic World*.

Dr. J. D. Scrimgeour is professor of English at Salem State University and the author of five books of verse and two of nonfiction, including *Themes for English B: A Professor's Education In and Out of Class*, which won the Association of Writers and Writing Program's Award for Nonfiction. He was selected as the inaugural poet laureate of Salem and began serving his term in 2025. One of his ancestors, Mary Towne Eastey, was put to death during the witch trials, while another, Thomas Perkins, sat on the jury that found her guilty. He is grateful to Molly Hackett for her lines that inspired his poem, "Salem."

Dr. Donna A. Seger is professor of history at Salem State University and the author of *The Practical Renaissance: The Quest for Information in Early Modern England*.

Dr. Margo Shea is professor of history at Salem State University. She is the author of *Derry City: Memory and Political Struggle in Northern Ireland* and several articles and chapters in anthologies on heritage, memory, and collaborative practice in public history.

Brian Valimont received master of arts degrees in anthropology from the University of Alabama and history from Salem State University. He has worked as an active field archaeologist for twenty-five years, searching for, investigating, and documenting Native American and Euro-American historic archaeological sites across North America.

Maryann Zujewski worked for the National Park Service for over thirty years. She is currently the Northeast regions' education program manager supporting eighty-three national parks in states from Maine to Virginia in their efforts to provide equitable and inclusive place-based learning experiences.

Index

Note: Page numbers in italics indicate figures.

1619 Project, 47, 58n1
1754 census, 50

abolitionist movement, 5, 124, 129–131, 133, 137n10, 165; Emilio and, 139–143; Remond family and, 103, 105, 107, 109–110, 118–119, 119–120n10
Aborn, Joseph, 52
Aborn, Samuel, 52
the *Achilles*, 80
Adams, Abigail, 35
Adams, Charles Francis, 130
Adams, Gretchen, 137n10
Adams, John, 35–36, 68, 70, 71, 123
Adams, John Quincy, 103, 105
Africa, 68, 171, 172, 173, 226
African Americans, 3, 5, 50, 101–114, 112n2, 139; "Black Picnic" tradition and, 164–169, *167*, 188; citizenship and, 110–111; free people, 97–99, 101–114, 133, 141; passing as white, 133; at Salem State College, 251–252; segregation and, 108, 109; suffrage and, 205; tradition of black picnics and, 164–169; transition from enslaved to free, 95–100; in Union army, 139–143, 143n5. *See also specific individuals*

African-descended population, 50
"African Jubilee," 165
African Methodist Episcopal churches, 165–166, *167*
"African Schools," 106
Africans, enslaved, 12, 47–60, 116
Agawam, 17
air raid wardens, 234–235
Air Raid Warden's School, 234
Air Warden's Manual, 233
Akerman, Lucy Evelina, 127
Alabama, 128
Alinsky, Saul, 247
Alley, John, 90–91, 92, 94n29
Almy, Bigelow, and Washburn, 206
Almy, James F., 206
Almy, Lurana Bigelow, 206
Almy's, 291
"alternative facts," 263–264, 268n34
American Anti-Slavery Society, 5, 105, 109, 139, 205
The American Architect, 190
American Gazette and Constitutional Journal, 53
Americanization, 155, 162n40
American Revolution, 5, 54, 67–68, 69–78, 79–83, 287

American Woman Suffrage Association, 205–206
Amsterdam, 85
Anderson, Terry, 252n2
Andersonville Confederate prison, 135
Andover, Massachusetts, 165
Andrew, John, 134, 140
Andros, Edmund, colony of, 64
Anglo-Dutch Wars, 62
antebellum era, 110
Anthony, Susan B., 205
anti-Catholicism, 146, 147–148, 155–156
Antietam, Battle of, 133
anti-immigrant sentiment, 147–148, 155–156
anti-Irish sentiment, 147–148
anti-"papist" sentiment, 148
antiquarianism, 190–204
anti-segregation movement, 205
antislavery movement, 205. *See also* abolitionist movement
Anti-Slavery Society of Salem and Vicinity, 106, 118, 139, 205
antisuffrage associations, 125
antisuffragists, 125, 207–208
Appleton, William Sumner, 201
Arawaks, 50
architecture, 68, 123, 220, 254, 289; Colonial Revival and, 190–204, *192*; Federal-era houses, 275, 276. *See also specific structures*
Arkansas, 128
Arlington, Massachusetts, 76
armory, 214
Arnold Constable, 202
Art Commission of the City of New York, 195
artisans, 70, 72–73, 96
Asia, 64, 68, 170–183. *See also specific locations*
Asian immigrants, 149
Asiatic Bank, 288
Asiatic Building, 288
assimilation, 150, 155, 156–158, 162n40, 198
Assisi, Italy, 153
Association for the Relief of Aged and Destitute Women of Salem, 124–125
Atlanta, Georgia, 133, 195
Augustin, Peter, 102
Azores, 61

Babcock, Cecelia Remond, 111–112n1, 113n23
Bacon, Edwin, 190

Bailey, Ronald, 54, 58n2
Baker, Charlie, 258
Baker, Emerson, 267n25
Baltimore, Maryland, fire in, 195
Banishment Act, 77
Baptist Church, 168
Barbados, 20, 50, 61, 62
Barbarick, Ray, 239–240
Barrett, John, 219
Barr, James, 54
Barry, Kenneth, 234
Barton Square Unitarian Church, 194
Barz-Snell, Jeffrey, 285, 292
Bass River, 22
Batchelor, George, 194
Battery Wagner, 141
Baumgartner, Kabria, 106
Becket Street, 198
Beckett, Daniel, 106
Bell, Alexander Graham, 124
Bell, Michael Mayerfeld, 281–282
Bentley, William, 54, 56, 81, 146
Bermuda, 77
Beverly Bridge, 223
Beverly Farms, Massachusetts, 232
Beverly, Massachusetts, 15, 21, 53, 76, 165–166, 184, 231–232, 240–241
Bewitched statue, 7, 258, 260, 267n21, 285, 292
bicycle clubs, 125
Bilbao, 80, 82
Billings, Thomas Henry, 44
Bishop, Bridget, 33–34, 280, 286
Black community, 54. *See also* African Americans
Blackhall, Charles H., 217
Black Heath pits, 130
"Black Picnic" tradition, 5, 164–169, *167*
"Black Republicans," 128
Bodnar, John, 160n17
Bogle, Robert, 102
Bombay, India, 179
Booth, John Wilkes, 135
Booth, Robert, 117
Booth, Robert A., Jr., 38
Bosch, Juan, 270
Boston and Maine Railroad Station, *287*, 291
Boston Daily Globe, 208
Boston Gazette, 51
Boston Globe, 38, 186, 195, 206, 218, 229
Boston, Massachusetts, 68, 70, 124, 146, 154, 166, 208, 214; "African Jubilee" in,

165; fire in, 195; railroad to, 288; Route 128 bypassing, 219; Salem as bedroom community for, 222; on V-J Day, 240–241
Boston Massacre, 71–72
Boston Navy Yard, 231
Boston Port Act, 67, 69, 72
Boston-Salem railroad line, 288, 289
Boston Street, 37, 38
Boston Tea Party, 67, 69, 72
Boston Traveler, 111
Bowditch, Nathaniel, 2, 31–32, *31*, 89
boycotts, 71–72, 73
the *Bradford*, 71
Bradford, William, 48–49
Brandeis University, 252n7
Bridge Street, 146
British America, 15–16, 18–20, 67. *See also* Colonial Revival; witch trials; *specific locations*
British Empire, 165
British regulars, 76
Britton, David, 51
Broad Street Cemetery, 81
Brooklyn Museum of Art, 199
Brooklyn, New York, 185
Brooks, Lisa, 17
Browne family, 70
Browne, William, 71, 72, 73, 75, 77
Brown, Glenn, 195
Buchanan, James, 127
Buddhist immigrants, 160n17
Buffum, Joshua, 37
the Bulge, Battle of, 231
The Bulletin of the Society for the Preservation of New England Antiquities, 196
Bunker Hill, Battle of, 76
burial practices, 179–181
Burlak, Anne, 228–229
Burnham's Quadrille Band, 166
Burns, Margo, 262–263, 265, 268n35
Burroughs, George, 34, 35
Byrne, Julia, 162n40

Cabot family, 67
Cabot, Francis, 72, 77
Cabot, Laurie, 258
Caeser, 53
Calcutta, India, 85
Calef, Robert, 34–35, 37–38, 39
Cambridge, Massachusetts, 18, 19, 208
Cambridge University, 43

candy, 115
cannons, 75
Canton, China, 99
Canton (Guangzhou), China, 85, 88, 90, 171, 172
Cape Ann, 11, 184
Cape Mount, 57
the Caribbean, 20, 49–50, 54–55, 57, 68, 71, 115–116, 119. *See also specific locations*
Carlin, Ruth, 235
Carolinas, 82. *See also* North Carolina; South Carolina
Castle Hill neighborhood, 151
catering, 102, 103, *104*, 107
Catholic clergy sex abuse scandal, 157
Catholicism, 144–163
Catholics: Canadian, 147; Catholic ethnic enclaves, 149–155, 163n55 (*see also specific churches*); French-Canadian, 152, 154; German, 147; immigration of, 144–163, 162–163n46; during interwar years, 156–157; Irish, 148, 151, 159–160n11; Italian, 145, 152–155; multiethnic, 144–163; Polish, 151–152, 153–154
Catholic schools, 154, 162n42
Cedar Mountain, Battle of, 133
Centennial Exhibition (1876), 191–192, *192*
Centennial Grove (Essex), 165
"Century of Progress" Exposition, 202, *202*
Chamberlain, Samuel, 202
Champlain, Samuel de, 28–29, *28*
Chancellorsville, Battle of, 133
Chandler, Joseph Everett, 198
Charitable Mechanic's Association, 124
Charles II, King, 44
Charles I, King, 18, 44
Charleston and Savannah Railroad, 142
Charleston, South Carolina, 127–128, 142, 279
Charlestown, 18, 19, 22
Charter Street, 220
Charter Street Cemetery, 292; Welcome Center, 274
Chase family, 55, 88
Chelsea, Massachusetts, 166, *167*, 195
Chestnut Street, 101, 208, 216
Chicago, Illinois, 192, 193, 195, 202, *202*
Chickataubut of Neponset, 18
China, 6, 84–94, 170–183, *175*, *178*, 254
China trade, 69
Chornesky, Maurice, 240

Christian Indians, 21
Christianity, 19. *See also specific sects*
Christopher Columbus Society, 157
Church, Benjamin, 75
Church Street, 85
citizenship, African Americans and, 110–111. *See also* suffrage movement
City Art Museum in St. Louis, 202
city planning, 215–217, 222, 223. *See also* urban renewal
civic engagement, 3, 7
Civil War (England), 64
Civil War (U.S.), 3, 5, 127–138, 139–143, 165; African American regiments in, 134; Salemites killed in, 135; Union war effort, 134–135; veterans of, 188, 289; war effort, 134–135
climate change, 271–272
Cloyce, Sarah, 256, 257
coal, 129, 130, 214, 223
Coast Division, 142
Coast Guard Air Station, 223
Coast Guard Women's Reserve, 240
coffee, 55
Cogswell, William, 131, *132*, 133, 135, 136
Cohasset, 53
Cohen, Lizabeth, 224n10
Cold War, 246, 270
Collegiate Defense Committee, 237, 241
Collins Cove, 223
Collins, Francis X., 221
Collins, John, 221
colonialism, 171–181. *See also* English settler colonists
"colonial" material culture, 199–202
colonial narrative, 6
Colonial Revival, 190–204, *192*
"Colonial Village," 202
Colonial Williamsburg, 199
"Colored Peoples Picnic," 166, 168, 188. *See also* "Black Picnic" tradition
Committee on Ancient Memorials, 289
Communist Party, 228
Community Preservation Act, 260
Compromise of 1850, 128
Conant, Roger, 11
Concord, Massachusetts, 18, 198
Coney Island, 185
Confederacy, 135
Confederate army, 140–142
Confiscation Act, 77

congestion, 218, 292
conscription, 131
Continental Army, 68, 76
Continental Congress, 73, 79, 123, 287
Conway, Kellyanne, 263, 268n34
Cooperative Council, 241
Corcoran, John, 133
Corcoran, Robert, 254, 260, 261, 264–265
Corey, Martha, 255
Cornwallis, Charles, 76–77
Corwin, George, 287
Corwin, Jonathan, 192
Corwin, Sheriff, 34
cotton, 128–129, 130, 135, 136
cotton economy, 128, 129, 136
Cotton Textile Act, 229
Cotton Textile Code, 226
county conventions, 73
County Kerry, 146
County Street, 84, 85
Court of Common Please, 62
Court of Oyer and Terminer, 33
Cousins, Frank, 191, 193–195, 196–198, 199–200, 201, 202, 203n9, 204n16
Cowasuck Band of the Pennacook-Abenaki, 16, 22, 24
Cox, Sallie Belle, 184
Cranch, Mary, 35
Cranch, Richard, 35
Crittenden, John, 130
Crombie Street Sabbath School Society, 127, 136
Cromwell, Oliver, 44, 45
Crowninshield, Benjamin W., 58
Crowninshield, Caspar, 133
Crowninshield, Elizabeth, 95, 98
Crowninshield family, 67, 71, 73, 77
Crowninshield, George, 55
cultural identity, 50
Cummings, Abbott Lowell, 220
Curtis Companies, 198
Curwen, Samuel, 77
Cushing, William, 53
customs laws, 70, 71
Cutler, Jim, 280
Cutshamake, 22

Daland, Benjamin, 51–52
Dalton, Bill, 239
Danersk, 201

Daniel Low and Company store, 200–201, 289, 291
Danvers Alarm List Company, 258
Danvers, Massachusetts, 36, 38, 67, 76, 117, 127, 164; Rebecca Nurse Homestead, 257–258, 264–265
Danvers Witchcraft Victims Memorial, 265
DAR (Daughters of the American Revolution), 262
dark tourism, 274, 276–277
Darwin, Charles, 172–173
Davis, Henry Winter, 130
D-Day, 231
Declaration of Independence, 53, 123
deCourcy, Elisa, 174–175
Defreace, J.H.A., 166
deindustrialization, 229, 267n28, 270, 271
Demarara, 56
demographics, changing, 6, 156, 194, 215, 269–273 (*see also* immigration)
demolition, 219, 220, 291
Derby, Elias Hasket, 54–55, 68, 69, 76, 80, 95–99, 171
Derby, Elizabeth Crowninshield, 95, 98
Derby family, 58, 67, 73, 77, 95–100. *See also specific individuals*
Derby House, 50–51, 95
Derby, Martha, 98
Derby, Richard, 53
Derby, Richard, Jr., 71, 72, 77
Derby, Richard, Sr., 70–71
Derby, Rose, 5, 54, 95–100
Derby, Sabe, 5, 54, 95–100
Derby Square, 221, 291
Derby Street, 53, 70, 85, 125, 144, 151, 152, 223
Derby Wharf, 70, 171, 275
desegregation, 103
the *Desire*, 48, 49, 54
DesRochers, Robert, 51, 52
digitization initiatives, 4
disease, 16, 18
distilleries, 70, 96, 116
"distinction" policy, 108. *See also* segregation
Dixon, John, *74*
Dodge family, 58, 71, 73
"Do-It-Yourself Walking Tour," 219
Dolliver, Ann, 62, 64n3
Dominaco (Havana), 54
Dominican Republic, U.S. intervention in, 270–271

Dominicans, 214, 229, 269
Dorchester Colony, 11
Dorsey, Thomas, 102
Doubleday Page and Company, 195
Douglas, 52
Douglass, Frederick, 124, 205
Dow, George Francis, 191, 198, 199–200, 201
Downing, George, 102–103
Downing, Thomas, 102, 103
the draft, 236–237, 247, 252n7
Drake, Samuel G., 21
Dr. Edna McGlynn Collection of World War II letters, 233
Dred Scott v. Sandford, 110, 128
Driscoll, Kimberly, 40
Du Bois, W.E.B., 102
Dunkin, Elizabeth, 54
Dwight, Wilder, 133

Eames, Rebecca, 38, 39
Earle, Alice Morse, 197
East Africa, 226
Eastern Railroad, 288
Eastey family, 266n6
Eastey, Mary, 256, 257, 259
East Female School, 106
East India Company, 62, 64
East India Mall and Parking Garage, 222
East India Marine Hall, 85, 103
East India Marine Society, 2, 103, 107
East Indiamen, 68
East Indies, 1, 73, 84, 85, 254. *See also specific locations*
Echo Grove (Lynn), 165
Eckstorm, Fannie Hardy, 22
education, 106, 272; of African Americans, 108; Catholic schools, 154; public schools, 103, 106, 108; school suffrage bill, 206; segregation and, 108
Edwards, Susan, 159n1
Egypt, 170, 179
Election and Training Day, 109
Election Day, 133
Election of 1879, 205–210
electric power, 214
electric street lights, 290–291
Eliopolous, Christopher, 241
Eliot, John, 19
Elkins, Henry, 54–55
El Punto, 271–272. *See also* "The Point"

Emancipation Day, 165
Emancipation Proclamation, 133
Emancipator and Weekly Chronicle, 165
Emergency Quota Act, 156
Emilio, Luis Fenollosa, 5, 134, 135, 139–143
Emilio, Manuel, 139
Emmerton, Caroline Osgood, 191, 198, 199–200
Endecott, John. *See* Endicott, John
Endicott, John, 11–12, 48, 103, 289
Endicott Street, 153
energy sources, 214, 215, 223, 226–227
England, Civil War in, 12
English Language Learners, 272
English settler colonists, 15–16, 18–19, 20
enslaved persons, 12, 47–60, 99, 116, 129; enlisted in Union army, 143n5; fugitive, 52–53, 54, 143n5; indigenous, 48–49, 50; literacy and, 52
entrepreneurialism, 7
environmentalism, 215
the *Essex*, 80
Essex County, 23, 73, 129, 131, 193, 278. *See also specific locations*
Essex County Convention, 73
Essex Gazette, 36, 51, 52, 77
Essex Historical Society, 4
Essex Institute, 2–5, 36, 191–194, *192*, 198, 199, 204n16, 219, 222. *See also* Peabody Essex Museum
Essex Institute Council, 219
Essex, Massachusetts, 165
Essex Street, 79, 103, 131, 136, 193, 219, 222, 232, 234, 286, 289, 291
eugenics, 181
Europe, 68, 170–183. *See also specific locations*
Evans, Walker, 289
evolution, theory of, 172–173
executions, 33–34
extraterritorial history, 6, 7

Fairfield, Rebecca, 57
Fairfield, William, 57
Farnam, Anne, 191
Farnum, Henry A., 135
Farrell, Jeannie, 277
the *Favourite*, 55–56, 60n33
Federal-era houses, 275, 276
federal funds, 217–218, 221, 223
Federal Street, 147, 158, 206, 222

Feldmann, Erica, 279
the *Felicity*, 56–57
Felt, John, 70, 75, 77
Female Book and Tract Society, 125
Fenollosa, Manuel, 135, 139
Fenwick, Joseph, 154–155
ferries, 186
Fifteenth Amendment, 205
Fifty-Fourth Regiment of the Massachusetts Volunteer Infantry, 133–134, 140–141, 142–143, 143n5
Fifty-Ninth Regiment of the Massachusetts Volunteer Infantry, 73
Fine, William, 237
First Church of Salem, 12, 13, 43, 48, 62, 117, 258, 285, 288–289
First District Court building, 222
First Massachusetts Volunteer Infantry, 133
First Thanksgiving, 47
Fischer, Gayle, 124
fisheries, 7, 49, 96, 119
Fish Street, 165
Flat Iron Building, 235
Flayderman, Benjamin, 201
Fletcher, Alexander &Co., 87
Fletcher, Francis H., 134
"Floral and Historical" parade, 213
Florida, 128, 142
Flynntan, 261
Folger, Jeff, 255
Ford, Henry, 199
Ford's Theater, 135
Forest River Park, 199, 223, 236
Fort Lee, 242
Fort Pickering, 223
Fort Wagner, 134, 141, 142
Foster, John, 29, *30*
Foster, Robert, 70, 75, 77
Foucault, Michel, 279–280
Fourteenth Amendment, 110
Fourth Massachusetts Battery, 188
Framingham, Massachusetts, 165
Francis, Edwin, 250
Frank Cousins Art Company, 194, 203n9
Frank Cousins's Bee-Hive, 193, 203n9
Frank Leslie's Illustrated Newspaper, 192
Franklin, Benjamin, 80
Freedom's Journal, 105, 112n2
freeholders, 73
free people, 97, 98–99, 101–114, 133, 141
free-soilers, 129

French Canadians, 144, 147, 149–150, 152, 154, 158, 214, 227, 250–251
French Guiana, 57
Frey, James, 135
Frick estate, 232
Front Street, 102
Frye, Peter, 71, 72, 73
"Frye's Tavern," 201–202
Fugitive Slave Act, 110
Furey, Thomas, 285
furniture manufacturers, 201

Gaddis, John Lewis, 27–28
Gage, Thomas, 67–68, 72, 73, 75, 77, 287
Gallows Hill, 5, 33–42, 213, 222, 260
Gallows Hill Project Team, 39–41, 41n1, 267n25
Gardner family, 71, 73
Garland, Joseph, 185–186
Garrison, William Lloyd, 5, 105, 119–120n10, 139, 165
genealogy, 254–268, 266n9
the *General Pickering*, 80, 81, 82
George Washington Bicentennial, 202
Georgia, 55, 128
Gerber, Louis, 291–292
Gerber's Restaurant, 291–292
German Catholics, 147
Gettysburg, Pennsylvania, 36; Battle of, 133
ghost stories, 275, 277, 280–281
ghost tourism, 5, 275, 277, 278–279, 280–281
Giard, Theresa, 275
Gibbons, Edward, 19
G.I. Bill, 241
Gibralters, 115
GIS, 39
Gist, Christopher, 39
globalism, 7
Glory, 134
Gloucester, 61
Gold Rush, 124
Goldwater, Barry, 247
G.O.P. Women of Essex and Middlesex County, 188
Gore, Christopher, 103
Gothic Revival depot, 218
Goths, 259
Gouldsboro, North Carolina, 140
Grafton, Joseph, 55–56
Grafton, Joshua, 55–56

the *Grand Turk*, 69, 76, 171
Gray, "Billy," 68
Great Depression, 217, 218, 235
"great" parade, 213
"Great Pastures," 216
Great Puritan Migration, 63–64
Great Salem Fire of June 1914. *See* Salem Fire of 1914
Great Yarmouth, England, 256
Greek Revival, 196
Greek Revival architecture, 289
Greenfield Village, 199
Green, Lorenzo Johnston, 96
Gregory, Dick, 247
grief tourism, 276–277
Grimké sisters, 124
Griswold, Almira C., 208
"Grotesque, Antiques, and Horribles" parade, 213
Grotto of Our Lady of Lourdes, 158
Groves, C. Dexter, 242
Groves, Jane Pearl, 242
GTE Sylvania, 217, 222, 242
Guinta, Matthew, 231–232
Guyana, 56

Haas, Anton de, 236
Halloween, 38, 216, 254–255, 261, 266n1, 274, 280–281, 292. *See also* "Haunted Happenings"
Hamilton Hall, 101, 102, 103, 105, 108
Hamilton, Massachusetts, 165, 166
Hancock, John, 192, 193
Hanno, Barbra, 260, 267n21
Haraden, Jonathan, 5, 68, 76, 79–83
Hardesty, Jared, 98
Harmony Grove Cemetery, 143
Harmony Grove (Framingham), 165
Harrington, Michael, 221
Harvard University, 43
Hathorne, Daniel, 2
Hathorne homestead, 291
Hathorne, John, 2, 71, 278, 286–287
Hathorne, Nathaniel, Sr., 1, 2
Hathorne, William, 2, 286
"Haunted Happenings," 38, 216, 254–255, 259–261, 274, 280–281, 291
Haunted Happenings Halloween festival, 7
Haus Witch, 279
Havana, Cuba, 54–55
Hawaii, 231

Hawthorne Boulevard, 147, 158
Hawthorne, Hildegarde, 289
Hawthorne, Nathaniel, 89, 147, 152, 191, 195, 198, 201, 277–278, 289; "Alice Doane's Appeal," 36; biographical background of, 1–2; "The Custom House," 1, 85; *House of Seven Gables*, 261, 278, 282–283n14; "Old Salem" and, 123–124; *Scarlet Letter*, 1, 85
Herbert Street, 150, 152, 221
Heritage Plaza East and West, 291
Heritage Plaza–East Urban Renewal Area, 219–220
heritage spaces, 274, 275. *See also specific sites*
heritage workers, 276
Higginson, Ann, 62, 64n3
Higginson, Francis, 11, 12, 13, 43, 61
Higginson, Francis (grandfather), 288
Higginson, Francis (grandson), 62
Higginson, Henry, 62
Higginson, John, 6, 12, 61–64, 64n3
Higginson, John, Jr., 12, 61–64
Higginson, Nathaniel, 61–62, 63, 64n3
Higginson, Sarah (sister of John Jr.), 61
Higginson, Sarah (wife of John Jr.), 62
Higginson Square, 108
Higginson, Thomas, 62
Highland Avenue, 222
High Street, 106, 153
Hindu immigrants, 160n17
historical landmarks, 275
historic house tours, 213
historic preservation movement, 7
Historic Salem Inc., 38, 219–220, 221
history: historical truth, 263–264; history lectures, 213; labor history, 226–230, 270; "living history," 199, *200*; maritime history, 2, 6; oral histories, 37, 232–235, 254, 255, 256–257, 264; public history, 7; Salem haunted by, 277–280; social history, 5–6, 7
Hocus Pocus, 51
Hodges, John, 52
Holyoke, Edward Augustus, 37
Honduran immigrants, 271
Honey Hill, Battle of, 142
Hong Kong, 85
Hooper-Hathaway House, 198
The House Beautiful, 197
House of Seven Gables, 51, 125, 216, 254, 261; Colonial Revival and, 190, 195, 198–199, 201–202, *202*; House of Seven Gables Historic House Museum, 116
House of Seven Gables Settlement Association, 191, 198, 223
house tours, 213
Howard's Grove (Saugus), 165
Howard Street Athenaeum, 109
Howe, Julia Ward, 205
Hubbard, William, 29
Hunter, George William, 173
Hurley, John, 188
Hurley, William, 128
Hutchinson, Anne, 44
Hutchinson family, 70, 72
Hutchinson, Thomas, 70, 71
Huxtable, Ada Louis, 220, 221
Hygrade Incandescent Lamp Company, 217
Hypes, Shelby, 267n25
Hytron Radio and Electronic Corporation, 242

Idlewood Grove (Hamilton), 165, 166
Immaculate Conception Church, 147, 148, 150, 152, 158, 159–160n11
immigrants, 229; Asian, 149; Buddhist, 160n17; Canadian, 144, 145, 149–150, 161n26, 214, 227, 250, 251; Caribbean, 144; Catholic, 144–163; Dominican, 269–270; Eastern European, 145; French-Canadian, 149–150, 161n26, 214, 227, 250, 251; Hindu, 160n17; Honduran, 271; Irish, 146–147, 270; Italian, 145, 152–155, 270; Jewish, 149, 160n17, 270; Latin American, 269–270; Mexican, 271; Muslim, 160n17; Orthodox Christian, 160n17; Polish, 149, 161n27, 161n28, 227; Salvadoran, 271; from Southern and Eastern Europe, 149
immigration, 3, 5–6, 125, 184, 194, 198, 215, 229; chain migration, 271; changes in, 149–155; economic growth and, 145–146; French-Canadian, 158; labor and, 48. *See also* immigrants
Immigration Act of 1924, 156
imperialism, 165, 170–183
indentured servants, 48
India, 64, 84, 170, 171, 179–181, *180*
"Indian Deed," 5, 12
Indian Ocean, 226
India Wharf, 85
indigenous history, 3, 5, 11. *See also* Native Americans

industrialization, 3, 125, 128, 129, 149, 215, 229
Industrial Recovery Act, 226
Intolerable Acts, 72
Ipswich, Massachusetts, 17, 61, 165
Irish Americans, 227
Irish Catholics, 146–147, 148, 151, 159–160n11
Irish immigrants, 270
Italian Catholics, 152–155
Italian immigrants, 270
Ives, Nathan, 279

Jackson, Andrew, 103, 105
Jacobs family, 37
Jakarta, 85
James, Henry, 190
James Island, South Carolina, 141
Jamestown, Virginia, 47
Japan, 231, 232
Jefferson Avenue, 158
Jefferson, Thomas, 31; death of, 123; embargo of, 58
Jenney, Edgar W., 201
Jewell, Franklin, 133
Jewish immigrants, 149, 160n17, 270
Jews, 233
Joane, 18
Johnson, George, 133
Johnson, Lyndon B., 246
John Ward House, 199, *200*
Jolly, Martyn, 174–175
Jonathan Corwin House ("Witch House"), 219
Jones, Henry, 102
Jones, John Paul, 82
Jordan, Carolyn, 252
Judicial Center, 222
the *Julius Caesar*, 80
Juniper House, 187
Juniper neighborhood, 242
the *Jupiter*, 116–117
"just war," enslavement and, 49

Kansas, 143n5
Kansas-Nebraska Act, 128
Kansas Territory, 128
Karpen, 201
Kasson, John, 185
Keenan, John, 260–261
Kennebec River, 22

Kennedy, Ted, 246
Kentucky, 206
Kilham, Walter, 216
Kimball, Eric, 55
Kimball, Fiske, 204n16
King Philip's War, 20, 21, 29, 35, 62
kinship networks, 17–18
Kinsman family, 6, 84–94. *See also specific individuals*
Kinsman, Ecca, 84, 90, 91–92
Kinsman, Nathaniel, 84, 85, 86, 88, 89–90, 91–92
Kinsman, Natty, 84
Kinsman, Rebecca Chase, 84, 85, 86–87, 88–92
Kinsman, Willie, 85
Kinston, Battle of, 140
Klondike Club, 157
Know-Nothing Party, 147–148
Koleman, Donald, 220
Ku Klux Klan, 156, 188
Kunstler, James Howard, 275
Kuntsler, William, 247

labor, need for, 48
labor history, 226–230, 270
labor unions, 227–228
Ladies Home Journal, 202
Lafayette, Marquis de, 103
Lafayette Street, 70, 131, 144, 150, 217, 239
Laight, Ellen B., 207
lantern slides, 172–180, *175, 178*
La Pointe, 158, 214, 216, 229, 269, 271
Larrabee, William, 133
la survivance, 150
Latin America, 270. *See also specific locations*
Latin Americans, 269
Latinos, 269–272
Lawrence, Clarissa, 106
Lawrence, Massachusetts, 226
leather, 217, 261
Ledge Hill, 37, 38
LeJee, William, 87
Lenox, Charles, 5, 107
Lenox, John, 110
Lenox, Nancy, 101, 114n8. *See also* Remond, Nancy Lenox
Leslie, Alexander, 69, 73, 75, 76, 287; Retreat of, 69, 77
Lexington and Concord, Battle of, 69, 71, 76
The Liberator, 101, 165

Liberty Tree Mall, 291
Lincoln, Abraham, 128, 131, 133; assassination of, 135–136; calls for raising of African American regiments, 140; Emancipation Proclamation and, 133
Lindall family, 70
literacy, among enslaved people, 52
Little, Arthur, 191
Little Canada (Petit Canada), 150
"Little City Hall," 291–292
Little Italy, 153
Little Round Top monument, Gettysburg, Pennsylvania, 36
Littleton Massachusetts, 18
"living history," 199, *200*
Loan and Fund Association, 288
The Log, 236–237, 241, 246–248, *249*, 250–251, 252n7
London, 77, 85
looms, automatic, 227
Louisiana, 128, 143n5
Lovett, Mary, 240
Lovin' Spoonful, 247
Low, Daniel, 190, 191, 193, 200
Lowd, Emma B., 206, 207
Lowe, Daniel, 37
Lowell cloth, 226
Lowell, Massachusetts, 19, 123–124, 226
Low, Seth, 200–201
Loyalists, 67, 70, 72, 73, 77
Lyceum, 125
Lyceum Hall, 124
Lynde, Benjamin, 72, 164
Lynde, Benjamin, Sr., 164, 168n1
Lynde family, 70. *See also specific individuals*
Lynde Street, 70
Lynn & Boston Railway Company, 166
Lynnfield, 21
Lynn, Massachusetts, 18, 21, 61, 165, 166, *167*, 188, 226
Lyon, Martha, 40
Lyons, Maritcha Remond, 113n23

Macao, 84, 85, 86, 87, 90, 92
Mack Park, 37
Madeira, 61
Madras, 62
Maine, 17
Malden, Massachusetts, 166
Mall Street, 146
mapping Salem, 27–32

Marblehead, 21, 55, 61, 72, 75, 76, 117, 223
March to the Sea, 133, 142
Margin Street, 153
Marine Corps Women's Reserve, 240
maritime economy, 70, 171; decline of, 6, 171, 291; eclipsed by Boston and New York, 129
maritime history, 2, 6
marriage alliances, Native American, 17–18
Marshall, Mary Joseph, 113n23
Marsh, George Rumney, 18
Marsh, James Rumney (a.k.a. James Quananpohit or Muminquash), 21
Martinique, 56, 82
Mary Queen of the Apostles Parish, 158
Masconomet, 17, 21
Mason David, 75
Mason, David, 70, 72
Mason, John, 77
Massachusetts, 107; abolition of slavery in, 128; Know-Nothing Party and, 147–148; Pilgrims settling in, 47; Puritans settling in, 47; slavery in, 47–60; suffrage movement in, 205–210
Massachusetts Act to Provide for the Instruction of Youth, 106
Massachusetts Anti-Slavery Society, 105, 165
Massachusetts Anti-Suffrage Association, 208
Massachusetts Association Opposed to the Further Extension of Suffrage to Women, 207
Massachusetts Bay, 17
Massachusetts Bay Colony, 12, 44; charter of, 18, 21; government of, 18
Massachusetts Board of World's Fair Managers, 193
Massachusetts Body of Liberties, 43, 49–50
Massachusetts Constitution of 1780, 53, 97
Massachusetts Fifty-Fourth Regiment, 5, 124
Massachusetts General Court, 56, 62, 67–68, 71, 72, 73, 75
Massachusetts Government Act, 67, 69, 72, 73
Massachusetts legislature, 109, 168; school suffrage bill and, 206; tourism committee, 261
Massachusetts Militia, 292–293n13
Massachusetts (people) at Ponkapoag, 16, 18, 19, 24
Massachusetts Slave Census, 13

Massachusetts Supreme Judicial Court, 53, 97
Massachusetts Tax Inventory, 96
Massachusetts Tercentenary, 199, 202
Massachusett Sunksqua, 16, 17–19, 21, 22
Massachusetts Volunteer Infantry, 133–134, 137n14, 139–143. *See also specific divisions*
Massachusetts Woman Suffrage Association, 206
Massasoit, 17
Mather, Cotton, 34, 35
Mathew, Theobold, 207
Mayflower, 264
Mayflower Society, 262
McGlynn, Dr. Edna, 237, 239
McIntire District, 275
McIntire, Samuel, 68, 105, 196, 197, 201–202
McKim, Mead, and White, 191
McLauglin, Kara, 261
Mechanic Hall, 133
Medford, Massachusetts, 16
meetinghouses, 286–288
Melish, Joanne Pope, 97, 98, 118
Melish, John, 68
memorial spaces, 275
Menotomy Hill, 76
Men's Athletic Association, 241
merchants, 54, 61–64, 70, 72, 73, 95–96, 148
Merchant's Bank, 288
Merimack River Valley, 17
Merrimack River, 17, 19, 22, 123, 129
Merritt, Henry, 117
Metacomet. *See* Philip, King
Metropolitan Museum of Art, 199, 201
Mexican immigrants, 271
Mexico, 229
Micmac, 16
Middlesex County, 129
Miles, Tiya, 276–277
militiamen, 62, 73, 75–76, 131, 137n14. *See also* Salem Militia
militias, 131. *See also* Salem Militia
Miller, Arthur, 262, 263
Mill Hill, 102
Mill Pond, 102, 105
mills, 226. *See also* Pequot Mills
Mill Street, 105
Minton, Henry, 102
Mississippi, 128

Missouri Compromise, 128
MIT (Massachusetts Institute of Technology), 191, 264
Mobile, Alabama, 130
modernization, 218
molasses, 55, 70, 71, 96, 116
money merchants, 72
Montgomery, Elizabeth, 267n21
Morrison, Dane A., 3
Moulton, Seth, 268n35
Mullanski, Dennis, 231
Muminquash, 21
municipal suffrage, 207
Murrow, Edward, 233
Museum of Fine Arts, Boston, 199, 201
Museum Place Mall, 222
museums, 274. *See also specific museums*
Muslim immigrants, 160n17
Mystic River, 16, 17, 18, 21, 22

NAACP, North Shore branch of, 168
Nahant, 18, 21
Nahumkeke, 22
Nanepashemet, 16, 17, 22
Nanjing (Nanking), China, 170–183
Nanjing University, 170, 173
Nantucket, Massachusetts, 192
Nashoba, 18
Natick, Massachusetts, 15, 19, 21
National Association of Cemetery Superintendents, 188
National Historic District, 158
National Historic Preservation Act, 220
National Industrial Recovery Act, 229
National Park Service, 95, 96, 214; Visitor's Center, 274
National Textile Workers Union, 228–229
National Woman's Relief Corps Committee, 206
National Woman's Rights Convention, Worcester, 205
National Woman Suffrage Association, 205
Native Americans, 15–25, 43–44; conflict among, 20; conversion to Puritanism, 19; dispossession of, 15–16; dwindling population of, 18; enslavement of, 20–21, 48–49, 50; hired as short-term labor, 48; land sales in Essex County, 23; warfare among, 16–17. *See also specific groups*
nativism, 147–148, 156, 162–163n46
natural gas, 214, 223

Naturalization Act of 1790, 110
Naumkeag, 11, 12, 16, 22, 103
Naumkeag Steam Cotton Company, 58, 128–130, 136, 146–147, 150, 195, 217, 222, 226–230, *228*
Navy Women's Reserve, 240
"negro cloth," 129
"Negro Election Day," 50, 164, 168, 168n6. *See also* Election and Training Day; Election Day
Nelson, Richard, 264, 265
nepotism, 70
New Bern, North Carolina, 140
Newbury, Massachusetts, 21
Newburyport, Massachusetts, 197, 288
New Deal, 226, 229, 233
Newell, Margaret Ellen, 48, 49
New England Anti-Slavery Society, 105
New England Colony, 12; maps of, 29, *30*
New England Dry Goods Men, 188
New England Historic Genealogical Society, 259
New England Women's Auxiliary Sanitary Commission, 135
New Hampshire, 17, 188, 288
New Model Army, 44
Newport, Rhode Island, 107–108
"New Salem," 216
New York City, New York, 103
New York Times, 110, 195, 220, 221
Nichols, Martha Ann Proctor, 35
nighttime tours, 275
Nineteenth Amendment, 208
the North, 128–130. *See also specific locations*
North Bridge, 69, 75
North Carolina, 128, 139, 140, 143n5
North Church, 75
Northend, Mary Harrod, 191, 196–200, *200*, 201
Northend, William Dummer, 131
Northern industrialists, 128, 130
North River, 11, 216, 218, 286
North Shore, 15–16
Northshore Shopping Center, 218, 219, 291
Norton, Irene, 232, 234–235
Norton, Mary Beth, 4
Nourse Monument Association, 257–258
Nova Scotia, 16, 17, 77
Noyes, Nicholas, 34, 286
Nurse family, 37, 254–257

Nurse, Rebecca, 36, 37, 38, 254–257, 260, 262, 264–265
Nutting, Wallace, 197–198, 201

Obed, 53
Oceana, 84
Old Burying Point Cemetery, 259, 280
"Old Castle," 218
Old China Trade, 84
Old Home Week, 290, *290*
"old planters," 11–12
"Old Salem," 123, 190–204, *192*, 216, 289
Old Town Hall, 221
Oliver, Andrew, 70, 71
Oliver family, 70, 72
Olustee, Battle of, 142
"Operation Bootstrap," 270
oral histories, 5, 37, 232–235, 254, 255, 256–257, 264, 282–283n14
Ordinance of Session, 127–128
Organization of American Historians, 96
Orientalism, 172–181
Oriental Office, 288
Orthodox Christian immigrants, 160n17
Osgood, Charles, 89
Osgood, Joseph, 136
Osram Sylvania, 261
Otis, James, 70
Our Father Free Christian Association, 166
Ousamenquin, 17. *See also* Massasoit

Pagans, 259
Paine, Ralph Delahaye, 81–82
Panama Canal, 231
Parker Brothers, 222, 261
Parliament (UK), 67, 70, 71, 72
Parris, Betty, 263
Parris household, 50
Parsis, 179
Parsons, R. C., 135
Passaconaway, 17
Patriots, 72–73, 76
Paul Revere House, 202
Pawtucket, Rhode Island, 226
Pawtuckets of Wabanaki heritage, 11, 12, 16, 17, 18, 19, 22
Peabody Essex Museum, 3–4, 36, 81–82, 214, 232–233, 254, 259, 261, 274. *See also* Phillips Library
Peabody, Massachusetts, 218

Peabody Museum, 2, 4, 219, 222; Ernest Dodge wing, 222. *See also* Peabody Essex Museum
Peace Parade, 242
Pearl Harbor, attack on, 231, 232, 233–234, 237
Peirce, Mr., 48
Peirce, William, 49
the *Pembrock*, 54–55
Pennacook, 16, 17, 19
Pennsylvania, 130, 226
Pepper, John, 115, 119
Pequot House, 202
Pequot Mills, 58, 129, 130, 136, 214, 222, *228*, 242, 290
Pequots, 19, 48, 54
Pequot War, 48–49
"period rooms," 199, 200, 201–202
Perkins, Frank S., 289–290
Perley, Sidney, 37–39
Peter, Elizabeth, 45
Peter, Hugh, 6, 12, 43–46, 45n1, *45*, 48, 288
Peterson, Elizabeth, 39, 41n1, 267n25
Phelps, Jonathan, 51
Philadelphia Museum of Art, 199, 201
Philadelphia, Pennsylvania, 73, 192
Philip, King, 20, 30. *See also* King Philip's War
Phillips family, 67
Phillips, James Duncan, 288
Phillips Library, 61, 82, 233
Phillips, Tom, 39, 267n25
Pickering family, 73
Pickering, Timothy, 68, 71, 75, 76, 77
Pickering Wharf, 223
Pickman, Benjamin, 77
Pickman, Benjamin, Sr., 71
Pickman family, 58, 67
Pickman Street, 70
Pickman, William, 77
Piemonte, Rev. Pietro, 153
Pilgrims, 47
Pineault, John, 241
Pine Street Quaker Meeting House, 85, 88
Pingree, David, 129
"Pioneers' Village," 199
pirates, 64
Pitman Debating Society, 236
Pitman, J. A., 172
Pittston, Mine, 22
Plans Commission, 215–216, 217, 222, 223
Plimoth Plantation, 199

Plummer Hall, 192, *192*
Plummer Home for Boys, 235
"The Point," 158, 214, 216, 229, 269, 271
Poland, 236
Polish-Americans, 152
Polish immigrants, 149, 151–152, 153–154, 161n27, 161n28, 227
the *Polly*, 55
Pompey, King, 168n1
Pope, Bathsheba, 255
Pope, Samuel, 35
Pope Street, 33, 37–38, 40, 260
Poquanum, 18
porcelain, 171
Porter, Samuel, 77
Portland, Maine, fire in, 195
Port Royal, South Carolina, 142
Portsmouth, New Hampshire, 82, 201
postcards, 180, *180*, *186*, 199, *287*
Praya Grande, 88
"Praying Indian" township, 19
Prescott Stret, 153
preservation, 7, 190–204, 216, 219, 220
Pride's Purge, 44
Privateer Act, 79
privateering, 7, 68, 77
privateers, 64, 68, 69, 77, 79–83, 96
the *Probius*, 84
Proctor family, 37, 73
Proctor, John, 35, 36, 255, 263
Proctor's Ledge, 5, 33, 35, 37–41, 265, 281
Proctor's Ledge Memorial, 40–41
Proctor's Ledge memorial, 260
Proctor Street, 33, 38, 260
Proctor, Thorndike, Jr., 35
Progressive Era, 215–216, 223
Proprietors of the Great Pasture, 36
Proprietors of the Town Commons, 35
Prosser, James, 102
Protestantism, 145. *See also specific sects*
Protestants, 148, 194
Providence, Rhode Island, 131
Provincial Congress, 68
public history, 7
public schools, 272
Puerto Ricans, 214, 229, 269–270
Puerto Rico, 270
Punchard, John, 51
Puritanism, 2, 19, 137n10
Puritans, 34, 47, 61–64, 144, 190, 194, 278, 286, 289

Putnam, Caroline, 110. *See also* Remond, Caroline
Putnam, Caroline Remond, 111–112n1, 113n23
Putnam, Ebenezer, 77
Putnam-Hanson House, 201
Putnam, Joseph Hall, 113n23
Putnam, Rufus, 106
Pynchon, William, 164

Quakers, 2, 63, 86, 118, 286
Qua, Lam, *88*
Quebecois immigrants, 149–151. *See also* French Canadians
the *Quero*, 71
Quinn, David, 29

racial identity, 50
racial inequality, 133, 134
railway lines, 124, 288
Ray, Benjamin, 39, 41n1, 267n25
Raymond, Benjamin, 53
Reader's Digest, 237
Reading, 21
Reagan, Ronald, 245
Reardon, Elizabeth, 220
Reardon, Michael, 234
Rebecca Nurse Day, 258
Rebecca Nurse Homestead, 257–258, 264, 265
Rebuilding Commission, 217
The Records of the Salem Witch-Hunt, 263
re-creation, 199, *200*
Red Cross, 232, 291
redevelopment districts, 291
Redmond, Sarah Parker, 106, 111–112n1
rehabilitation, 220–221
religious freedom, 47
Remond, Caroline, 106, 109, 110, 111–112n1, 113n23
Remond, Ceceilia, 111–112n1, 113n23
Remond, Charles Lenox, 105–109, 111–112n1, 113n19, 114n8, 124, 205
Remond, Cornelius, 111–112n1
Remond family, 109–114, 111–112n1, 139. *See also specific individuals*
Remond, John, 5, 101–114, *104*, 111–112n1, *111*, 112n8, 113n23, 114n8
Remond, John Lenox, 107, 111–112n1, 114n8
Remond, Maritchia J., 106, 111–112n1, 113n23

Remond, Mary, 111–112n1
Remond, Nancy (daughter), 109, 111–112n1, 112n8, 113n19, 113n23
Remond, Nancy Lenox (mother), 101, 105, 109–110, 112n8, 114n8
Remond, Sarah Parker, 5, 105, 106, 109–110, 111–112n1, 113n23
Remond, Susan H., 111–112n1, 112n8, 113n23
The Remonstrance, 207
The Report of the Massachusetts Commissioner to the Centennial Exhibition at Philadelphia, 192
Republicans, 131
residential shifts, 222–224
Restoration, 44
Retire Becket House, 198
reunions, military, 187–188
Revere Beach, 185–186, 187, 188
Revere, Paul, 70
Revolution of 1688, 64
Rhode Island, 43, 103, 107, 228
Rhode Island Republican, 107
Rice, C. B., 258
Rice, Isaac, 103, 107
Rice, Ruth B., 107
Richard, Mark, 149
Richardson, Judith, 279
Riley, Phil M., 196
Riordon, Mrs. Ty, 234–235
Roach, Marilynne, 38, 39, 41n1, 267n25
Roanoke Island, North Carolina, 139
"Roast Meat Hill," 102
Robinson, William, 55–56, 57
Romney Marsh, 18
Roosevelt administration, 226
Roosevelt, Franklin Delano, 229
Ropes family, 58
Ropes, Jonathan, 72
Ropes Mansion, 51
Ropes, Nathaniel, 72
Rosenthal, Bernard, 59n18
Route 128, 219, 223, 291
Rowley, Massachusetts, 4, 82, 233
Royalists, 45
Royal Navy, 76, 77
royal power, opposition to, 70–71
rum, 55, 70, 96, 116
rum distilleries, 70, 116
runaway slave advertisements, 52, 53
Russian Immigrant Aid Society, 125

Sablock, Peter, 39–40, 41n1, 267n25
The Sacred Heart Review, 148
"the sacred," notion of, 279–280
sagamores, 15, 16, 17
Salem Academy of Music, 125
Salem Athenaeum, 2
Salem Cadets, 127, 131
Salem Camera Club, 176
Salem Chamber of Commerce, 258
Salem City Council, 81
Salem Committee of Correspondence, 73
Salem Committee of Safety, 77
Salem Common, 62, 63, 236
Salem Covenant, 44
Salem deed, 15–16, 22
Salem Defense Committee, 234
Salem depot, 288. *See also* Boston and Maine Railroad Station
Salem Equal Justice League, 208
Salem Equal Suffrage League, 207
Salem Evening News, 39, 155, 172, 173, 188, 227–229, 242
Salem Female Anti-Slavery Society, 105, 139
Salem Fire of 1914, 6, 151, 153, 195–196, 198–199, 215, 216–218, 227
Salem Freedman's Aid Society, 124
Salem Gazette, 103–104, 116, 117, 134, 288
Salem Harbor, 68, 184, 215, 222–224
Salem Harbor Power Station, 223
Salem High School, 290
Salem Historic District Study Committee, 220
Salem Hospital, 222
Salem Jewish Association, 246
Salem Light Infantry, 103, 111, 131
Salem Lyceum, 206
Salem Marine Society, 82
Salem Maritime National Historic Site, 50, 95–96, 99, 214, 218, 223, 275
Salem, Massachusetts, 55, 61, *167*; American Revolution and, 5, 54, 67–68, 69–78, 79–83; as bedroom community for Boston, 222; bicentennial of, 123; as Catholic city, 146; changing demographics of, 6, 156, 166, 194, 215, 269–273; City Seal of, 8n2; Colonial Revival in, 190–204; as commercial and retail center, 218; commercial cosmopolitanism of, 68; contemporary, 213–214; deindustrialization of, 229, 267n28, 270, 271; development and redevelopment of, 3, 5, 6–7, 215–225, 285–286; economic decline of, 1–2, 6, 171, 291; economic revival of, 260–261; as haunted by its history, 277–280; as a heterotopia, 279; incorporation of, 67; industrial identity of, 129; as major seaport, 117, 171; mapping, 27–33, *28*, *30*, *31*; maritime hegemony of, 68, 117, 191; as merchant city, 54; officially becomes a city in 1836, 124; policy of nonimportation of British goods, 71; population of, 12–13, 67, 146, 166, 184, 215, 217, 271; provincial census and, 12; quadricentennial of, 3–4; residential shifts in, 222–224; as "society of societies," 124; suburbanization of, 222; tercentenary of, 213, 291; urban evolution of, 124, 222–224, 286; on V-J Day, 240–241
Salem Militia, 62, 75, 76
Salem Mission, 166
Salem Newsletter, 239, 240
Salem Normal School, 6
Salem Observer, 104, 133, 136
The Salem Pilgrim: His Book, 289
Salem Post Office, 218, 231, 288
Salem Rebuilding Commission, 289
Salem Redevelopment Authority (SRA), 219, 220–221, 223; Design Review Board, 220
Salem Register, 107–108, 110, 127, 129, 135, 136
Salem Savings Bank, 288
Salem School Board, 206–207
Salem School Committee, 106
Salem State College/University, 97, 170, 222, 241, 260; African Americans at, 251–252; Afro-American Society, 251–252; Archives and Special Collections (SSU Archives), 6, 159n1, 233; Bowditch Hall, 251; French-Canadian students at, 250, 251; History Department, 255; *The Log*, 246, 247–248, *249*; Music Department, 252; Salem's Trials: Lessons and Legacies, 255; in sixties, 6, 245–253; Student Government Association, 251–252; student strike at, 249, 250; "Valentine's Day Manifesto," 251; Vietnam War protests at, 246–248, 252; women's activism at, 250, 252; Women's Center, 248, 250. *See also* Salem Teachers College
Salem's Trials: Lessons and Legacies, 255
Salem Teachers College, 236; becomes Salem State College in 1960, 241; "Roll of Honor," *238*; students serving in World War II from, 236–242, *238*

Salem tunnel, 288
Salem United Inc., 168
Salem Willows, 5, 166–168, *167*, 184–189, *186*, *187*, 223, 242
Salem Witch Museum, 258, 264
Salem Witch Trials Memorial, 259, 260, 265, 280, 281, 292
Salem Woman Suffrage Club, 206, 207
Salem Youth Commission, "Salem: The Home Front, 1941–1945" project, 232–233
Salenius, Sirpa, 110
the *Sally*, 55, 80
Saltonstall School, 217
Salvadoran immigrants, 271
San Francisco, California, fire in, 195
Santa Chiara, 153
Sargeant, John, 77
Saugus, Massachusetts, 18, 21, 165
Savage, Sarah, 62
Savage Thomas, 62
Savannah, Georgia, 142, 279
schools, 272
"school suffrage" initiative, 206
Schubert Club, 125
Schulman, Bruce, 245
Schultz, Nancy L., *Salem: Place, Myth, and Memory*, 3
scientific racism, 172–173, 181
Scip, 52
Scopes trial, 173
Scott, Dred, 128
Scott, Henry, 103
Seaman's Bethel, 150
seaports, 69
secession, 127–131
secessionists, 127–129
Second Civil War (England), 44
Second Massachusetts Volunteer Infantry, 131, *132*, 133, 135, 136
Second Regiment, *132*
segregation, 108, 109
Selective Training and Service Act, 236–237
Sergeant, John, 75
Servicemen's Readjustment Act, 241
Seven Years' War, 70
Sewall, Samuel, 35
sewing circles, 135
shamans, 18
Shanghai, 170, 172, 173, 175, 177
Shaw, Robert Gould, 133, 134, 140, 142
Shawsheen Grove (Andover), 165

Shea, Margo, 275
Shearman, James L., 113n19, 113n23
Shearman, Nancy Remond. *See* Remond, Nancy (daughter)
Sheehan, Robert, 237
Sheffield, Deliverance, 45
Sherman, Sarah E., 206, 209n8
Sherman, William Tecumseh, 133, 142, 207
shipbuilding, 43, 96
shipwrecks, 115
Shoe and Leather Reporter, 217
shoe industry, 217
shopping centers, 218, 219, 224n10, 291
Shore Line Drive, 223
Sierra Leone, 56, 57
silk, 171
Silsbee, Marianne, 112n8
Sisters of Notre Dame, 148
Sixty-Fourth Regiment of Foot, 73, 75
Skelton, Samuel, 43, 61
Slater, Samuel, 226
"Slave for Sale" advertisements, 51–52
slave labor, 129, 130
slavery, 5, 47–60, 94n29, 96–97, 116, 118, 127, 128; advertisements and, 51–52; concentrated in coastal cities, 51. *See also* enslaved persons
Slavery Abolition Act (British Empire), 165
"slave(ry) trade," 54–57, 58n2
slave trade, 54, 55, 57, 116; decline of in Salem, 57–58; laws against, 56; Trans-Atlantic Slave Trade Database, 55, 60n33. *See also* "slave(ry) trade"
slave trade vessels, insurrections on, 57
small pox, 18
"Smile and Work Club," 188
Smith, Frank, 188
Smith, Joshua Bowen, 103
Smith, Maggie, 280
Smith's Grove (Ipswich), 165
social Darwinism, 172–173
social history, 5–6, 7
social justice, 254–268, 280
Society for the Preservation of New England Antiquities, 201, 258
Society of Friends, 286
sojourner migration, 161n26
Sons of the African Society, 99, 164–165
Soochow (Suzhou), China, 177
the South, 127–129. *See also specific locations*
South America, 56, 171. *See also specific locations*

South Carolina, 55, 127–128, 141, 142, 143n5
South Church, 105
South Edisto River, 142
Southern cotton interests, 128
Southern planters, 129, 130
South Essex Sewage District treatment facility, 223
South River, 286
South Salem, 216, 217
Spain, 61
Spanish-American War, 289
Spartanburg, South Carolina, 229
Spencer family, 118–119
Spencer, Mary, 5, 115–120
Spencer, Mary (daughter-in-law), 118
Spencer, Thomas, 117–118
Spicer, Sean, 268n34
spices, 171
Stage Point, 150
Stamp Act, 70, 71, 287
Stanton, Edwin, 134
Stanton, Elizabeth Cady, 205
State Normal School, 170
steam power, 129, 214, 226, 227
Ste. Anne's Parish, 151, 153–154, 158
Sterling, Colin, 275
Stevens family, 37–38
Stevens, George, 166
Steward, Moses, 35
St. James Catholic Church, 147, 148, 158, 159n10
St. John Paul II Shrine of Divine Mercy, 158
St. John the Baptist Church, 151–152, 157, 158
St. Joseph's Catholic Church, 144–145, *145*, 149–151, 154, 157, 159n1
St. Joseph's Credit Union, 150
St. Joseph's Hall, 125, 157
St. Joseph Society, 152
St. Louis Museum of Art, 199, 202
St. Mary's Catholic Church, 146, 152–155, 157, 159n7
Stone, Lucy, 205, 206, 207
Stowe, Harriet Beecher, 139
St. Peter's Episcopal Church, 98, 279
St. Peter Street, 219
street culture, 275
street names, 70. *See also specific locations*
strike of 1933, 226–230
strikes, 290
Stroyer, Jacob, 166, 168n7
St. Thomas Catholic Church, 159n2

Students for a Democratic Society, 247, 252n7
suburbanization, 222
suffrage movement, 205–210
sugar, 49, 54, 55, 96, 115–116, 117, 118, 119
sugar islands, 115–116, 119
sugar plantations, 49, 116, 270
Sullivan, Edward, 237
Sullivan, Joseph, 237
Summer Street, 85, 88, 234
Sumner, Charles, 133
Sun Chuan-Fang, 173
Sunday Herald Traveler, 218–219
sunksquas, 17
Swampscott, Massachusetts, 21, 153
Symonds, John, 37

Tahattawan, 18
Taney, Roger, 128
tanneries, 261. *See also* leather factories
Tarbell, Ida, 227
"Tarrentines," 16
tarring and feathering, 71
tea, 73, 85, 171
temperance movement, 124, 206–207
Tennessee, 128
Tenth Connecticut Regiment, 141
Texas, 128
textile economy, 129, 226, 227. *See also specific materials*
thanatourism, 276–277
Thayer, John, 146
Thirteenth Amendment, 165
Thirty-Second Massachusetts Volunteer Infantry, 135
Thompson, George A., 118–119, 119–120n10, 128
Thompson, William O., 282–283n14
Thorton, Tamara, 31–32
Tierney, John, 251–252
Tinti, William, 221
Tituba, 50, 59n18, 263
Tories, 77
tour guides, 275–276, 278, 282–283n14
tourism, 5, 7, 191, 213, 215, 219; dark tourism, 274, 276–277; ghost tourism, 5, 275, 277, 278–279, 280–281; grief tourism, 276–277; history and, 254, 258–259, 260, 269, 274–283; Massachusetts legislature and, 261; thanatourism, 276–277; witchcraft tourism, 38, 258–259

tours, 275–276
Towne family, 265. *See also* Towne Family Association (TFA); *specific individuals*
Towne Family Association (TFA), 256–257, 260, 262, 264, 266, 266n9
Towne, Joanna, 256–257
Towne, Mary. *See* Eastey, Mary
Towne, Rebecca. *See* Nurse, Rebecca
Towne, Sarah. *See* Cloyce, Sarah
Towne, William, 256–257
Town House Square, 285–293, *287, 290,* 292–293n13
Townshend Acts, 71
trade, 54–55, 61–64, 70, 72, 96, 117, 171, 254; China trade, 69; maritime trade eclipsed by Boston and New York, 129; Old China Trade, 84; Revolutionary War and, 68, 77; "slave(ry) trade," 54–57, 58n2; slave trade, 54, 55, 56, 57–58, 116. *See also* maritime economy; "slave(ry) trade"; slave trade
Trans-Atlantic Slave Trade Database, 55, 60n33
transportation, 6, 215
trolleys, 166, 186, 223, 288
Trower, John S., 102
Trujillo, Rafael, 270
Trump, Donald J., 263, 268n34, 268n35
Truth, Sojourner, 205
Turner family, 70
Turner-Ingersoll mansion, 198, 282–283n14
Turner, John, 72, 116
Turners Seafood, 280
Turner Street, 116
Turtle Island, 15
Twenty-Fifth Massachusetts Voluntary Infantry, 140
Twenty-Fourth Massachusetts Voluntary Infantry, 141–142
Twenty-Third Massachusetts Voluntary Infantry, 139–140, 143
the *Tyrannicide*, 80, 82
Tyson, Amy, 276

Ukrainian Catholic Church, 159n2
Union army, 131, 135, 139–143
Union Bethel Church, 105–106
unionists, 128–129
unionization, 270
Union navy, 135
Union Street, 128
United Shoe factory, 231
United Textile Workers Local 33, 227–228

Universalist Society, Danvers, 127
University of Virginia, Scholars Lab, 39
Upham, Charles W., 81
Upham, William P., 257
urban development, 3, 5, 6–7, 215–225, 285–286
urban fires, 195. *See also* Salem Fire of 1914
urbanization, 149, 195
urban renewal, 7, 217, 218–222
U.S. Census Bureau, 123–124
U.S. Congress, 130, 220
U.S. Department of Housing and Urban Development, 221
U.S. House of Representatives, 130
U.S. Marines, 270–271
Usovicz, Stanley J., 292
U.S. Sanitary Commission, 134–135
USS *Constitution*, 131
USS *Jonathan Haraden*, 82
USS *Massachusetts*, 231
U.S. State Department, 110

Vaillancourt, Mrs. Blandine, 242
Vans, William, 77
V-E Day, 240
Vermette, David, 156
Vermont, 17
veterans: of Civil War, 135, 142–143, 188, 289; disabled, 135; reunions of, 187–188; of World War I, 289–290; of World War II, 241–242, 289
Vickers, Daniel, 2, 117
"Victory Cottage," 291, 292–293n13
Victory Gardens, 236, 239
Vietnam War, 246–248, 252
Virginia, 47, 58n1, 128, 130
Virgin Islands, 82
"virgin soil epidemics," 16
V-J Day, 240–241

Wabanaki, 16, 17, 22
Walker, Quock, 53, 54
Walnut Street, 147
Walsh, Louis S., 162n42
Walter George Whitman Collection, 170, 171
Wamesit, 19, 21
Wampanoag, 17, 20, 30
Wampanoag alliance, 17
wampum, 19
Ward family, 73
Ward, Mary G., 206, 207
war effort (Civil War), 134–135

Ware, William Rotch, 191
Warner, Anna L., 207
War of 1812, 58, 68
Washington, George, 68, 71, 192, 287–288
Washington Street, 70, 113n23, 198, 218, 222, 286, 287, 292–293n13
waterfront, 222–224. *See also* Salem Harbor
water power, 227
Watertown, Massachusetts, 19
Webb, Martha, 92
Webcowet, 18
Wenepoykin, 5, 15–26
Wentworth-Gardner House, Portsmouth, New Hampshire, 201
West African tradition, 54
West Indies, 54, 61, 62, 70, 96, 115–116. *See also specific locations*
West Virginia, 226
Wetmore and Company, 85, 90
Wharton, Richard, 61
Wharton, Sarah, 61
Whicher, Joseph, 75
Whigs, 67, 71, 72. *See also* Patriots
White family, 58
Whitehall, North Carolina, Battle at, 140
White, John, Jr., 53
White, Joseph, 56–57
Whitman, George, 174
Whitman, Mary, 174
Whitman, Mrs., 173, 174
Whitman, Walter G., 6, 168n6, 170–183, *175, 178, 180*
Whittier, John Greenleaf, 87, 127, 257–258
Wiccans, 258, 259
Wide Awake clubs, 131
Wiesel, Elie, 259
Williams, Abigail, 263
Williams family, 71
Williams, Roger, 12, 18, 43, 44, 288
Williams, William, 164–165, 168
Williston, W. D., 133
Wilmington, North Carolina, 140
Wilson, Deborah Buffum, 286
Wilson, Pat, 260
wind turbines, 214
Wine Islands, 61
Winter Island, 62, 223
Winthrop, John, 11–12, 47–49
"Witch City" branding, 3, 7–8, 193, 254, 258–259, 265, 274–283, 285
Witchcraft Heights, 38, 222
Witchcraft Hill, 35–36. *See also* Gallows Hill

witchcraft industry, 258–259
witchcraft tourism, 38, 258–259. *See also specific museums and memorials*
Witch House Museum, 39, 274
"Witch Memorial Land," 38
witch trials, 2, 5, 7–8, 50, 62, 64, 129, 191; bicentennial of, 193; descendants of victims, 5, 254–268; memorial to, 280 (*see also* Witch Trials Memorial); social justice lessons of, 260–266; tercentenary of, 1992, 7, 280, 292; tourism and, 277–278; victims of, 282, 286 (*see also specific individuals*)
Woman's Day, 184
Woman's Journal, 206
Women's Army Corps, 240
women's issues, 248, 250
women's suffrage, 125, 205–210
women's suffrage associations, 125
Wonderland Park, 185–186
Wood, Robert, 71
Woods, Mr., 240
Woodward, Geoffrey Esty, 259–260
Woodward, William Elliot, 259
Worcester, Battle of, 44
Worcester Insane Asylum, 135
Worcester, Massachusetts, 205
Works Progress Administration (WPA), 218; soup kitchens, 235; Writers' Project, 233
World Anti-Slavery Convention, 107, 205
World's Columbian Exposition, Chicago, 1893–1894, 192, 193
World War I: Liberty Loan drives, 291, 292–293n13; veterans of, 289–290
World War II, 6, 152, 157, 229, 231–244, 291; air raid wardens, 233–234; maritime threats during, 233; Peace Parade after, 242; Salem's students serving in, 236–242, *238*; Selective Training and Service Act, 236–237; veterans of, 241–242, 289; wartime deprivations during, 235–236, 239

Yawata, 18
Ye Old Pepper Companie, 115, 119
Yorktown, surrender at, 76
Young Men's Christian Association, 124

Zanzibar, 226
Zoll, Samuel F., 221, 223, 233, 235
Zwick, Edward, 134

www.ingramcontent.com/pod-product-compliance
Lightning Source LLC
Chambersburg PA
CBHW052051230426
43671CB00011B/1871